Made by
TAIWAN

Booming in the
Information Technology Era

Made by
TAIWAN

Booming in the
Information Technology Era

edited by

Chun-Yen Chang
President, National Endowed Professor
National Chiao Tung University, Taiwan

Po-Lung Yu
C. A. Scupin Distinguished Professor
School of Business, University of Kansas, USA;
Distinguished Professor, Institute of Information Management
National Chiao Tung University, Taiwan

World Scientific
New Jersey • London • Singapore • Hong Kong

Published by

World Scientific Publishing Co. Pte. Ltd.

P O Box 128, Farrer Road, Singapore 912805

USA office: Suite 1B, 1060 Main Street, River Edge, NJ 07661

UK office: 57 Shelton Street, Covent Garden, London WC2H 9HE

British Library Cataloguing-in-Publication Data
A catalogue record for this book is available from the British Library.

MADE BY TAIWAN
Booming in the Information Technology Era

MIC

ISBN 981-02-4779-6

Printed in Singapore by Uto-Print

Contents

Preface

In 1960 Taiwan's electronics industry was virtually nonexistent. Today, Taiwan is the third largest production center in the world for integrated circuits (ICs) and personal computers (PCs), next to the United States and Japan. In 1998, the Taiwan ranked first in the world in the following industrial outputs: mouses (60%), motherboards (61%), keyboards (65%), scanners (84%), monitors (58%), network cards (39%), power supplies (66%), graphic cards (31%), notebooks (40%), and CD-ROM (34%).

These achievements have attracted worldwide attention, and in the last decade there has been a marked increase in curiosity about Taiwan's economic success in the global marketplace. People want to know how Taiwan built an economy that is resilient, flexible and adaptable to the extraordinary changes in the information era. They are curious about how Taiwan's economy successfully survived the Asian financial crisis in 1998 and the rose successfully from the 1999 big earthquake in Taiwan.

Many executives of international companies want to know how businesses are operated in Taiwan and how to do business in or with Taiwan. Many industrial researchers want to know how Taiwan not only survived, but also prospered, in the economic crisis. They also want to know how Taiwan's industrial structures developed so that developing countries can learn from Taiwan's patterns and develop their own economies, which could be stronger than Taiwan's.

For every living thing, including industries, there are cycles—birth, growth, maturation, decline, and death. Many farsighted scholars and economic planners are interested in how Taiwan's economy can continue to grow, how to prevent its decline, and how it can maintain its competitive edge.

This book intends to provide answers to the above questions and cover most aspects of IC/ PC development of Taiwan. To do so, we invited 13 leading experts and their associates, some of whom worked with CEOs of large companies, to contribute their ideas and observations. Each of the authors examines the Taiwan experience—both failures and successes—and points out areas where Taiwan needs to change in order to continue its progress. The reader won't find the facts about Taiwan's growth sugar-coated. What they will discover is a realistic assessment of a nation that has succeeded against impressive odds. Our hope is that Taiwan's stories can help stimulate other countries to achieve a better state that enhances their people and the quality of their lives.

Our intention in writing this book is to offer the Taiwan Experience to others, but not in the spirit of offering a model for others to follow lock-step. For those countries interested in doing business with Taiwan, we offer insight into Taiwan's way of doing business and its organizational culture. For nations struggling to create an economic niche in a world where business is increasingly global, we offer a look at how Taiwan developed from a small, occupied island into one of the strongest industrial nations in the world.

The book looks at Taiwan and how it evolved from an agricultural economy, then to an export arm for large corporations, to its current economic niche in the information age. In addition, readers will gain a broader, global perspective of the electronics industry—who the players are, which countries dominate in certain areas—so readers and countries aspiring to learn about succeeding in the international marketplace get a glimpse of the marketplace as a whole.

We don't propose that other countries follow Taiwan's footsteps exactly. Each nation has its own characteristics and its own economic destiny. This destiny is shaped by many forces—natural resources, the character of its people, its government, its history, and its economic status.

What we can offer is a look at how Taiwan harnessed its unique characteristics to create a niche in an international economy. As it developed, Taiwan looked to successful countries for useful models and industries and adapted much of what it found. Some efforts faltered, some succeeded strongly, and this book looks both at Taiwan's false starts and achievements, for there are lessons in both. Readers interested in helping developing countries can analyze Taiwan's evolution, failures, and successes and learn from Taiwan's experiences as they shape their own economic future.

General Outline

The book is divided into six general parts:

1.   **Overview.** Chapter 1, "The Development of Taiwan's IC Industry: An Overview," gives us a historical view of Taiwan's four decades of growth.

2. **Management Innovation,** Chapters 2 and 3, examine the organizational structure, strategic innovations, and financial incentives underlying Taiwan's growth.

3. **IC/PC Industries,** Chapters 3 through 8, is a look at the specific industries Taiwan has focused on in its bid for a favorable international niche.

4. **Technical and Capital Innovation,** Chapters 9 and 10, focus on innovations in the IC/PC industry that have played a major role in Taiwan's economy.

5. **Education and Government Policy**, Chapters 11 through 12 look at educational and governmental practices that underpin Taiwan's economical initiatives and growth.

6. **Culture and People**, Chapter 13, focuses on five specific cultural life experiences that shape Taiwan's character and soul, which are the building blocks of Taiwan's economy.

Depending on individual interest, the reader could flexibly choose any sequence of chapters to read this book. Those who want to know the general view of the development process could start with Chapter 1, then delve into those chapters that are most interesting to them. For those who believe that history, geography and life experiences can shape a people's character and their ways of doing business, we strongly recommend they read Chapter 13 first, then Chapter 1, then those chapters that most interest them. Indeed, Ms. Phyllis Siefker, our English editor, who has more than 20 years of experience in journalism and English writing, strongly recommends that non-Taiwanese read chapter 13 first. By doing so, the reader can catch the Taiwan spirit and form a cultural context for the remaining chapters.

In order to give the reader an effective picture of the entire book, we offer the following Synopsis of Each Chapter.

Chapter 1: The Development of Taiwan's IC Industry: An Overview

In 1960 Taiwan's electronics industry was virtually nonexistent. Today, Taiwan is the third largest production center of the world of IC (integrated circuits) and PC (personal computers). Taiwan's path to its present status was not always smooth, but it was no accident. Taiwan's government held a paramount role in determining the nation's economic future and systematically charted the nation's goal to become a high-technology center.

The authors, Chen-Yen Chang, and Po-Lung Yu, divide Taiwan's economic development into five major events that coincided with developmental stages of Taiwan's integrated circuit (IC) industry. In the first stage, Taiwan's government concentrated on the resources needed to make the transition to high-tech industries. One pivotal decision was the establishment of NCTU, which expanded to offer advanced laboratories for research into semiconductors, lasers, computers, and telecommunications. After NCTU acquired expertise in high technology, it diffused it to other educational systems, broadcasting the education needed to make the transition.

In its second phase, NCTU graduates tried to transfer its technological success to the marketplace. At the same time, Taiwan expanded its effort and focus to importing technology and forming alliances with high-tech companies in the United States. Taiwan also decided on a specific industry focus and aggressively recruited Taiwanese in America to return and join the industrial revolution their homeland was about to undergo. During this phase, ERSO, Taiwan's powerhouse of electronics research, was successfully built.

In the third phase, as Taiwan acquired better management and marketing knowledge, the nation was ready to establish its own industries. The first was United Microelectronics Corporation, which manufactured digital watches, calculators, TV wafers, and music ICs. UMC's unqualified success in the IC business encouraged other companies to expand into the growing IC market. In Taiwan's fourth phase, TSMC, the first professional manufacturer, was created, focusing on foundry operations. TSMC's success spawned the birth of multiple IC-related industries in Taiwan. In the fifth phase, management and operations evolved as multiple small and medium-sized businesses sprang up to form a cohesive supply chain that established Taiwan as a world-class player.

The chapter also looks briefly at the primary characteristics of Taiwan's IC industry: vertical disintegration, the use of company stocks to reward performance, and technological development, all of which also are covered in more detail in subsequent chapters.

Chapter 2: The Three Vs of Global Competitiveness

Today's business arena is global, and industries achieve success by strategies that make them competitive on an international scale. Han-Lin Li and Jia-Jane Shuai analyze the basic strategies Taiwan's IC companies have utilized to enhance their global competitiveness.

Professors Li and Shuai call these strategies the Three Vs—vertical *dis*integration, virtual integration, and a value-shared bonus system.

Disintegration is the polar opposite of the vertically integrated company in which one company controls and owns virtually every aspect of the production and supply chain. In disintegration, small- and medium-sized companies divide production into specialized stages. In Taiwan, this was an arrangement that reflected the Taiwanese "motorcycle" mentality (see Chapter 13) in which every person wants to be in charge, is willing to take educated risks, and is confident about the ability to succeed. Each company develops core competencies and expertise that allow it to excel in its field, better utilize its capacity, and reduce manufacturing cycle time.

This kind of arrangement could be chaotic, with hundreds of independent businesses functioning separately. In Taiwan, however, a strategy of virtual integration pulls together the disparate parts into an integrated global supply chain of specialized, professional knowledge.

In discussing the Third V, the authors introduce us to a concept, different from stock option, that attracted talented technical people from around the world to Taiwan—the value-shared bonus system. Under this system, employees become company stockholders and are paid generous bonuses in company stocks. This strategy has been a highly successful way of attracting expert talent, building company loyalty, motivating employees, and achieving wealth for a great number of people.

Chapter 3: Employee Profit Sharing and Stock Ownership Attracts World-Class Employees

In a high-technology environment, intellectual capital is paramount. To attract engineers and technical talents to Taiwan and keep them there required a special incentive. This incentive is the third V mentioned in Chapter 2—the bonus system.

Taiwan recruited educated engineers and technical personnel, concentrating on students who had gone to the United States for their education then stayed in America's high-tech industries. A financial carrot, the ability to earn more money, was a major factor in enticing Taiwanese back to their homeland.

In this chapter, An-Pin Chen and Shinn-Wen Wang details the evolution of this plan in which employees own company stocks. As with other areas of Taiwan's development, the stock ownership and profit sharing plan evolved through several stages. Taiwan's government has been an essential part of the country's economic growth, so it is not surprising to find that the government was the first to promote profit sharing and stock ownership. As in other aspects, the government looked abroad to find models for growth, found a model of stock ownership in the U.S. and Europe, and adapted it to the Taiwan's needs. Before it became an industry standard, the government subsidized several efforts to evaluate the impact when employees shared in both stock ownership and profit bonuses.

After United Microelectronics' success in profit sharing and stock ownership, both local and foreign talents joined the company. As other companies adopted this incentive plan to attract and retain employees, it soon became an industry expectation. The author examines the numerous advantages for Taiwan's companies and the country's competitive edge as well as the obvious advantage of enhancing employee wealth.

The authors also looks at the "dark side" of profit sharing and stock ownership. One consequence is a diminished company loyalty, as bright talents put a stock value on themselves and are open to the highest bidder. Research shows profit sharing and stock ownership was the primary determinant for employees when they decided to join (or leave) a company. In addition, because of the structure of the stock system in Taiwan, where there is no such thing as stock splits, companies must grow consistently and significantly in order to remain profitable. Overall, concludes Chen and Wang, the system has been a positive stimulant for Taiwan's international success.

Chapter 4: The Integrated Circuit Industry: A Technological Powerhouse

The Integrated Circuit (IC) industry is fast becoming Taiwan's most important manufacturing sector. This chapter looks at the development of the IC industry, the factors that propelled the industry, the models that drove this growth, and trends.

Charles V. Trappey and Hubert Chen take readers on a tour of this vital industry's development. Taiwan's IC industry began with IC packaging in the 1960s. At that time Taiwan was an exporting center. In 1973, with the global oil crisis and rampant inflation, the export industry faltered, and Taiwan's government sought ways to stimulate the economy. At this time, Taiwan's government began a concerted effort to develop its high-tech industry, and the IC industry showed favorable promise. Through the next two decades, Taiwan's IC industry expanded, and in 1999 there were about 150 IC-related companies with 50,00 employees.

Taiwan's rapidly growing, evolving microelectronics industry is seen as the result of the country's educational system. The educational, governmental, and business sectors of Taiwan are intimately linked in the quest for prosperity and success. The first electronics companies were the result of technology and talent transfers from government research institutions, and the educational system is finely tuned to the evolving needs of industry.

This chapter also gives a brief review of some of the prolific literature about Taiwan's economic success. One of the models emphasizes the role of the Science Park Model. As shown throughout this book, the establishment of the Hsinchu Science-based Industrial Park was a critical ingredient in Taiwan's success story. Under this model, adapted from America's Silicon Valley, an industrial park was established adjacent to major universities and research facilities. The park provides infrastructure and significant services for its tenants. The services include power, water, and sewers, modern housing, training for employees, schools for children, recruiting services, and considerable tariff and tax advantages for businesses. In the park, significantly, research is demand-motivated and responds to industry needs.

The authors finish with a look at the challenges Taiwan's IC industry faces and finds two main needs—to increase the industry's competitive edge and to gain more global market share. To meet these challenges requires expanded internationalization, more emphasis on research and development, and expanded science-based industrial parks.

Chapter 5: IC Foundries: A Booming Industry

This chapter looks further into the booming Integrated Circuit Industry in Taiwan. Two Taiwan semiconductor manufacturing companies are ranked in the top 10 of the top 200 emerging market companies, Taiwan Semiconductor Manufacturing and United Microelectronics Corporation. In 1999, Taiwan occupied about 67 percent of the world's IC foundry market, so the industry has become a mainstay and signature industry for the nation's economy.

David Muh-Cherng Wu looks at the evolution of the IC foundry business, from the first dedicated IC foundry company in 1987 to the present. The first foundry, Taiwan Semiconductor Manufacturing Company, was the result of an Industrial Technology Research Institute (ITRI) research project. The

project existed to establish advanced semiconductor fabrication technology
to supporting emerging IC design houses. To make the venture successful,
three strategies were formulated—the company should be a dedicated IC
foundry; it should be a joint venture with an international semiconductor
company, and all research institute resources should be transferred to the
company. The strategy was successful, and the chapter tracks the
development of TSMC from a research project to its present status as the
aspiring largest semiconductor company in the world.

The chapter also takes a closer look at another Taiwan powerhouse,
United Microelectronics, as it grew to become the second largest IC foundry
in the world. In examining these companies, the author analyzes the reasons
for the success of Taiwan's IC foundry industry, including the tightly
integrated supply chain composed of the hundreds of companies.

Chapter 6: Taiwan's IC Packaging Industry: A Local Success Story Goes International

IC packaging was Taiwan's first step into the high-technology arena. The
packaging industry began 30 years ago as a low-cost production arm for
European and American companies. Over three decades, the industry has
established a presence of its own, ranking second in the world in capacity
and expanding at an average compound growth rate of 40 percent.

Pao-Long Chang and Chien-Tzu Tsai look at this industry's development
and the competitive factors that forged its successful growth. Originally
Taiwan stressed low cost, and European, American, and Japanese
semiconductor companies established factories in Taiwan's export
processing zones. In the 1980s, as American and Japanese companies battled
for control of the semiconductor market, Taiwan established specialized chip
OEM factories. These factories provided strategic turnkey services, and they
became highly competitive specialized post-processing partners in the
international arena.

Taiwan developed a niche in the high-tech marketplace. Taiwan was not
a technology leader, but due to what the authors call its "fast-follow"
capability, it quickly captured and utilized mainstream technology for mass
production. Its success in this industry illustrates a hallmark of Taiwan's
industry—responding immediately to market changes and being able to
produce products that fill those needs without delay. Again, government
worked hand in glove with the industry, utilizing its R&D to create the

technology and competence industry needed. Chang and Tsai summarize Taiwan's competitive advantages in the industry as a fast-follow strategy, a production capacity that ranks number 2 in the world, and a world-class customer response system. These attributes—the ability to respond quickly and quickly meet challenges—are essential features of Taiwan's industries on all levels.

Chapter 7: The Notebook Niche

Taiwan leveraged its competencies to create a successful niche in the computer industry. These attributes include flexibility, competence in medium technology, assembly orientation, and cost-driven and customer-driven focuses. By excelling in this specific sphere, Taiwan has carved out a distinctive niche within the international industrial system. The characteristics that are part of Taiwan's cultural Habitual Domain (see Chapter 13) are particularly suited to producing information products. Taiwan ranks third in the world in information product production, after the United States and Japan. Within information projects, Taiwan has found the specialized niche of notebook computers to be a lucrative, competitive one.

The overall notebook computer industry is comprised of design, component sourcing, manufacturing, distributing, marketing and servicing. Within this chain, Taiwan found its niche in manufacturing.

Jen-Hung Huang examines the characteristics of the notebook computer industry—high entry barriers, short product life cycle, and low price elasticity. Taiwan began its notebook computer industry by selling products to medium and small customers and built its competitive strength along the way. In 1994, when Inventec began manufacturing notebooks for Compaq, Taiwan became the *de facto* manufacturing center for notebook computers in the world. Taiwan's notebook computer industry achieved an annual growth rate of 34.7 percent in 1999, more than twice the world market growth rate.

Huang gives a SWOT analysis of the industry in Taiwan. Notebook computer manufacturers in Taiwan play a key role in the international value chain of notebook computer products and distribution, but the role is filled with challenges, especially high customer bargaining power that results in constantly decreasing profits and a lack of control over some key components. He also gives us personal glimpse at one of the powers behind the notebook industry, Pi-Lee Lin. Mr. Lin, who founded Quanta, stresses a "turtle culture." For Mr. Lin, to emulate the turtle means being humble, stable, and making sure progress every step of the way. Quanta's turtle culture is an emerging one in Taiwan, as the company seeks to create a unique, international company with diverse cultures.

Chapter 8: Desktop PCs: A Project Management Revolution

Technological sophistication, talented workers, a successful incentive system, and government support all are important components in Taiwan's success. But they are just components without a management system that can respond almost instantly to the continual changes in information systems products. In the personal computer market, life cycles are short, demand is unstable, and price declines are inevitable. This chapter looks at Taiwan's ability to supply the demanding global market for personal computers through project management and lightning-speed engineering.

Chyan Yang attributes Taiwan's ability to remain competitive and profitable in this environment to the project manager, the person who shepherds a product through its entire life cycle. Yang looks at project management's phases—what each phase entails, and how this system allows industries to respond to changes quickly. He gives readers a look at the methodology that makes it possible to adopt changes quickly, yet economically, in an industry where Taiwan has set quality standards.

The product manager (PM) system evolved at acer, and most companies have adopted the system, modifying the system to conform to their needs. The essence of the PM system is to divide development into phases, each of which is assigned to a PM, who is responsible for delivery of the product. A PM watches all activities that are related to on-time delivery of the product. The first activity is the marketing proposal, which contains a market requirements survey and an impact report that specifies the impact on existing products. Next comes the planning phase, where the emphasis is on creating a product development schedule and creating a working engineering sample.

After phase two, phase three, R&D, takes over, with the emphasis on costing down or featuring up a product. In phase four, design verification testing (DVT), engineers fix hardware, software, and firmware bugs. Phase five assesses a product's manufacturability for mass production and successfully ends with a committed manufacturable design. In the next phase, six, QVT or quality verification testing, pilot runs detect all possible flaws. Finally, in the last phase, the product is mass produced.

Throughout the process, the PM, aided by essential workflow application software, maintains a flow and quality control that has earned Taiwan's production capability its place in the international marketplace.

Chapter 9: Competing in the Knowledge Game: Intellectual Property Rights

As Taiwan evolved from a production and export arm of foreign companies to a major player in information products, the issue of intellectual property rights became more and more important. Intellectual property rights—copyright and patents—were not part of Taiwan's culture, but became so during the 1970s as Taiwan entered into trade negotiations with the U.S. Beginning in the 1980s, Taiwan reinforced the idea among the burgeoning industries of Taiwan.

Taiwan first was motivated simply to avoid copyright and patent infringement suits from international companies. Soon, however, their motivation changed as Taiwan stressed research and development and invented products and processes that could become an important source of income. This shifted the emphasis to Taiwan's protecting its own intellectual property. Taiwan's engineering technology is its strongest technological asset, and Taiwan in 1999 ranked 11th in engineering innovations worldwide.

As Shang-Jyh Liu notes in this chapter, the key to technological competitiveness lies not only in developing an innovative product: The product also must become an industry standard at the beginning of a product's life cycle. The chapter looks at product life cycles and the rewards and risks of innovation. Through an increase in patents in the U.S. and internationally, Liu shows Taiwan's evolution to a sophisticated player in the knowledge arena, especially in manufacturing processes. The author also proposes some international alliances to benefit Taiwan and other Asian nations and looks at one possible future, one in which Taiwan would evolve from a manufacturing center to a technology service center and locus for technological innovation.

Chapter 10: Investment: The Life Blood of Growth

The government put Taiwan on the path to technological expertise, but industrial growth must be fueled by investment. The sources of these investments changed over the decades, starting with government backing and seed money, then expanding as companies were able to secure their own, independent financing. The appetite of industries that grow and change constantly is voracious, but Taiwan has managed to create around 200 OCT firms and a gross domestic product of more than 9.3 trillion NT dollars (US $1 is about NT$33). It is a market where the total par value of all listed stocks is about 3.6 trillion NT dollars, the total par value of outstanding bonds 450 NT billion dollars, and where a newly emerging venture capital industry has accumulated 110 billion NT dollars.

Taiwan's strengths are in its PC and IC industries, and a public that has one of the highest savings ratios in the world has supported these home industries. Taiwanese have a savings rate of 24 percent, and this impressive savings rate has fueled the economy that made these savings possible. Taiwan's financial system comes under scrutiny as well and is seen as a system that has successfully performed its function—transferring public funds to manufacturing sectors—despite some debate over its efficiency.

The author, Chih-Young Hung, points to other factors responsible for Taiwan's ability to successfully fuel its industry with investments, including a trade surplus that enabled a high level of savings. Hung also gives insights into the two types of funds providers. One is the "unorganized" financial source, which consists of a direct transfer of funds from lender to borrower. The "organized" segment, on the other hand, which introduces an intermediary bank, bond market, stock market, or venture capital funding source, is supplanting the older forms of credit as industries become larger and the investment stakes higher.

Chapter 11: The Industrial Park: Government's Gift to Development

The government planned and financed the beginning of Taiwan's conversion from exporter to a major manufacturer for companies around the world, including its growing local industries. The government also created the center for Taiwan's revolution into the 21st century, the Hsinchu Science-based Industrial park (HSIP). Taiwan built the park for the sole purpose of making high-technology industries a reality for a nation whose traditional economic bases were eroding.

In 1980, Taiwan chose Hsinchu as the location for this experiment in economics because the country's primary academic and research institutions were there to provide the research, human resources, and technological knowledge necessary to guide Taiwan's industry into a new era. HSIP was a locus for everything Taiwan envisioned for itself and attracted talents from around to world to make Taiwan's vision a reality.

At the beginning of the economic transition to high-tech industries, Taiwan looked overseas for successful models and adopted the example of Silicon Valley, a community where academia and industry worked closely, sharing talent and ideas. The result was HSIP. HSIP is devoted exclusively to high-tech industries, and companies who do business in the park must meet one of several criteria that put them in the high-tech category. Industries fall into one of several categories—integrated circuits, computers and peripherals, telecommunications, opto-electroncis, precision machinery, or biotechnology.

Pao-Long Chang and Chiung-Wen Hsu's look at the Hsinchu Science-based Industrial Park takes readers through the park's industrial growth, the considerable government tax and financial incentives for companies to locate in the park, and the government incentives for higher education and technological training needed to make high-tech industries succeed.

Companies are eager to join the Park, and readers see why as the authors see how the Park is organized to provide a one-stop service for HSIP enterprises. These services include attracting investments, testing products, necessary certifications, passports, taking care of immigrant affairs, issuing certificates of tax exemption, issuing business registration, managing storage and transportation, and bonding warehouses—a veritable wealth of services that ties the hundreds of businesses together into a cohesive unit.

Chapter 12: Intellectual Capital in the Information Industry

In traditional economic theories, the essential industrial activity investments are land, labor and capital, and their costs are computed as rent, wages and interests. Traditional theories fail to evaluate human brainpower, or "intellectual capital," which is the knowledge and skill that provide a competitive advantage. Richness of intellectual capital and human resources is the reason Taiwan, a small island with few natural resources and only 23 million people, was able to become the third largest world producer of information hardware and achieve the 19th highest GDP among the 192 countries of the world.

In this chapter, Gwo-Hshiung Tzeng and Meng-Yu Lee examine how Taiwan built its intellectual capital into its major asset. One of the means was the Hsinchu Science-based Industrial Park and its alliance with the National Chiao Tung University (NCTU), National Tsing Hua University

(NTHU), and the Industrial Technology Research Institute (ITRI). Although Taiwan may have adapted the park's model from America, what is unusual about Taiwan's venture into technology is the enduring, international, deep sharing of knowledge for the benefit of a nation's progress.

The authors chart the incentives to bring high-tech Taiwanese back to their homeland and retain them, especially profit sharing. Incidents that helped reinforce Taiwan's characteristic crisis consciousness (see Chapter 13) drove many Taiwanese away from their land. The unconditional surrender of Japan at the end of World War II resulted in Taiwan's return to the Republic of China (ROC). The February 28 Incident, White Terror and the Formosa Incident resulted in the death of more than 120,000 persons, mostly from the educated elites. Most intelligent Taiwanese at one time left their native land for greener pastures and challenging work environments. As the authors point out, Asians and Taiwanese form a large percentage of Silicon Valley engineers. These, coupled with the large number of Taiwanese students in the United States, formed a natural bond. At first associations of ex-patriots focused on learning and helping with employment. In the 90s their focus shifted to technology, capital, business ideas and business management experience. US-educated Taiwanese engineers created an invisible social and economic link between Silicon Valley and Hsinchu. As Taiwanese in America shared their experiences with their cousins in the homeland, capital, technology, creativity, and marketing crossed international boundaries, infusing Taiwan with advanced economics, which the country quickly absorbed. Returning Taiwanese did more than provide educated labor; they were responsible for creating almost half the industries in Hsinchu Science-based Industrial Park.

The authors also examine the work ethic of Taiwan, a country in which people would "rather become king of small domain than a follower in a huge dominion," and which holds the world's record for longest work hours and lowest unemployment rate. It is also a country where education is treasured and continual, and where industries join in the educational effort when public universities fall short of industry needs.

Chapter 13: Five Life Experiences that Shape Taiwan's Character

Every people and every country is unique, shaped by historical, economic, and environmental forces that blend in a singular way to create a national "habitual domain" or worldview. Professor Po-Lung Yu developed the concept of Habitual Domains (HDs) for personal and organizational growth, and in Chapter 13, applies the idea of habitual domains to a people, the Taiwanese. Professor Yu and Professor C. Y. Chiang-Lin show how the five singular experiences of the Taiwanese people, along with Taiwan's geographical conditions, shaped the country's cultural Habitual Domain and therefore its economic destiny.

A look at five Taiwanese life experiences will shed perspective on the rest of the book, which details how the shape of Taiwan's economy reflects national moral principles and values—its habitual domain. Yu and Chiang-Lin examine Taiwan's cultural characteristics or historical events and how they developed the dominant values in Taiwan's culture. One might be tempted to label these values "positive" or "negative," but in evaluating a people, it is wise to simply accept them as realities when building an organization or an economy. The five experiences are (i) **reverence for knowledge and higher education**, (ii) **the ubiquitous motorcycle,** (iii) **a crisis consciousness** from four hundred years of foreign occupation, plus its proximity to Mainland China, (iv) **compulsory military service** for all young men, and (v) **the experience of students studying abroad, then returning.** These five life experiences not only shape Taiwan's character or habitual domains but also strongly impact the competitiveness of Taiwan business.

In addition to looking more closely at the events that shape Taiwan's habitual domain, the authors offer suggestions for Taiwan's further development. To upgrade the Taiwan economy and habitual domain, the authors say individual HDs must be upgraded and suggest specific ways Taiwan needs to enlarge its HD to meet future challenges. These include broadening the educational system, improving the traffic infrastructure, improving law enforcement, and preventing a deterioration of Taiwan's core values.

Acknowledgements

We would like to thank the thousands of people who have contributed to the buildup of Taiwan's IC/PC industry, including researchers, teachers, advisers, government leaders and officials, businessmen, hard-working engineers, professionals and workers. Without their hard work, this book of Taiwan story would have been impossible to write.

To all authors and their assistants we also want to send our heartfelt thanks. No matter how busy they were, they always tried to be helpful, offering encouragement, drafting and cross-reviewing manuscripts and turning them in time,

Finally, we are very grateful to Ms. Phyllis Siefker for her effort in editing the English of the entire book. Her work has made the book read smoothly and easily. We also want to thank Ms. M. C. Wang of National Chiao Tung University and Mr. Frank C. S. Liu of the University of Kansas for their assistance in keeping the book finished on schedule.

Part 1: Overview

Part I: Overview

Chapter 1

The Development of Taiwan's IC Industry: An Overview*

Chun-Yen Chang

President and National Endowed Chair Professor
National Chiao Tung University
HsinChu, Taiwan,ROC

Po-Lung Yu

School of Business, University of Kansas
Lawrence, Kansas 66045-2003 and
Institute of Information Management
National Chiao Tung University
HsinChu, Taiwan, ROC

1.Introduction

In the early 1960s, Taiwan's electronics industry was virtually nonexistent. Today, Taiwan's Integrated Circuit (IC) design industry is ranked second in the world. Its total revenue in 1999 was over US$ 1.5 billion and is estimated to grow at a rate of 22 percent. The total output value of Taiwan's IC industries in design, fabrication, and packaging in 1999 was over US$ 15.4 billion, and was estimated to grow to US$ 17.8 billion in 2000. See Figure 1 for the detailed output value of design, fabrication, and packaging in recent years.

* Acknowledge: We are grateful to Ms. Mei-Yu Wu, Garling Wang of National Chiao Tung University and Mr. C. S. Liu of University of Kansas for their helps and assistance in drafting this article.

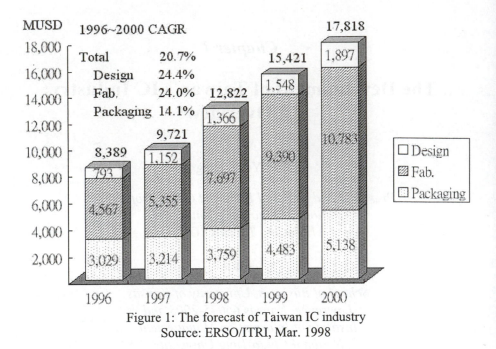

Figure 1: The forecast of Taiwan IC industry
Source: ERSO/ITRI, Mar. 1998

The IC industry is capital-intensive, and the investment in production capacity, including equipment and buildings, is enormous. In 1998, the world's total capital investment was about US$ 21,825 billion, 15 percent of which was in Taiwan. Taiwan's investment ranked third in the world, next to the United States and Japan. See Figure 2 for details.

Indeed, Taiwan currently is the third largest production center of the world. The change from nonexistence in the early 1960s to it status as the third largest production center is almost a miracle. Thousands of people, including scholars, engineers, entrepreneurs, labor and the government have contributed to make this happen. Certainly, luck, which usually favors hard-working people, is also an important factor.

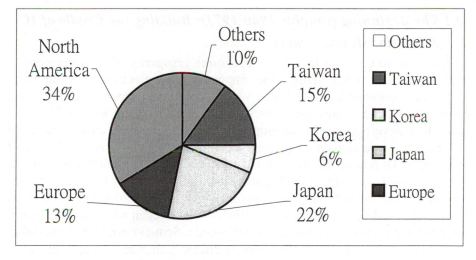

Figure 2: The pie chart of the capital investment in semiconductor equipment, worldwide, 1998

In this chapter, we will first sketch an historical overview of Taiwan's IC development, which is characterized by five major events. Then in Section 3, we will describe three important management characteristics that have contributed to the success of Taiwan's IC industry. Finally, sections 4 and 5 give a brief perspective for the future and conclusions.

2. An Historical Overview of Taiwan's IC Development

It takes soil, sunshine, seed, water and time to grow trees. So does it take these elements to grow forests. Just as in growing trees and forests, it has taken time, effort and luck to cultivate a good environment in which Taiwan's IC industry could be established and flourish. This section sketches five major events that coincided with the developmental stages of Taiwan IC industry over the last four decades. These five events will give a snapshot of Taiwan's IC development.

2.1 The Beginning (roughly 1960-1973): Building the Cradle of IC Professionals and Leaders

In order to survive and to achieve economic prosperity, the government of Taiwan around 1960 sensed the importance of electronics technology, especially semiconductors. There was a consensus among scholars and government leaders that the semiconductor would be the key to Taiwan's economic development. To develop an IC industry required an abundance of competent professionals, including technicians, scholars, researchers and engineers. To realize this end, in 1958 the government established National Chiao Tung University (NCTU) at Hsinchu. The university had only one institute, the Institute of Electronics, which offered courses related to electronics and semiconductors. In 1963, NCTU began to conduct research on producing semiconductors and established a Semiconductor Lab in 1964.

The establishment of the Semiconductor Lab was a major event in Taiwan's semiconductor research and development where the silicon planar technologies were developed, which is considered the fundation of today's IC manufacturing technologies in Taiwan. To signify its importance, Mr. Chiang, Ching Kao (son of Mr. Chiang Kai-shek, who later became the President of Taiwan, ROC) made a special trip to visit the Lab in 1964 (See Figure 3). In 1966, the first IC was successfully fabricated at NCTU by Professors H. C. Lin[*], C. Y. Chang and S. F. Guo.

Since then, teaching and research on semiconductors have become the focus of the NCTU's Institute of Electronics. NCTU established the Department of Electronic Engineering and offered doctoral study for bright students. These events accelerated semiconductor development.

During that time, NCTU actively recruited scholars and internationally prominent professors within and outside Taiwan to participate in teaching and research on Electronics and Information Technologies. More than 20 professors from MIT, Cornell University, Bell Labs, and IBM were invited to engage in teaching, research, and development projects.

Shortly, a number of the most up-to-date, advanced laboratories was established in NCTU to study semiconductors, lasers, computers, and telecommunications. These laboratories quickly attracted a number of first-class scholars and students to NCTU, where they enthusiastically studied, researched and made breakthroughs in semiconductor technology and

---

[*] H. C. Lin, a visiting professor at NCTU in 1966, while he is the manager of Molecular Electronics Division of Westinghouse Inc.

science. This was evidenced by the number of publications on semiconductors in international journals [3, 4] and by the fact that in 1965 the Lab could successfully manufacture ICs.

Figure 3. Mr. Ching-Kuo Chiang (Minister of National Defense at that time) visited the Sintering Furnace in the Semiconductor Research Lab, 1964.
Persons shown in the picture from left to right are Dr. Chun Yen Chang (the author)(張俊彥), Dr. J. J. Chang (張瑞夫), Ching-Kuo Chiang (Minister of National Defense at that time)(蔣經國), Chih-Yih Chang(Dean)(張去疑)

Since 1964, NCTU has continuously produced a number of distinguished IC professionals, researchers, and industrial leaders. In 1977, NCTU expanded the Lab into the Semiconductor Research Center to further promote semiconductor research and study.

After about a decade of success, NCTU shared its successful experiences with other major national universities, including National

Taiwan University (NTU), National Tsing Hua University (NTHU), and National Cheng Kung University (NCKU).

In this way, IC research and development was diffused from the successful "tree" (NCTU) into a forest (other major universities and industrial IC research labs). At present, NCTU is still one of the most prominent research centers in Taiwan and around the world. The number of research papers published in the professional journal IEEE by major research institutes reflects this effect. Table 1 shows the number of publications by NCTU and comparable universities in IEEE in recent years.

Year University	1998	1997	1996
NCTU	102	87	88
NTU	61	57	64
MIT	79	94	17
Stanford	62	76	84
UCB (Berkeley)	49	54	83
U of I (Illinois)	69	86	70
UCLA	66	48	42

Table 1: The number of papers published on IEEE Journal by NCTU and by other universities.
Counts on first author's institute only.

In addition, at least 40 percent of Taiwan's IC industrial leaders are alumni of NCTU, as shown in the Appendix, which lists the leaders of top electronic companies and computer corporations and their affiliations. It is, therefore, not an overstatement that NCTU is the cradle of Taiwan's IC industry.

2.2 Building the IC Power House (roughly 1974-1979)

From IC lab success to IC industry success was still a long journey. This is illustrated by NCTU's first unsuccessful commercial venture. In 1970, an NCTU team formed Fine Product Micro Electronics Corporation, the first silicon-based transistor manufacturing company in Taiwan. This corporation was established by NCTU graduates because of the Semiconductor Lab's technological successes. These native professionals and engineers worked hard, but hardly very successfully, because they lacked the right product implementation strategy. The firm was eventually acquired by Walsin Lihwa Corp. in 1987. Fine Product Micro Electronics Corporation did train and produce a number of IC engineers and technicians who focused on bipolar IC technology. Many of them subsequently joined the Electronics Research and Service Organization (ERSO) of the Industrial Technology Research Institute, which later became the powerhouse of Taiwan IC industry.

In order to accelerate the growth of the Taiwan electronics industry, the government decided* that importing available technologies from the United States was the best way to develop the IC industry quickly. To execute this decision, Dr. W. Pan wrote the IC Development Proposal. With strong support from the Minister of Economic Affairs, Mr. Y. Sun, Dr. Pan formed the Technical Advisory Committee (TAC) in the United States, and the Industrial Technology Research Institute established the Electronics Industrial Research Development Center (EIRDC) in 1974. Dr. Pan established the TAC in the United States because of the number of Taiwanese students with advanced degrees in Electronics and Electrical Engineering that had studied and then worked there after graduation. Being in the United States would provide easier access to these highly trained technical professionals to recruit them to participate in TAC or ERSO projects.

TAC drafted letters inviting large IC companies to enter into technology cooperation, evaluated competitive proposals, and participated in negotiations with IC companies. In addition, TAC also cooperated with other consulting companies to list design, mask, and process equipment so that an IC research and manufacturing factory could be built and operated successfully. It also provided direction for technology development and participated in training personnel and technicians.

EIRDC was the predecessor of the ERSO (the Electronics Research and Service Organization). Mr. P. Kang was the Director of the center, and Prof. T. Hu of NCTU was a specially invited researcher and Vice-Director. For simplicity, we will use ERSO to mean both EIRDC and ERSO.

---

* This was decided jointly by Y. Sun, Minister of Economic Affairs; Y. Kao, Minister of Transportation; H. Fei, Secretary-General of the Executive Yuan; S. C. Feng, Chief officer of Telecommunication; C. Wang, the President of the Industrial Technology Research Institute; P. Kang, the director of Telecommunication Research Institute, and W. Pan, the Director of RCA Research Lab.

With TAC's assistance and screening, ERSO successfully recruited researchers and engineers from Taiwan and from abroad, including those who studied and worked in the United States. These included Prof. D. H. Hu, graduate students from NCTU, engineers, and employees of Fine Product Micro Electronics Corporation and the Institute of Telecommunications. Dr. T. Y. Yang, C. Shih, and C. Chang, recruited from the United States, became important leaders in the Center and in the IC industry.

The Centers' main goal was to nurture and build the IC industry and to import and transfer advanced IC design and manufacturing technologies from the United States, starting with digital watches.

IC technology is divided into unipolar and bipolar. Because the large number of parameters of elementary parts in bipolar make it difficult to manufacture, based on TAC's suggestion, the Industrial Technology Research Institute chose the relatively easier unipolar technology. Although unipolar manufacturing technology was still under development at that time, it showed many potential advantages over that of bipolar.

Simplicity in manufacturing was not the only evaluation criterion. Unipolar includes CMOS (Complementary Metal Oxide Silicon)[*] and NMOS (N-type Metal-Oxide-Silicon). CMOS is more adaptable to the working environment, uses less electricity and creates little noise, which makes CMOS suitable for such products as satellite communication and digital watches. TAC reasoned that, because CMOS was in the growth stage of the product life cycle and the manufacturing technologies of CMOS were still immature, it was easier to reach the learning curve and to gain a competitive advantage over that of NMOS. At that time, it was not easy for Taiwan to manufacture CMOS, and the risk of failure was quite high. After much consideration, however, Prof. D. H. Hu, the executing leader of the IC Development Proposal, decided to focus on introducing CMOS technologies. Seven companies submitted proposals for technology transfer and cooperation. With the evaluation criteria established by TAC, TAC selected RAC and Hughes as the two final candidates. An evaluation committee consisting of H. C. Fang, D. H. Hu, C. Y. Duh, T. Wen, and C. Y. Chang was formed choose the partner, and the committee chose to cooperate with RCA.

RCA guaranteed the non-defective yield to be at least 17 percent within six months after the personnel, engineers and technicians were trained and

---

[*] CMOS was invented by Dr. C. T. Sah, who has made significant support and help to Taiwan IC development.

the manufacturing plant in Taiwan was built according to specifications. To many people's happy surprise, the non-defective yield after six months of operation achieved 70 percent, far better than the RCA's expectations.

The success of IC manufacturing at ERSO then was copied to Taiwan's IC companies by technology transfers and ERSO's assistance.

It is evident that Prof. D. H. Hu's critical decision to introduce CMOS technologies to Taiwan and the selection of RCA as the cooperative partner had a great impact on the development of Taiwan's IC industry. It is also clear that ERSO played a vital role in the industry's development.

2.3 Planting and Nurturing a Successful IC Tree (roughly from 1980 to 1986)

After the success of IC manufacturing, ERSO continued its research and development into mask production and commercialization and gradually increased its engagement in production and sales. In order to retain its primary role of research and to reduce its manufacturing role, the ERSO transferred its IC technologies to private or non-governmental companies. There were three proposals to reach this goal:

To charge royalties for using the technologies;

To appraise the value of the technologies and invest that value in the private companies;

To form a new company to produce and sell ICs and keep ERSO's main mission of research and development for cutting edge technologies.

In the end, ERSO adopted the third proposal. This prompted the establishment of UMC (United Microelectronics Corporation) in 1979 and built a sound foundation for the continued growth of Taiwan's IC industry. Indeed, UMC was the first privately owned IC manufacturing company and the first authorized corporation in the Science-based Industrial Park in Hsinchu, which is to be described shortly.

On September 20, 1979, the planning office of UMC was established at the Industrial Technology Research Institute for the purpose of upgrading the electronics industry in Taiwan. The planning team was lead by Dr. C. Y. Du, the President of Orient Electronics Co. and R. Tsao etc. In October 1979, UMC decided to build its company in Hsinchu's Science-based Industrial Park. UMC was formally organized and established in May 1980 and became the first domestic company to develop and to produce CMOS.

It took two years—from October 1979 to November 1981—to complete the transfer of technologies from ERSO to UMC. There were three stages in this time: a planning stage, a construction stage, and a manpower training stage. ERSO played a vital role in transferring the technology. It offered UMC its professional knowledge and rich experiences and assisted in planning tasks, construction, technology transfer, manpower training, and product authorization.

UMC built its plant in Hsinchu's Science-based Industrial Park to manufacture digital watches, calculators, wafers used in TVs, and muHSIP ICs. It began mass production in April 1982. In November of the same year, UMC reached a break-even point and had 380 employees and sales of US$ 4.69 million. By June 1983, UMC's monthly sales exceeded US$ 2.47 million. That year its annual sales reached US$ 27 million, and it employed 610 people. Its products were sold not only in Taiwan, but also exported to Hong Kong, Korea, and the United States. In 1985, its sales reached US$ 33.04 billion, with profits of US$ 5.45 million. This ranked UMC 183rd in sales among Taiwan's top 500 privately owned corporations and number one in profitability.

As the only IC corporation in Taiwan, UMC achieved its goal of upgrading technology through mergers, acquisitions and joint ventures. UMC purchased Unicorn Microelectronics, a small R&D company in Silicon Valley in the United States, as its listening post. It also transferred technologies and co-developed with other research organizations within and outside Taiwan. For instance, in 1984, 3μm CMOS technology was transferred from ERSO. Also, through co-development with two small U.S. companies, Mosel and Quasel, UMC successfully developed 1.25μm CMOS technology, which resulted in manufacturing 16K and 64K SRAMS in 1986. In the same year, UMC collaborated with SMC on computer terminal IC technology and co-developed 1.25μm technology with the United States-based TRW.

UMC's success instilled confidence in Taiwan's IC industry, and more IC-related companies were built. As a consequence, more skilled human resources and technologies were developed and more knowledge about managing the IC industry accumulated, which formed the foundation in which Taiwan's hi-tech industries could flourish.

In 1984, a team led by R. Tsao had proposed a foundry business plan to the board of director of UMC, but was not approved.

2.4 New Species (roughly from 1987 to 1994)

The success of ERSO and UMC encouraged development of more IC-related products and industries, and as IC-related companies sprouted up, new types of management and operations evolved.

The most significant one was the IC Foundry of TSMC (Taiwan Semiconductor Manufacturing Company) in 1987, the first professional IC foundry in the world*. From 1985 to 1986, Dr. Morris Chang, then chairman of the Industrial Technology Research Institute, successfully executed a plan to turn the VLSI Lab into a foundry and to establish TSMC. The creation of TSMC made a considerable impact on Taiwan's information technology and semiconductor industries. Because TSMC is a foundry, it does not have its own branded products but offers its customers professional manufacturing services. As a result, customers' product designs could enjoy more protection from being copied, and TSMC could obtain steadier usage of its capabilities. TSMC's success prompted many IC design and manufacturing companies to spring up, including MOSEL, SiS, MXIC, and Winbond. Since then, the Taiwan IC industry has successfully moved into the international market. With a worldwide presence, TSMC is well-known for its excellent IC foundry work, and many IC corporations around the world have been eager to do business with them.

2.5 The Flourishing Forest (roughly 1990 to Present)

In the 1970s, as ERSO established its technical competence and experimental IC factory, Taiwan was a follower in IC technology and could not compete with the United States and Japan. However, Taiwan did have a competitive advantage in operations and manufacturing because of abundant well-trained, educated engineers and technicians who were willing to work from 7 a.m. to 11 p.m. to get jobs or projects done (See Chapter 13 for further discussion).

To leverage Taiwan's dedicated human resources to make Taiwan's IC design and manufacturing competitive in the world, the government planned and built a special industrial park-Hsinchu Science-based Industrial Park (HSIP) in Hsinchu. The park was created close to ERSO and adjacent to two leading universities, National Chiao Tung University (NCTU) and National Tsing-Hua University (NTHU). The two leading universities and ERSO

---

* It was also claimed by UMC that the first foundry proposal was made in 1984 by UMC's management team.

provided an abundance of well-trained people for the IC and related industries.

With special attention to the needs of the IC and related industries (See Chapter 8 for further discussion), HSIP provided an excellent infrastructure and environment for these types of companies to operate and grow. In 1980, UMC, the first company, built its factory and offices at HSIP. Later, TSMC and hundreds of other companies built their factories and offices there.

Because of their proximity, the companies at HSIP form supply chains, in which they both compete and cooperate in IC production and operations. They have the advantages of cost efficiencies in production and of effectiveness in management. In worldwide competition, they opened a winning window.

These hundreds of IC and related companies in HSIP survive and prosper as trees in a forest. The Taiwan government now is trying to copy this successful HSIP experience to other areas for building new IC and PC "forests."

Let us summarize the five events and stages of development in an historical perspective:

The Beginning (roughly 1960-1973): At NCTU directed by Drs. J. J. Chang, C. Y. Chang and Prof. S. F. Guo, Institute of Electronics was established in 1958. In 1964, the Semiconductor Laboratory was built within the institute.The institute fostered the interest of a number of faculty members and graduate students, who made IC in the laboratory and created confidence and interest in IC development. After almost a decade of development, NCTU diffused its knowledge of semiconductors and copied the curriculums to other national universities. NCTU is the cradle of Taiwan's IC industry and has heavily influenced many contemporary industrial leaders.

Building the IC Power House (roughly 1974-1979): The Electronics Industrial Research and Development Center, established on September 1, 1974, by the Industrial Technology Research Institute, was renamed ERSO (Electronics Research and Service Organization) in Aprill 1979. ERSO actively recruited well-educated and trained scholars and professionals from the United States and Taiwan. Professor D. H. Hu led the CMOS Proposal to success. Through cooperation with RCA, ERSO successfully built an IC manufacturing factory for experiment and research. The technologies developed at ERSO were later transferred to private companies, so many IC industrial leaders have very close ties with ERSO.

Planting and Nurturing a Successful IC Tree (roughly from 1980 to 1986): With the technologies and management transferred from ERSO, the first authorized corporation, UMC, under the direction of Hsien-Chi Fang, C. Y. Duh and R. Tsao, was built and successfully operated in the Science-based Industrial Park at Hsinchu. The success of UMC encouraged many start-up IC companies in Taiwan.

New Species (roughly from 1987 to 1994): Dr. M. Chang and his associates built TSMC, the first professional IC manufacturer, which focused on foundry operations. TSMC's success generated many new IC-related industries in Taiwan, and Dr. M. Chang is honored worldwide as the Father of Foundry.

The Flourishing Forest (roughly 1990 to present): Through vertical integration and other management innovation to be discussed later, hundreds of IC and PC companies have been built and flourish in the Science-based Industrial Park at Hsinchu. The competitive and cooperative relations among these companies inspire more innovation and continuous improvement in the IC industry.

3. Some Characteristics of Taiwan's IC Industry

After an historical overview of Taiwan's IC industry, let us now discuss some characteristics of Taiwan's IC industry: vertical disintegration, performance shares, and independent technology development.

3.1 Vertical Disintegration

Taiwan's IC industry has a unique infrastructure of vertical disintegration. Vertical disintegration means dividing an industry into several segments, from upstream to downstream, with each firm concentrating on certain functions of certain segments (See Figure 4). The firms in the sequence of segments comprise supply chains. Semiconductor manufacturing segments are marketing, designing, masking, manufacturing, testing and packaging.

Vertical disintegration is not confined to high-tech industries; it has been used by other industries and is a common structure in Taiwan. This concept of vertical disintegration in IC production also has emerged in the United States; however, the infrastructure of the United States is not as fine as that of the Taiwan IC industry. Mr. R. Tsao, Chairman of UMC, and Mr.

S. Shih, Chairman of Acer, exercise this vertical disintegration in their operations.

Vertical disintegration has many advantages, including technology specialization and advancement, management simplification, economy of scale, precise prediction of each cycle time which gives in turn the precision of inventory measures, etc. and flexibility and quickness in responses.

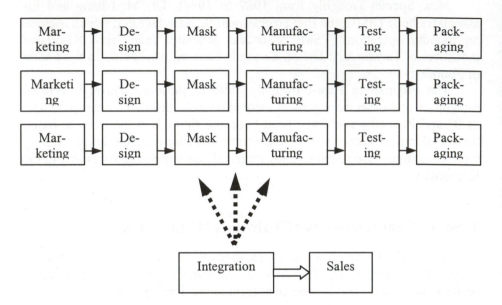

Figure 4: Vertical Disintegration

The core value of vertical disintegration derives from management efficiency and effectiveness in each firm of each segment of the supply chain. Because each firm is responsible, sink or swim, for its operations and its specialized core technology and management, each firm is highly motivated to continuously innovate to compete with other firms. As a consequence, each firm's core competence in technologies and management is continuously improved and upgraded, which creates a competitive advantage for the firms and for the industry. In recent years, many information technology companies, including TSMC, UMC and Acer, have enthusiastically promoted global logistics systems and management and set up affiliates overseas. Vertical disintegration therefore has expanded geographically, and global operations have gradually formed.

Vertical disintegration enjoys the following features:

As each segment has a shorter operation time than the entire supply chain, it is easier to predict, calculate, and control the flow of inputs and outputs.

Each firm in the supply chain is more flexible and quicker to respond to the changes in external events.

Inventory cost can be reduced to a minimum.

In order to compete successfully, each firm has a strong desire to upgrade its equipment and know-how.

Vertical disintegration can shorten the time to bring products to the market.

Vertical disintegration improves operational efficiencies and effectiveness.

Business risks can be reduced to as much as one-third of that of IDM (independent design manufacturing) companies, while financial leverage can be increased.

Vertical disintegration can greatly improve cost effectiveness.

Freely choice of each segment for an integrator to form a most efficient chain.

The above features can be explained as follows:

Every segment mentioned above can be viewed as an independent firm. Because of the adoption of vertical disintegration, the product life cycle in each segment is shortened. The input and output flow of each segment can be predicted and managed more accurately. In order to compete in the infrastructure of vertical disintegration, professional management is needed. Through outsourcing, firms obtain stable supplies of materials and other resources such as marketing channels, business information, increased operational efficiency, and shortened delivery time to the market. Business risks are, therefore, lowered, and cost effectiveness is increased. For a more detailed discussion along this line, please see Chapter 2 of this book.

In Taiwan, most semiconductor firms only engage in some segments, or a few functions of a segment of the supply chain. Myson Technology Inc., for instance, only engages in design, Taiwan Mask only manufactures masks, TSMC only engages in wafer manufacturing, and ASE Group only does packaging. TSMC was the first company to do foundry work without involving design and marketing. Taiwan's semiconductor industry, therefore, can be viewed as an excellent example of vertical disintegration. More examples of vertical disintegration in Taiwan semiconductor industry are presented in Table 2.

	Upper stream	Upper stream	Middle stream	Downstream
Business Activities	IC design	mask	wafer manufacturing	IC testing packaging
Representative Firms	Etron, VIA, ALI	Taiwan Mask	TSMC, UMC	ASE Group, SPIL

Table 2: The vertical disintegration in Taiwan semiconductor industry.

The number of vertically integrated IC companies in Taiwan is small. Winbond and Vanguard International Semiconductor are two companies that choose this kind of operation.

3.2 Performance Shares: Employees Sharing Bonuses and Becoming Shareholders.

Performance shares have been used by Taiwan's IC industry as an effective means to attract hi-tech talents around the world, including many from IBM, Motorola, AT&T, and TI, to actively participate in IC operations and management to create value (profit) and share value (profit).

Performance shares work as follows:

At the end of each fiscal year, the company decides on a certain percentage (once UMC used 18 percent) of its net profits or retained earnings for bonus sharing among employees. These shares are awarded according to certain established criteria, such as position (duty and authority), seniority, and performance evaluation.

Instead of giving a cash distribution as a bonus, an equivalent number of shares of new stocks calculated at par value are issued to employees. For instance, if an employee merited a bonus of $10,000, and the par value of each stock is $10 per share, the employee would receive 1,000 shares for his/her bonus. If the market value of the stock is $100 per share, the real value of the bonus issued is $100,000 ($100 x 1,000).

There are a number of advantages for using Performance Shares in Taiwan's businesses:

The company does not have to pay cash for employee bonuses, so the company increases its working capital for business expansion.

Because the stock's market value is usually much larger than its par value, the real value of the bonus is much larger than the announced value. Many hi-tech company employees receive more compensation from "bonuses" than from their regular salary. Their annual incomes therefore far exceed those of employees of companies that do not exercise Performance Shares. In this way, performance shares become a principal appeal for attracting productive employees. This attraction is reflected in the results of a recent PanAsia Human Resource Bank Internet survey about what strategies corporations use to attract new employees (see Table 3). Although it was not scientific, it could indicate some important attributes that interest potential employees.

Employee Welfare	1,514 votes	30.55%
High Salary	1,258 votes	25.38%
Performance Shares	981 votes	19.79%
Working Environment	967 votes	19.51%
Corporation Popularity	236 votes	4.76%

Total：4,956 votes

Table 3: The attributes that enterprises employ to attract talents
(See http://www.9999.com.tw/vote0689.htm .The table is a translation from Chinese.)

Once employees receive their bonus shares, they become more concerned about and closely tied to their company's ability to make more profits. Employees are more devoted to operations, are loyal to the company and are willing to work hard so the company can make more money, which results in their making more money for themselves. They are no longer workers with a fixed salary. Companies can encourage employees to work harder with the employees' new role as owners. As a result, employees' bonds and loyalty to the company are strengthened. The relation between management and labor can improve along with productivity. For a more detailed discussion on performance shares please see Chapter 3 of this book.

3.3 Emphasizing Independent Development of Technology

From the very beginning, Taiwan has emphasized developing its own technology. If technology had to rely on foreign countries, Taiwan's IC industry would not grow as much as it could. This emphasis on the independent development of technology led to the establishment of TSMC and UMC, some of the leading foundries in the world.

Big companies such as TSMC and UMC never purchase manufacturing equipment wholly from foreign companies. Because Taiwan's IC industry leaders believe IC development would be restricted if foreign companies controlled all technologies, they always try to contribute some new technology to the process. The successful development of Taiwan's semiconductor industry is to a large degree due to this spirit of self-reliance and hard work in accumulating new technologies and research. With independent development, Taiwan's IC companies can collaborate in R&D, share intellectual assets, and make strategic alliances with large firms around the world on an equal footing. They have been so successful at this that today many foreign companies actively seek collaboration with Taiwan's IC companies.

4. Future Prospects

By 2000, global collaboration and competition had become mainstream management strategies in the IC industry. As an example, in March 2000, UMC and Hitachi collaborated in setting up a 12-inch wafer lab and a new company, Trecenti, which in Latin means 300 (300mm equals 12 inches). The company's ambition is almost fully expressed by its name. In April of the same year, Winbond and Toshiba decided to co-develop a new generation of highest density DRAM products that will need $0.13\mu m$ trench DRAM technology and to produce 512Mb DRAM or beyond. The collaborations between Winbond and Toshiba and between UMC and Hitachi show that Taiwan's semiconductor technology is as prominent as those of world-class firms. It also shows that Taiwan's IC industry is strongly motivated to upgrade its technologies, continuously and as fast as possible; otherwise it may not survive, let alone prosper.

Taiwan's semiconductor industries have come a long way to become so competitive with world-class corporations as to be able to co-develop future technologies with them. In collaborations between UMC and Hitachi and between UMC and IBM, Taiwan's IC companies can develop future Sub-0.1 μm technology. The staffs of IBM and Hitachi were surprised to find technologists from Taiwan were as creative, self-motivated, and as productive as those from Toshiba and Siemens, also partners of IBM. Sometimes they find Taiwan IC technologists outperform others.

It can be expected that the output of Taiwan's wafer foundries will continue to grow in the next decade, and the worldwide IC competition will increase. Global supply chains and alliances, such as between Winbond and Toshiba, UMC's selection of Hitachi as its joint venture partner, and TSMC and Phillips' co-investment in a plant in Singapore, show the determination of Taiwan's IC industry to survive and prosper in worldwide competition. Unless extraordinary events occur, we expect Taiwan's IC industry to maintain its prominent presence around the world in technology, production, and business.

In the future, Taiwan cannot be solely dependent on her strength of manufactory Global operation strategy should be emphasized to utilize the resources globally. (c.f. Philips, Nokia 's strategy is use of 20% domestic while 80% of abroad resources including human resource.)

Second, Taiwan should develop her own "product" strategy in which I.P. is essential.

Third, Taiwan should develop her own consumer's " brand ". Like Acer (#1 in Italy, Mexico and #3 in mainland China), especially in mainland China .

The above are interrelated as illustrate in Figure 5.

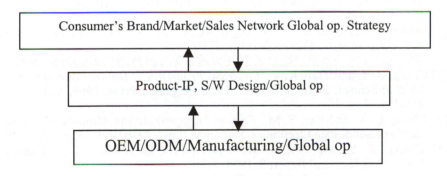

Figure 5:From Consumer's Brands to Global Operations

Through the strategy of promoting brand, Product and OEM, Taiwan would be survived in the next decades.

5. Conclusion

We have sketched some main events in the development of Taiwan's IC industry. Taiwan has been lucky in the sense that it has successfully negotiated each event, which involved many unknowns, uncertainties and challenges. We also roughly outlined some features that have characterized the IC industry's management and development. Finally a future perspective of Taiwan IC industry is provided.

More detailed discussions on innovations in strategic management, operations, manufacturing, government policies, technology development, capital resources, human resources, and competitive characteristics of Taiwan's people are systematically described in the following 12 chapters. By carefully studying them, readers can better understand Taiwan's IC-PC industries and find ways to improve their high-tech industrial development or to outperform Taiwan.

References

[1] Su, L. Y., *There Are Storms and Attached Friendship: The 20 years Path of ERSO*, ERSO, ITRI, 1994.
   蘇立瑩, "也有風雨也有情—電子所二十年的軌跡", 工業技術研究院電子工業研究所, 1994.
[2] Huang, C. S., *President C. Y. Chang of NCTU Teaches to be Millionaires, not to be Handsome Men*, Wan-PaoWeekly, 2000.
   黃靜雪, "交大校長張俊彥 不教帥哥只教富豪", 萬寶週刊 2000/6/5→6/11.
[3] Chang, C. Y. and Tsao, K. Y., *Electrical Properties of Diffused Zinc on SiO2-Si MOS Structures*, Solid-State Electronics, Pergamon Press, 1969, Vol. 12, pp. 411-415.
[4] Chang, C. Y. and Sze, S. M., *Carrier Transport Across Metal-Semiconductor Barriers*, Solid-State Electronics, Pergamon Press, 1970, Vol. 13, pp. 727-740.
[5] Chang, C. Y. and Sze, S. M., *Development of bipolar I.C.*, Ching-Ling Foundation Technical Report 8, 1975.
[6] Yang, T. Y. and Chen, F. L., *Natural Choice in Competiving Enterprices*,Industrial Times Publisher,1998.
   楊丁元，陳慧玲, "物競天擇" ,工商時報,1998。

Appendix

The founders of Taiwan top electronics corporations

Corporation	CEO*/COB* Founders
UMC	R. Tsao/ NTU, NCTU(F*) J. Huan/NCTU(F)
TSMC	M. Chang/MIT, Stanford(F) F. C. Tseng/NCTU, NCKU(F)
WB	Y. C. Jiao/NCTU(F, COB) C. C. Chang/NTU(CEO)
Mosel	N. Tsai/NCTU, NTU, Stanford(F) H. Hu/NCKU(COB)
Micronix	D. H. Hu/NCTU, NTU(COB) M. Wu/NCKU, Stanford(F)
PW Chip	J. Huang/NCTU(F), K. C. Tsai/NCTU
Acer-Semi	S. Shih/NCTU(F)
WSC	K. Chiu/NCTU, NCKU(F, CEO) R. Chang/NTU(CEO)
Mosel-Siemens	H. Hu/NCKU(F, CEO), N. Tsai / NCTU, NTU

The founders of Taiwan top computer corporations

Corporation	Founder
Acer	S. Shih/NCTU(F, CEO)
Mitac	F. Miao/UCB(F) S. Tu/NCTU(CEO) L. Su/NCTU S. Duh/NCTU F. S. Tsai/NCTU
Quanta	P. Lin/NTU(COB)
Leo	M. J. Chien/NCTU(COB)
UMAX	C. J. Huang/NTU(COB)
ASUS	C. T. Shih/NCTU, NTU(COB)

* CEO: Chief Executive Officer
* COB: Chairman of Board
* F: Founder

Part 2: Management Innovation

Chapter 2

The Three Vs of Global Competitiveness

Han-Lin Li and Jia-Jane Shuai

Institute of Information Management
National Chiao Tung University
HsinChu, Taiwan, R.O.C

O14

L63

L22

G30

M50 M31

1. Introduction

Recently, the success of Taiwan's IC industry has captured the world's attention. As both entrepreneurs and researchers examine the successful competitiveness of Taiwan's semiconductor industry, many have focused on the history of the industry's development [2][7][11] or the role of the government [2][3]. This chapter analyzes the basic strategies Taiwan's private IC companies have utilized to enrich their global competitiveness. We call these basic strategies the 3V strategies, because they comprise Vertical disintegration, Virtual integration, and a Value-shared bonus system.

Figure 1 shows briefly the effects and results of 3V strategies on Taiwan's IC industry. The vertical disintegration strategy results in enhanced technical proficiency, improved capacity utilization, and reduced manufacturing cycle time. The virtual integration strategy integrates Taiwan's IC companies into a global supply chain, accumulates professional knowledge, and helps fund-raising. The value-shared bonus system has the multiple effects of reducing conflicts with employees, attracting global talents, and achieving win-win results for employees and shareholders. The effect of these three strategies is exceptional productivity, profitability, and marketability of Taiwan's IC industry.

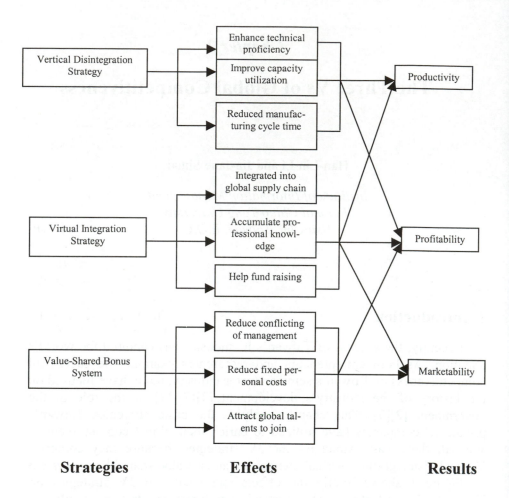

Strategies   **Effects**   **Results**

Figure 1. Strategy-Effect-Result relationship

2. Vertical Disintegration Strategies

Since its beginning in IC packaging in the 1960s', Taiwan's
semiconductor industry has been characterized by a *disintegration* network.
This characteristic helps explain why Taiwan's IC industries have been able
to adapt more rapidly than others to stresses caused by market changes.

Historically, Taiwan's government discouraged concentrations of Taiwanese businesses and relied on state-owned enterprises. As a result, resulting industrial organization was less concentrated, and most firms are small and medium-sized enterprises.

This situation contrasts sharply with the status of major world IC companies, which had their own internal vertically integrated systems before 1980. After that, with the rapid growth of personal computers and the break-up of such huge telecommunication enterprises as AT&T, small Taiwan IC companies faced a whole new frontier of business opportunities. Since no single Taiwan IC enterprise had the resources to establish internal integration on a massive scale, the small and medium-sized enterprises have divided the workload and developed close cooperation. The result is a vertical disintegration coupled with virtual integration.

As the globalization trend continues, the vertical disintegration growth model has gradually replaced the older, traditional vertical integration growth model. Integrated device manufacturers (IDMs), responsible for all aspects of production, found they were no longer competitive due to the difficulty of integrating resources and the complexity of management [1].

This vertical disintegration strategy has resulted in three major effects: (1) enhanced technical proficiency, (2) improved capacity utilization, and (3) reduced manufacturing cycle time.

(1) Enhanced Technical Proficiency:

The semiconductor industry is divided into five specialized sectors: IC design, mask making, wafer processing (fab), IC packaging, and testing. In Taiwan, there are 115 IC design houses, five mask manufacturers, 20 wafer manufacturers, 36 packaging companies, and 30 test firms (see Figure 2).

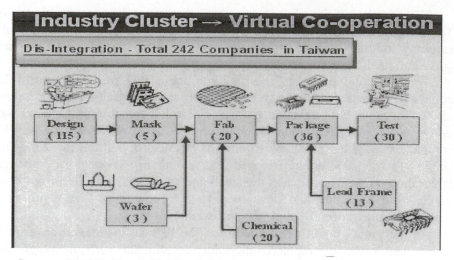

Source: ERSO (April 1999), digitimes (*www.digitimes.com.tw*)

Figure 2: The IC industry cluster in Taiwan

Because each company in the production chain operates independently, it can concentrate on its specialized role, resulting in increased proficiency in and management simplicity. As a result of each company focusing on its core competencies, each sector has grown an average of 30 percent annually (Table 1).

Item	2001 Forecast	2000	1999	1998	00/99 Growth Rate
Industry Revenue	880	675	405	283	59.2%
IC Design	128	97	64	47	31.1%
IC Manufacturing	616	469	257	169	77.0%
Foundry	388	279	146	94	99.3%
IC Packaging	105	85	65	54	28.8%
IC Testing	309	24	19	13	27.0%
Product Revenue	356	287	175	123	63.5%

Source: ITIS (Apr. 2000)[6]

Table 1. Taiwan IC Industry Revenue (billions of NT dollars)

(2) Improved Capacity Utilization

Capacity utilization is the single most important factor influencing productivity in the IC industry. In a vertically integrated system, because each sector has only one end user, it becomes inflexible in adjusting to changes in demand. In contrast, the vertically disintegrated system has multiple users, allowing a flexibility in response to changes in demand.

An additional factor in improved utilization is management. Because each sector of the production chain in a vertically disintegrated system operates independently, management is simplified and improved production techniques can receive more attention. The result is increased yield rates of products. Because of improved flexibility to users' demands and the proficiency in yield control, capacity utilization can be improved significantly.

(3) Reduced Manufacturing Cycle Time

In the highly competitive electronics industry, time to market is critical to success. With the shortened product cycles, speed is often the best selling point. The additional pressure of compressed supply chains makes manufacturing flexibility and turn-around time critical. Under the disintegrated industry cluster, increased efficiency in each production sector results in the shortest possible cycle time.

Since technical disintegration contributes to the service level and the competitive yield rate, the result is a shortened cycle time, higher capacity utilization, and higher profits. As each sector develop strong competitiveness, the industry as a whole becomes strongly competitive.

Another factor causing the reduced cycle time is owing to the aggregation of IC companies in Hsinchu Science Industrial Park. The aggregation of related IC companies could reduce the cost of information communication, the cost of transportation, and the cost of bureaucracy. Which attracts up, middle and down steam companies located at the same area thus to form a complete supply chain system. For instance, following the development of fab fundry industry, the number of fabless IC design companies has increased at annual rate of 30%(Table2). Most production processes of IC industry have been completed in the home country(Table3).

	1992	1993	1994	1995	1996	1997	1998	1999
Number of Company	59	64	65	66	72	81	115	127
Sales (billions of NT)	9	12	13	19	22	36	47	74
Growth (%)	30	36	6	56	13	67	29	58
Investment /Sales(%)	10	23.5	15.5	15.9	15.5	17.3	13.5	15.4
R&D/Sales(%)	10.1	9.5	10	12.2	9.5	8.8	9.4	8.9

Source: ITIS (Apr. 2000)

Table 2. Fast Growth Fabless in Taiwan

	Wafer				Package		Test	
	Taiwan	Singapore	Korea	Other	Taiwan	Other	Wafer Test in Taiwan	Finish Good Test in Taiwan
1998	72.3%	24.9%	2.3%	0.5%	100%	0%	36.2%	38.1%
1999	91.2%	5.8%	2.4%	0.6%	98.8%	1.2%	67.5%	36.2%

Source: ITIS (Apr. 2000)

Table 3. Taiwan Fabless Production Outsourcing

3. Virtual Integration Strategies

In an industry distinguished by specialized, separate enterprises, virtual integration of these independent enterprises becomes critical. An important factor affecting the success of Taiwan's IC industry is its virtual integration into a global IC supply chain. There are mainly five integration options for an IC industry[10]:

• To construct a fab factory requires integrating these facets: architectural design, construction and building engineering, installation of mechanical, electrical, water purification, gas and water supplies, and clean room systems.

• To develop a manufacturing process it is necessary to integrate a photolithography system, iron implanters, diffusion furnaces, thin film deposition and cleaning equipment, and etching and other apparatus.

• To produce a single IC component, it is necessary to integrate the processes of design, mask making, assembly, and testing.

• To manufacture IC equipment requires another complex chain of integration since the equipment is produced by a variety of specialized companies around the world.

• To assemble electronic components into systems for computers, communications and industrial applications require the integration of various sources around the world by a huge number of downstream companies.

Vertical disintegration and virtual integration are trends that have moved the industry for two decades; why then have these trends led to strong competitiveness for Taiwan's IC industry and not for IC industry in other countries?

Taiwan's IC industry has been able to virtually integrate the five IC sectors into a global IC supply chain because of two major reasons: technical specialization and knowledge management. UMC is a good example of technical specialization. In 1983, UMC was only capable of 5-micron process technology; today UMC owns 0.18-micron process technology. Because of UMC's accomplishments in the techniques of copper interconnectors and low-k dielectrics, it now leads the majority of Japanese and American manufacturers[10].

In the last decade, Taiwan's IC industry has capitalized on its knowledge management – the ability to concentrate its expertise on one sector and utilize that expertise. TSMC is an example of knowledge management where the vertical separation of the manufacturing process into specialized sectors has made operations more manageable and simpler, allowing knowledge in manufacturing and management to accumulate and accelerate.

At TSMC, there are several levels of technical evaluation committees. An engineer aspiring to be a senior engineer or manager is required to submit a formal document to a related technical evaluation committee. This document describes the applicant's professional technical knowledge and management experience that have improved one's previous work. The technical evaluation committees organize the knowledge and disseminate it to relevant engineers and managers. This knowledge can then be "smart copied" to teach junior engineers to improve their work, to buy new equipment, or to build a new fab factory. This knowledge management system assures internal knowledge is utilized, resulting in industrial self-learning and improvement. The result is for TSMC is that is has become the largest IC foundry company in the world.

Adopting a virtual integration strategy has resulted in three significant effects:

(1) Integration into a global IC supply chain

Since each sector in a virtual integration system is exposed to the harsh realities of global competition, each company needs to continually improve its core competencies in order to be integrated into a global IC supply chain. For example, three of the top ten worldwide IC foundry companies are Taiwan companies (see Table 4).

1999	1998	Company	1998 Sales	1999 Sales	Sales growth rate %	Market Share %
1	1	TSMC (Taiwan)	1,522	2,263	48.7	30.1
2	2	UMC (Taiwan)	1,130	1,784	57.9	23.8
3	3	Chartered Semiconductor	450	708	57.3	9.4
4	5	Texas Instruments	240	400	66.7	5.3
5	4	IBM	380	300	-21.1	4
6	8	ANAM Semiconductor	110	294	167.3	3.9
7	10	Seiko Epson	100	164	64	2.2
8	7	Sharp	179	150	-16.2	2
9	12	Sanyo	79	141	78.5	1.9
10	33	WSMC (Taiwan)	4	120	2976.9	1.6
		Total Top 10 for 1999	4,194	6,324	50.8	84.3
		Other Companies	1,147	1,182	3.1	15.7
		Total Market	5,341	7,506	40.5	100

Source: Dataquest, 2000/07, ITIS 2000/11

Table 4. Top ten IC Foundry Worldwide (in millions of US dollars)

(2) Accumulated professional knowledge

As each sector in a virtual integration system develops a high level of proficiency, it is more convenient to accumulate its professional knowledge in management and technology.

(3) Help in fund raising

IC industry is a highly capital intensive industry. Due to the continued improvement of the IC designs and manufacturing process, outdated equipment has to be replaced to new generation technology and products. A continuous and large amount of capital is needed to upgrade the facilities, lower product costs, thus to maintain competitive advantage.

Because each company of the production chain can raise funds independently, it is easier to reach the necessary capital scale to be competitive. With the growth profit, Taiwan's IC industry increases the capital investment necessary to update equipment and expand its capacity. The appeal to investors is strong; according to Dataquest in 1998, three of the top ten companies worldwide in terms of investment were located in Taiwan (Table 5). While compared with the leading countries in the world, Taiwan's IC industry also has the highest capital investment rate in terms of sales percentage (Table 6).

1996 Rank	1997 Rank	1998 Rank	Company	Amount (US $Billions)	97~98 Change %
1	1	1	Intel (USA)	3.70	-18%
11	4	2	Motorola (USA)	1.55	-14%
13	5	3	Siemens (Germany)	1.35	-21%
21	17	4	UMC Group (Taiwan)	1.31	46%
6	7	5	NEC (Japan)	1.25	-21%
24	20	6	AMD (USA)	1.20	53%
10	10	7	IBM (USA)	1.20	-14%
18	14	8	TSMC (Taiwan)	1.09	-8%
19	15	9	Winbond (Taiwan)	1.08	9%
9	9	10	Toshiba (Japan)	1.03	-26%

Source: Dataquest 1999

Table 5. 1998 IC Capital Investment by Company

	1994	1995	1996	1997	1998	1999
U.S.A	21%	23%	23%	18%	19%	17%
Japan	16%	21%	22%	20%	14%	17%
Europe	19%	24%	24%	22%	20%	22%
Korea	26%	40%	45%	51%	16%	34%
Taiwan	32%	63%	58%	63%	60%	62%

Source: WSC, VLSI Research 99/11

Table 6. IC Capital Investment as % of Sales

4. Value-Shared Bonus System

Most of Taiwan's IC companies let employees receive their bonuses in the form of company stocks, which are created from the companies' retained earnings converted into capital. This so-called employee value-shared bonus system has been another major factor in the success of Taiwan's IC industry and has attracted excellent international talents to Taiwan.

The multiple effects of the value-shared bonus system on Taiwan's IC industry are as follows:

(1) Reduce conflicting of management

Since employees become company shareholders, many problems of conflict between management and labor are eliminated. With employees in this type of system highly motivated and productive, the result is a win-win situation for employees and shareholders. UMC's last 15 years experience serves as an example of increased earnings: On an annual basis, with the agreement of the shareholders, 0.43% of the company's shares have been released to employees. Since implementing an employee value-shared bonus system, the original shareholders have enjoyed an average annual return of 14.5 times their investment.

(2) Reduce fixed personal costs

Enjoying the increase in value from their stocks, the employees could accept much lower base salaries.This gives Taiwan semiconductor industry the most competitive fixed salary cost structure among the world. Also if companies are not making money, the employee will not be get good paid either, this cause employees full of enterprising spirit.

(3) Attract global talents to join

Even though the base salary is low, once the company makes money, the employee annual income will be much higher than those of in USA, Singapore and Japan. Taiwan's IC companies therefore are in a strong position to attract global industry talent. Professionals attracted by this system are highly entrepreneurial as well as highly skilled workforce.[10]

Because the annual income of employees surpasses that of workers in USA and Japan, Taiwan's IC companies are in a strong position to attract global industry talent. Professionals attracted by this system are highly entrepreneurial as well as highly skilled.

Comparing with the bonus-share system, the stock option system means to allow employees to purchase certain among of company stock, in which the selling price is the stock market price on that day or discount of that market price. In order to keep the employees within the company, this option can be exercised within 5 years; so, the employee can exercise their right next year using original price is the stock price is not good this year. The biggest difference between the value-share bonus system and the stock option system is that the former one rewards employees for their achievement from last year. Employees under this system may leave the company after obtaining his share of stocks. The later one asks employees to work hard for the future, which encourages the employees' to stay with the company longer to wait for the raise of companys stock price.

The value-shared bonus system contributes a lot for the growth and strong of Taiwan semiconductor industry. Many companies in Taiwan have adopted the same system in order to attract talents. However, after many years implementation, many side impacts have appeared. The most obvious one is this system has cause the traditional industries hard to raise capital and attract talents.

Most of high tech employees treat the value-shared bonus system as a short cut to earn big money, therefore when consider changing jobs, they are always looking for high bonus company.

5. Profitability and Marketability of Semiconductor Companies

The performance of a company can be measured by two criteria. The first is profitability -- a company's ability to generate revenue in terms of its labor, assets, and capital stock. The second is marketability -- a company's performance in the stock market as measured by revenue, profit, and market share. (Table 7)

Performance	Measurement
Profitability	Sales
	Employee production value
	Capital return ratio
	Asset return ratio
	Gross profit ratio
Marketability	Market share
	Market value (Stock price)

Table 7: The measurements of profitability and marketability

Financial indicators are critical and the most possible to measure. Sales revenue is the leading indicator. There also are some intermediate variables such as service level or customer satisfaction. For simplification, we envelop these intermediate variables in the item "sales."

(1) Profitability

Table 8 lists the 1997 and 1998 profitability index for Taiwan's IC design, manufacturing, and packaging sectors. For each sector, the index includes the average employee production value, the capital return rate, the gross profit, and the net profit for 1997 and 1998.

The world market recession from 1996 to 1998 significantly lowered IC demand, and many overseas IDM companies suffered losses. Taiwan's IC industries show two different stories. Foundry companies such as TSMC and UMC are still profitable, but most of the IDM companies (e.g., Winbond and MXIC) and DRAM companies (e.g., Vanguard and Nan Ya) are not profitable. The average IC manufacturing net profit fell from 23.5 percent in

1997 to 9.5 percent in 1998, and the average IC design net profit fell 44.4 percent, from 16.9 percent in 1997 to 9.4 percent.

Item	IC Design		IC Manufacturing		IC Testing/Packaging	
	1997	1998	1997	1998	1997	1998
Average Employee production Value (In NT thousands)	10,840	11,200	5,650	5,660	1,990	2,580
Gross Profit rates	30.9 %	29.1 %	24.8 %	24.9 %	37 %	32.7 %
Net Profit rates	16.9 %	9.4 %	23.5 %	9.5 %	24.6 %	34.6 %

Source: ITIS (June 1999)[6]

Table 8. The Profitability of Taiwan IC industry

(2) Marketability
Even though there was an overall decline in profits, the IC industry was still the most profitable industry, which has resulted in a public preference for this sector's stock. Despite the recession, Taiwan's semiconductor industries increased their global market share as well as their revenues (Table 9).

Year	Taiwan IC Industry %	Revenue Growth %	Taiwan DRAM %	Revenue Growth %	Taiwan Wafer %	Revenue Growth %
1996	7	7	5	0.3	-	-
1997	8	18	8	37	-	-
1998	9	-3	11	-5	7.3	77
1999	10	27	16	67	7.8	20
2000(E)	12	43	18	99	9.5	39

Source: WSTS (Feb. 2000) [http://www.semiconductorbiz.com/]

Table 9. Global Market Share

(3) The performance of Taiwan's companies and overseas IDM companies

Table 10 compares the profitability and marketability of Taiwan's IC industry with the 1999 *Fortune* 1000 IDM companies, ranked by revenue. Comparing profit after tax to net sales, the TSMC is 34% and UMC is 36%, both signifcantly higher than the other companies.

This shows TSMC has performed creditably in labor profitability and capital profitability. According to the Hambrecht & Quist report on January 27, 2000, TSMC is the third largest semiconductor company in the world by market capitalization, following only Intel and Texas Instruments.

(4) Future Trends

The weakness of the vertically disintegrated companies in the past was their lack of financial strength, small size, and lagging technology [5]; however, the three-year (1996-1998) downturn in IC industry gave Taiwan the opportunity to catch up with the most advanced IDM companies. Now Taiwan is in an ideal position to benefit from the current worldwide "disintegration" trend. As system companies and IDMs focus on their core competencies, they will seek specialized sectors as partners. The Internet as a business-to-business link will accelerate the formation of strategic partnerships across nations and across oceans.

There are three issues that will affect the competitiveness of Taiwan's IC industry in the future: (1) an emphasis on R&D, (2) retention of superiority in production capacity, (3) and the internationalization of the financial market. Fully integrated to the global supply chain, Taiwan can create a unique position of global competitiveness.

The industry competitiveness is not determined by the cost it saves but the value it brings. Take IC cost for example, making a chip cost much more comparing with design, assembly or testing process. In a semiconductor value chain, the understanding of markets, the skills for integration, and the design of IC chips raise the most value. Therefore, some US semiconductor companies choose to focus on this part of value chain since they have only limited resources. They work together with Taiwan foundry business to do manufacturing but still can play major roles in the world-wide semiconductor industry.

Company	1999 Fortune 1000 Revenue Rank	Employee (1)	Capital (2)	Sales (3)	Profits (4)	Market Value (5)	Productivity by employee (3)/(1) in thousands	Productivity by employee (3)/(1) in thousands	Profitability by employee (3)/(1) in thousands	Profitability by employee (3)/(1) in thousands	Marketability by employee (3)/(1) in thousands	Marketability by Profit (5)/(4)
Intel	39	70,200	32,535	29,389	7,314	457,200	418.6	0.903	104.2	0.225	15.5	62.5
Texas Instruments	180	38,197	9,255	9,468	1,406	135,300	247.9	1.023	36.8	0.152	14.3	96.2
National Semiconductor	698	11,600	901	1,957	-1,010	12,100	168.7	2.172	-87.	-1.121	6.2	-11.98
TSMC	N.A.	5,908	3,847	2,285	955	81,700	386.8	0.594	161.6	0.248	35.75	85.5

Source: Organized from Fortune, TSMC and UMC annual report

Table 10. The Comparable Performance Result

(in millions US dollar - except employee numbers)

6. Conclusion

In this chapter we examined the three key success strategies of Taiwan's IC industry, i.e., vertical disintegration, virtual integration, and value-shared bonus system. The vertical disintegration strategy results in enhanced technical proficiency and reduced mamufacturing cycle time. The virtual integration strategy integrates IC companies into a global supply chain and accumulates knowledge. The value-shared bonus system attracts global talents and reduces conflicts with employees.

References

[1] Bailey, D. E., "Challenges of Integration in Semiconductor Manufacturing Firms", *IEEE Transactions on Engineering Management*, Vol. 46, No. 4, November 1999.

[2] Chang, P-L and Chiung Hsu, "The Development Strategies for Taiwan's Semiconductor Industry," *IEEE Transactions on Engineering Management*, Vol. 45, No. 4, November 1998.

[3] Chang, P-L, S. S. C. Lung, and C-W Hsu, "The Evaluating Model for the Technology Needs of Taiwan High-Tech Industries," *International Journal of Technology Management*, Vol. 18, 1999.

[4] Choung, J-Y, "Patterns of Innovation in Korea and Taiwan,." *IEEE Transactions on Engineering Management*, Vol. 45, No. 4, November 1998, Nos. 1/2.

[5] Christensen, Clayton M, "The Drivers of Vertical Disintegration," *International Journal of Technology Management*, Vol. 18, Nos. 1/2, 1999.

[6] Taiwan Industrial Technology Information Services, *Current IC Industry Survey*, June 1999.&2000

[7] Liu, S-J, "Industrial Development and Structural Adaptation in Taiwan: Some Issues of Learned Entrepreneurship," *IEEE Transactions on Engineering Management*, Vol. 45, No. 4, November, 1998.

[8] Loch, C., S. Lothar, and C. Terwiesch, "Measuring Development Performance in the Electronic Industry," *IEEE Engineering Management Review*, Summer 1998.

[9] Tilley, K. J., and D. J. Williams, "An Assessment of the Electronics Industry in Southeast Asia," *IEEE Transactions on Components, Packaging, and Manufacturing Technology-Part C*, Vol. 20, No. 4, October 1997.

[10] Tsao, R. H. C., "A Discussion on the Global Competitiveness of Taiwan's IC Industry," UMC Group, March 1999.

[11] Yuan, B. J.C., M. Y. Wang, "Analysis on the Key Factors Influencing Competitive Advantages of DRAM Industry in Taiwan," *International Journal of Technology Management*, Vol. 18, Nos. 1/2, 1999.

Chapter 3

Employee Profit Sharing and Stock Ownership Attracts World-Class Employees

An-Pin Chen and Shinn-Wen Wang

Institute of Information Management
National Chiao Tung University
HsinChu, Taiwan, ROC

1. Introduction

This chapter examines Taiwan's employee profit sharing and stock ownership system, including its merits and weaknesses, and compares this system with other employee reward systems. In addition, the profit sharing and stock ownership system is seen as a factor enhancing the international competitive strength of Taiwan's IC/PC industry and contributing to the growth of Taiwan's enterprises. The chapter also looks at the impact of this stock ownership system on cultural and social habits, including employee values. Finally, it anticipates future developments.

2. The present situation in Taiwan's IC/PC industry

Early in the 50s and 60s embryonic models of a research and development park existed. The most representative models were the research parks in the United States, including the ones near Stanford University in California, the Boston-Cambridge area, and North Carolina. These parks carry out technology research, development, innovation, and the cultivation of new technological business, with manufacturing facilities situated in a separate industrial district. These parks reflect a planned development trend in land utilization.

In Taiwan, KRP in Kyoto, which had been an old gas refinery, and KSP in Sun Nai state, which had been an old factory, were being rebuilt as innovation, research, and development areas. When the Hsinchu Scientific Industrial Park (HSIP) was established in Taiwan 20 years ago, its objective–to cultivate high-tech companies–was reached successfully. Presently the five to six percent research and development density inside the scientific park is much higher than the average of one percent in other areas [1].

This cultivation of high-tech companies and research has changed the complexion of Taiwan's industries. In 1997 Taiwan's Electronic Research & Service Organization, Industrial Technology Research Institute (ERSO/ITRI) pointed out that during the introductory stage of Taiwan's integrated circuit industry, IC had almost no relationship with the global silicon cycle (Table 1.). Before 1990, Taiwan's industry was in the formative stage and contributed little to Taiwan's Gross Domestic Product (GDP) [2].

After 1990 Taiwan's IC industry began a growth trend that has persisted into the 21st century. In 1990, Taiwan IC industry only contributed 2.5% to the GDP; however, by 1994 its contribution had risen to 10.9% and by 1995 was up to 17.6%. This increasing contribution to the GDP reflects the important role Taiwan's IC industry plays in national and international economics. The scale of IC industry became large enough that Taiwan's economy was affected by the international silicon cycle. In 1996, the global silicon cycle reached a low point when IC production dropped 11 percent from the previous year. Reflecting this cycle, Taiwan's IC production value dropped by nine percent. As its importance and size increases, global market trends affect production, planning and logistics in Taiwan. This close and interactive relationship illustrates the increasing role Taiwan's IC industry plays in world economics [3], and the same situation is true for the PC industry (Remark 1).

During the upgrading of Taiwan's industry, it was obvious that high-tech industry would be a mainstream industry, along with the electronics information industry. In 1994 when Kes Rood Technology Taiwan LTD. (KRTT) was established, Taiwan officially entered the age of the 8" fountry [4] and spurred an investment fever in the domestic IC industry. Following that, Taiwan Semiconductor Manufacturing Co. LTD. (TSMC) announced it would invest US$12.9 billion to build 8" and 12" semiconductor wafer fab and other IC factories like United Microelectronics Corp. (UMC), Winbond, Macronix International Co., Ltd. (MXIC), Mosel and Vitelic followed over the next 10 years. TSMC followed up by announcing a cross-century investment plan amounting to NT$1,600 billion. If the investment of packing and testing factories is included, investments in the entire IC industry reached US$64.52 billion.

There were some obstacles to growth; as a result of the global IC recession and Asian monetary storm. Some domestic companies slowed their investment pace, some moderated their progress, and some conducted strategic changes such as UMC' acquisition of semiconductor wafer fab in Japan (Nippon Steel Corporation Yawata Works, NSCYW). Generally, however Taiwan's industry continued constructing domestic IC chip factories. Based on statistics of the World Semiconductor Commission (WSC), the speed of investment of Taiwan IC industry in recent years will exceed that of other advanced countries. Capital expenditures were about 60 percent of operating income from 1995 to 1998, much higher than that of other advanced countries. As the IC industry becomes the backbone of Taiwan's economy, its investment plans will have a strong relationship to the overall competitive strength of the manufacturing industry, and its development will lead to growth for the entire economy.

The important fact that economic development in developed countries has changed from a reliance on land, natural resources, capital investment, and cheap labor to intelligence capital means innovative technology and intelligent manpower are the keys to competitive strength [5]. In areas where technology innovation can be cultivated, apart from research and development departments of various enterprises, national laboratories, research and development corporations and academic institutions, the system requires many inter-supplementary arrangements [6].

Taiwan's HSIP and ITRI played an important role in developing Taiwan's technology industry and became a classic example recognized all over the world for facing dynamic changes in technology, rapidly replacing industry structures and allocating and enhancing competitive resources. Other successful models comparable to the HSIP can be found in the Silicon Valley in the USA, Sophia Antipolis in France, the Oxford Scientific Park in Great Britain, and KSP in Sun Nai state and KRP in Kyoto.

The Sophia Antipolis area in the south of France occupies 2,300 hectares, with an area four times the size of HSIP, with only 100 more companies than HSIP's 260 companies. Of the 19,000 people working in Sophia Antipolis, only 40 percent are laborers; most are involved in technological research and positions requiring brainpower.

Of HSIP's 65,000 employees, the percentage of workers with masters and doctoral degrees is much higher than other areas. Like other developed countries, Taiwan has evolved from the perspiration advantage of manufacturing to the inspiration advantage of R&D, continuing the enhancement of Taiwan's competitive strength. Porter [5] calls this the "Diamond System," and it is not unique to Taiwan. In recent years, Scandinavian countries have strengthened their technological abilities impressively. The percentage of Sweden's investment in R&D to national income is the highest in the world. Eighty percent of the multinational companies in Sweden have established R&D facilities and have demonstrated their technological richness more than any other country in the OECD.

Another example in which high-tech employees served as the core for a city's development is the Oxford Scientific Park, which was established in 1991. Presently there are 710 high-tech companies in the Oxford district and 28,000 employees. In England, this ranks second to Cambridge, which has 1,300 companies with 35,000 employees. The Oxford scientific park is the product of a cooperative venture by Magdalene College, which donated land, and Prudential Insurance. The park's purpose was to commercialize technology developed at Oxford University. Presently there are 40 innovative companies in Oxford Scientific Park, around one-third of which are biotechnology and one-third are in information electronics. Sharp's European laboratory considered around 30 locations before they chose Oxford Scientific Parkas their base.

This was a change of focus for Oxford. Previously the university paid little attention to the product value and market opportunities of their research. Ten years ago the university established an intellectual property rights and technology transfer office and actively encouraged scholars to commercialize their technology and encouraged professors to establish businesses. This began interactive opportunities among academicians, the transfer office, researchers, business creators and venture capitalists, creating an environment attractive to many high-tech companies.

First-class talents in research and development have certain criteria for an ideal environment—sufficient space, a high quality of living, excellent communication facilities, and convenient traffic and flow of goods. Tax incentives are primary enticements for industries that focus on research & development.

Taiwan's HSIP is based on the same interactive model, with NCTU, National Tsing Hua University (NTHU), and ITRI serving as the intellectual and research and development nucleus for the park's knowledge and growth (Remark. 2). This model was essential to Taiwan's growth and success in the high-tech environment. For Taiwan nowadays, because of labor shortages and the high price of land, more than 60 percent of computer peripherals are manufactured overseas. In order to conduct work with more value in the expensive land and to provide a higher living quality, Taiwan has depended on the establishment of high-tech industries. In recent years, Taiwan's high-tech industries continue to create economic miracles for Taiwan and to attract first-class talents.

Taiwan is only one of the advanced countries employing this interactive model, and they all face similar problems such as talent shortages, upgrading their industries and investment. In this competitive global environment, Taiwan has managed to attract excellent talents. The key to this attraction and therefore to Taiwan's ability to excel in competition with other high-tech recruiters is Taiwan's employee profit sharing & stock ownership system.

	1986	1990	1994	1995	1996
GDP	$71,380	$161,160	$242,590	$264,632	$272,446
GDP/Capital	$3,669	$7,918	$11,487	$12,490	$12,733
Manufacturing/GDP(%)	39.4%	33.3%	29.0%	28.1%	28.0%
Electronics/manufacturing	10.1%	14.0%	16.1%	18.4%	19.6%
IC Industry/electronics (%)	--	2.5%	10.9%	17.6%	18.4%

Ref: [2]

Table 1. Analysis on level of importance of Taiwan's IC industry growth rate
(Output value Unit: million US$/year)

3. Theory and General Concepts of Profit Sharing and Stock Ownership for Taiwan Employees

To explain Taiwan's profit sharing and stock ownership system, this section will start with basic concepts and definitions. It then will analyze and compare the reward systems of Taiwan's IC industry. Profit sharing and stock ownership can be divided into three levels including "profit sharing," "stock ownership" and a combined "profit sharing & stock ownership" [7]:

3.1 Concepts and comparisons

Profit sharing or bonuses

It was pointed out at the International Profit Sharing Meeting in Paris in 1899 that profit sharing means companies shall appropriate a certain percentage of profits as a reward to general employees of an enterprise. This reward is based on negotiation, and once the appropriation percentage and ratio are decided, the employer cannot change them. In Taiwan's regulations, when a company has no profit, dividends and bonuses cannot be allocated. When the earnings reserve for the year exceeds 20 percent of total capital, in order to maintain stock prices, the excess can be appropriated as a stock dividend or bonus.

Stock ownership

Employee stock ownership means that employees can become stockholders in their own company, and this ownership is limited to stock availability. This is different than the USA. Company stocks held by employees are based on various methods of reward, negotiation and support and used to promote a company's direction or policy. Employee stock ownership means that an enterprise provides beneficial terms so employees can become stockholders in the company. As stock ownership means a possible gain in wealth, employees are willing to bear the risk inherent in an enterprise's operation.

Taiwan-style employee profit sharing & stock ownership systems (TSE-PSSO)

Profit sharing & stock ownership mean profit sharing combined with stock ownership. Apart from allocating bonuses to employee in the form of cash or checks, enterprises issue stocks as part of employees' bonuses. This way employees can not only earn bonuses from the company revenue, they can also acquire ownership. In addition, these benefits are taxed on the stock's face value, not its market value. Since the taxation system is of such importance, the next section will examine it.

Employee stock ownership allows employees to become stockholders of their company based on the following methods [8]:

Purchasing of stocks by employees who are stockholders

When a company issues new stocks in the form of cash capital increases, and when the stocks reserved for subscription by employees is larger than the maximum legal 15 percent, companies can apply the method of forfeiture on purchases by the original stockholders to allow employees to purchase stock.

Payment by new stocks during allocation of employee profit sharing

When the company allocates profits, the allocation amount shall be based on company regulations. Apart from cash payments, profit sharing also can be paid in the form of new stock issues, which means "employee profit sharing and stock ownership". Companies normally use both methods so employees can afford expensive stocks while retaining enough cash to pay their taxes.

Transfer of stocks owned by present stockholders to employees

When the company is not issuing new stocks, if it intends for employees to invest in the company, the company can negotiate with present stockholders to transfer some of their stocks to employees.

When the company is conducting cash capital increases, a certain percentage of stocks is reserved for priority subscription by employees

Article 267 of the Company Act specifies that when a company issues new stocks, except when approved by supervisory institutions, 10 to 15 percent of new stocks shall be reserved for subscription by employees. A special case approved by the supervisory institution might be overseas Chinese returning to conduct investments based on foreign investment regulations. If an overseas Chinese or foreign investment comprises more than 45 percent of a business' total capital, the regulation reserving a certain percentage for employees is not applicable.

Comparisons among various systems and TSE-PSSO

Profit sharing can increase employees' income, and stock ownership can allow employees to enjoy stock dividends. Because of the relationship between profit sharing and stock ownership, employees also can become stockholders, so such a system possesses the merits of profit sharing and stock ownership. However its effectiveness is dependent upon whether the stock ownership system is adequate. On the surface they are the same, yet there is a difference, and they can be conducted separately or together. Obviously, profit sharing & stockholders system is strongly related to TSE-PSSO. The following shows how profit sharing, stock ownership, TSE-PSSO, year-end bonuses, production bonuses, ESOPs and stock options differ [9].

Table 2. Comparisons among profit sharing, stock ownership, TSE-PSSO, year-end bonus, production bonus, ESOP and stock option

Ref. [7], [10], [11] and this research

Employee profit sharing
Condition:
(1). Allocation target is limited to company employee.
(2). The company has to have after-tax profits after deducting loss supplements, various public reserve appropriations, and dividend allocations.
(3). The percentage of employee profit sharing should be stipulated in the company's regulations; however, the allocation percentage to various employees is not stipulated. Normally the board of directors can be authorized to decide this.

Merits:
(1). Both employees and company benefit, management and operating efficiency are enhanced.
(2). Profit sharing payable to the employees is the allocation of profit and in accounting should not affect the company's acquisition capability.
Demerits:
(1). Improper allocations of profit sharing may cause arguments and employee-management problems.
(2). Employee profit sharing allocated from profits cannot be listed as an expense when reporting for income tax, and there is no income tax deduction benefit.
(3). Employee cannot be satisfied when there is no yearly profit sharing.
(4). Cash payments cannot carry out the function of employee savings or savings retirement funds.

Employees stock ownership
Condition:
(1). Stock ownership is limited to stocks of the servicing company.
(2). When employee stock ownership is conducted in the form of cash capital increases, based on the regulation of company law, employees should first appropriate 10% to 15% for stock purchases.
Merits:

(1). Owns enterprise operating rights and can participate in stockholders' meetings.

(2). Combination of employee and employer as one. Increases employees' sense of participation and belonging. Employee and employer disputes can be reduced.

(3). It is easier to attract excellent talent.

(4). There is an increased source of interest-free long-term capital.

(5). Can easily reach the regulation of stock ownership dispersal of supervisory institution.

(6). The employee acquiring stock ownership has comparatively little or no tax burden.

Demerits:

(1). When the stock ownership system is improper, it may cause injustice or fighting for benefits.

TSE-PSSO
Condition:

(1). A system that combines profit sharing and stock ownership.

(2). The company could decide the ratio of profit sharing to stock ownership.

(3). Employees are allowed to obtain stocks without any taxation.

Merits:

(1). Simple and convenient procedure through account transfer without transaction costs.

(2). By reflecting the operation's performance, remuneration will be adjusted, which increases the flexibility of labor costs.

(3). Harmonious relationships between labor and management and reduced operating cost.

(4). Reallocation of income.

(5). Enhancement of social status.

(6). Employees are stockholders of the company; therefore the difference between blue color and white color status can be reduced.

Demerits:

(1). Same as profit sharing and stock ownership.

(2). To draw on the strengths of each to offset the weakness of the other.

(3). Flexible to modify.

Year-end bonus (Quarters, Festivals)
Condition:

(1). A year-end bonus can be treated as part of the company's total expenses, and the company will not them deduct from it business income tax.

(2). Normally a year-end bonus is calculated based on the basic salary in certain months. No matter how much it profits an employee, the year-end bonus will always be issued. To employees, it is equivalent to a fixed income.

(3). Generally the year-end bonus will be issued before spring vacation.

Merits:

(1). Doing something for the occasions.

(2). Employees would be more concerned about how the company is run.

Demerits:

(1). Disagreement of opinion on annualized benefits between the employer and employees often causes arguments.

(2). It's an extraneous expense for the company, especially while its profit margins are low.

(3). Employees compare with other companies.

(4). No excess return.

Production (performance) bonus
Condition:

(1). Production bonus are given to employees based on certain performances such as enhancing work efficiency, achieving a production quota, improving product quality, reducing costs, or improving service performance with the result that the enterprise exceeds its profit forecast.

Merits:

(1). To reward employees to improve production performance.

(2). Allocating profits according to the performance of employees.

(3). The basis of merit systems.

Demerits:

(1). It may cause injustice or fighting for benefits because of differences between evaluating systems of various departments.

(2). Managers and employees face the pressure of evaluations.

ESOP (Remark 3)
Condition:

(1). Allowing debt.

(2). Taxation is up to the 25% limits.

(3). Having to invest on spots issues from the company over 51%.

(4). May consider combining a stock & profit sharing plan with a cash retirement plan.

Merits:

(1). Allows leveraging with lower interest rate.

(2). Enhancing willingness to work.

(3). Paying back principal and interest through leveraging with debt and pre-tax income and stock dividends.

(4). Attracting good intention stockholders.

(5). Inviting excellent talents and decreasing liquidity of employees.

(6). To avoid being taken over.

(7). Increasing investor profits.

(8). To preserve the value of assets

(9). Increasing the company's cash flow

(10). Employees need not pay taxes on stocks until they realize profits through selling the stocks.

Demerits:

(1). The stock price may not be correlated with results.

(2). Diluted stock prices.

(3). The strain of being recovered by stocks.

(4). High costs.

(5). Increased risk of trust fund.

(6). Risk of employees to mass excessively.

(7). Most of the time employees have to sell stocks to pay the taxes.

Stock Option (Remark 4)

Condition:

(1). Companies are allowed to issue stocks to raise funds and to reward employees.

(2). Employees could buy allocated stocks according to the issue-date price.

(3). Employees obtain stocks by stages.

(4). There are options to get the stocks or not.

(5). Credit line extensions for company.

Merits:

(1). The price of stocks would be higher if the costs of running the company continue to grow.

(2). Employees have to be at a job for a long period to get rewards; 3. Rewarding for employees for long-term employment.

(3). Matching the benefits with stockholders and employees.

(4). To attract the talents with extended credit.

(5). To raise funds for enterprises.

Demerits:

(1). Need a long term to rise the price of stocks.

(2). Stockholders' equity can be diluted.

(3). Influences of stock price to be diluted.

(4). Employees may get no benefits while the company is not doing well.

(5). Allocating stock quotas for employees can cause disagreements.

3.2 Tax Planning for profit sharing & stock ownership

The purpose of companies in implementing an employee profit sharing & stock ownership system is to benefit employees by giving them stock profits. Because of tax considerations, enterprise owners must pay close attention to tax planning. Since tax planning is so important for TSE-PSSO, this section will describe the principles of tax planning for profit sharing & stock ownership systems and compare them with other employee reward methods.

Tax planning principles

The essence of tax planning for employee profit sharing & stock ownership is to transform taxable income into tax-free income or delay the time of tax payments. For example, if profits payable to employees take the form of cash, it is considered income. However, if the company allocates employee profit sharing, which can be considered deferred payments of non-allocated cash capital increases, and employees have no income tax burden the year they receive the profit sharing. When these stocks are transferred and cashed in at face value, employee shares are calculated as salary income (required to be deducted from salary income). The part in excess of face value is considered securities transaction income and starting in 1990, is exempted from income tax. Generally speaking, factors to consider in employee profit sharing & stock ownership tax planning are as follows.

If the company adopts the method of prize money rewards or undertakes the price variance of employee stock ownership purchase, the company's portion can be reported as an expense and deducted from income taxes. However, if the company's regulations stipulate payments of employee profit sharing, it is deemed a profit allocation and cannot be considered an expense and treated as a tax deduction. The ultimate purpose of an enterprise's operation is to create maximum benefit for its stockholders. Although expenses concerning employee bonuses and stock rewards can be listed as a company tax and can be deducted from income taxes, they reduce the stock's profit capability and affect the value of the company stock. The tax burden of employee stock ownership differs depending on the method of stock acquisition, as shown below:

Tax burden ⠀⠀⠀⠀Method of acquisition	When the stock is acquired	When the stock is disposed
Cash purchase	No tax burden problem	Disposal price minus issue price leaves securities transaction income (tax exempt)
Employee stock profit sharing ⠀⠀⠀⠀Conforms to deferred tax levy regulations ⠀⠀⠀⠀Does not conform to defer tax levy regulations	No tax burden problem Face value is salary income	Face value is deemed as salary income tax Disposal price minus face value leaves securities transaction income (tax exempt) Disposal price minus face value leaves securities transaction income (tax exempt)
Utilization of employee purchase rights ⠀⠀⠀⠀Remuneration cost shall be borne by the company (corporation or stockholder) ⠀⠀⠀⠀Remuneration cost shall be borne by the individual stockholders who transfer out the stocks	Issue price minus purchase price leaves salary income (other income) Transferor is levied with gift tax and transferee shall be exempted from tax.	Disposal price minus issue price leaves securities transaction income (tax exempt) Disposal price minus issue price leaves securities transaction income
Transfer from the original stockholder ⠀⠀⠀⠀Market price transfer ⠀⠀⠀⠀Sub-market price transfer	No tax burden Transferor is levied with gift tax and transferee shall be exempted from tax.	Disposal price minus purchase price leaves securities transaction income (tax exempt) Disposal price minus purchase price leaves securities transaction income (tax exempt)

Ref. [12]

Table 3. Comparison of tax burden under employee stock ownership method

3.3 Research and Studies on Profit Sharing & Stock Ownership

Research and studies from European countries and America support the importance and influence of the profit sharing & stock ownership system on enterprises. Studies on the relationship between ESOP and excess return include [13], Stulz (1988), Harris and Raviv (1988), [14], and Chang (1990). Studies that focus on performance improvement, including [15], [16], [17], [18], [19] and [20] studies start from the viewpoint of ESOP's influence on stock prices. Research on ESOP's added value include Defourney, Estrin and Jones (1985), who conclude profit sharing increases the cost of doing business but does not improve production capability. On the other hand, stock ownership could improve production capability. Fitzroy and Cable (1980) say that profit sharing can provide a connection between employee effort and remuneration.

Under the stock ownership system, employees are stockholders. The major expectations of this arrangement are that employee turnover will be reduced and the overall profit would be increased through the joint efforts of employees and the employer. By both parties' receiving profits, the opposition between employees and employers is reduced or resolved. Because of this, a system that includes the merits of profit sharing and stock ownership can increase labor productivity, reduce employee turnover rate and reduce supervisory costs, while resolving employer-employee disagreements. Defourney, Estrin and Jones discovered that profit sharing could increase productivity; however, there is no significant influence on the size of productivity. The stock ownership system will promote productivity, but pressure needs to be kept on the policy to facilitate its success.

Svejnar and Jones (1985) concluded the profit sharing and stock ownership system has a positive and significant impact on an enterprise's productivity. Svejnar and Conte (1988) confirmed profit sharing and stock ownership's contribution to productivity, but the magnitude depends on the quantity of stocks owned. Fitzroy and Kraft also discovered that profit sharing systems could increase productivity, increase operating income, and reduce employee turnover rates [21]. The above results of research are listed in Table 4.

Researchers & Papers	Investigation information				Dependent Variable	Explanation Variable	Results
	Period	Country	Industries	Samples			
R1	--	USA	Selected Industries	--	Excess Return	*E1*	*D1*
R2	--	Taiwan	Top 500 service industry, manufacturing industry	500	Performance of subjective judgment Financial performance	*E2*	*D2*
R3	1976 | 1989	USA	Selected Industries	276	Major reason for running ESOP in American enterprises.	*E3*	*D3*
R4	--	USA	Polaroid	--	Excess Return	*E4*	*D4*
R5	--	USA	Selected Industries	--	Influences of stock price for announcing ESOP.	*E5*	*D5*
R6	--	USA	Selected Industries	165	Excess Return Effect of stock price	*E6*	*D6*
R7	--	USA	Selected Industries	--	Stock Price	*E7*	*D7*
R8	--	USA	Selected Industries	--	Enterprise performance	*E8*	*D8*
R9	--	Taiwan	Companies that are running ESOP.	--	Employees liquidity Production capability	*E9*	*D9*
R10	--	USA	Selected Industries	--	Major reason for running ESOP in American enterprises.	*E10*	*D10*
R11	1978 | 1979	France	Construction industry Printing industry Machinery industry	430	Added-value	*E11*	*D11*

R12	1975 | 1980	Italy	Manufacturi ng industry	315 316	Added- value	*E12*	*D12*
R13	--	England	--	40	Added- value	*E13*	*D13*
R14	1977 | 1979	West Germany	Metal manufacturi ng industry	65	Added- value Total essential productivity profit sharing	*E14*	*D14*
R15	1974 | 1976	West Germany	--	42	Added- value	*E15*	*D15*

Ref: [7], [11] and this research

Table 4. Excerpts of result of literature research

Symbolic notes:
R1: [13]; Stulz(1988); Harris and Raviv(1988); *R2*: [15][16]; Chang (1989); Chang and Mayers (1992); *R3*: [14]; *R4*: [14]; *R5*: [17]; *R6*: [19]; *R7*: Gordon and Chang (1990); *R8*: [17]; *R9*: Zheng B. W. (1989); *R10*: [22]; *R11*: Defourney, Estrin & Jones (1985); *R12*: Svejnar & Jones (1985); *R13*: Svejnar & Conte (1988); *R14*: Fitzroy & Kraft (1987); *R15*: Fitzroy & Cable (1980).

E1: 1. Tax preferential; 2. Stock price; *E2*: ESOP; *E3*: 1. To improve welfare of employees; 2. Avoiding to be taken over; 3. Decrease salary of employees; *E4*: ESOP; *E5*: 1. Effect of taxation for ESOP; 2. Effect of distribution for ESOP; *E6*: ESOP; *E7*: Announcing takeover speculation for ESOP; *E8*: 1. ESOP; 2. Participate in-style management; *E9*: Employees be the shareholders; *E10*: 1. Welfare of employees; 2. Tax preferential; 3. Production capability of employees; 4. Taking over by ill emotion; 5. Bankrupt crisis; *E11*: 1. Profit/employee number; 2. Employee percentage; 3. Employee participation degree; 4. Employee capital percentage; *E12*: 1. Capital amount; 2. Employee number (based on whether they are member); 3. Cooperative plan personnel percentage; 4. Employee profit allocation figure; 5. Employee loan amount; 6. Loan preparation fund amount; *E13*: 1. Labor total work hour; 2. Fuel & electricity expense; 3. Abstract variables include; 4. Profit sharing; 5. Employee participation and wage decision; 6. Non management level indirect enterprise stock holding percentage; 7. Employee participation in group negotiation percentage; 8. Company bankruptcy employee appeal right on asset; *E14*: 1. Capital amount; 2. Blue collar work hour; 3. White collar work hour; 4. Time abstract variables; 5. Profit sharing; 6. Total essential productivity; *E15*: 1. Capital amount; 2. Blue collar work hour; 3. White collar work hour; 4.

Amount/employee number; 5. Employee capital percentage; 6. High low participation abstract variable; 7. Time abstract variable.

D1: 1. Tax preferential isn't the notable factor for excess return; 2. To compensate for salary of employees, welfare decreasing isn't the remarkable factor for explaining the stock price; *D2*: Performance of subjective judgment and financial performance of ESOP companies are better than non-ESOP ones; *D3*: 1. To improve welfare of employees (74.6%); 2. Avoiding to be taken over (19.6%); 3. Decrease salary of employees (5.8%); *D4*: Positives excess return for ESOP companies.; *D5*: 1. If tax effect were greater than distributed effect than stock price would be raised; 2. If tax effect were smaller than distributed effect than stock price would be declined; *D6*: Announcing day for ESOP obtains 3.66% excess return.; *D7*: Remarkable positives reactions of stock price; *D8*: ESOP combined with participate in-style management cause the notable improving performance of companies; *D9*: Decreasing the liquidity of employees; *D10*: Welfare of employees (91%), Tax preferential. (74%), Production capability of employees. (70%), Taking over by ill emotion, Bankrupt crisis; *D11*: 1. Employee participation increase enterprise production; 2. Profit sharing can increase enterprise production but its effect on productivity is not large; 3. Stock ownership can enhance productivity but this policy needs enforcement to be successful; *D12*: 1. Profit sharing has positive and significant influence on productivity; 2. Stock ownership will have positive and significant influence; *D13*: 1. Employee participation can enhance enterprise productivity.; 2. Employee stock ownership influence depends on the quantity of stock ownership; 3. Union will have positive influence on productivity; *D14*: 1. Profit sharing can increase productivity and operating amount can be increased; 2. Profit sharing can reduce employee turnover rate; *D15*: 1. Profit sharing can increase productivity; 2. Profit sharing can reduce production cost; 3. Stock ownership can reduce opposition between employee and employer; 4. Increase employee participation and enhance efficiency.

4. Legal Aspects of Taiwan's Employee Profit Sharing & Stock Ownership

This section will discusses the regulations governing Taiwan's employee profit sharing and stock ownership system as well as its origins, direction, and room for flexibility.

4.1 The system's history

The relationship between labor and management is one of the most important issues in running a business. Since the Second World War, because of the losses resulting from conflicts between labor and management, various countries in Europe and the USA have established methods for handling labor and management disputes. Through promoting union and employee profit sharing & stock ownership, it was hoped that the relationship and cooperation between labor and management could be improved. The results were successful, and developing countries soon adapted the idea. In addition, due to the popularity of capitalism in Europe and the USA, the difference between the poor and rich was growing. Because of this, the Anti-Trust Act and Company Act were established, which allowed general enterprises to offer stocks to the public instead of stocks being controlled exclusively by the capitalists. As employees were able to become part of the enterprise by holding company stocks, this allowed the interests of labor and management to merge [10].

Taiwan advocates equivalent fortune and democracy and promotes labor and management cooperation. This has developed over time, and this section will analyze how the system evolved from a disappointing beginning to UMC's successful implementation of profit sharing and stock ownership [11].

Promotion and guidance period (1945-1975)

In its early stages, although the governing party, the Kuomintang, promoted profit sharing and stock ownership (Remark. 5), the results weren't very successful. In 1945, the governing party of Taiwan announced its Labor Policy Outline, which promoted employee profit sharing and stock ownership. After that, various parties and government departments, companies, officials and academic fields started to promote the idea, and a promotion and guidance period took place for 30 years, from 1945 to 1975. The most important draft proposal was the "Draft proposal of a profit sharing system outline for public and private operating," which included: 1. Purpose of stipulation, 2. Percentage of profit sharing, 3. Calculation basis for profit sharing, 4. Method of payment, 5. Percentage of stock ownership, and 6. Reward for excellent performance. This proposal established many of the relationships and percentages being implemented today—for example, basing the percentage of profit sharing on 10 to 20 percent of total profit and reserving not less than 10 percent of newly issued stocks for employee to purchase.

Period of promotion on important points (1976~1982)

The special distinction of this stage was that the governing party and government cooperated to select large enterprises to subsidize to promote the venture. In November 1965, the governing party convened the 11th National Representatives Meeting, which passed a regulation that included "protection of labor rights, promotion of profit sharing and stock ownership, and promotion of labor and management cooperation". The employee profit sharing & stock ownership motto was changed from "promotion and guidance" to "promotion" and promotion became more aggressive. The most important points were "essentials of profit sharing & stock ownership promotion," "important measures on labor benefits enhancement" and the sixth amendment to the Company Act. The main promotional targets were large enterprises. The most significant promotion occurred at Ta-Tung Company, which in 1946 started to retain part of its newly issued stocks for employees to purchase. However, the company kept the stocks in trust so employees could only obtain stocks after they ended employment.

The derivative innovation period (1983~2001)

The largest reformer at this stage was UMC. Since 1983, UMC employees have been able to obtain company stocks from a profit sharing plan. This benefit attracted first-class talents from Taiwan and abroad to UMC. As a result, in a very short time, UMC was able to compete with TSMC and solidify its steps onto the international stage. With UMC's success, other companies began implementing the plan to attract and retain first-class employees.

As the monetary system, accounting system and related laws and regulations of Taiwan have remained conservative, there have not been a lot of variations to the basic system. It is believed that when the government actively promotes Taiwan as an Asia-Pacific Monetary Center and joins the World Trade Organization (WTO), domestic financial markets will become more active, and related financial products and coping measures will become less strict (Remark. 6). At that time, employee profit sharing & stock ownership system innovation will take place.

The US employee profit sharing & stock ownership was promoted for 53 years (1886~1939) before its profit sharing & stock ownership entered a feasible implementation stage. It has been 55 years since Taiwan began to employ the system. Although Taiwan adopted the concepts from Europe and the USA, it has evolved into a unique system adapted to Taiwan's industrial needs.

4.2 The legal aspect of employee profit sharing & stock ownership system

Article 235 of the Taiwan Company Act (Remark. 7) specifies that companies must stipulate the percentage or ratio of employee profit sharing. Also Article 267 specifies that "when business units issue new stock, employees should purchase 10% to 15% of the total amount of new stock". Because of this act, employee stock ownership is not just a benefit enjoyed by electronic industry employees.

The profit sharing and stock ownership system evolved to fit the nation's needs. After the province was simplified (Remark. 8), Taiwan's government organization became flat and parallel, eliminating layers of signing units and departments. As a result, policy implementation has become clearer. This organizational simplification, paired with a flexibility of legal revisions, has created a more responsive regulatory environment. If there is an urgent needs for a law's immediate implementation, as long as a draft proposal can be sent to Legislative Yuan for three readings, the proposal doesn't encounter serious obstacles, and after it goes through a public notification, a law can be become effective immediately. This occurred when Taiwan was facing the monetary storm. At that time, a "company act revision on part of articles draft proposal was proposed," under which the treasury stock system could be included to save the monetary market.

4.3 Related coping measures and assistance to law revision

Taiwan needs to be internationalized to become an Asia-Pacific Logistics Management Center and enhance its competitive strength. At the same time, talent, capital, technology and materials need to be able to enter and exit Taiwan rapidly and conveniently. To enable this, certain laws, regulations, and policies must be broadened. For example, Taiwan proposes to develop an Asian-Pacific Monetary Center, a multi-media center, an expedition center and a manufacturing center. However, it is difficult for foreign multinational companies to function under present laws and regulations, which work against the attainment of these national goals. Under current regulations and laws, foreigners can only be employed in Taiwan for a period of two to three years. Because of this, foreign companies are discouraged from developing in Taiwan on a large scale or for an extended period of time. In this situation, employers in Taiwan end up training workers but not being able to reap the benefits. This increases the costs of business operations and of major government construction projects. This applies to house servants as well. When foreign workers have to pay brokerage fees, but can only stay in Taiwan for a limited time, they simply take off when their work visas expire and continue to work in Taiwan illegally, increasing the problem of illegal workers.

Because of this situation, a revision of Article 49 of the Occupation Service Act was presented to "extend the employment period of foreigners in Taiwan and reduce the cost to employers of labor replacement". This would extend the period of stay for white-collar foreign employees to three years each time. After the period expires, employers can apply for extensions, with future stays limited to one year, with an unlimited number of extensions. For foreign workers and servants, the longest period would be 3.5 years. The hope is that this would enhance Taiwan's competitive strength.

Another measure that would have a profound influence on Taiwan's industry is a national defense military service alternative. High-tech professionals with high academic qualifications such as masters and doctoral degree are the most sought after employees, but these talents must serve in the military service for several years. In response to political pressure from the opposite side of the strait, Taiwan has implemented compulsory military service, but this system has never changed, despite the fact there has been no war for more than 50 years. Under a national defense refinement proposal, the military could cultivate high-tech talents (Remark. 9), and these people would not have to interrupt their research. It also would help attract outstanding overseas talents to return to the country without worrying about the problem of military service. Instead of serving in the traditional military, high-tech talents can choose to work in the Industry Technology Research Institute, the Chung-Shan Institute of Science and Technology, or the Academia Sinica, concentrating on technology research and development. The scope of research would be limited to an area related to national defense. The academic institution can broaden the scope to include going abroad to conduct research. Young men also can serve in private technology companies like TSMC, Acer, and the Institute for Information Industry.

The head of Academia Sinica, Lee Yuan Chieh, recognizes that economic war waged with technology is becoming a substitute for military combat. In a global competitive economy, people can contribute to their country's service in ways other than through military service. Some European countries allow people to participate in social services, national defense services or scientific research to serve their country, and Taiwanese also could contribute in different capacities.

The substitute service promoted by Taiwan in 2000 made it the first country outside Europe to implement substitute service. This alternative service would encompass all males, not just those with high academic qualifications, a fact that will significantly impact Taiwan's industries.

From this overview, it can be seen that measures and regulations related to employee profit sharing & stock ownership in Taiwan can be modified in response to changing requirements of people and industries. This is one of the important factors in large companies like TSMC and Acer's willingness to remain here [23].

5. Unique merits of profit sharing & stock ownership systems and international competitive strengths

Article 235 of the Taiwan Company Act clearly points out that a company must appropriate a fixed employee profit sharing percentage, and presently that percentage is around 10 to 15 percent [41]. However, in recent years, when UMC breathed new life into a system that has been used in this industry for a long time, it started a fever of duplication. Not only did UMC lay down the ground rules for attracting talents to Taiwan industries, it also created a high-tech legend in the park.

Whether looking at the academic environment or industrial conditions, Taiwan's salary and land in its early stage development could not be compared to that of Europe and the USA. Even excellent native talents were happy to take every opportunity to study and work abroad, a fact that was reflected in the slang saying: "Come, come, come, come to NTU (Remark. 10); go, go, go, go to the USA". Taiwan could not attract first-class international talents to join its industry. Facing the fact that the best talents were leaving Taiwan for greener pastures, UMC decided it had to provide a superior, more practical system to attract and retain superior, high-tech employees. To achieve this end, the company was the first to provide employee profit sharing and the ability to acquire company stocks through capital increases transferred from profits. In order to keep employees from buying and selling immediately, which would have an erratic effect on company stock prices, UMC locked the acquired company stock for a while (Remark. 11) and then released it to market. This is now the most popular employee profit sharing & stock ownership system in Taiwan's high-tech industry [24]. The broad implementation of employee profit sharing and stock ownership systems in Taiwan has been successful in attracting first-class talents for its high-tech industries. This not only enhances the Taiwan's global competitive strength, it also helps internationalize Taiwan and improve its international image.

What is unique about the Taiwan employee profit sharing and stock ownership system, giving it such influence? The following lists some key reasons:

5.1 Employees could obtain excess tax preferential returns

TSE-POSS has been in HSIP for the last 10 years. According to Taiwan's stock system, each stock belongs to a stockholder. Since there are no index option commodities in Taiwan, enterprises have to withdraw a fraction of their annual returns for employee stocks. For example, if the annual return is NT$200 million, 10 percent of this return is for employee profit sharing, and employees are taxed NT$10 for each stock. The market price of these stocks, however, may be worth many times NT$10. This constitutes an excess return for employees but not for the company. This innovative system rewards employees and has had the effect of attracting excellent talents to Taiwan.

5.2 Promotes cooperation between labor and management and establishes a mutually beneficial relationship

If we separate remuneration into "business creation" and "job remuneration," the traditional emphasis of employee profits-sharing systems has been on "job remuneration". This means employees can obtain only small adjustments to their base salary, with considerations for years of service and performance. Throughout the employee's life, the remuneration is insignificant compared with what the employer receives. A company owner can acquire favorable subsidies, etc. (Remark. 12) and amass a fortune through its employees. This "business creation remuneration" further increases the distance in wealth between owners and staff. Although this problem is not peculiar to Taiwan and exists in industries in other countries, it became a pressing issue in Taiwan as it sought to upgrade its industries. Traditional industries relied on a minor number of excellent leaders or managers who led hard-working employees to attain a certain performance level. Today's technology industries need specialized fields in which to innovate, research and develop new technologies. This requires technologically sophisticated employees, who are in high demand throughout the world. This creates a strong mutual dependency between company owners and employees.

The employee profit sharing and stock ownership system blurs the line between employee and employer, and progressively "employees" become "employers". The speed of this role change is in direct relation to the individual employee's contributions to the company. This kind of arrangement is similar to the policy of "whoever wants to farm will have land" implemented when the R.O.C. Government moved to Taiwan. This system has allowed high-tech industries to be exempt from the labor and management antagonism and strikes that characterized traditional industry. With a harmonious relationship between employee and employer, the company can enjoy a longer, more productive life span. The system's success is based on the principle of mutual advantage [25]. As enterprises opens the profit-sharing door, employees increase their own and the company's benefits [26].

5.3 A common life full of internal gathering force

An internal gathering force comes from two sources. One is the enhancement of overall operating performance from being a stockholder. The second is the sense of honor that results from successful competition among peers. Usually Taiwan's technology industry does not pay extremely high base salaries to retain its talent; instead profit sharing and stock ownership systems reward employees for the entire year. Using TSMC as an example, in 1999, on the average, each employee was allocated 20 stock certificates (Remark. 13). Every employee knows very clearly what each cycle must achieve in order to maintain a qualified rate, reduce the cost of failure, and create better profits. This community spirit originates from benefits to oneself and others.

Secondly, in the Taiwan technology industry, especially the high-tech industry, as profits become high, more and more industries are founded in the profitable field. The result is intense competition among companies in similar industries, such as that seen between TSMC and UMC in chip consignment processing and CMC and Ritek in CDR production [27]. This competitive model is a strong and powerful. To the people in the occupations, becoming the leader of the industry has its perks and intensifies employees' sense of loyalty.

5.4 Ability to recruit world-class and first-class talent

Talent is the lifeblood of a company, especially in high-tech industries. Famous national universities and research institutes near HSIP such as the National Chiao Tung University (NCTU), National Ching Hua University (NTHU), and the Industry Technology Research Institute have created a unique cooperative environment between industry and academia similar to the relationship between America's Silicon Valley and Stanford University. NCTU, which emphasizes applied science, and NTHU, which emphasizes research in foundation sciences, provide academic resources and a research environment for international talents attracted to the park by high profit sharing and stock ownership. In addition, the Technology of Industry Institute, a semi-government research organization, offers facilities for research and technological development. These resources accelerate technological innovation as well as research and development. Development personnel and engineers in the park have access to the best academic choices. In addition, in recent years there has been an active establishment and expansion of space for employees who want to obtain a degree or earn credit hours.

In addition to HSIP, Tainan Scientific Industry Park (TSIP) has adopted the "successful copying" model to create a second high-tech paradise in Taiwan. The model employed in TSIP is similar to the HSIP [28]. On its perimeter are National Cheng Kung University (NCKU) and National Sun Yat-san University (NSYSU), important places for cooperation between academia and business. Another consideration is that most of the companies in the park provide excellent, comfortable living environments for employees.

5.5 Smooth advance and retreat with rich flexibility

Taiwan's employee profit sharing & stock ownership system is flexible so companies can make adjustments based on their individual environments.

Profits can be retained and allocated at a later period, or profit allocations can be based on a cash method. In addition, employees' profit sharing percentages can be adjusted. Stock prices for employee stock ownership can either adopt or not adopt the face value as the standard.

The percentage of employee profit sharing & stock ownership, as well as the scale and amount, can all be adjusted and controlled flexibly. As far as how many stocks can be allocated to employees, the evaluation method adopted also is quite flexible and can include academic and work experience, performance, special performance, years of service, etc.; all of these potentially can be included in determining allocation. An example is UMC, where the percentage allocated for employee profit sharing percentage started at 25 percent, dropped to 12 percent, then dropped again to eight percent [29].

5.6 Co-sharing of profit and establishment of a win-win performance

The following figures illustrate the win-win situation created by co-sharing of profits. UMC implemented employee profit sharing & stock ownership in 1983. With the exception of an operating loss in 1990, the enterprise experienced profits every year, and every year profit sharing & stock ownership occurred. UMC yearly profit stock allocation percentage is as follows (based on the calendar year):

Year	Earnings stock allocation Percentage	Year	Earnings stock allocation percentage
1984	34.6%	1991	(Earnings not allocated)
1985	(Earnings not allocated)	1992	21%
1986	15%	1993	15%
1987	37%	1994	25%
1988	28%	1995	50%
1989	27%	1996	93%
1990	25%	1997	30%

Ref: [42]

Table 5. Earnings stock allocation percentage

Based on this stock allocation percentage, if the founding stockholders of UMC had held on to their stocks until now, their original cost per stock would be only $0.27. Based on the closing price of NT$92 on June 5, 2000, the stock's income rate is 340.74 times the original investment. In addition, starting from 1984, stocks from profit sharing by employees of UMC had accumulated to 365,819,879 stocks, occupying 6.58 percent of actual paid up capital in 1999 (NT$56 billion). Had employees started in the allocated profit sharing stock at the beginning and participated in profit allocation every year, their accumulated stock holdings would occupy 18.52 percent of the company stock (up until 1999). Presently, management-level employees at UMC (those with titles of deputy manager and above) hold 12 percent of the company's stock. This is larger than any corporation stockholder and sufficiently exemplifies the company style of professional leadership [29]. Acer group is another example. General Manager Stan Shih released stocks to employees in 1980. By the end of 1988, 60 percent of the company's stock had been transferred to employees, and his personal stock dropped from 63 percent to less than 15 percent [30].

In UMC's 15 years of experience with employee profit sharing & stock ownership, an average of 0.43 percent of the stocks are released every year so employees can participate in profit conversion to capital increase. Because of this, employees have become stockholders and created a 14.5 times income rate every year. This creates a considerably significant win-win effect [31]. The situation is the same for TSMC [32].

Companies also can allow employees to participate in profit sharing during the construction of a new factory or they can conduct a cash capital increase. The company can release a fixed percentage for employees to subscribe to stocks, with the stock price normally one-third to one-eighth of the market price. The most obvious examples are the construction of HSIP, the third factory of MXIC, the sixth and seventh factories of TSMC, and the fifth factory of UMC [33].

Worth noting is Nan Ya Plastic Co. Ltd., which is the largest private enterprise in Taiwan and is considered the giant of traditional industries in Taiwan. Due to loss of talent, they adopted the profit sharing & stock ownership system in their new company, Nan Ya Printed Circuit Board Co. Ltd.

5.7 Enhancement of management performance

Somebody has called the "enterprise spirit" of Taiwan a "motorcycle spirit" because everyone wants to be a boss so they can work in their own style. Because of this, there is an abundance of strong small- to medium-sized enterprises. Employee profit sharing & stock ownership leverages this desire for independence and responsibility. Each employee acts as if he or she were operating his or her own company, so behavior is self-initiating and responsible. Managers in upper-level positions can personally attend to their own matters with the knowledge that their subordinates are performing their duties under their own initiative and eliminating any adverse practices. This kind of management can be handled effectively and simply, as can be observed from two sides–a system side and a work enthusiasm side.

TSMC is an example, with its company emphasis on honesty. There is no falsity of their work or in the performance of their research. Because of the reputation TSMC has built for honesty, large international companies such as Intel hand over design drawings of important CPU and IC components to TSMC for consignment processing. In regard to employee work dedication, TSMC engineers frequently work overtime until 9 or 10 p.m. [34]. At Acer Communication (ACERCM), an affiliate of the Acer group, engineers work the same [35]; in fact this enthusiasm and dedication to long hours is a common practice in the park instead of the exception. The same is true for engineers of companies in Software Park. The effect of this personal sense of responsibility is exemplary performance.

5.8 Decreasing resistance to change and enhancing enterprise

In the Harvard Business Review [36], Paul Strebel is of the opinion that a yearly wage system makes employees unwilling to work harder then their boss. In particular, employees will create a bottleneck to change if the company is facing re-engineering of its workflow. These cases are found at many international companies that are undergoing enterprise resource planning (ERP), global supply chain management (GSCM) and knowledge management [37]. In these cases, employee resistance causes most of the failures. On the contrary, many successful cases come from well-executed employee reward systems. TSE-POSS plays an important role in helping enterprises that face changes and re-engineering.

5.9 Solution to the problem of succession

Under the employee profit sharing & stock ownership system, if employees retain their allocated stocks, they have the chance to become major stockholders of a company. The company grows and continues because it can choose the most qualified managers. In traditional Taiwan industries, the most frequent complaint concerning operations is caused by "family businesses". Stocks reside in the hands of family members, and relatives fight among each other for company positions. This often results in the wrong persons operating the company, which causes operational problems or the loss of talented employees. As a result, the growth of this enterprise will face a bottleneck [43].

UMC is an example of a company that transcended this situation. When it was established, a large capital investment was required, and the founding stockholders held most part of stock. After this stage, the president, Tsao Hsin-cheng, decided to progressively reduce original stockholders' holdings so the company could grow more quickly. Under this method of accumulated employee stock holdings, employees became the largest stockholder group and now own more than half of the director seats. They have the leading function regarding operating rights so the company can avoid the situation of ignorant people leading experts. Furthermore, UMC has stringent integrity rules, a benefits system, a strict commendation and reprimand system, a retirement plan, and prohibitions against employing relatives. Not only can the company avoid unstable management as a result of competing small groups or private forces, leadership succession can be achieved by selecting the best talent to lead the enterprise. Former President Tsao Hsin-cheng saw this principle enacted when he was succeeded by President Shun Ming-chi. UMC is frequently cited as a model case for domestic technology industries.

5.10 The treasury stock system

In 1987, the stock market crashed, marking in history what was later known as "Black Friday". Treasury stocks (Remark. 14) at that time proved their robustness by surviving the adverse situation. The treasury stock system had been discussed in the country for long time, dating back to October 1997, when Taiwan first encountered the power of monetary storms. A group of international speculators stuck with NT dollars sold short in large amounts. In order to maintain the NT exchange rate, the Central Bank of China supplied US dollars without limit. Although the exchange rate stabilized, interest rates kept climbing until at one point the short-term interest rate reached 11 percent. The prosperity the Taiwan stock market enjoyed after crossing the 10,000-point barrier in October 1997 ended and dropped back to 6,000 points. Industries, academics and government advocated amendments to the Security Transaction Act. A priority concern to stop the fall was the inclusion of the treasury stock system. The act went through the first and second readings. In January 14, 1999, after the Legislative Yuan was rumored to pass a third reading of that law, the stock market rose 220 points as a result, illustrating the effects of public anticipation. Finally, Legislative Yuan passed a third reading of the act on June 30, 2000 (Remark. 15).

In the US, treasury stocks are purchased by a company for the following reasons:

(1). For the use of stock options, profit sharing and employee stock purchase rights;

(2). To be used as convertible special stocks or convertible company bonds;

(3). As a company balance capital investment or company stock price adjustment;

(4). As a pre-purchase action for acquisition of another company's stock in an exchange;

(5). To reduce the number of stocks circulating outside in order to increase the profit per stock;

(6). To reduce the number of stocks held by investors to prevent acquisition by another company;

(7). To be used for stocks issued as stocks so the dividend can be used for stock allocation without payment.

In the US, the success of the improved treasury stock system can be credited to the fact that the US stock market system is healthy and regulative laws and measures are complete. Because of this, defects can be reduced to a minimum. However, in Taiwan there is a threat that the treasury stock system will become the tool for major stockholders and companies to control stock prices (Remark. 16).

After the employee profit sharing and stock ownership system allowed employees to become major stockholders, under special situations they also serve a stabilizing function similar to the treasury stock system. Through group efforts and confidential talks, employee will decline to sell their stocks so the circulation of stocks decreases, which has a positive effect on the stock's price. The biggest difference between the treasury stock system and employee efforts is that the company openly operates the treasury stock system, and employee efforts can be carried on inside the company. In this circumstance, as long as employees have confidence in the company, certain functions can be carried out.

5.11 The impact on traditional industries

A strategy of stock allocation in the technology industry results in a circulation of talent within the same industry. This puts pressure on traditional industry to offer the same types of benefits in order to attract employees. Presently, China Steel, the first private company that is a former government-owned company to propose employee stock ownership, is awaiting approval from the National Operations Commission to implement a stock allocation plan. China Steel's human resource department head, Weng Chao-tung, points out that China Steel cannot afford to stay outside this industry trend.

Weng Chao-tung acknowledged that the technology industry's stock ownership system has made a lot of multi-millionaires of young managers, and this has affected the attitude of managers and employees in traditional industries: "To people who have to work so hard for several tens of years, sometime they feel so inferior". However, although employees in traditional industry are jealous, they have obstacles to overcome if they want to cross over into the high-tech industry.

Taiwan President Group Chairman Kao Ching-yuan points out that employee profit sharing and stock ownership has not had a large impact on the President Enterprise Group because employees in the President Group have found it difficult to make the jump to a technology industry. However, Kao Ching-yuan admits that if the President Group decides to enter into the high-tech industry, it will adopt the high-tech industry's profit sharing & stock ownership system, or it will allow employees to purchase stock before the stock is listed on the market in order to attract talent.

5.12 Creating competitive strength

Presently, Taiwan's largest industry is the technology industry, and the main competitors are companies in the USA, Japan, and Korea, etc. Compared to the employee profit sharing and stock ownership system, there are significant differences among employee fringe benefit systems in various countries. Systems in Korea and Japan are quite rigid, and employees have no stock ownership, so they are purely employees. Employee salary is mostly decided by years of service, and the scale of adjustment is not large. Although both Japan and Korea have hard-working people, it is difficult under this system to stimulate staff morale and to initiate an employee spirit of innovation and creation. This system contrasts significantly with the rich vitality and unlimited remuneration brought by Taiwan employee profit sharing & stock ownership. In the 21st century, systems with a clear employer bias will find themselves merging into a system that yields better competitive strength.

Generally three types of fringe benefits comprise the US employee fringe benefit system: founder's stocks, stock options, and high salaries compared with salaries in Taiwan. Face value of US stock can be self-stipulated, unlike Taiwan, which regulates that one stock certificate equals 1,000 stocks, with a NT$10 per-stock face value. At the same time, US stocks do not have the restriction that technology stocks cannot exceed 15 percent. Because of this, normally when a US technology company is established, it decides how many stocks the founding stockholders want to have and the price of each stock. After the stock is on the market, the market determines its value, and stocks cannot be then transferred to employees at various symbolic prices or free of charge.

At this time, through stock options, stocks cannot be given to employees directly. When hiring employees, in order to employ first-class talents and to allow them to devote themselves to the company for a long time, normally companies use stock options as the main chip. Under this method, it is stipulated that after a certain number of years of service to the company, employees can purchase a certain percentage of company stocks. Generally this purchase price is based on the closing price of the stock the day the employee started working for the company. Every couple of years, the company conducts a stock option plan and implements the plan, with the stock price of that day as the purchase price. It is a gamble; if the stock price raises on the date the employee reports to work or when the stock purchase plan commences, employees can earn stock profits. Conversely, if the stock price drops, stock options become abstract. This kind of system is like long-term stock purchase certificates in that losses are limited, but potential profits are unlimited.

From the perspective of employee motivation to enhance overall operating performance and create competitive strength, the US founder stock system and stock options can be too excessive on one hand and too insufficient on the other hand. This can be seen by comparing company founders Yang Chi-yuan and Bill Gates. After their companies became successful, they immediately became billionaires. There were also network concept stocks or Internet companies like Netscape that were unprofitable and had low operating amounts, but their stock prices rose. Netscape was listed on the market after the company had been established for six months, the stock price quickly rose to 3 billion US dollars, and every employee momentarily became extremely rich. Another example is e-Toys.com. After it was listed, it was well liked by investors, and stocks rose US$60. Looking further, valinux.com, which provided integrated services, rose 800 percent after it was listed on the market. The main impetus for these stock increases was the hot trend established by Linux. Such stories were common in the USA, and founder stockholders or company employees found it was a quick way to become rich.

Compared with the employee profit sharing and stock ownership system, the speed and scale of becoming rich was too quick and too strong, so, from the angle of a company's long-term operations, it is not worth encouraging. The natural consequence of these success stories was that many companies were established for the purpose of listing the company on the market. Then the stock would be sold or the company would be acquired by another company after the stock had price had increased. The founders and employees then would retreat after they had earned a lot of money. In this way, they imposed considerable damage on the operation and growth of the company, employees, and customers. This is illustrated by the behavior of the presently established ISP companies and numerous network companies (.com) and portals.

In comparison, if TSMC, for example, had implemented the US stock ownership system in Feb. 11, 2000, the employee stock purchase price would be set at NT$210, the closing price of that day. Since most Taiwan employees' profit sharing and stock ownership is calculated on a face value of NT$10, the difference would be 21 times the purchase price. If the Holystone stock price in April 12, 2000, were adopted as the starting date and its closing price was NT$948, the price difference would be as high as 95 times its original value. Therefore from the angle of motivation, it is far worse than employee profit sharing and stock ownership.

In Taiwan, employee profit sharing and stock options possess reasonable co-sharing of profits so that employees can be proud of being "new techno rich," without the defects of the US-style stock system, which includes an insufficient long-term motivation. At the same time, under minimum employee operating costs, industries can respond flexibly to the economic cycle, and the tempo can be adjusted so company operations can be either shrunk or expanded. Because of this, even though overseas companies offer higher salaries and stock options, they cannot prevent first-class talent from coming to work in Taiwan. With first-class talent, first-class technology, first-class equipment, and a first-class system and work environment, Taiwan's explosion in competitive strength becomes the competitive strength of the industry and of the nation. This kind of competitive strengths is the result of the broad promotion of employee profit sharing and stock

6. Negative effects caused by employee profit sharing & stock ownership and hidden worries

This section reviews business culture, social style, and the reasonability of employee profit sharing and stock ownership so that worries hidden under the bright appearance of the economic miracle created in Taiwan can be revealed. By looking at problems, the unrevealed dark side can be illuminated and appropriate adjustments can be made to the system so that Taiwan can write a brighter page in the 21st century. First we will look at the impact and hidden worries caused by employee profit sharing and stock ownership from the viewpoint of the enterprise.

6.1 Looking from the industry viewpoint

Taiwan's technology industry is striving to promote employee profit sharing and stock ownership systems. Although these systems have resulted in performance that has strengthened both individual and national competitive strength, there are shady defects hidden beneath the luxurious corona. This section examines the impact of the employee profit sharing and stock ownership system on enterprise cultures, employee work attitudes, and social style.

Employee loyalty is facing a test

There is a battle for talent, especially experienced engineers. The popularity of talent snatching is causing instability and discomfort in the industry. Domestic electronic industries issue stocks that are not yet on the market to employees for subscription or directly allocate stocks in large amounts as year-end bonuses to attract talent.

"Presently the whole market is fighting for experienced people," a senior Acer computer engineer says. In order to attract excellent talent, each company is handing out excellent terms in order to build an attractive work environment. Of all benefits, however, stock allocation is the most direct and the most effective. As an example, Asutek used the price of 700 stock certificates to attract a group of Acer computer employees. United Integrated Circuits Corp., which just established its factory, promised engineers that they would own 300 stock certificates after three years. There are even rumors that operators of Winbond Electronics already earn assets of NT$2 million. These rumors more or less have been overstated; however, rumors circulate, and when outsiders talk about profit sharing and stockownership in the park, they cannot disguise their envious feelings.

UMC, starting in 1996, lured senior vice-presidents from its competitors TSMC and Winbond. UMC also lured away the senior vice-president of Chartered Semi-Conductor in Singapore. As a result, many main staffers of semiconductor companies are putting a price on themselves, waiting for buyers. Their minds are unfocused, and work ethics are damaged. The general manager of UMC rationalizes these moves by comparing them to the National Basketball Association: "The turnover of employee is like the turnover of NBA players. Players and teams take what they need, and the mutual flow of talent is normal". The consequence, however, yields discomfort within the same industry.

Apart from the effect on employee morale, talent acquisition through profit sharing and stock ownership is the nightmare of many enterprises. In recent years, the scientific park has established many chip factories that not only offer large amounts of stocks, they also offer better job titles. This combination has induced some semiconductor senior employees to leave their companies to join the new firms.

Normally talent snatching of industry senior management is conducted individually, but the effect goes beyond one talent. After remuneration and salary have been negotiated, the person will leave immediately. Not only does the company lose a senior manager, the manager's team also often departs with the manager. As the cultivation of senior staff requires considerable time, the loss of important staff members exacts a tremendous toll on the company.

One personnel officer in charge of a semiconductor factory mentioned that recently another company in the same industry snared the company's senior staff. He angrily scolded: "There is no integrity. They just want to show clearly that they will use money to buy your death". From this, one can see that employee loyalty is facing many challenges. In the past, semiconductor factories like Vanguard International Semiconductor and Commonwealth Electronics were most loved by new employees. After training for one to two years, they would have gained experience and would jump to a company that offered better profit sharing & stock ownership and a higher stock market price. In this way, the job selection standards are salary, benefits, stock ownership, stock market price, work environment, name and ranking. From this, one can see that employee loyalty is facing many challenges.

The lost sense of personal worth and psychology based on size of reward

As stock prices of traditional industries in Taiwan have not performed well, even when these industries allow employees to own stock, their employees are not that interested. Instead, young talents want to join technology industries. As a result, traditional industries have increased their reliance on foreign workers [43].

According to the Council of Labor Affairs, Executive Yuan Republic of China (CLA), the period in which domestic enterprises implemented employee stock ownership was concentrated between 1989 and 1991. At that time, the Taiwan stock market was booming, and the willingness of companies to implement employee profit sharing and stock ownership was closely related to the prosperity of the stock market. Generally speaking, after domestic enterprises obtain a profit, they adopt three methods to reward their employees: 1) a direct cash reward that means profit sharing; 2) a combination of cash and stock; 3) issuing stock and allowing employees to own stock to substitute for cash profit-sharing. Presently, mostly enterprises adopt a non-payment method of conversion of profit to capital increase, conversion of capital reserve to capital increase, etc., to allocate stock to employees. The system used by United World Chinese Commercial Bank (UWCCB) is an example. If the company plans to give a NT$20,000 bonus to employees, the bank will issue 2,000 UWCCB stock certificates (in NT$10 face value). By calculating at the market price of about NT$60 for UWCCB stock, employees of UWCCB actually obtain an annual reward that is an increase of six times the stocks' value.

In addition, enterprises also can use the method of cash capital increase payable stock allocations to issue stock certificates. That means that when the company is conducting a cash capital increase, part of the stock will be reserved for employees to purchase. Employees can purchase this stock at the undertaking price. If it is a company that is not listed on the market, employees generally purchase company stock either based on NT$10 face value per stock or a price higher than NT$10 and agreed to by the stockholders. No matter which method is utilized, the difference in stock prices after the stock is on the market generally creates quite a large fortune for employees. In the principle of following benefits, young engineers will select a company based on whether the company allocates stocks. In the last few years, UMC established many subsidiary companies and adopted the strategy of high stock allocation. The personnel department head of a UMC subsidiary acknowledges, "Many people come to work here because of the stock".

A senior engineer at MEMC Electronic Materials, Inc. (MEMC) points out that based on his experience, stock is a big temptation to young engineers. At this time, MEMC cannot provide this kind of benefits and has trouble retaining employees. For the first half year of this year, the turnover rate of MEMC employees reached eight percent and was equivalent to the turnover rate of the entire previous year. From the employee's perspective, if the work content and work environment are similar, it is reasonable to select a company with a higher remuneration. What is troublesome to enterprise operators is the comparisons that privately go on among employees. A speaker from Winbond Electronics, Chang Chi-yuan, points out that many engineers in the park were classmates and during private chats inevitably will compare how they are doing. Since each company's profits differ, as does the stock allocation, when these comparisons take place, a psychology of imbalance results. One engineer working in the park expresses, "Salary and stock earned by operators of TSMC are higher than what our engineers can earn," and he feels helpless and wronged.

From the point of view of the system, few people will deny the overall merits of employee stock ownership. The head of human resources of Taisil Electronic Materials Corp. (TEMC), Hung Por-kai, views employees becoming company stockholders as positive. He points out that issuing stock not yet listed on the market to employees at a very low price shows care and concern for employees and is a means by which the company can obtain their recognition and loyalty. One department manager of a large domestic factory asks excitedly when talking about employee stock ownership system,

"Don't you feel it is great to allow employees to share in the performance of the company?"

Beneath the emphasis on stock ownership system, however, these good intentions and methods have generated negative effects. A well-known venture capital company president comments on the down side of this type of incentive: "Employees are fighting for the money of stockholders, and the minds of employees become wild".

Changes in values–people follow stocks

A personnel department head of a foreign company admits that the stock ownership strategy of domestic technology industries has generated a strong absorption effect on talent. As a result, foreign companies with no similar system will have difficulty finding excellent talent. What makes these personnel department managers feel uneasy is the attention many people pay to stocks: "Have these people ever thought, when that industry can no longer earn so much money, what they will search for?"

Of course, not every foreign company is in an adverse position in the fight for talent. The branch company of US Intel this year started to issue stock options on stock listed in the US stock market to domestic employees so that every employee has the right to own company stock. Intel's Asia Pacific's salary department manager Pat Gurren indicates that the reason they adopted this system in Taiwan was to allow employees to own stock and to share the profits of the company.

Allowing employees to share profits and own stock progressively will become a global trend, especially for the high-tech industry. There are indications that without a profit sharing & stock ownership system, a company cannot find excellent talent. In addition, employees also need a system to encourage them to stay with the company and to share the honors together.

Examples of impact on enterprise culture by these newly rich employees are displayed continuously in the park, and it becomes more and more obvious that employees go where the stock is.

Impact on enterprise culture by newly rich employees. It is easy to go from frugality to excess spending, but it is difficult to go from excess spending to frugality

At the same time enterprises are striving to gain the hearts of their employees, they worry that terms they are using will damage the culture inside the company. Acer Computer offers an example of the consequences of this practice. In 1981, Acer opened stocks to employees. When the company stock started to trade on the market in 1988, the reference market price was NT$47. At the time Acer was booming, and stock prices rose 100 dollars more before the rise stopped.

In his book Restructuring of Acer [35], Acer Group President Stan Shih points out when stock prices rose quickly, the culture of Acer, which had been "simple and practical," started to loosen up. The increase in wealth generated a "comfortable syndrome," in which the organization became complacent, and a "large rice pot attitude," meaning no separation of responsibility and authority. In order to restore the common people's culture and hard-working spirit of Acer, Stan Shih conducted two Lung Tang exercises in 1988 with the purpose of reminding employees not to change from frugality to luxury because of their increase in stock values.

Apart from worry about the damage to company culture, the employee stock ownership system also puts pressure on enterprises to constantly grow. This can be summarized as, "If there is no growth, any talk is empty talk, and there won't be a good chance of good profit sharing for employees". Winbond Electronics speaker Chang Chih-yuan says, "At this time, the cruel test occurs between enterprises whether they are good or bad".

A road of no return

Profit sharing and stock ownership is a road of no return. Once an enterprise starts down that road, it must continue forward and maintain an excellent performance in order to retain its employees. Issuance of stocks seems to help enhance employee loyalty; however, once an enterprise's profit-making capability drops, the system is truly tested. In spite of this, overall, this kind of pressure has more merits than drawbacks. Although some companies with poor structure will be eliminated, from the perspective of the larger environment, industry competitive strength is enhanced.

Besides pressures to grow, enterprises that adopt capital increase methods to allocate stock have to face the problem of dispersion of stock rights and the dilution of stockholders' profits. The result of continuous allocation of stock to employees is an enlargement of stock capital, which decreases the profit for each stock and dilutes stockholder profits.

On the other hand, the enlargement of stock capital means that chips of company stock are reduced, and as more stocks circulate outside, that stock's ownership becomes more dispersed. Due to too many chips circulating outside, it is not easy for stock prices to rise. Looking over the long term, an enterprise could no longer bear the consequence of a continuous dispersal of stock rights. Conversely, stock options that have been issued in the US technology industry do not have the above-mentioned problem.

No matter how the system is designed, for now, retaining the hearts of employees through stocks is a kind of win-win strategy. Stocks are just a means, however. Taiwan's Philips Human Resource and Management Center general manager points out that, based on the theory of Maslow's hierarchy of needs, money can only satisfy people to a certain degree. On a higher level, people need self-realization. Therefore, apart from creating high salaries, enterprises should also provide smoother communication channels and space for growth.

Even though the system has some negative consequences, the primary reason Taiwan's high-tech industry has achieved what it has is the emphasis on honesty and seriousness. Most of the engineers are working silently and hard.

6.2 Looking from the viewpoint of the fair taxation principle

At TSMC, employees are exempt from taxes when they obtain stock through a stock allocation. The purchase is based on a face value of NT$10 and, based on the average market price in June 2000, stocks were worth 16 times that amount. The tax levy, however, is only based on NT$10 per share instead of NT$160 per share. Under Taiwan's accumulated taxation, the difference is more obvious. Even if a stock is issued at excessive prices and discounted 1/3 of its face value, there is still a distance from the actual income tax levy. Because of this, on the basis of taxation, both companies that implement an employee profit-sharing system and their employees can obtain a tax benefit. From the employee's point of view, the employee experiences an accumulated effect. From the position of the company, tax reductions and cost reductions contribute considerably to financial statements.

From the angle of social justice and fairness, however, it is obvious that there are deficiencies and an unfair taxation basis. Others industries, such as traditional industries, laborers, farmers, soldiers, government servants, and teachers, are taxed on what they actually earn. However, practically, in terms of income, most people cannot make more than this group of the "technology newly rich," and this is a potential hidden worry in the society.

6.3 *Looking from the viewpoint of stockholders' rights and benefits and enterprise operations*

Every year, a fixed percentage of profits or capital reserve has to be appropriated for profit sharing and stock ownership or stock allocation. Following increases over the years, stock capital will continue to expand, and stock ownership will concentrate in the operating group of the company. Naturally, this will dilute the values of the stocks, and this dilution has a negative effect on stockholders' benefits. Furthermore, under the pressure for a continuous expansion of stock capital, a company must earn a higher profit than last year in order to obtain earnings per share (EPS) similar to last year. If this doesn't occur, the financial statement may make it appear that the company's operation is worse than last year. In order to reach the goal of continual operation for the company, there has to be a balance between maintaining a first-class operating or technical team and an accounting performance that company operations will pay attention to. Undeniably, this is a hidden worry inherent in the system. Too little an appropriation percentage cannot attract and retain employees, but too large an appropriation percentage will cause stock capital to expand too rapidly.

Many Taiwan traditional industry stocks already suffer this problem. Taiwan does not have a stock split system like the USA, which is one reason this problem exists. From the perspective of companies such as TSMC or UMC, the continuous building of new factories, enhancement of production capability and rates, continuous expansion of sales, recruitment of new talent, and implementation of policies like diversified operations and investment can almost eliminate the effect caused by this problem. Another example is the Acer group, which has established subsidiary companies to implement their operating strategies. This method allows the group to create greater added value in various industries or in research and development through thinning and simplifying. It can completely offset the problem caused by expansion of stock capital. Even so, many high-tech companies are seeking a solution to this problem.

7. Study and analysis on actual proof of employee profit sharing and stock ownership system

This section analyzes the results of a questionnaire and field interviews that substantiate the viewpoints presented in this chapter [8].

7.1 Study on the IC industry manufacturers in HSIP

The study is primarily based on interviews with employees from 236 high tech companies in Taiwan HSIP who attend on-the-job classes at NCTU. This sample includes 92 companies in the integrated circuits industry, 44 companies in computer and peripheral industries, 36 in communication industries, 35 in optical electronic industries, 16 in optical electronic industries, and 13 in the biotech industry. Companies include UMC, Mosel Vitelic, Winbond, MXIC, Promos, MTI, and Lucent Technologies Taiwan Telecommunications Co. Ltd. (LTTT). Other companies are identified as Company A, Company B, and Company C. Employees of these companies were limited by company regulations from discussing their companies' situation to outsiders, so the symbols A, B, and C are used to represent them.

Interviews mainly focused on the employee reward systems of companies listed on the market. These systems include appropriation of a fixed percentage of salary to purchase stock, issuance of cash bonuses, purchase of stock during factory construction, purchase of stock for cash capital increases, free allocation of stock, conversion of earnings to capital increases for employee profit sharing, stock options, bonus systems etc. The results are indicated in Table 6.

These interviews show considerable similarity among key employee reward systems, such as employee profit sharing and stock ownership systems, and there is only a slight variation in appropriation percentages and methods. There are some differences in related systems, however overall these differences are not large because they are all in the same general field. Because they are in the same industry, there is more competition and comparison among employees and among companies, which results in similarities among companies. In addition, the 236 companies in the park can be classified into six large industry types, so it is understandable that there are "observations and learning" within companies in the same industry.

The following compares 11 companies on nine reward system dimensions:

Table. 6 Taiwan HSIP listed companies' employee reward system[1] comparison table[2]

Company: Microelectronics Technology Inc. (MTI)
Annual Salary: 12 Months. In addition, a year-end bonus of 1.5 months full salary.
Fixed percentage appropriation from salary for stock purchase:
  a. 10 percent (maximum/every month, two chances a year to revise the appropriation percentage.
  b. For employees who have served for two full years, company will calculate the number of stocks purchased and help employee to buy another half of that number. For example, if the employee had 100 stocks, the employer would buy 50. The employee does not have to pay.
  c. For employees with less than two years service, stock ownership belongs to the company. The number of stocks purchased by employees will be based on the stock price of that time to convert into cash that is paid to the employee.

Company: Mosel Vitelic Group
Annual Salary: 14 months, including year-end bonus of one month.
Fixed percentage appropriation from salary for stock purchase:
  a. 10 percent of employee stock bonus percentage with a maximum of 50 percent. The balance shall be a cash issue.
  b. Employees must serve for three years before they can take away purchased stock.
Issue of cash bonus:
  a. Quarterly bonus. One quarter as a unit is based on the decision of the company operator and is divided into .5, 1, and 1.5 months.
  b. After the company has appropriated 10 percent reserve funds, that 10 percent shall be employee bonuses.
  c. The bonus base figure is the salary base amount.
Factory construction stock subscription:
  a. Cash stock subscription, technical stock subscription.
  b. Stocks should be held at least three years.
Cash capital increase: Low-price cash increase.
Reward system: Marriage, funeral benefit fund, construction performance, long service, full attendance, type of station, special, in-charge, patent proposals, performance improvement rewards.

Company: Company A
Annual Salary: 14 months.
Cash capital increase: Low price cash increase requires being locked in for three years. If the employee leaves the company, the stock will be taken back and the company shall purchase back at a 6 percent annual interest. Retained earnings of every year changed to capital increase shall be taken back at NT $10 per certificate[3].
Allocation of stock without payment: Stock allocation based on academic and work experience and is allocated over three years[4].
Retained earnings converted to cash capital increases for employee profit sharing: 15 percent[5].

Company: Winbond
Annual Salary: 14 months.
Reward system: Three festivals, quarter, performance, special, special project reward.

Company: UMC
Annual Salary: 14 months.
Issue of cash bonus: *Simplex system*: Receive full month salary cannot join profit sharing; *Profit sharing system*: Deduct a certain amount from monthly salary and amount is based on the job position and each year profit sharing can be enjoyed.

Company: MXIC
Annual Salary: 14 months.
Issue of cash bonus: Including appropriation of earnings, employee bonus: 15%, dividend: annual interest 10%, director and supervisor: 2% and shareholder bonus: balance.
Allocation of stock without payment:
Stock options: Fixed amount of stock warrant to employees and will be given in 4 years.
Reward system: Mid-term and seasonal motivation, year end bonus, patent reward, proposal reward, long service commendation, model colleague commendation, overseas travel subsidy.

Company: Company B
Annual Salary: 14 months.
Issue of cash bonus: Including appropriation of earnings, employee bonus: 15%, director and supervisor: 5% and shareholder bonus: 80%.
Allocation of stock without payment: Stock allocation based on job position and performance examination.

Reward system: Quarterly bonus, year-end bonus (2 months, including basic and performance examination reward).

Company: Promos Technologies
Annual Salary: 14 months.
Cash capital increase: Available stocks for employees = (position class-1) × 10.

Company: LTTT
Annual Salary: 14 months.
Fixed percentage appropriation from salary for stock purchase: Employees may buy company's stocks, referencing daily market price, using 6% salaries of every month, and 4% subsidized by company.

Company: Holtek Semiconductor Inc.
Annual Salary: 14 months.
Allocation of stock without payment: For employee served for full 2 years will obtain 1/4 and for full 2.5 years 1/4 and full 3 years 1/2.

Company: Company C
Annual Salary: 14 months.
Allocation of stock without payment: 1~3 certificate every year and about more than 10 certificates for 2~3 years.
Reward system: Three festivals (the Mid-Autumn Festival, the Dragon Boat Festival, the Spring Festival), Christmas, birthday, traveling allowances, year-end bonus: 3 months.

Remarks:
　1. Issue of bonus and market value ranking: TSMC, UMC, Winbond, Mosel Vitelic, Promos and MIC.
　2. See Worldwide Semiconductor Manufacturing Corporation (WSMC), United Semiconductor Corp. (USC), TSMC, UMC, Powerchip Semiconductor Corp., Winbond, Promos, Nan Ya Printed Circuit Board Co. Ltd., MXIC, Texas Instruments-Acer Incorporated, Vanguard and Mosel Vitelic.
　3. First stage

No. of subscribed certificate	Subscription price (per share)	Subscription cost (10,000)	Estimate market value in June 2000 (10,000) (Based on NT$70)	Investment benefit
200	20	400	2,990	7.4
300	20	600	4,490	7.4

4. Second stage

Academic qualification	Academic base figure	Academic base figure counting from the second year
Bachelor	12	3
Master	13	4

For example, master degree graduates with five of years of service can obtain about 35 stock certificates in three years.

P.S. Company A, Company B and Company C are head of Taiwan IC Industrial group that asked this research keeping secret (or confidential) of the company name and also not allowed the employs to discuss the reward system personally.

7.2 Questionnaire research result analysis

The purpose of this research is to conduct the following research analysis and investigation:

Research Method

(1). To investigate employee profit sharing and stock ownership in Taiwan and stock options that that popular in Europe and the USA. What is the attraction to high-tech talent and the effect of employer stock ownership plans?

(2). To compare simple profit sharing, stock ownership implemented by traditional industry, and the merits and demerits of traditional profit sharing and stock ownership.

(3). To look at other levels of employee motivation, enhancement of competitive strength, and related problems derived from the implementation of employee profit sharing and stock ownership systems by various companies in the park. In addition, the views and suggestions of the interviewed employees will be combined to seek a solution.

Sample data

Altogether there were 70 questionnaires issued, resulting in 40 effective questionnaires. The questionnaires were mainly based on random testing on employees in the Taiwan HSIP area. Industries include the integrated circuit industry, the computer and peripheral industries, biotechnology, the optical electronic industry, the financial corporation and finance industries. The following describes the questionnaire results.

Research questions on actual samples

Most welcomed employee reward system

This questioned employees of Taiwan's high-tech industry about the most attractive employee reward system. There were 40 effective questionnaires. There are seven types of employee reward systems, including profit sharing, stock ownership, profit sharing and stock ownership, stock options, cash benefit measures (bonus for three festivals, performance bonus, for example), retirement fund appropriation systems, and other systems not listed. Out of these, profit sharing and stock ownership occupied 67.5, profit sharing occupied 12.5 percent, cash benefit measures occupied 7.5 percent, stock options and retirement fund appropriation systems both occupied 5 percent apiece, stock ownership occupied 2.5 percent, and other systems not listed occupied 0 percent. These are indicated in the following diagram:

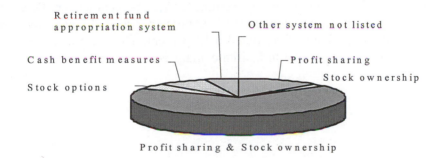

Fig 1. The most attractive employee reward system

The most attractive employee reward system was the combination of employee profit sharing and stocks, favored by 67.5 percent of the respondents, followed by profit sharing with 12.5 percent. The difference between the two preferences is very large, more than 50 points. It is obvious that the employee profit sharing and stock ownership system is the most highly valued by high-tech dream chasers.

*Main factors employees consider in deciding whether to remain in their
original company or change*

This question sought the main considerations high-tech industry employees
take into account when they decide whether to remain with their original
company or change to another company. There were altogether 98 valid
selections for this part. Considerations can be grouped into 11 factors: an
excellent employee profit sharing and stock ownership system, excellent
work team, work interests, personal emotional pressure, personal factors
(close to home, etc.), a high salary, a large space for personal growth, a large
space for personal expression, good company prospects, and other factors.
The results indicate that an excellent profit sharing and stock ownership
system was the most important consideration for 21.43 percent of the
respondents. The second most important consideration, a good company
future, was chosen by 18.27 percent. A large space for personal growth
occupied 12.25 percent. Work interest scored 10.2 percent, and an excellent
work team tied with high salary to account for 7.14 percent apiece. Personal
emotional pressure only accounted for 1.02 percent, personal factors for 3.06
percent, and "other factors" occupied 6.12 percent. These are arranged and
showed in the Fig. 2 in order to facilitate analysis:

Fig. 2 Main considerations for remaining in the original company or changing to another company

It is obvious that employee profit sharing and stock ownership is the main factor for determining whether an employee decides to stay or leave. Because of this, the high or low rate of deployment and manpower turnover is dependent on the system itself. What is worth noticing is the second main factor, those for whom the company's favorable prospects were paramount. The percentage occupied by good company prospects, 18.27 percent, and that of excellent profit sharing and stock ownership, 21.43 percent, are similar, which illustrates that profit sharing and stock ownership supplement good company prospects. Looking back at the early establishment of TSMC, the company allowed employees to have profit sharing and stock ownership at a face value of NT$10, and at the end of year the company used stock allocations to reward their employees. Employees immediately wanted to sell out as soon as they received their rewards, primarily because the company's prospects did not appear optimistic. This created an atmosphere of doubt and fear, so employees favored cash issues. Today it is completely different, as TSMC President Chang Chung-mau said, "For the semiconductor industry one cannot see a dark cloud within the next 10 years". With such company prospects, naturally employees are willing continue to work there.

For traditional industries in Taiwan, although they are weakened and their future prospects are doubtful, they also intend to build themselves up. Even with employee profit sharing and stock ownership, however, they fear they cannot produce results similar to high-tech industries like the electronic information industry. This illustrates the importance of prospects.

Employee profit sharing & stock ownership as a motivator

In statistics based on 32 effective questionnaires, the majority agreed that employee profit sharing and stock ownership is the most valued motivator. Of usable responses, 87.5 percent agreed, and only 12.5 percent disagreed, supporting the fact that employee profit sharing and stock ownership is the most effective method for motivating employees. Please refer to Fig. 3.

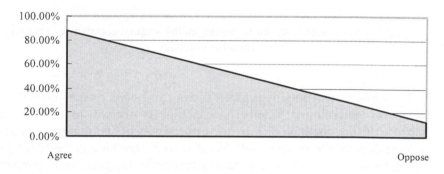

Fig. 3 Employee profit sharing & stock ownership is the most effective method for motivating employees

The relationship between employee profit sharing & stock ownership and
company or industry competitive strength

Employee profit sharing and stock ownership can create competitive strength for a company or an industry, as emphasized throughout this chapter and supported by the questionnaire. The survey, with 30 effective votes, shows 96.7 percent agree with that there is relationship, while only 3.3 percent disagreed. Respondents' reasons to support this relationship were as follows: Employee profit sharing and stock ownership can enhance productivity, encourage research and development and innovation, strengthen the willingness to obtain patents, increase employee stability, reduce deployment rates, allow personal participation in company growth and profit sharing, and provide a sense of being one's own boss. Although the structure under different job cultures and company systems is different, the objective is quite similar—the creation of competitive strength and enhancement. Please refer to Fig. 4.

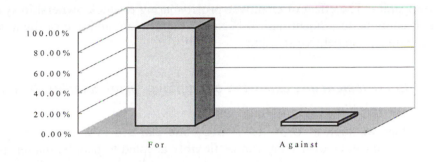

Fig 4. Opinion that employee profit sharing and stock ownership can create competitive strength for the company or industry

8. Prospects and Vision

After the successful promotion of employee profit sharing & stock ownership in Taiwan, in recent years this has become a global trend. Various countries will base their systems on different practices and related systems and stipulate slightly different employee profit sharing & stock ownership methods so as to achieve a maximum effect. In Taiwan, many foreign countries are following this practice in order to recruit excellent talent. In the foreseeable future, domestic high-tech industries will continue to set up factories in Southeast Asia, Mainland China, Europe and the USA in order to absorb local talent and to conduct localization. The same system will definitely be extended to various places in the world (Remark. 17). As mentioned in this essay, this is a "road of no return". The future will see transformed and more attractive employee profit sharing & stock ownership systems so as to strengthen competitive benefits.

8.1 Continuous fermentation of effect of employee profit sharing and stock ownership

The electronics industry originated the profit sharing and stock ownership system. The impact spread beyond the information industry to impact traditional industries. Through foreign capital it has expanded to foreign companies. The effect of employee profit sharing & stock ownership system still continue to ferment until it becomes mainstream and one of the aspects of national competitive strength.

8.2 Improvement and extension of employee profit sharing & stock ownership

Whether we look at UMC or TEMC, one can see how employee profit sharing and stock ownership can be flexibly adapted to people, matter, time, place, and objects. It is obvious that there is still a lot of room for change, and companies have a broad avenue of expression for innovative ideas, as long as these changes don't conflict with legal and accounting principles.

When stock options are combined with an employee profit sharing and stock ownership system, employees are more assured of profits and have a stronger sense of safety. This is the case with United Electronics' commitment to newly employed engineers that at least one stock certificate will be allocated if they stay one year, at least 20 for two years, etc. This helps eliminate employees' sense of uncertainty and assuages their desire to anticipate results. In addition, by coping with ADRs (American Depository Receipts) or GDRs (Global Depository Receipts) models, a stock purchase can be transferred to the stock market of other countries in order to obtain better profits. As an example, ADRs issued by TSMC in the USA can be combined with the employee profit sharing and stock ownership system. This allows employees to participate in the issuance of company ADRs or GDRs. Also, just as in the combination of employee profit sharing and stock ownership with a warranty of a company stock target, various combinations of new financial products could result.

8.3 Strengthening of global competitive strength

According to the annual Global Competitive Strength report published by the International Management Development Institute, Lausane, Switzerland (Remark. 18), Taiwan's position in the global economic competitive strength ranking has dropped to number 22 from number 18 the previous year because of its "unstable political situation and continuous budget deficit". Once again USA and Singapore are listed as number 1 and number 2 respectively. Hong Kong slipped to number 14, and Japan dropped to number 17.

The report points out that over half of Asian countries have "gone back on the right track". In 1997, during the explosion of the Asian monetary crisis, Singapore showed its "high flexibility"; its economic growth last year was 5.4 percent and is rising this year. After the Asian monetary crisis, South Korea immediately started its "most significant economic recovery," and its ranking rebounded strongly to rise by 10 positions to number 28. European countries occupy positions three through 10 in global competitive strength in the following order: Finland, Holland, Switzerland, Luxembourg, Ireland, Germany, Sweden, and Iceland. The massive investments Scandinavian countries have made in technology have strengthened their competitive position, and these countries have become global leaders in the development of hand phones.

No country or industry can delay building and strengthening its global competitive strength. The alternative is to be drowned in a flood of competition. The struggle is no longer country against country or company against company. Today is the age of chain competition–competition between supply chains and supply chains or between demand chains and demand chains that crosses national boundaries. The bases for these chains are companies or factories with excellent leadership and professional first-class technical teams at their nucleus. The most successful will have excellent company systems, and among these systems, the most crucial is how employees can participate in company profits. Employee profit sharing and stock ownership plays an essential role in maintaining and strengthening the whole system. It is believed that in this century, the employee profit sharing and stock ownership system will be a bright pearl valued by all people in this world.

Remarks

Remark. 1
Some major global forecast organizations like WSTS, IDC, SIA, IC Insights and Dataquest made forecasts on 1999's global IC growth rate. They are 6.6%, 8.5%, 9.1%, 10.0%, and 11.8%, respectively, and were optimistic about the future of the

global IC industry. After the recession of the global IC market in 1996, DRAM price dropped dramatically, and Taiwan's IC product production value dropped 7.4%, but industry production value growth was 9.5%, which was related to the growth of 40.4% for chip consignment processing. The annual growth rate of IC chip consignment processing values, industry production values, and product production values were 50.4%, 31.7%, and 15.2%, respectively, in 1997 and 11.4%, 14.3%, and 16.3%, respectively, in 1998. Although the growth rates were not as good as before, they still exceeded the global market. In regard to 1999, the electronic industry forecast the annual growth rate for IC chop consignment processing values, industry values and product production value at 49.4%, 24.3%, and 6.4% respectively. The requirements of the IC market will slowly increase, and future development should be quite optimistic [38].

Remark. 2
The innovation cultivation center established by NCTU and NTHU is the bridge for many professors to enter industry. Correspondingly cheap site rental, tax favors, and management fees combine results of academic research into industrialization. Apart from obtaining excellent social appraisals and low cost and related subsidies, school talents can be utilized to create business creation models. Presently the promotion has been quite successful, and many companies were encouraged to enter HSIP or had listed their stocks on OTC. This is the best sample of cooperation between industry and academia [39].

Remark. 3
ESOP is an American-style employee profits sharing & stock ownership plan, and it's a benefit programs that is tax-preferential and allows for debt leverage. A company establishes a trust fund in which it places cash or stocks for employees every year, and this fund must be commissioned by a professional financial institution. Employees can acquire stocks while retiring.

Remark. 4
The enterprise gives the option to employees to buy stocks on an irregular schedule. The purchase price is based on the market price on that day, or more than 85 percent of market price. Employees could buy or sell the stocks in five years while the stocks are rising or falling.

Remark. 5
In May 20, 2000 the new President is a Progressive Democratic Party member, and therefore the present governing party is the Progressive Democratic Party. The previous government party was the Kuomintang (KMT).

Remark. 6
Presently, it is estimated that the index option will be introduced in Taiwan. Combined index mobile debenture has been implemented so that the debenture market can be more active. There is already quite a scale for warrant. After joining WTO, the market will become more active.

Remark. 7
Article 235: Distribution of dividend and bonus, unless otherwise specified, shall be based on percentage of stock hold by various stockholders. The set of regulations should stipulate the percentage of distribution of profit to employees, but this is not limited to companies approved through the business central supervisory institution's special proposal. This is not applicable to government-operated businesses, apart from special approval by the supervisory institution of that business and stipulated in the set of regulations.

Remark. 8
Suitable jurisdictions will determine whether it will be governed by the central or local government.

Remark. 9
This is an important change in academic research and education reform. This originated in the Technology Policy Symposium at the meeting of the Academia Sinica in July. At that time 61 members of the academy endorsed the suggestion and presented it to the Administrative Yuan to review the requirements of the national military service. Also they recommended the military service system should be loosened in order to absorb excellent talents [40].

Remark. 10
NTU is the abbreviation for National Taiwan University. In Japan's occupational period it was called Imperial University and in the past it was the most famous university in Taiwan.

Remark. 11
Normally it shall be one to two years.

Remark. 12
Tax-exempt favors for companies in the park.

Remark. 13
Issued by direct stock ownership type, and market price at that time was about NT$156/stock and 1 certificate = 1,000 stocks.

Remark. 14
Treasury stock or inventory stock: company buys back stock issued by itself but the stock will not be cancelled. Instead it will be resold, hence the name "treasury stock". In other words, after the company bought back the treasury stock and has them resold, or when the company did not conduct capital reduction and cancellation, the stock the company kept on hand is called treasury stock. Conversely, if the stock has been cancelled, it becomes un-issued stock. There are many reasons why a company buys back stock it issued. It can be issued to employees as an extra reward or used to maintain the stock's market price. As previously mentioned, treasury stock is stock that has been approved and issued and is held by the company. If the stock presently is held by stockholders, it will be called stock circulating outside. During the period the company holds the treasury stock it cannot enjoy stockholder rights such as dividends, votes, priority purchases of new stocks, and allocation of residual property.

Remark. 15
The "security transaction law term 2 of article 28 draft proposal" presently under examination in Taiwan Legislative Yuan will further increase the applicable area of treasury stock. Under the following situations, companies listed in the market or on the counter can buy back their own stock: 1. To transfer stock to employees; 2. To cope with issuance of stock company right certificates, enclosed stock rights company bonds, enclosed stock purchases of special stock, convertible company bonds or convertible special stocks to be used for stock transfer; 3. Due to factors beyond the company's financial or sales control that can have an important influence on stockholders' equity and it is necessary to protect company credit and rights.

Remark. 16
The president of UMC, Tsao Hsin-cheng, recognizes that once treasury stock is opened it would be like the opening of Pandora's box in that the consequence couldn't be imagined.

Remark. 17
Mosel Vitelic indicates in June 5, 2000 that they would build a 12" wafer fab in Quebec in Canada or in Europe.

Remark. 18
Ranking of Taiwan competitive strength for the latest seven years (Switzerland Lausane Institute IMD): 11 (1992), 11 (1993), 22 (1994), 14 (1995), 18 (1996), 24 (1997), 18 (2001). In 1997, Taiwan's competitive strength dropped to No. 24 globally. However, in the 1997 IMD nations Competitive Strength Report, Taiwan only has one item, "science and technology," that rose. Obviously high-tech industry is still the central force of Taiwan's competitive strength.

References

[1] Wen, Z. D., "To be in the ascendant for Science Park of Wisdom and Innovation," Institute of Technology Management, National Cheng-chi University, 1999.

[2] Lin, Michael M. K. and Trappey, Charles V., "The Development of Taiwan's Integrated Circuit Industry," IEEE Transactions on Components, Packaging, and Manufacturing Technology--Part C, Vol. 20, No. 4, October, 1997.

[3] Tilley, Kevin J. and Williams, David J., "An Assessment of the Electronics Industry in Southeast Asia," IEEE Transactions on Components, Packaging, and Manufacturing Technology--Part C, Vol. 20, No. 4, October, 1997.

[4] Sesser, Stan, "Asian Technology," The Asian Wall Street Journal, Tuesday, December 28, 1999.

[5] Porter, Michael E., *The Competitive Advantage of Nations*. America: Free Press, 1990.

[6] Xu, Z. H., *National Innovation System and Competition*. R.O.C.: Linking Publishing Corp., April 1999.

[7] Lee, J. H., *Theory and Practice on Employ Stock Bonus and Ownership*. R.O.C.: Tsing-hua Management Science Series Publishing Co., Ltd., Jan. 1992.

[8] Chen, An-Pin and Wang, Shinn-Wen, "A Unique Employee Stock Bonus Distribution in Taiwan Hi-Tech Industry," working paper, 2001.

[9] Nevitt, Peter K., "Project Financing-ESOP," working paper, 1999.

[10] Chen, J. F., *The Employee Profit-Sharing and Stock-Ownership Plans in the Republic of China*. R.O.C.: Chinese Culture University Publisher, Jan. 1982.

[11] Lee, Y. C., *The Research of feasible, Tax Effect and Distribution Effect of Employees Ownership Plans*. R.O.C.: Unpublished Thesis, National Sun Yat-Sen University, June 1994.

[12] Xue, M. L., "Laws and Taxation Planning of Employees Profits Sharing and Stock Ownership Systems," working paper, 1994.

[13] Dhillon, Upinder S. and Ramirez, Gabriel G., "Employee Stock Ownership and Corporate Control: An Empirical Study", Journal of Banking and Finance, Vol. 18, pp. 9-26, 1994.

[14] Bruner, Robert F. and Brownlee, E. Richard II, "Leveraged ESOPs, Wealth Transfers, and Shareholder Neutrality: The Case of Polariod," working paper, 1990.

[15] Chen, L. Q. and Weng, N., "The Study on the Feasible of Employees Stock Ownership Plan in State-Operated Enterprise," Management Review, Institute of Business Administration, National Cheng-chi University, 1992.

[16] Chen, L. Q. and Weng, N., "The Study of the Relationships between Employees Stock Ownership Plan and Performance of Enterprise," Management Review, Institute of Business Administration, National Cheng-chi University, pp. 81-102, 1992.

[17] Pierce, J. L. and Furo, C. A., "Employee Ownership: Implications for Management," Organizational Dynamics, pp. 32-43, Spring, 1990.

[18] Chaplunsky, Susan and Niehaus, Greg, "The Tax and Distribution Effects of Leveraged ESOPs," Financial Management, pp. 29-38, Spring, 1990.

[19] Charg, Saeyoung, "Employee Stock Ownership Plans and Share Holder Wealth: An Empirical Investigation," Financial Management, pp. 2-11, Spring, 1990.

[20] Charg, Saeyoung, "Managerial Vote Ownership and Shareholder Wealth: Evidence from Employee Stock Ownership Plans," Journal of Finance Economics, August 1992.

[21] Wu, J. S., "The Research of Employ Stock Bonus and Ownership Plans," Council of Labor Affairs, Executive Yuan Republic of China, April 1988.

[22] GAO, "ESOPs-Benefits and Cost of ESOP Tax Incentives for Broadening Stock Ownership," GAO, 1992.

[23] Shih, Stan, "Me-Too is not My Style," www.acer.com.tw, 1999.

[24] Tsao, Robert H. C., "A Discussion on the Global Competitiveness of Taiwan's IC Industry," Working Paper, March 1999.

[25] Yo, P. L., *Habitual Domains*. R.O.C.: China Times Publishing Company, July 1998.

[26] Blanchard, Ken and Bowles, Sheldon, *Gung Ho!*. R.O.C.: Harvard Management Services Inc. June 1998.

[27] Yang, D. Y. and Chen, H. L., "High-Tech Industrial Ecological," Commercial Times, April 1997.

[28] Luo, M. Z., *Semiconductor Industrial Competition advantages of R.O.C.— The Research of the Management Tactics of Integrated Circuit Manufacture Factories*. R.O.C: Unpublished Master Degree Thesis, Institute of Technology Management, National Chiao-Tung University, Feb. 1998.

[29] Tsao, Robert H. C., *A legend of UMC*. R.O.C.: Commonwealth Magazine, June 1999.

[30] Shih, Stan, *Acer--Leader, Tactic, Culture*. R.OC.: Commonwealth Magazine, Jan. 2000.

[31] Ma, W. Y., "The Research of Human Resource Problem in Science Park," Journal of Economics and Finance in Taiwan, 6, 34, June 1998.

[32] Yang, A. L., "A god-father of IC— An Tactics Autobiography of Mou Chang," Commonwealth Magazine, April 1998.

[33] Wang, S. Q., *Dreams of Cisco in Taiwan*. R.O.C.: Business weekly Publications Inc., June 1998.

[34] Chang, Mou, *An Autobiography of Mou Chang (Part I), (Part II)*. R.O.C.: Commonwealth Publishing Co., Ltd., May 1998.

[35] Shih, Stan and Lin, Wennie, *Reengineering Acer*. R.O.C.: Commonwealth Publishing Co., Ltd., July 1997.

[36] Strebel, Paul, *Change*. R.O.C.: Harvard Business Review, 1998.

[37] Lee, Hau. L., Bollington, Corey, "The Evolution of Supply-Chain-Management Models and Practice at Hewlett-Packard," Interfaces, providence, Vol. 25, Iss. 5, Sep/Oct, 1995.

[38] Luo, D. X. and Iv, J. H., "The Analysis of Resource Manipulation via Semi Conductor Industry Development," Journal of Forum on Industries, Jan 2000.

[39] Web site 1: http://www.cc.nctu.edu.tw/~incubate/intro.html, 2001.
[40] Web site 2: http://www.moi.gov.tw/W3/conscip, 2001.
[41] Web site 3: http://www.dfmg.com.tw., Industrial Economics Database of FibrNet, 2001.
[42] Web site 4: http://www.umc.com.tw, 2001.
[43] Web site 5: http://www.sciencela.org/hcsbip.htm, 2001.

Acknowledgement

The authors of this research would like to thank the students of on-the-job credit course class of NCTU for answering the questions proposed by this research. Many thanks to the many employees and managers in HSIP who joined this research. The writers are grateful for their help that is so perfect. Thanks very much to all of you and any suggestions are welcome.

Part 3: IC/PC Industries

Chapter 4

The Integrated Circuit Industry:
A Technological Powerhouse

Charles V. Trappey

Department of Management Science
National Chiao Tung University
HsinChu, Taiwan, ROC

Hubert Chen

Electronic Research and Service Organization
Industrial Technology Research Institute
HsinChu, Taiwan, ROC

(Taiwan)
014
L11 L63
M11 032
038

1. Introduction

The rapid growth of the Taiwan Integrated Circuit (IC) industry has been attributed to many factors, including government support, the successful attraction of overseas technology and capital, and the workforce provided by local laboratories and universities. This chapter looks at the industry's development and the factors that have been cited as contributing to the industry's success. Recommendations for continued growth and profitability in the global marketplace are provided.

Table 1 shows several important trends for the growth and development of the Taiwan IC industry. First, the IC industry continues to expand and is becoming the most important manufacturing sector. Whereas traditional manufacturing continues its decline as a contributor to the Gross Domestic Product (GDP), the electronics industry covers more than a quarter of all

Taiwan manufacturing and continues to grow. The IC industry is the largest contributor to the electronics industry producing more than a quarter of the electronics industry output.

Before 1990, Taiwan's IC industry was in the introductory stage and offered little more to the economy than hope for a brighter future. After the successful launch of the sub-micron consortium in the Hsinchu Science-based Industrial Park, the IC industry was firmly planted and started to grow. The consortium established the IC industry as a player in the international marketplace, and during the period of 1990 to 1994, reached the point where the global silicon cycle began to influence managerial decisions and market performance. In other words, the global demand cycle began to affect the industries nurtured by the government and the Hsinchu Science-based Industrial Park. The world production of ICs reached a five-year low in 1996, declining 11 percent from 1995. Taiwan experienced a similar drop, as production levels followed the silicon cycle and fell nine percent from the previous year. These data indicate that as the IC industry became a larger contributor over time to the GDP, Taiwan's economic prosperity was increasingly linked to trends in global demand.

Year	GDP (Billion USD)	GDP/Capita (USD)	Manufacturing/ GDP (%)	Electronics/ Manufactur -ing (%)	IC Industry/Electro -nics (Estimated %)
1986	75.4	3,897	39.4	13.0	~
1987	101.6	5,192	38.9	13.6	~
1988	123.1	6,223	37.1	14.1	~
1989	149.1	7,455	34.6	14.8	~
1990	160.2	7,918	33.3	15.9	3
1991	179.4	8,769	33.3	15.6	5
1992	212.2	10,274	31.8	15.6	8
1993	224.3	10,757	30.6	16.7	10
1994	244.3	11,613	29.0	17.7	11
1995	264.9	12,488	27.9	19.8	18
1996	279.6	13,073	27.9	22.5	18
1997	290.2	13,449	27.8	23.0	20
1998	267.2	12,268	27.4	24.4	23
1999	288.7	13,152	26.4	25.9	24

Table 1. The IC industry's impact on the prosperity of Taiwan [1]

There are five sections to this chapter. The second section provides an historical perspective of the IC industry. The history covers the 1960s, when the IC packaging industry was born; the 1970s, when ITRI's electronics lab was set up; the 1980s, when IC manufacturing and IC design came of age; and the 1990s, when Taiwan enterprises gained global status and market share. The third section summarizes factors credited with making the IC industry successful in Taiwan and has two sub-sections. The first sub-section is a review of the literature, whereas the second sub-section presents an updated version of a planning framework used by the Industrial Technology Research Institute/Electronic Research and Service Organization (ITRI/ERSO). The ITRI/ERSO framework uses quantitative data to make plans and predictions. The fourth section highlights the emergence of new IC technologies, strategies, and market developments. Finally, the fifth section presents a new framework to explain the factors underlying the success of Taiwan's IC industry.

2. The History of Taiwan's IC Industry

Taiwan's IC industry began in the 1960s with IC packaging, the industry process whereby pre-manufactured wafers are packed into lead-frames and substrates to form the chips used in computers and other electronic devices. Packaging involves molding the chips into small components that can be mounted on boards that are fitted into electronic devices such as personal computers. Packaging requires less technology and more labor than wafer fabrication and much, much less technology than logic design. Since Taiwan had little IC technology in the 1960s, packaging was used as a test case to demonstrate that there was a viable and sustainable market. By 1970, the government supported several laboratories to transfer the necessary technologies to build the fabrication and manufacturing facilities for an upstream supply chain. By the 1980's, IC fabrication sites and IC design laboratories completed the supply chain, forming the first nascent IC industry in the Hsinchu Science-based Industrial Park (Hsinchu SIP or HSIP).

1960s -- IC Packaging

During the 1960's, Taiwan's Gross National Product was about $237 US dollars per capita. Industry was concentrated in commerce (46 percent) and manufacturing (31 percent). Although agricultural contributed 23% to the economy, the manufacturing sector was developing and creating a shift in the economic structure. The trend at the time was to build the textile, plastic, glass, and paper industries through government incentives. The greatest incentives were given to companies that attracted advanced technology and patents that would increase the production of exports. A special industrial zone was set up in Kaoshiung in 1966 to facilitate the export of domestically manufactured goods and to reduce the trade deficit. Kaoshiung Electronics Company and Phillips Taiwan set up facilities in the HSIP and were the first to package ICs.

1970s -- ITRI's Electronics Laboratory

The first global oil crisis occurred during 1973, causing a 23 percent rise in domestic prices, an inflation rate of 41 percent, and a decline in the economic growth rate to one percent. During the 1970's, Taiwan's agricultural sector was in decline and although the manufacturing sector had grown and was a major contributor to the economy, Taiwan's overall exports were badly hit by the rise in inflation. The government sought new ways to stimulate the economy by increasing public spending on six major transportation projects. In addition, a 10-year national development plan was formulated to improve infrastructures and facilities, to speed up industrial modernization, and to build heavy industries such as steel, copper, iron, aluminum, shipbuilding, automobiles, machinery, and petrochemicals.

The development of Taiwan's IC industry began in 1974 when the Industrial Technology Research Institute founded the Electronic Research and Service Organization (ERSO). ERSO was the launch point for the IC manufacturing industry and provided the basic laboratories and personnel for the transfer of technology. A key milestone for ERSO was a 1976 project with RCA to transfer CMOS IC technology. The project was instrumental in demonstrating the feasibility of industry and government working together to build a new industrial sector. During 1979, regulations governing the establishment of science and industrial parks were written and the first IC industries began to build facilities in Hsinchu.

The 1980s -- IC Manufacturing and Design Industries Launched

During the 1980's, Taiwan was affected by the global recession, resulting in falling demand for Taiwan's products and a decrease in private investment. With government backing, the United Microelectronics Corporation (UMC) was founded and represents the first step towards moving the electronics industry from IC packaging into IC manufacturing. Taiwan continued to adjust the industrial structure by promoting the information and electronics industry through incentives and regulations. The regulation called "Encouraging Investment Conditions and Requirements" had a positive effect on the investment climate and helped to build the electronics sector in spite of the global recession.

When America's telephone monopoly was dismantled, the newly formed regional companies began to send orders to Taiwan firms to manufacture telephone parts and telecommunications equipment. Orders from the "Baby Bell" companies helped UMC and others in the Science Park survive a difficult start-up period during adverse economic conditions. The Taiwan Semiconductor Manufacturing Company (TSMC) was established in 1987 and began the island's first IC design business and created the dedicated semiconductor foundry industry. As a result of the formation of UMC and TSMC, the foundation for the IC industry was completed. Taiwan began making computers, PC peripherals, and communications devices and to create products that boosted the demand and increased overall IC production.

1990's -- Building the IC Industry Supply Chain

During the 1990's, Taiwan aggressively developed the electronics industry and added support industries to the supply chain. After 30 years of development, the design and manufacturing supply chain system was completed with over 150 related IC companies, as shown in Figure 1. The workforce exceeded 50,000 employees, most of whom are college educated and bi-lingual. Table 2 shows investment commitments at the end of the 90's almost reached 80 billion U.S. dollars, setting a record for growth and using up all of the land in the Hsinchu industrial park. The IC firms began planning and building facilities in the Tainan Science-based Industrial Park (TSIP).

Research and development investments in the global IC design industry typically account for 11 percent of a company's total expenses. By comparison, Taiwan's IC R&D expenses accounted for less than five percent since local companies are large-volume OEM production. The next decade of development will show greater emphasis on the creation of intellectual property and greater investment in research.

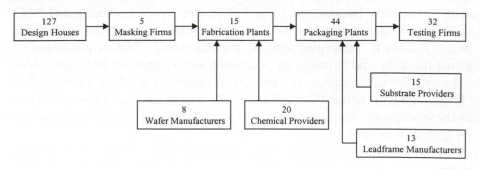

Figure 1. The ERSO/ITRI [1] diagram of the Taiwan IC industry supply chain

The building of IC facilities inside the Hsinchu SIP is declining since there is no more space. However, industrial development in and around Hsinchu and in Hsinchu County is underway and companies are building facilities in Ju Bei and in the nearby river valley area. Tainan, on the other hand, is drawing firms south because there is an available and educated workforce, ample space, water and power.

3. An Overview of the Literature and Models Describing the Industry

The literature explaining the development of Taiwan's IC industry is extensive due to the great financial and technological success achieved over the last thirty years. Many authors have studied and continue to study Taiwan's IC industry in hopes of formalizing the knowledge and replicating the success in other parts of the world. This literature review compiles the results of a sample of academic articles and provides diagrams of factors underlying the success of Taiwan's IC industry. This section also presents ITRI's analysis of the industry trends and future directions. Finally, by combining the abstracted diagrams with ITRI's results, a new framework of factors is proposed to represent Taiwan's successful creation of a technological powerhouse.

Companies	Investment, billion US$	Factory	Location	Comment
Macronix	$ 7.2 over 10 years	1 12" Fab 2 or 3 12" Fabs	Hsinchu SIP Tainan SIP	System on a chip
Mosel	$ 3.6	1 12" Fab Packaging & Testing	Tainan SIP Tainan SIP	
Nan Ya	$ 3.6	1 8" Fab 2 12" Fabs	Linkou	
Powerchip	$ 1.2	1 12" Fab	Hsinchu SIP	DRAM
Acer	$ 9.0 over 10 years	3 12" Fabs	Tainan SIP	Expansion of the 8" Fab
TSMC	$ 14.5 over ten years	1 8" Fab	Tainan SIP	8" constructed 7/1997
UMC	$18.8 over ten years	1 8" Fab 5 12" Fabs	Tainan SIP	Joint venture strategy
Winbond	$ 5.8 over ten years	1 8" Fab 2 12" Fabs	Tainan SIP	Mass production 8" Fab
WSMC	$ 3.6	2 12" Fabs	Tainan SIP	
ASE	$ 11.9 over 13 years	Assembly House Test House	Tainan SIP	BGA, CSP Packaging, Testing
Total	$ 79.2	24 to 25 12" Fabs 4 8" Fabs	Majority in Tainan	

Table 2. IC industry production is moving south to the Tainan Science Park [1]

Academic Articles and Reports

This section uses a sample of articles to represent the knowledge that has emerged to explain the successful creation of the Hsinchu Science-based Industrial Park and the local IC industry. Although the articles are a convenience sample and not an exhaustive review of the literature, the authors stopped the analysis when the information started to repeat. The search demonstrates that there is consistency in what people say has led to the successful development of the Taiwan IC industry.

Education, Culture, and a Diversified Business Infrastructure

Kuo [2] asserts that Taiwan's rapid growth of the microelectronics industry is attributed to the strength of academic institutions that provide training in electronics, the diverse business infrastructure supporting the semiconductor industry, and strong cultural links to the US, Europe, and Japan. Kuo categorizes semiconductor research and development across academic institutions, government-funded development groups (e.g., the Electronic Research Service Organization), and manufacturing groups. Academic institutions have kept up with the growth of the industry and continue to deliver skilled technologists, engineers, and managers as well as offer continuing education courses through professional training centers like the Tze Chiang Foundation. Manufacturing groups take a strong interest in continuing education and offer in-house training courses and professional career development.

The growing diversification of the infrastructure has led to a strong base for global operations. Although the industry started off with labor-intensive IC packaging, a balanced portfolio of manufacturing, design, masks, wafers, materials, frames, and chemical companies has emerged. Given a balanced industry infrastructure in a managed environment, Taiwan has been able to attract investment from local enterprises. Companies in Taiwan have also leveraged educational and cultural ties with the United States and Japan to form alliances and build joint ventures with global microelectronics firms.

Public/Private Initiatives and Technology Diffusion

Williams and Cho [3] studied the growth dynamics of the Hsinchu Science-based Industrial Park and investigated whether the Taiwan cluster was due to entrepreneurial tradition or a close relation to the California business and educational systems. That is, the California Silicon Valley is believed to be the result of the industrial ecology of a complex of firms, venture capitalists, universities, and private sector partners. In studying the California model, Williams considers contributory factors from the industrial ecology, the firms, the venture capital companies, and the university and private sector partners that created dynamism for growth. Unlike Silicon Valley, William notes, the Hsinchu Science Industrial Park was developed as a matter of public policy, with the creators intending to leverage existing technology and accelerate its diffusion into the private sector. Thus, Williams attributes much of the success of Taiwan's high tech industry to the "management of the diffusion of technological innovation rather than the generation of new knowledge itself."

The process by which an industrial structure is created using the proposed model is that high-tech core capabilities are created via the public sector (e.g., ITRI). These sites act as engines for diffusing technology to industry. Then a park is created with an administration that sets industrial policy, regulates, and guides development. With support from the government, private sector investment is sought to build new companies in the park, then these companies are privatized. Once the companies are shown to be successful, they are placed on the stock exchange.

Asian Trends in the Electronics Industry: The Flying Geese Paradigm

Das [4], in a report covering the growth of the electronics industry in Asia, proposes that Asia's electronics industry development resulted from technology transfers, direct foreign investment, and the formation of subsidiaries by transnational corporations. The technology transfers resulted from increased Original Equipment Manufacturing (OEM), whereas the increased investment flowed from overseas Chinese firms (often with links to the US) and Japanese consumer electronics firms. Das calls the development the "flying geese paradigm," where newly industrializing economies are awarded simple assembly opportunities but move into more sophisticated operations as technology is transferred via OEM contracts. As the market grows, strategic partnerships are formed. With increasing production, investments and overseas technology transfer and support accumulates, and firms move into the creation and development of branded electronic goods.

Leveraging and Diffusing Technology Creates New Technology

The Taiwan Industrial Technology Research Institute (ITRI) and the Electronic Research Service Organization (ERSO) formed a consortium in 1990 to develop 8-inch wafer, 0.5 micron mass-production technology using 16 MB DRAM and 4Mb SRAM as the driving technology. The project was designed to foster technology transfer from a government-sponsored lab (with a budget of $247 million dollars for four and a half years) to industry. The method of transfer was through licensing. The government provided research funding and formed the advisory committee, ERSO/ITRI coordinated the scientists and technologists, a users' league supplied the foundry services, and the consortium members (who ultimately received the technology and the license to use it) worked to co-develop the technology and processes. After the technology was released, the users' league paid foundry fees, and the consortium members paid license fees to the government. In addition to recouping some of the research and technology costs, more than 40 academic publications, 400 technical reports, 100 patents, and 50 workshops were delivered to the Science Park community as an indirect outcome [5].

The Foundry Paradigm and Virtual Fabs

The foundry industry is leading the development of the Taiwan semiconductor industry into the 21st century [6]. Foundries are developing core competencies in the areas of process technology, advanced and flexible manufacturing, and customer service. As the foundries become more specialized and service oriented, IC design houses and Integrated Device Manufacturers (IDMs) realize fewer incentives to use in-house facilities.

The trend toward specialization and away from vertical integration is referred to as the dis-integration of the IC industry or the foundry paradigm. Dis-integration and specialization cause firms to place greater emphasis on information, product life cycles, and time-to-market. However, information must be protected and shared between firms under the foundry paradigm, making intellectual property and information systems critical components. Virtual fabs that make use of the latest computer integrated manufacturing techniques are capable of handling many customers simultaneously. Information technology bridges distances and speeds up information transfer, making the foundry seem like an integral part of the fab-less design houses and IDMs. Finally, virtual fabs become the central link between the players of the IC industry and facilitate business between subcontractors and customers in the integrated supply chain.

New Methods of Operation Require Upgrading Safety

The emerging virtual fabs that are integrating the IC supply chain are larger in scale than ever before. Foundries use flexible manufacturing technologies that require less permanent facilities for which it is more difficult to set up fire and smoke control systems [7]. With increased operating times (24 hours per day), larger value orders, and stricter requirements for cleanliness, the risk of fire becomes an ongoing concern. Fire not only causes loss of life, loss of production up and down the supply chain, and the destruction of extremely expensive machinery and facilities, but it also can create a wave of panic among investors that destroys confidence in the industry.

Porter's Diamond applied to the DRAM Industry

The authors Yuan and Wang, [8] study the Taiwan DRAM industry using Porter's Diamond [9]. The diamond is a research framework that looks at factory production, market demand, the existence of related and supporting industries, and government policy. Using the framework as a guide to develop a structured questionnaire, data were elicited from DRAM manufacturers, related semiconductor firms, and related channel members such as ITRI and venture capital firms. The results, based on responses from 67 companies, show that the factors most strongly influencing production are technical manpower, electricity, and water. Respondents also indicated that the market demand for personal computers and workstations has a direct impact on the demand for DRAM. Another key factor is the state of development of support industries such as IC equipment manufacturers. The government policies that have the greatest impact are strategic industrial planning and the development of science-based industrial parks. In terms of industry-level development, it is critical for companies to acquire technology, raise funds, form strategic alliances, and develop corporate strategies.

Timing is Critical to the Science Park Model

Xue [10] argues that Taiwan implemented the science park model at the right time of industrial development. Science parks are necessary since traditional labor-intensive businesses declined in importance as industry moves toward a knowledge-based economy. When industry was at an early stage in the labor-based economy, Export Processing Zones (EPZs) are introduced because of the comparative advantage of labor. The processing zones help to shield industry from competition. As industry develops, particularly if the export processing zones focuses on a significant strategic mix, the exchange rate will make exports less competitive, tariff rates will fall, and the export-processing zone loses its advantages. If these conditions are met, industry will move to the next stage, which requires the construction of science parks. The evolution described by Xue is illustrated in Figure 2.

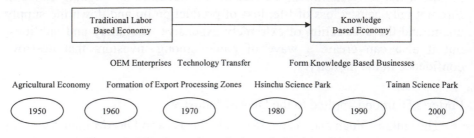

Figure 2. The formation of a knowledge based economy

After the EPZs began to lose their comparative advantage in Taiwan, the Industrial Technology Research Institute (ITRI) was created to conduct applied research and transfer the results to industry. Following the creation of ITRI, the Hsinchu Science Based Industrial Park provided an environment for research and development, trained local talent, and recruited experienced scientists and engineers that were educated abroad. The park also promoted the development of the high-tech industry according to formal plans and written policies.

Xue indicates that Taiwan's science park model was successful because of its emphasis on social, institutional, economic, and technical factors. In terms of social and institutional factors, the park established an Administration Bureau to develop the infrastructure, provide services (power, water, and sewers), and implement policies mandated by the National Science Council. Human resources were considered a social and institutional priority, meaning that the Park spent considerable amounts of training park employees, providing schools for children, recruiting talent from abroad, and providing modern housing. Economically, the Park worked with the government to provide financial services, such as providing investment capital for returning professionals, holidays, and tariff-free imports for components that would be part of a re-export program. Management also allowed foreign and Taiwan government investment in Science Park companies.

The science park holds a different view of R&D than the view commonly held by research universities and laboratories -- that is, R&D must be demand-motivated. Industry, working hand-in-hand with the park, identifies shortcomings in process technology or opportunities in product development. Government also supports the demand-motivated R&D by sponsoring annual awards for product development.

Universities play an active role in the R&D process by supplying students, faculty, laboratory equipment, and computing facilities. In addition to faculty consulting, both ITRI and local universities seek licenses and apply for patents. In conclusion, Xue points out that ITRI plays a dual role of developing innovative technology for the high tech-industry and integrating existing technology to improve manufacturing processes and product quality. The success factors cited by Xue are:

- Active government involvement via the National Science Council and the Ministry of Economic Affair's provision of land, tax breaks, tariff plans, and investment incentives.
- Accumulation of knowledge and skills by recruiting people with knowledge and an entrepreneurial spirit. Likewise, knowledge was accumulated through the creation of export processing zones in related industries.
- The science parks focus on manufacturing and demand-motivated R&D (applied research rather than fundamental research). The demand-driven R&D allows the ITRI to focus on specific processes and product development projects that potentially have the greatest impact on the regional economy.
- The Hsinchu Science Park administration, even though a public organization, has independence and authority to administer and implement policy.

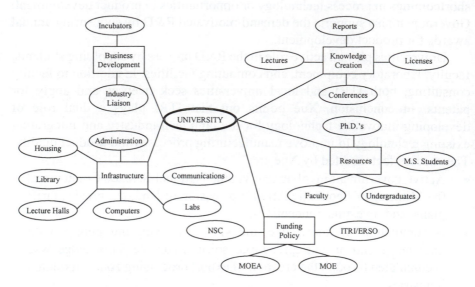

Figure 3. University linkage to funding, resources, infrastructure, business
development, and knowledge creation

The Role of Information

The authors Yuan, Wang, and Wang [11] support the argument that information is critical to the success of enterprises. To fully develop the semiconductor industry, Taiwan should support the continuing development of corporate business information services. According to the authors, the Industrial Technology Information Service (ITIS) is Taiwan's largest government funded provider but there are other sources such as ITRI, the Institute for Information Industry (III), the Taiwan Economic Institute (TEI) as well as numerous privately funded institutes and market research companies.

Business information in Taiwan is derived from newspapers and magazines, seminars, exhibitions, competitors, and associations. The major sources of purchased information come from periodicals and seminars. Many of the companies surveyed by the authors are interested in knowing development trends, industry ties, and technological developments. The services that Taiwan companies find of interest are seminars on industrial activity, real time information, and access to professional databases.

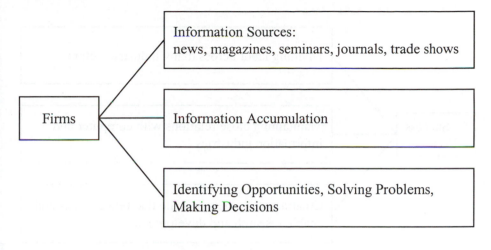

Figure 4. Information and the success of firms

A Manufacturer's View of IC Industry Success Factors

An executive from Winbond semiconductor manufacturing credits a clear division of labor among firms as a factor of success [12]. Taiwan's wafer and foundry suppliers have a unique position in the industry because of two factors—a clear division of labor and an industry closely tied to the information industry. The executive stresses that core technology development and economies of scale are what really impacts the IC industry. The economies of scale enable firms to reduce manufacturing costs and justify R&D investment. Hsu further states that the IC industry can boost development through partnerships with foreign companies and through internal technology development. Hsu's model is shown in Figure 5.

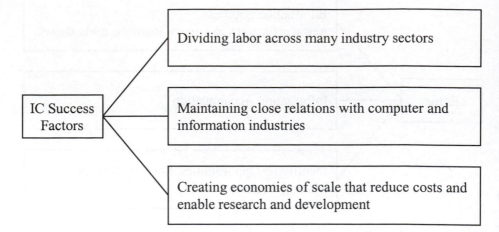

Figure 5. The division of labor across industry sectors is important to success

Rules of the Technology System

The authors Hung and Wittington [13] explore the question of why some national industries are successful but others are not by looking at the fit between national systems and technology. The authors note that the Taiwan national system of industry began with the state governing the market. However, the creation of large-scale conglomerates was avoided to ease tensions between the state and the population, which sometimes held different political views or pursued projects with conflicts of interest. Figure 6 shows that under the national system, the local population developed small and medium-sized enterprises (SMEs), but these enterprises had to conform to the rules of the ruling party to succeed (Taiwan's national system of production).

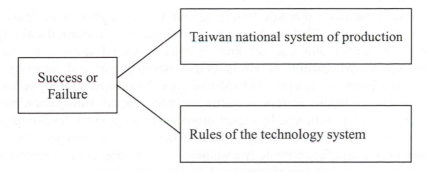

Figure 6. The politics of industrial development

The authors argue that when SMEs conform to the rules, i.e. have party support via the national system, then it is easier to survive against large conglomerates.

Business Strategies

Yuan, Chang, and Lo [14] argue that semiconductor industries have followed four common business strategies:
1. Foreign integrated device manufacturers form strategic alliances with local IC manufacturers to increase process technology. The alliances reduce the risk of patent infringement and develop licensing in the industry.
2. Strategic alliances with IC design houses allow for increased production.
3. Strategic alliances with equipment manufacturers allow for collaborative improvement of mass production capabilities.
4. Strategic alliances with upstream and downstream partners stabilize orders and profits.

In addition to strategic alliances, the authors identify other steps for the industry to pursue. They argue that the semiconductor industry should place greater emphasis on the development of process technology. As a result of the increase in R&D and domestic development of technology, companies should apply for patents and build up a culture of intellectual property creation and protection.

Micromanagement Leads to Failure

Lin [15] maintains that key factors behind Taiwan's growth are human capital (interpersonal relations, business networks, and education), the ability to seek out finance and markets, and an entrepreneurial spirit. Likewise, government's participation in infrastructure development and supportive policy formulation are essential to industrial growth in the technology sector. Successful government entrepreneurship includes import substitution and resource allocation, followed by expert promotion and product development (Figure 7). Government support fails when market competition is micromanaged, and the technology commercialization process is abandoned due to bureaucracy and the splintering of the research effort.

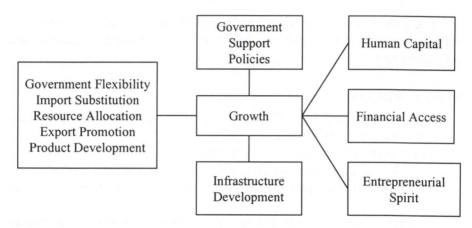

Figure 7. The importance of human capital, financial access and entrepreneurial spirit

Technology Needs

Chang, Lung, and Hsu [16] identify a methodology for evaluating technology needs, choosing appropriate research areas, and then developing technology for diffusion to industry. The methodology consists of three steps. The first, choosing appropriate research areas, identifies "products that have great market demand but lack local/domestic technologies to design and manufacture." The second step involves studying the technology gap between foreign and domestic industries. If the gap is not too large, the third step is taken and government-supported research institutes bridge the gap and transfer the technology to industry (Figure 8).

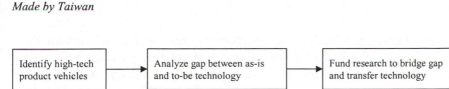

Figure 8. Evaluating technology needs is the first step toward success

The ERSO/ITRI Index Model

ITRI/ERSO models and analyses the Taiwan's IC industry by studying various indices across IC design, IC manufacturing, and IC packaging. This section provides a brief introduction to the use of these indices for drawing conclusions and forming industrial strategy [1].

Marketing Index

The marketing index studies imports, exports, and local production across the sectors of manufacturing, design, and packaging. As shown in Table 3, the Taiwan IC market is growing at a high rate, ranging from 30% to over 47% in recent years.

Units: Million USD	1998	1999	99/98	2000	2000/99
Revenue	8,450	12,512	48%	17,299	38%
IC Design	1,398	1,973	41%	2,792	41%
IC Fabrication	5,051	7,959	58%	11,136	40%
Foundry Services	2,797	4,525	62%	6,636	47%
IC Packaging	1,610	1,995	24%	2,597	30%
IC Testing	391	585	50%	773	32%
Production Value	3,652	5,407	48%	7,292	35%
Domestic Sales (%)	50%	43%	~	43%	~
IC Market	8,181	10,609	30%	13,698	29%

Table 3. Taiwan IC industry market indices [1]

Technology Index

Taiwan's IC technology development can be divided into two categories -- domestic R&D and technology transfers from foreign nations. Domestic R&D focuses primarily on memory products, including 16 megabyte DRAM, 1 megabyte synchronized SRAM, 64 megabyte ROM, and 16-megabyte flash memory. Taiwan produces some microcomponents such as IC sets for PC's and micro-controllers. Technology transfers from foreign countries include DRAM and design and manufacturing process technology, with the main focus being computer kernel transfers such as RISC processors. Many companies are aggressively forming strategic alliances with related companies in the US, Japan, and Europe. Alliances allow Taiwan industries to receive more advanced product design and manufacturing processes, which stimulates the international competitiveness of domestic firms. Table 4 and Table 5 list Taiwan's IC memory product technologies, which include memory and IC packaging, and compare them to other countries. Both tables compare Taiwan's level of technology to the technology level of the leaders.

Item	Taiwan's Technology Level	World Leading Manufacturers	Leader's Technology Level
DRAM	128M mass production (0.18μm), 256M pilot production (0.18μm)	Samsung, Micron	256M mass production (0.18μm), 1G Sample
SRAM	4M mass production (0.18μm), 8M, 16M	Samsung, NEC	16M mass production (0.18μm)
ROM	128M mass production	Samsung, MXIC	128M mass production
EPROM	8M mass production	STM, Atmel	32M mass production
Flash	16M mass production	Intel, Fujitsu, AMD, Sharp	256M mass production

Table 4. Taiwan IC memory technology [1]

Item	Measure Index	Taiwan's Technology Level	World Leading Countries	Leader's Technology Level
BGA	Pin Count	700-pin mass production	US, Japan	1156-pin mass production
QFP	Lead Pitch	0.3-0.4mm mass production	Japan	0.25-0.4mm mass production
TSOP	Thickness	Mass production 1mm	US, Japan	1-0.5mm Mass production
TAB-OLB	Lead Pitch	Mass production 45mil	Japan	40mil mass production
Flip-chip	Pin Count	1000-pin	US, Japan	2300-pin Mass production
CSP	Pin Count	256-pin mass production	US, Japan	768-pin Mass production

Table 5. Taiwan IC packaging technology [1]

5. IC Industry Trends and Strategies

Taiwan has become one of the major IC producers in the world with a comprehensive supply chain and world-class manufacturing and design. The IC industry has contributed greatly to Taiwan's high technology industrialization and an upgrading of the overall industrial structure. Other industrial sectors such as textiles, chemicals, steel, and machinery have aggressively diversified into the IC industry, underscoring the importance of this sector in Taiwan's economy.

The DRAM and foundry businesses are the two key players in the industry by market size. Since these two businesses face international competition, a key issue is controlling these businesses' technology for long-term growth. Currently, companies in Japan, Korea, and the US control the DRAM market. Strategic alignments among companies and countries are being established to build the infrastructure.

Taiwan is the founder of the pure foundry business, a production base where a company produces but does not design, and TSMC and UMC are examples of this type of specialization. These foundries' success has encouraged Singapore, Malaysia, Thailand, China, and Israel to join in and build foundaries. The key factors for foundry competitiveness includes quality, service, capacity, and, most importantly, manufacturing technology. Both government and industry are increasing efforts to build global networks and improve intellectual property protection. These efforts include:

- Aggressively building patent databases, recognizing companies' ownership of patents and intellectual property, analyzing technical trends, and facilitating the granting of rights between aligned companies and research institutions that carry out government-granted research.

- Improving the environment and standing of intellectual property by helping resolve disagreements, fully utilizing government-owned intellectual properties, granting rights among international companies, and developing and co-owning patents.

The IC industry is entering into the sub-micron era. Levels of difficulty and complexity have increased extraordinarily, as have uncertainties about technologies, manpower, and investment costs. With the current levels of complexity, the risk is too large to bear for a single company, so Taiwan's IC manufacturers are forming cooperative arrangements by:

- Participating in international conferences and trade shows to better understand future product and technology requirements.

- Joining in R&D with international organizations organizations, companies, and research institutes and by training more technical personnel.

- Inviting internationally known technical experts to join R&D and research projects locally.

Although Taiwan's IC industry was affected by the 1996 downturn in the silicon cycle, it is still the top performer and ranks highest in profits. Table 6 lists goals for IC industrial development. In 1996, the total IC production value was 3.324 billion US dollars, which accounted for about 3% percent of the global market. IC producers were ranked number four globally and domestic sales accounted for about 18% percent of Taiwan's total production. ERSO/ITRI forecasts that Taiwan's IC production will exceed 10 billion US dollars by the year 2002, and its global market share will reach 4 percent and satisfy 25 percent of Taiwan's domestic market.

Index	1996, million US$	2002 estimate, million US$
Industry production	$ 6,276	$ 26,090
IC Design	$ 793	$ 2,675
IC Manufacturing	$ 4,567	$ 16,360
IC Packaging	$ 916	$ 7,055
Production Value	$ 3,324	$ 10,855
Global market share (%)	3%	4%
Taiwan self supply (%)	18%	25%

Table 6. Predictions for Taiwan's IC industry development [1]

In order to achieve the forecasted levels, Taiwan's IC industry must respond to new challenges and competition. The main challenges are twofold -- to increase the industry's competitive edge and to increase global market share. In general, there are three factors affecting the industry's competitiveness: leadership in product technology R&D, operation and business management, and the industrial environment and infrastructure. Companies must make a long-term commitment to technology R&D and business/operational management to survive. The industry must expand product lines and find new ways to add value to products. Furthermore, internationalization in business management and cooperation is needed to survive fierce global competition. A better infrastructure is needed as well, including more space, water, electricity, and roads. Taiwan must react in three ways to achieve competitive advantage:

1. Internationalization. This includes internationalization of the financial market, technology transfers and international alignment, professional training for global business management, and attracting domestic and international experts and professionals.
2. Emphasizing R&D, strengthening intellectual property protection, and retaining superiority in production capability
3. Continued government support in expanding science-based industrial parks, providing long-term resource planning for water, electricity, land, manpower, and transportation, as well as provide financial support for R&D projects.

In order to increase market share, Taiwan's industries must reach out and seek customers. The Asia-Pacific region is the most promising market in the near future, particularly China, where global IC manufacturers are fiercely competing with each other. There are three ways to expand market share:

1. Improve the cross-strait (Taiwan-China) relationship.
2. Actively develop Taiwan's downstream electronics industry in order to increase the demands for IC products. Also, participate in the government's National Information Infrastructure (NII) project to create new markets through electronic commerce.
3. Explore new markets. Align with developers of new electronic products.

Conclusion

The educational infrastructure of Taiwan appears to be the driving force or the primary link between factors underlying the successful development of the IC industry. Viewing Figure 9, there is a convergence point linking the educational infrastructure to the park infrastructure, the technology diffusion infrastructure (ITRI), and technology creation. The importance of the educational infrastructure, as discussed by Kuo [2], Williams [3], Xue [10], Lin [15] and others, cannot be under emphasized as the driving force for new enterprises and economic development. Technology can be bought and OEM production can be sustained, but a well-educated workforce builds the long-term advantage. The creation of new firms via university incubators and the simultaneous provision of capital and guidance supports the need for promoting life-long education and training. Given these observations, it is clear that the Taiwan education system has to attract the best minds to develop technology and sustain the growth of the IC industry. With the on-going dis-integration, specialization, and coordination re-shaping the supply chain, it is also critical to develop a sound legal and financial system to create and protect intellectual property. Otherwise, Taiwan will have little more to offer other than a place to manufacture goods. With so many available and low-cost manufacturing locations around the world, the correct strategy is to focus on creating new knowledge and transforming that knowledge into new materials, processes, and products with brand names.

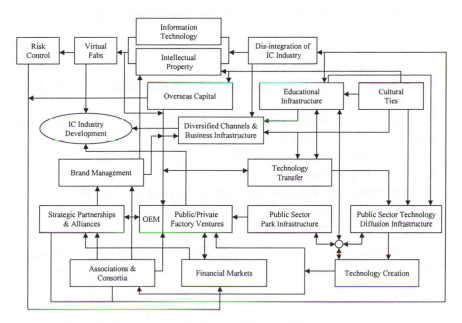

Figure 9. Factors contributing to Taiwan's IC industry's success

Reviewing the Framework

The success factors in Figure 9 overlap with factors recommended to develop Science Parks and the IC industrial base in Hong Kong and China. Professor Lin, the Vice President for technology development at the Hong Kong University of Science and Technology, provides a framework describing the direction that Hong Kong should take to develop high technology businesses in China (Figure 10). Professor Lin emphasizes the importance of four critera underlying industrial and business technology development: material, designs, processes, and quality. The importance of these criteria are further leveraged through the correct application of information technology. Hong Kong has certain limitations, including too few universities and too little electronics research and development. Evaluating the emerging business opportunities in the region, Lin proposes several steps to move Hong Kong into a position of technology leadership:

- Hong Kong must re-affirm government commitment to developing science and technology.

- Proactive policies are needed to encourage private investment.
- The education infrastructure must be strengthened and education expenditures increased.
- Greater investment in R&D is required, and more research collaboration with China is necessary.
- An institute is needed to supply technical guidance and assistance to industry.
- Science Parks are needed, specifically a network of parks to link Hong Kong and China and to act as incubators for high-tech ventures.
- Businesses must take the initiative to do R&D, develop brands, and seek market opportunities.
- The university reward system must be altered so that faculty will integrate with society.

Figure 10.depicts Professor Lin's framework.

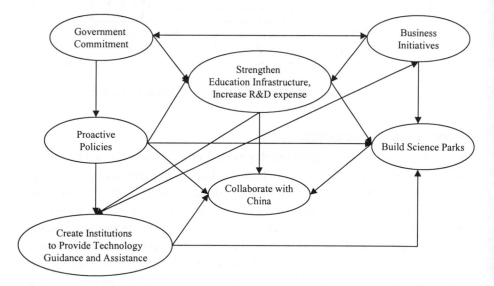

Figure 10. The success factors planned for Hong Kong and China to develop Science Parks and an IC industrial base.

The factor diagram derived from the literature (Figure 9) matches many of the ideas put forth by Professor Lin. The formalized knowledge about the factors underlying Taiwan's IC industry success can be derived from the literature. However, replicating the success in other parts of the world depends greatly upon having a well-educated workforce to build and maintain the infrastructure.

References

[1] ERSO/ITRI Project, An internal report compiled by Hubert Chen and staff at the Electronic Research and Service Organization, Industrial Technology Research Institute, Hsinchu, Taiwan, 2000.

[2] Kuo, J.B., "Microelectronics R & D Blossoms in Taiwan," *Circuits and Devices,* , pp. 31-34, 1995.

[3] Williams, J.A. and Cho, D.-S., *Tiger Technology, The Creation of a Semiconductor Industry in East Asia*, Cambridge University Press, Cambridge, U.K., 2000.

[4] Das, Dilip K., "The Dynamic Growth of the Electronics Industry in Asia," *Journal of Asian Business*, Vol. 14, No. 4, pp. 67-99, 1998.

[5] ERSO/ITRI Project, An internal report compiled by Michael Lin and staff at the Electronic Research and Service Organization, Industrial Technology Research Institute, Hsinchu, Taiwan, 1997.

[6] Tseng, F.C., "Semiconductor Industry Evolution for the 21st Century," *Symposium on VLSI Circuits Digest of Technical Papers*, IEEE, pp. 1-4, 1999.

[7] Liu, Eddy, "Risk vs. Investment: A Semiconductor Industry Tradeoff," *IEEE Proceedings*, , pp. 156-160, 1998.

[8] Yuan, J.C., and Wang, Y.W., "Analysis of the Key Factors Influencing Competitive Advantages of DRAM Industry in Taiwan," *International Journal of Technology Management*, Vol. 18, Nos. 1/2, pp. 93-109, 1999.

[9] Porter, M.E., *The Competitive Advantage of Nations*, N.Y., The Free Press, 1990.

[10]Xue, Lan, "Promoting Industrial R&D and High-tech Development through Science Parks: The Taiwan Experience and its Implications for Developing Countries," *International Journal of Technology Management*, Special Issue on R&D Management, Vol. 13, Nos. 7/8, pp. 744-761, 1997.

[11]Yuan, J. C. Benjamin, Wang Ming Yen, Wang Chen Chien, "Demand for Business Information Services of Firms in Taiwan: A Case Study of Hsinchu Science-based Industrial Park and Hsinchu Industrial Park," *Journal of Engineering and Management*, Vol. 6, 349-372, 1999.

[12]Hsu, Chung S., "A Word from Management: Taiwan's Industry in Expansion," *Winners,* Vol. 6, No. 1, 1995.

[13]Hung, Shih-Chang and Whittington, Richard, "Playing by the rules, Institutional Foundations of Success and Failure in the Taiwanese IT Industry," *Journal of Business* Research, 47, pp. 47-53, 2000.

[14]Yuan, Benjamin, Chang, Chun-Yen, Lo, Mei Chen), "Strategies of the Semiconductor Industry in Taiwan," *IEMC, IEEE,* pp. 541-545, 1998.

[15]Lin, Min-Shyong, "Technology Trends of Microelectronics in Taiwan," IEMT/IMC Proceedings, pp. 1-9, 1998.

[16]Chang, P. L., Lung S.S.C., and Hsu, C.W., 'The evolution model for the technology needs of Taiwan high-tech industries." *International Journal of Technology Management*, Vol. 18, No 1/2, pp. 133-145, 1999.

[17]Leachman, Robert C., and Hodges, David A. "Benchmarking Semiconductor Manufacturing," *IRW Final Report*, IEEE, pp. 1-6, 1997.

[18]Mathews, John A., "A Silicon Valley of the East: Creating Taiwan's Semiconductor Industry," *California Management Review*, Vol. 39, No. 4, pp. 26-54, 1997.

[19]Lin Otto C. C., "The Future of Technology and Business Development in Hong Kong," Invited speech at the 96/97 Annual General Meeting, the Hong Kong Electronic Industrial Association, August, 1997.

[20]Liu Shang-Tyh, "Industrial Development and Structural Adaptation in Taiwan: Some Issues of Learned Entrepreneurship," *IEEE Transactions on Engineering Management*, Vol. 45, No. 4, pp. 338-348, 1998.

Biographical Summaries

Charles Trappey is a professor of marketing in the Department of Management Science and Associate Dean of the College of Management, at the National Chiao Tung University. He received a Ph.D. in Consumer Behavior from Purdue University and is active in electronic commerce research and trade area analysis.

Mr. Hubert Chen is Manager of the Strategic Planning Department under the Planning and Technical Marketing Division at the Electronic Research and Service Organization (ERSO). ERSO is affiliated with the Industrial Technology Research Institute (ITRI), Taiwan's center for research and technology development and transfer.

Chapter 5

IC Foundries: A Booming Industry

Muh-Cherng Wu

Professor, Department of Industrial Engineering and Management
National Chiao Tung University
HsinChu, Taiwan, ROC

1. How successful is Taiwan's IC Foundry

Semiconductor manufacturing is a very important industry in Taiwan. On Jan. 2000, two distinguished semiconductor manufacturing companies combined would occupy about 20 percent of the entire Taiwan Stock Exchange's market value [1]. These two companies are TSMC (Taiwan Semiconductor Manufacturing Co.) with US$50 billion and UMC (United Microelectronics Corp.) with US$33 billion in their market value.

TSMC and UMC run their semiconductor business in a non-traditional model, known as *dedicated semiconductor foundry* or briefly known as *IC foundry*. A dedicated semiconductor foundry manufactures integrated circuits (IC) for customers based on their proprietary designs. It focuses on manufacturing and will not involve itself with any IC design business that would pose a competitive threat to its customers. A traditional semiconductor manufacturing company, known as IDM (integrated device manufacturing), covers almost the full spectrum of jobs in making ICs— from design to manufacturing, packaging, and testing. Some IDM companies also may offer foundry services when they have excess capacity.

Taiwan is far ahead in the global IC foundry market, a booming sector in the semiconductor industry. According to an analysis (Table 1), Taiwan in 1999 occupied about 67 percent of revenue market share in the worldwide IC foundry market. The global IC foundry market in 1999 was about

US$6,700 million and accounted for 12 percent of the worldwide semiconductor market. IDC (International Data Corporation) estimates that the sales of IC foundries will keep increasing to 26 percent of the world semiconductor market by 2004 [2]. That is, one out of four ICs will be made by an IC foundry.

Year	1996	1997	1998	1999
Taiwan IC Foundry Revenue (US$ billion)	2.0	2.9	2.8	4.5
World IC Foundry Market (US$ billion)	5.0	5.1	5.4	6.7
Taiwan's Market Share	40%	56%	52%	67%

Table 1: Revenue and world market share of Taiwan's IC Foundries (Ref. 3)

The profit margin and return to stockholders of Taiwan's IC foundries seems quite remarkable. From 1995 to 1999 (Table 2), TSMC's average profit after tax to net sales was about 47 percent, and UMC's was about 40 percent. TSMC stock lauched initial public offering (IPO) in 1994, the market value of one common share at that time was about US$ 3.4. One IPO common share of TSMC, if not sold, as of June 2000 had become 9.6 shares with a market value of about US$ 43.6, or approximately 13 times its original value in five years [1]. Market value of UMC stocks likewise has been booming. The market value of one common share in 1994, if not sold, now has increased approximately nine times [1].

Year	1995	1996	1997	1998	1999
TSMC	52%	49%	41%	30%	34%
UMC	65%	34%	39%	24%	36%

Table 2: Profits after tax to net sales of TSMC and UMC (Ref. 4-8)

In the worldwide semiconductor industry, Taiwan has received highly regarded credit for the birth and growth of its IC foundry business. TSMC is the first company in the world to run on the dedicated IC foundry business model. UMC is the first company in the world that successfully switched from an IDM company to an IC foundry. These two companies are both very successful and have respectively achieved number 1 and number 2 market shares in the global IC foundry business. Their success also has considerably impacted the infrastructure of the semiconductor industry in Taiwan.

We might question the following issues. How did the IC foundry business happen in Taiwan? Why is the IC foundry business in Taiwan so successful? What are its impacts on Taiwan? What are its impacts on the worldwide semiconductor industry? Will Taiwan retain its lead in the IC foundry industry? What are the threats and opportunities to Taiwan's IC foundries? These questions will be analyzed in the following sections of this chapter.

2. Birth and Growth of IC Foundries

2.1 Fabless IC Design Houses

TSMC, established in 1987, is the first company in the world that claimed to be a dedicated IC foundry company. Before the establishment of TSMC, IDM semiconductor companies provided IC foundry services. The main customers of IC foundry services are known as *fabless IC design houses* (briefly known as *IC design houses*), which design ICs but do not have their own IC fabrication factories and have to outsource capacity from some of the IDM semiconductor companies. These IDM companies can be referred to as *part-time IC foundries* because they both design and manufacture IC products and might unavoidably become competitors of their IC design house customers in the market.

The relationship between fabless IC design houses and IDM semiconductor companies had been unbalanced. A typical IDM company had at least 10 or even 100 times the revenue and capital of a typical fabless IC design house. IDM companies therefore would have more bargaining power than IC design houses. IDM companies also design ICs and they would inevitably put higher priorities on producing their own products. Because of this, especially in economic upturns, it was very difficult for IC design houses to get manufacturing capacity, and the cost would become quite high when they could get it. With their strong bargaining power, some IDM companies might even be allowed to use their fabless customers' designs and manufacture products in IDM companies' brand. In this case, the intellectual properties of fabless IC design houses might not be well protected.

Fabless design houses in general were too weak in capital to establish a semiconductor fabrication factory (also known as *IC fab*). In 1987, the year when TSMC was established, there were 30 fabless design houses in Taiwan, and their total revenue was about US$25 million. A typical 6" IC fab (a factory where ICs are made on a 6" silicon wafer) at that time would cost about US$200 million. Fabless IC design houses typically had been started by engineers from the design departments of IDM companies or research institutes and were relatively weak in capital financing. Before the inception of dedicated IC foundries, the growing space for fabless IC design houses had been quite limited.

2.2 Birth and Growth of TSMC

The idea of establishing TSMC started from a VLSI (very large-scale integrated circuit) research project (1983-1988) funded by the government. The research project was implemented by the Industrial Technology Research Institute (ITRI), a non-profit research institute in Taiwan. This research project aimed to establish advanced semiconductor fabrication technology in order to support the emerging fabless IC design houses in Taiwan.

In 1985, Morris Chang, a senior executive with more than 30 years experience in the USA semiconductor industry, was appointed president of ITRI and was requested by the Taiwan government to establish an internationally competitive semiconductor manufacturing company. Prior to that, he was chief operating officer of the General Instrument Corporate Group and vice-president of Texas Instruments. The VLSI project in 1985 had successfully developed 2 um (micrometer) resolution technology for manufacturing IC in a pilot plant; however, the commercial state-of-art technology at that time was 1um.

Three strategies were formulated in establishing the new company, TSMC. First, the company should be a dedicated IC foundry. Second, the company should be jointly ventured with an internationally competitive semiconductor company. Third, resources involved in the VLSI project, including engineers, equipment, process technology, building, and land, should be transferred to the company in order to speed up the company's establishment.

The first strategy, a dedicated IC foundry, was to develop the market of fabless IC design houses. Fabless design houses had been in a weak bargaining position in outsourcing manufacturing capacity. A dedicated IC foundry would be more competitive than IDM companies in attracting orders from fabless IC design houses. If the IC foundry business model could be successfully implemented, this would encourage the establishment of new IC design houses, and the market of dedicated IC foundries would grow quickly.

The rationale for supporting the dedicated IC foundry strategy sounded promising; however, most local enterprises that were invited to invest in the new company hesitated. Quite a few of them, after joining the business venture because of the government's invitation, quickly sold their stocks within two years after the inception of the new company.

One main concern for the IC foundry strategy was that the company was destined from birth to have no IC products under its own brand. The concern was whether a semiconductor company without its own products could survive, especially when there had been no successful template on which to build. Another concern was that the total revenue of fabless IC design houses in Taiwan was only US$25 million in 1987, while a typical 6" IC fab would cost about US$ 200 million, which raised the question of whether the capacity of such a factory could be highly utilized. The loss of an IC fab, if too low in utilization, would be formidable.

The second strategy, entering into joint venture with an internationally competitive semiconductor company, had two main purposes. One was to maintain substantial orders from the venture partner. The other was to acquire advanced semiconductor manufacturing technology. This strategy sounded good but was very difficult to implement. Morris Chang, had contacted more than 10 internationally known semiconductor companies, but most of them showed no interest. Finally only Philips, the largest semiconductor company in Europe, was willing to participate in the joint venture.

The joint venture strategy was very important for TSMC to start up the IC foundry business. In the acquisition of orders, Philips had been a key customer of TSMC and once accounted for 17 percent of its sales. In the acquisition of technology, with the help of Philips, TSMC had a very good start in minimizing risks from any infringement on other companies' intellectual property (IP). By paying a percentage of net sales as IP royalty, TSMC was authorized to use Philips' patents. In addition, through Philips' cross-licensing arrangements, TSMC was authorized to use patents of some other internationally known semiconductor companies such as IBM, Intel, and Toshiba.

The third strategy, transferring resources of the VLSI project from ITRI to TSMC, was the quickest way to start up the IC foundry business. Experienced technical staffs in semiconductor manufacturing were limited in number, and 130 from the VLSI project were spun off from ITRI to become employees of TSMC. The Taiwan government also allowed ITRI to rent to TSMC all equipment, plants, and land that had been involved in the VLSI project. Moreover, TSMC was funded by ITRI, under the cooperative arrangement with ITRI, to continue the VLSI project until 1991.

The IC foundry business model, pioneered by TSMC, has proven to be very successful. Since its inception in 1987, TSMC have maintained a highly regarded record in revenue and net income (Table 3). TSMC's revenue was expected to reach US$ 5 billion by the end of 2000; its revenue has grown over 1000 times in 14 years. The number of employees has increased from 130 to 13,000.

	Revenue	Net Income
1987	4	-4
1988	33	5
1989	70	16
1990	82	-6
1991	167	19
1992	259	46
1993	466	161
1994	631	193
1995	1,088	567
1996	1,435	707
1997	1,532	625
1998	1,507	458
1999	2,263	759
2000	5,156	2,062

Table 3 Revenue and income of TSMC (US$ Million) (Ref. 1, 4-5)

It is estimated that TSMC, ranking by manufacturing capacity, might become the largest semiconductor company in the world in 2001. The annual capacity of TSMC 2000 was about 3.4 million 8" equivalent wafers and is expected to expand to 4.8 million in 2001. Due to the fast-growing demand of IC foundry services, TSMC has been aggressively expanding its capacity.

Two semiconductor companies in Taiwan, Worldwide Semiconductor and TSMC-Acer, were merged into TSMC as of July 2000 [2]. Prior to that, TSMC itself had constructed two 6" fabs and four 8" fabs in Taiwan during the last 14 years.

2.3 Growth of UMC in the IC Foundry Industry

UMC is the first company in the world that successfully transferred from an IDM company to an IC foundry. Ranked by revenue, UMC is the second largest IC foundry company in the world. The track that UMC moved on from an IDM company to an IC foundry was quite impressive and should have a credible position in the development of the IC foundry industry.

UMC, established in 1980, is the first private semiconductor company in Taiwan. The birth of UMC can be traced back to a technology transfer project carried out by ITRI in 1975. Through this project, ITRI contracted with RCA for the transfer of semiconductor design and manufacturing technology and established the first semiconductor pilot plant in Taiwan. Due to the local emerging demand for ICs, ITRI, under the support of the government, was asked to establish a private semiconductor company in 1980. Some management and technical staff in the technology transfer project were spun off from ITRI and became employees of the semiconductor company (UMC).

Since its inception, UMC had been an IDM company that in some cases also offered IC foundry services. In 1995, UMC decided to become a dedicated IC foundry company. That year, UMC entered into three joint ventures with some well-known IC design houses in the USA to establish three dedicated IC foundry companies in Taiwan. IC foundry services at that time accounted for only 30 percent of UMC's revenue, that is, 70 percent of revenue was in the IDM business.

At the time UMC strategically decided to turn into a dedicated IC foundry company, the IC foundry business had been growing rapidly for several years. The average annual growth rate of Taiwan's IC foundry market (1993-1995) was about 68 percent (Table 4), and the annual growth rate of the global IC foundry market (1993-1995) was about 52 percent. It seemed that a dedicated IC foundry business would keep growing and could become an influential business model in the worldwide semiconductor industry.

Year	1993	1994	1995
Total revenue (US$ M)	580	877	1,504
Growth Rate	82.1%	51.2%	71.5%

Table 4 Total revenue and growth rate of Taiwan IC foundry services (Ref. 9-10)

The idea of entering into a joint venture with world-famous IC design houses was very creative and pioneered by UMC in 1995. Through this strategy, UMC would assure orders from the IC design houses and share the risk of establishing the capital-intensive IC fabs. A typical 8" wafer IC fab would cost about US$1 billion. This idea also was proposed at a right timing. Fabless IC design houses at that time were in need of capacity and had retained quite an amount of cash from several years of growth. Capacity was so in demand that IC design houses had to pay cash in advance to book future capacity from IC foundries.

From the perspective of an IC design house, establishing an IC fab with 100 percent ownership would face some problems. First, the investment might be too large for an IC design house. Second, IC design houses have no manufacturing experience and might be less competitive in running a fab. Third, an IC fab in an economical scale has substantial capacity, which might exceed the demand of just one IC design house.

UMC implemented the idea of a joint venture in a very speedy way. In only four months, UMC contacted the top 10 IC design houses in the USA and came to an agreement with some of them to establish three dedicated IC foundry companies in Taiwan. These leading American IC design houses then became strategic allies of UMC. The reason for establishing three companies at the same time was to avoid competitors' duplicating this idea. With these alliances, there was little room left for competitors to form similar alliances. These alliances proved to be of very beneficial to the growth of UMC in the IC foundry business.

Turning down its path of becoming a dedicated IC foundry, UMC started to close its IC design departments, and relevant employees were spun off to establish independent fabless IC design houses. These IC design houses, operating under more freedom, have proven to be quite successful; two of them are in the top 10 list of Taiwan IC design houses.

UMC and the three joint venture companies were known as the UMC Group. Holtek, a semiconductor company, joined the UMC Group in 1998, and the four companies were merged into UMC as of January 2000 [7]. The performance of UMC or the UMC Group in the IC foundry business has been quite successful. The revenue of UMC as an IC foundry increased to US$1,696 million in 1999, about seven times higher than its IC foundry revenue in 1995, when UMC was an IDM company.

3. Why Taiwan's IC Foundries are so Successful

The IC foundry industry in Taiwan undoubtedly has proven quite successful, accounting for 67 percent of market share in the world. What accounts for the success of this industry in Taiwan? Some observations from the corporate perspective, the industry perspective, and the environmental perspective are discussed below.

3.1 Success Factors from Corporate Perspective

3.1.1 Leaders and Strategies

"A world filled with opportunities will create new heroes; a hero with vision will create a new world," says a Chinese proverb. Capable leaders are undoubtedly indispensable factors in the success of Taiwan IC foundries. Capable leadership in the new business of a dedicated IC foundry could be defined by two main criteria—credible performance in business and long-term experience in the semiconductor area.

Before founding TSMC, Morris Chang had been in the semiconductor industry for more than 30 years and had proven to be a successful executive. He had been vice-president of Texas Instruments' global semiconductor business. Before leading UMC to the dedicated IC foundry business, Robert Tsao, chairman of the board of directors of the UMC Group, had been in the semiconductor area for more than 20 years and had provided credible leadership for UMC for more than 15 years.

Strategies and vision are also very important. The visions and strategies of creating the IC foundry business model by TSMC and entering into a joint venture with fabless IC design houses by UMC have both proven to be successful. However, when these strategies were implemented, there were few followers. Vision undoubtedly is the first critical successful factor in establishing Taiwan's IC foundry industry.

3.1.2 Incentive Systems

People work most diligently when they work for themselves. Employees in Taiwan's IC foundries are highly motivated by an attractive incentive system known as a stock bonus system. In the stock bonus system, a percentage of a company's net income is given to employees as a bonus. This bonus, valued by the par value of common stock, is issued to employees in the form of common stock. The market value of a common stock might be 10 times higher than its par value, which creates incredible financial rewards to employees of IC foundries.

As an example, an engineer might be given a US$10,000 bonus. If the bonus were given in cash, it would be worth US$10,000; however, if the bonus is given in the form of stocks, the US$10,000 common stock in par value actually is US$100,000 if sold on the stock exchange market. A typical engineer with two years experience in the Taiwan IC foundry might get a stock bonus equivalent to US$100,000 in market value.

3.2 Success Factors from Industry Perspective

3.2.1 The Cluster Effect

IC fabs in Taiwan are located in a cluster. In 1999, there were 21 semiconductor manufacturing companies in Taiwan. Dedicated IC foundries accounted for more than 55 percent of total revenues, and most of the others were manufacturers of memory products. Most of these semiconductor factories are located in Hsin-Chu, a city in the northern part of Taiwan. There are several good reasons for the cluster infrastructure.

Resource sharing, whether intentional or unintentional, can reduce cost. The clustering of semiconductor factories helps establish a strong mutual support system through vendors. Semiconductor equipment is very expensive and requires high utilization, but to maintain high utilization requires a vendor to keep a supply of spare parts and maintenance engineers. The cost of providing good vendor services can be reduced if semiconductor factories are located in a cluster because international equipment vendors can devote more resources and consequently provide better support to Taiwan IC foundries.

A sportsman runs faster when another one is trying to overtake him. The clustering of semiconductor companies also provides a mutual benchmarking system for these companies. Benchmarking in profit, revenue, capacity, and process technology pushes the mutually competitive IC foundry companies to improve faster than they would otherwise.

3.2.2 The Demand Chain Effect

To run a successful business, you have to know your customers because they give you orders; but you also have to know your customers' customers because they give orders to your customers. Who are the customers of IC design houses?

Customers of fabless IC design houses are known as *systems companies*; that is, the products they produce are electronic systems, which involve ICs as key components. Typical examples of systems companies are those in the electronics industry, which produce personal computers, cellular phones, video players, etc. IC foundries need orders from design houses; design houses need orders from systems companies. Systems companies, design houses, and IC foundries therefore can be referred to as an IC demand chain.

	Taiwan	North America	Others
1994	30.5%	55.1%	14.4%
1995	36.6%	55.5%	7.9%
1996	40.8%	42.8%	16.4%
1997	47.5%	31.2%	21.3%
1998	34.9%	51.4%	13.7%
1999	38.3%	47.5%	14.2%

Table 5: Product shipping regions of Taiwan IC foundries (Ref. 11)

The success of Taiwan IC foundries in part is due to the fast growth of systems companies in the IC demand chain. Taiwan has been famous worldwide in the manufacturing of electronic products, particularly in personal computers. For example, about 40 percent of notebooks in the world (1998) are manufactured in Taiwan. These electronic products demand a large amount of ICs, which provides growth opportunities for IC design houses and subsequently provides growth opportunities for IC foundries. About 38 percent of the semiconductors fabricated by Taiwan IC foundries in 1999 were sold to local systems companies (Table 5).

3.3 Success Factors from Environment Perspective

3.3.1 Massive and High Quality Manpower

To successfully run the IC foundry business, high quality and massive manpower are very important. High quality manpower for this purpose could be characterized as well-educated, diligent, and adaptable employees.

Semiconductor manufacturing is continuously improving technologically and requires well-educated employees to develop new process technology. According to Gordon Moore, one of the founders of Intel Corp., the resolution of semiconductor technology will be reduced by half every 18 months. With this rapid rate of change, capable research and development staffs are essential to a competitive IC foundry.

Taiwan's culture has been highly valuing the importance of higher education, so large amounts of well-educated employees have been available in the human resource market. In the Hsin-Chu Science-Based Park where TSMC, UMC, and other high-tech companies are located, there were more than 80,000 employees in 1999. About 18 percent of these employees have Ph.D. or masters degrees, 45 percent have bachelors or junior college degrees, and 37 percent have high school degrees (Table 6). The percentage of highly educated employees in IC foundries is even higher than other high-tech companies.

	Ph.D./Master	College Degree	High School/Others
TSMC	23%	37%	40%
UMC	23%	36%	41%
HS-Science Park	18%	45%	37%

Table 6 Education Distribution of Employees in 1999 (Ref. 5, 7, 12)

Employees in Taiwan IC foundries are very diligent and adaptable. This might be partially due to the stock bonus system and partially be due to the culture of Taiwan society. Whatever the reason, diligent employees are very important for running a productive IC foundry. Semiconductor equipment is so expensive and has to be utilized at a high rate to reduce costs. Equipment in an IC foundry typically runs 24 hours a day, and employees have to work in shifts. Staffs, whether working in the daytime or at night, have to be alert and diligent. Whenever a machine malfunctions or shuts down, the problem has to be identified immediately and repaired as soon as possible to keep productivity high.

Employees in a successful IC foundry also have to be very adaptable to the constantly changing environment. IC foundries provide manufacturing services to many design houses, so they have to be able to adapt to the frequent demand changes of various customers. That is, production schedules may have to be changed, process routes may have to be modified, and equipment may have to be reset to accommodate a demand change from customers.

3.3.2 Government Support

Government support has been significant in promoting the birth and growth of Taiwan's IC foundry industry. Major contributions may be due to the establishment of ITRI (Industrial Technology Research Institute), and HSIP (Hsin-Chu Science-based Industrial Park).

ITRI, a research institute funded with many government projects, was assigned the mission of developing the semiconductor technology in the 1970s. Several large-scale semiconductor projects were carried out by ITRI, which then provided experienced managers and engineers to start up the semiconductor business in Taiwan. In fact, most of the leaders in semiconductor design/manufacturing companies once were employees of ITRI. Some of them joined the RCA technology transfer project (1976-1977), which subsequently promoted the birth of UMC and several other companies in Taiwan. Others joined the VLSI project (1983-1988) and became the founding employees of TSMC.

If ITRI is the incubator of Taiwan IC foundries, then HSIP is its cornfield. HSIP (Hsin-Chu Science-based Industrial Park) is an industrial park located in Hsin-Chu, and accommodated 292 companies, with more than 80,000 employees, in 2000. TSMC, UMC, and most other semiconductor companies are located in HSIP. Only science-based industries such as integrated circuits, computers, telecommunications, and some other promising industries are allowed to be located in the Park. Companies located in HSIP have benefited from government policies, including land leasing, building leasing, tax exemptions, low-interest loans, and research grants. HSIP has proven to be very successful in promoting the growth of science-based industries in Taiwan. The number of companies in HSIP in 15 years has increased from 50 to 292, and the combined sales revenue has increased over 50 times, from US$ 377 million (1984) to US$20,100 million (1999).

4. The Impacts of Taiwan's IC Foundries

The success of IC foundries in Taiwan has had a profound impact on the infrastructure of the semiconductor industry. First, fabless IC design houses have been booming since the inception of dedicated IC foundries. Second, a comprehensive IC supply chain has been established in Taiwan.

4.1 Growth of Fabless IC Design Houses

The business model of IC foundries has posted a significant milestone in the history of the semiconductor industry. In 1999, Morris Chang, referred to as the "father of the foundry business," was honored by the Fabless Semiconductor Association (FSA) with its first-ever "Exemplary Leadership Award." This award will be permanently named "The Dr. Morris Chang Award for Exemplary Leadership" in recognition of his outstanding contribution to the fabless semiconductor industry.

According to FSA, fabless companies have grown faster and maintained higher average gross profit margins than any other segment of the semiconductor industry. More than 350 fabless companies are now in business around the globe, and dozens of start-ups appear each quarter. The largest concentration of fabless companies is in the USA, followed by Taiwan and Israel, and there are dozens of small, start-up fabless companies in Europe.

Fabless IC design houses in Taiwan have grown so quickly because of the capacity support of dedicated IC foundries. Without the risk of outsourcing capacity, design engineers are encouraged to start up new IC design houses. As a result, the number of IC design houses in Taiwan has increased to 127 in 2000 and the total revenue has increased over 100 times in 14 years (Table 7).

Year	Number of Companies	Total Revenue US$ Million
1986	18	13
1987	30	25
1988	50	77
1989	55	205
1990	55	219
1991	55	272
1992	59	342
1993	64	444
1994	65	469
1995	66	729
1996	72	794
1997	81	1,267
1998	115	1,403
1999	127	1,981

Table 7 Growth of fabless IC design houses in Taiwan (Ref. 9-11)

4.2 A Comprehensive IC Supply Chain

The making of ICs requires several stages of effort, which include design, manufacturing, packaging, and testing. Manufacturing of ICs also needs raw materials (blank silicon wafers) and supporting materials such as photo masks and chemical gases. Packaging of ICs likewise needs supporting material such as lead frames. The aggregation of companies contributing to the making of ICs can be referred to an *IC supply chain*, a value chain for supplying ICs.

Taiwan has now established a comprehensive IC supply chain (Figure 1), which helps Taiwan provides a one-stop service for international customers to place orders for manufacturing ICs. In Taiwan (1999), there are 21 IC fabrication companies, 42 IC packaging companies, 33 IC testing companies, eight blank wafer companies, five photo mask companies, 20 chemical gas companies, and 11 lead frame companies. Among the 21 IC fabrication companies, in 1999, IC foundries accounted for more than 53 percent of the total revenue of these IC fabs (Table 8).

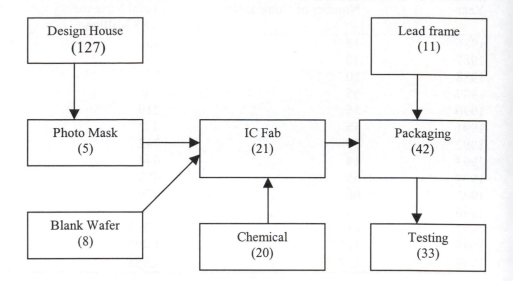

Figure 1: Number of companies in the Taiwan IC supply chain in 1999 (Ref. 11)

	IC Foundries	Other IC Fabs.
1994	36.6 %	63.4 %
1995	36.2 %	63.4 %
1996	44.6 %	55.4 %
1997	55.0 %	45.0 %
1998	55.4 %	44.6 %
1999	53.0 %	47.0 %

Table 8: Revenue percentage of IC foundries and other IC fabs. in Taiwan (Ref. 11)

IC foundries play only one role in the cast of making ICs in Taiwan, but undoubtedly a very critical role in helping create the versatile cast. Semiconductors produced by IC foundries or IDM companies need to be packaged and tested, and the rapid growth of IC foundries naturally provides great opportunities for IC packaging and testing companies. In 1999, the revenue of IC packaging increased to US$ 1,996 million (Table 9). The worldwide market share and ranking of the Taiwan IC supply chain are quite impressive (Table 10). IC foundries and packaging are both ranked No.1, IC design is ranked No.2 in the world.

Year	1996	1997	1998	1999
Design	793	1,252	1,398	2,248
Fabrication	4,567	5,283	5,051	8,027
Packaging	994	1,405	1,800	1,996
Testing	185	368	391	585

Table 9 Revenue of Taiwan IC Industry (US$ Million) (Ref. 11)

	Design Houses	IC Foundries	IC Packaging	IC Testing
Market Share	19.6%	64.6%	29.0%	28.0%
Ranking	2	1	1	N/A

Table 10 Worldwide market share of Taiwan's IC industry in 1999 (Ref. 13)

5. Future Threats and Opportunities

The IC foundry industry in Taiwan has proven to be very successful. Will Taiwan keep leading in the future? What are the threats and opportunities to the Taiwan IC Industries?

5.1 Escalating Investment

Maintaining leading-edge process technology is very important to IC foundries and IDM companies. The unit cost of fabricating an IC is essentially determined by the process technology, which can be characterized in two perspectives, *line width* and *wafer size*. Line width or resolution (often measured in um or micrometers) denotes the size of a transistor designed on an IC. The smaller the line width, the larger number of transistors could be built on an IC. Wafer size denotes the size of raw material (silicon wafer) on which ICs are fabricated. The larger the wafer size, the lower the unit cost of an IC. Since the invention of transistors, semiconductor equipment has been continuously improved to either reduce the line width or enlarge the wafer size.

In order to remain competitive, an IC foundry has to keep investing in new-generation semiconductor equipment; however, the unit price of the new-generation semiconductor equipment has been escalating. A typical 8" IC fab would cost US$1 billion, while a 12" fab on an economical scale would cost US$3 billion. It is estimated that the unit cost of an IC fabricated in a 12" fab with 0.13 um line width technology might be only one third of that fabricated in an 8" fab with 0.25 um technology. That is, an IC foundry resisting the fast migration to new-generation technology in the long run can never be competitive.

Large-scale investments seem to be mandatory for an IC foundry to be competitive in the market; however, it also seems quite risky from another perspective. One 12" fab in capacity is nearly equivalent to three 8" fabs. The capacity of a 12" fab is so large that its annual revenue for break-even might have to reach a substantial amount, say US$2 billion. Were there not enough orders for such a large-scale fab, the loss would be formidable, on the scale of a billion US dollars.

5.2 A Chain of Threats and Opportunities

"This is the most miserable time and is the most promising time." The trend of requiring a tremendous investment in the new-generation IC fabs surely is a threat to IC foundries; however, it also provides opportunities.

IDM companies, the other type of IC fabs, also face the same situation—an escalating scale of investment. In order to reduce the risk of investment, IDM companies tend to invest conservatively, that is, they may establish their in-house capacity at less than their forecasted demand, say 70 percent of their forecasted demand, and outsource capacity from IC foundries whenever the demand is higher than their in-house capacity. This conservative investment policy is beneficial for IDM companies because they keep their in-house fabs at a high utilization rate without losing the control of IC fabrication technologies.

The strategic outsourcing policy of IDM companies offers great opportunities to IC foundries. According to IDC (International Data Corporation), sales of foundry fabricated semiconductors in 1999 was about US$7 billion, accounting for only 12 percent of the worldwide semiconductor market; that is, the total sales of IDM companies accounts for 88 percent. This implies that IDMs would release 26.4 percent market share to IC foundries if they outsource 30 percent of their capacity. This market share in the future will account for 38.4 percent of the world semiconductor market. If the compound annual growth rate for the global IC market is 10 percent, and the 30 percent capacity outsourcing policy were fully realized in six years, the global IC foundry market in 2005 would be about US$35 billion, five times the sales in 1999. Sales revenue of US$35 billion implies the living space of over 15 IC fabs (12" wafer).

To capture the great opportunity of massive orders from IDMs, leading IC foundries undoubtedly would have to expand their capacity. The opportunity of IDM orders also brings out new threats, however. New participants in the IC foundry industry would come out to share the "big cake" and increase the global capacity of IC foundries. When the global semiconductor market is in an economic downturn, IDMs might have to take orders back from IC foundries, trapping some less competitive IC foundries in a very serious situation.

The future of Taiwan IC foundry will never be known until the future becomes a reality. Future opportunities chained with future threats indeed challenge Taiwan's IC foundries. How to capture the future opportunities in time while avoiding the potential threats is a very critical issue to the leaders in this industry.

References

[1] http://plan.tse.com.tw/
[2] Taiwan Semiconductor Manufacturing Co., *Prospectus for Issuing ADR*, 2000.
[3] Hu, G. "Current Status of Taiwan Semiconductor Industry," *Proceedings of the Prospects on the 21st Century's Electronics and Packaging Technology Seminar*, p. 3-7, Feb. 2000.
[4] Taiwan Semiconductor Manufacturing Co., *Prospectus for IPO*, Aug., 1994.
[5] Taiwan Semiconductor Manufacturing Co., *Prospectus for Issuing Bond*, Sep., 1999.
[6] United Micro Electronics Corp., *Prospectus for Issuing Bond*, May., 1996.
[7] United Micro Electronics Corp., *Prospectus for Merge and CapitalRaising*, Nov., 1999.
[8] United Micro Electronics Corp., *Prospectus for Issuing Bond*, March, 2000.
[9] Industrial Technology Research Institute, *Annual Report of Semiconductor Industry*, 1996.
[10] Industrial Technology Research Institute, *Annual Report of Semiconductor Industry*, 1999.

[11] Industrial Technology Research Institute, *Annual Report of Semiconductor Industry*, 2000.

[12] http://www.nsc.gov.tw/

[13] Industrial Technology Research Institute, *Investigation of New Opportunities for Taiwan IC Industries*, p. 6-3, 2000.

Acknowledgements: The author is grateful to Dr. M. S. Lin, Mr. Alfred. Wang of ITRI, Mr. Y. C. Huang of TSMC, Dr. F. T. Liu and Dr. Simon Yen of UMC for their helps and suggestions in drafting this article.

Chapter 6

Taiwan's IC Packaging Industry:
A Local Success Story Goes International

Pao-Long Chang

Institute of Business and Management
National ChiaoTung University
Taipei, Taiwan, R.O.C.

Chien-Tzu Tsai

Dept. of Industrial Engineering & Management
MingHsin Institute of Technology
HsinChu, Taiwan, R.O.C.

1. Introduction

As the trend of downsizing electronic products increases, so does the importance of the IC packaging technology. The packaging industry in Taiwan has gone through 30 years of development. In that time, the industry evolved from its beginning as a low-cost production arm for European and American companies to a ranking national presence based on Taiwanese factories. Today Taiwan's IC packing industry ranks second in the world in capacity. In recent years, the industry has expanded at an average compound growth rate near 40 percent and established close partnerships with large global IDM factories and IC design companies. The industry's competitive strategy in the international arena is partially attributed to its fast-follow strategy in technology. This Taiwan-based industry also has created a performance advantage in such logistical factors as capacity, delivery, quality, cost, and services. In this way, it has set itself apart from leading technology countries and new-entrant Southeast Asia countries that stress low cost. The IC packaging industry in Taiwan has established a unique strategic position in the global semiconductor supply chain. Its development and competitive factors are the focus of this article.

2.   A New Look at Packaging

The IC packaging industry had not attracted as much attention as the semiconductor manufacturing or the IC design sectors because of its relatively small operating scale and the fact that IC packaging processes were similar to traditional electronic fabrication and required relatively low-level technology. The total value of specialized packaging occupies less than one-tenth of the total output of the whole semiconductor industry. The packaging industry's importance in the electronics industry has increased in the last ten years with the demand for downsizing and mobile products as well as advances and breakthroughs in packaging materials and process technology. As a vice president of IBM, Paul Loa, predicted in the early 1990s, "Electronic fabrication technology, just like the silicon chip of the1980s, will make significant advancements in technology, leading the electronics industry into the 21st century." In May of 1999, the associate chief editor of *Semiconductor International* announced, "Electronic packaging, just like IC manufacturing, will decide the success of a product." Because of its increasing importance in the electronics industry, the packaging industry deserves further study.

The manufacturing process of IC products primarily can be divided into circuit design, photomasking, chip fabrication, and packaging, as shown in figure 1. In earlier periods, semiconductor companies were mostly IDMs (Integrated Device Manufacturers) because they took responsibilities for all these processes. As the industry expanded, with increased investment and more sophisticated technology, every critical process in IC fabrication became an area of specialization, forming its own sub-industry. Since the packaging industry is located toward the end of the semiconductor fabrication process, since packaging technology is not the core of IC fabrication, and labor costs were more significant in this process, industry players considered this portion the most readily detachable. In the 1950s, Philips began the move by setting up a factory in Singapore and transferring its packaging process there. In the 1960s, U.S. companies one after another followed suit, making investments in Asia and establishing packaging factories. In this way,

Taiwan's packaging industry was begun by large IDMs that transferred assembly lines from advanced countries to overseas sites. In 1966, the U.S. company Microchip established the first electronic packaging factory in Kaohsiung. In the same period, Texas Instruments (TI) and the Dutch company Philips Electronics successively set up factories there. Later, the Japanese company Sanyo established a packaging factory in the Taichung Export Processing Zone. Taiwan thus became an important base for IC post-processing for large international semiconductor manufacturers in their global division of labor.

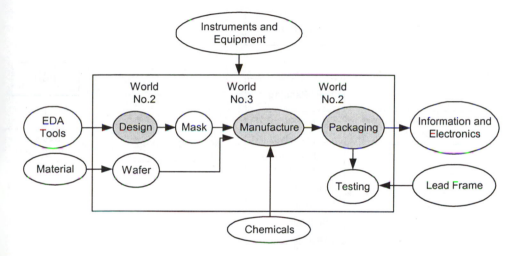

Figure 1. Semiconductor-Related Industry Processes and Industry Status of Taiwan

After 30 years of continuous development, this industry has gradually become the second largest in the world, dealing with most of the important semiconductor companies and design houses in the world either directly or indirectly. The Taiwan packaging industry has become an important partner in the global semiconductor supply chain.

3. The Development of Taiwan's Packaging Industry

This study's investigation of the specialized packaging industry does not attempt to cover all IC post-processing, but will focus on chip packaging as a sub-industry. Taiwan has developed a division of labor in related packaging processes, as shown in figure 2, which includes specialized producers of leadframe, substrate, testing, etc. This specialized division of labor and alliances among specialized industries has aided the development of post-processing in the semiconductor industry.

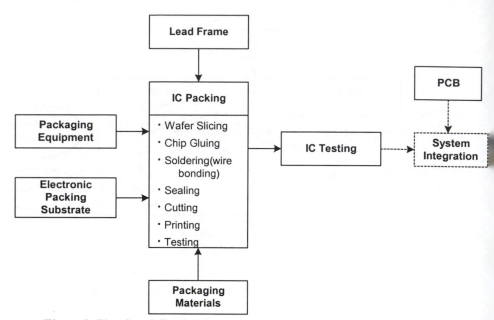

Figure 2. Fine Specialization Structure in Semiconductor Post-processing

As described above, the Taiwan packaging industry started to develop in the 1960s under pressure from European, American, and Japanese semiconductor companies to lower their production costs. Attracted by cheap manpower, foreign capital came in, established their factories, and brought in related production technology. At that time, most of the foreign-invested electronic packaging factories were located in the export processing zones, where they applied the technology transferred from their parent companies and accepted orders for export. They primarily acted as low-cost overseas extensions of their parent companies, so their growth was largely attributable to foreign investment by large international companies (refer to Table 1). As the semiconductor technology evolved, the industry gradually shifted from transistor assembly to IC packaging.

Producer name	establishing year	recapitulation
Kaohsiung Electronics	1966	packaging factory in Kaohsiung Export Processing zone established by U.S. company Microchip, engaging in transistor packaging
Philips Semiconductor Kaohsiung	1967	packaging factory established by Dutch company Philips
TI Taiwan	1971	packaging factory at Chunghe set up by U.S. company Texas Instruments, initially engaging in ceramic packaging
Siliconix Taiwan	1974	packaging factory set up by foreign company Siliconix, initially engaging in packaging of discrete parts
Sanyo Taichung	1976	factory set up by Sanyo of Japan for semiconductor packaging
Digital	1981	IC packaging factory at Tan Tze Export Processing zone
Motorola	1985	IC packaging and testing factory at Chungli set up by U.S. company Motorola and then merged by ASE

Data source: ITIS plan of ERSO, ITRI (Jun. 1998)

Table 1. The Establishment of Foreign-Invested Packaging Factories in Taiwan

In the 1980s, competition among semiconductor companies became increasingly vigorous, as U.S and Japanese companies battled for control of the market. This competitive situation resulted in global strategies that created a new look in the semiconductor market. In the late 1980s, specialized chip OEM factories sprung up in Taiwan, as a reaction to the industry strategy of global division of labor by specialization. Under this notion of an integrated supply chain that crosses national boundaries, the underpinning principle was, "Whichever party within the business processes can most efficiently and effectively perform a task should perform the task." In response to this trend, the Taiwan semiconductor industry evolved into specialized industries, including the packaging industry, to create a clustering of factories devoted to specialized subdivisions of the production process.

Backed by government support in investment financing and technology development, large numbers of locally invested firms sprang up, focusing on the competitive edge derived from increased capacity, faster delivery, better quality and service, and lower cost. Domestic firms became capable task performers in the global division of labor by specialization, laying the foundation for this industry's continuous growth. In addition to older companies like HuanYu, Orient Semiconductor Engineering (OSE), and LingSen, which had been established earlier, HuaShu was the first packaging company establishing itself in the HsinChu Science Park (1983). Advanced Semiconductor Engineering(ASE) and Siliconware Precision Industries (SPI), both ranked among the top five (refer to Table 2) in Taiwan packaging industry, were established one after another in this period.

Ranking	1998	1999
1	ASE	ASE
2	SPI	SPI
3	OSE	OSE
4	Caesar	ASE,TaoYuang
5	Chipmos	Greatek
Weight of Top Five	73.0%	72.9%
Weight of other industry companies	27.0%	27.1%
Total	100%	100%

Data source: ITIS plan of ERSO, ITRI (May 2000)

Table 2. Top Five IC Packaging Companies in Taiwan

In the 1990s, with the development of new packaging technologies and the booming IC industry in Taiwan, more packaging factories were established. Backed by investments in BGA and CSP technology and a strong promotion of quality and service, the size of the industry expanded remarkably, as depicted in Table 3. In addition to the growing number of firms during these years, the industry also experienced a 14 to 69 percent growth rate in business volume, and the specialized packaging industry as a whole reached NTD54.9 billion in annual sales. In addition to the expansion of local chip OEM factories and design houses, there was a significant increase in customers from North America, as shown in Table 4.

Year	1991	1992	1993	1994	1995	1996	1997	1998	1999
Number of players	7	10	10	10	12	14	17	25	38
Sales value (NTD100millions)	39	58	100	141	222	252	362	420	549
Growth rate		49%	69%	43%	59%	14%	44%	16%	31%

Data source: Author's work based on data sorted out from 1996 and 2000 Semiconductor Yearbooks

Table 3. Important Indicators in the Development of Locally Invested IC Packaging Industry in Taiwan

Type of customer		1998	
		Sales value	Sales amount
Local	Design house	34.4%	36.5%
	Manufacturing company	23.5%	29.1%
	Others	0.8%	0.7%
Foreign	Design house	28.4%	22.7%
	Manufacturing company	12.8%	10.4%
	Others	0.2%	0.7%
Total		100%	100%

Data source: ITIS plan of ERSO, ITRI (Apr. 1999)

Table 4. Distribution of Customers of Locally Invested IC Packaging Companies

In terms of product types, high pin-count QFP and BGA surpassed low pin-count DIP and PLCC. The SO series also were produced in significant quantities to match DRAM output, but BGA and other new types of packaging experienced the most remarkable growth, as shown in Table 5.

By combining chip fabrication and testing, packaging firms provided strategic turnkey services, which gradually made them a highly competitive specialized post-processing partner in the global semiconductor supply chain. These firms not only accepted packaging orders from the parent company, they also provided specialized packaging services to chip fabricators and IC design houses. These firms also aggressively sought the certification of more IDM factories.

Units in %

	PDIP		SO		PLCC		QFP		BGA		others		total
1994	58.4	35.7	18.7	16.9	7.1	9.2	12.3	36.5	0.3	0.4	3.2	1.3	100
1995	42	22.2	30.4	24.3	4.8	6.4	13.8	44.4	0.3	0.4	9	2.3	100
1996	33.3	15.7	37.7	26.5	3.9	401	18.4	50.8	0.1	1.3	6.5	1.7	100
1997	26.1	13.1	43.1	31.9	3.8	3.9	16.9	40.0	0.8	8.0	9.3	3.0	100
1998	21.3	10.8	42.1	29.9	4	3.6	16.5	33.7	2	17.6	14.1	4.4	100
1999	16.1	7.3	51.6	28.3	4.7	2.9	15.1	26	4.2	32.6	8.3	2.9	
99/98 growth rate	9.1	-11.6	77	23.7	69.7	5.3	32.2	0.8	203.3	142.1	-15	-13.8	%

Remarks: SO* primarily covers four types of products: SOJ/ SOP/ TSOP/ LOC
Data source: ITIS plan of ERSO, ITRI (May 2000)

Table 5. Product types of Locally IC Packaging Industry (sales amount/sales value)

The next section will elucidate the competitive strategy of the Taiwan packaging industry in the world market, and the fifth section will explore the main factors that contributed to the development of the industry's core competence.

4. Competitive strategies of the Taiwan Packaging Industry

The Taiwan packaging industry started to develop in the 1960s, using cheap manpower to attract foreign capital to set up factories and bring in related production technology. In the 1980s, however, Taiwan found itself losing its low-cost labor advantage to Southeast Asian countries. Foreign capital gradually dwindled, and after 1985, no foreign firms established new packaging firms. Taiwan also had to face the competition of technological advances in Europe, America, and Japan. Under these circumstances, Taiwan could not position itself either as a technological leader or a low-cost labor provider.

In this situation, as a result of the fierce competition among international semiconductor industries, a viable goal became specialized divisions of labor to attain scales of economy and cost advantages. Large semiconductor firms sought specialized partners around the world to create a global system to meet the competition. From a managerial viewpoint, strategic partners in the supply chain needed to provide lower-cost production, satisfy quality requirements, and match the requirements of diversity, flexibility, delivery, and capacity.

These partners also could offer add-on services, from ordering to post-sales processes, to meet the market demands for increasingly short product life cycles and changes.

Although Taiwan's packaging firms do not possess leading technologies, they do possess such advantages as fast-follow technical capability, appropriate quality level, and flexibility in response to market demands. Adding to these capabilities, domestic semiconductor industries became more comprehensive, and thereby benefited from capacity scales, control of total production costs, efficient delivery, and turnkey services in testing and packaging. Taiwan's packaging industry developed its role as a strategic partner, emphasizing fast-follow technology and integration of quality, cost, delivery, and capacity factors. All these factors helped the industry maintain a highly competitive position in the specialized international system. The relative advantages of this strategy and its overall competence are illustrated in figure 3.

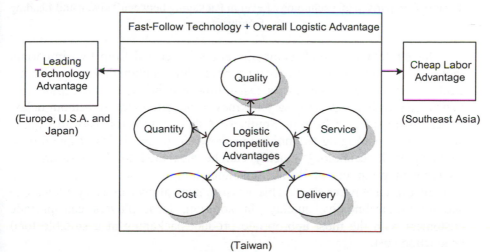

Figure 3. Competitive Strategy and Main Industry Advantage Factors of Taiwan's IC Packaging Industry

The competitive situation faced by Taiwan's packaging industry can be analyzed using Porter's framework of competitiveness consisting of five forces. Looking upstream, Taiwan does not have the advantage in the precision machinery, molding technology, or material processing required for IC packaging. While the U.S.A., Japan, and Korea have attained advanced technological developments like BGA, CSP and MCM packaging, Taiwan lags behind, as depicted in Table 6. In relation to competition from Southeast Asia, Taiwan has lost the advantage of low-cost labor. Lacking the technological advantages and the low-cost labor, the only path Taiwan could pursue to counter the competition was to concentrate on the customer. Taiwan's packaging industry strove to provide integrated quality, delivery, service, cost, and capacity factors to gain a foothold in worldwide competition.

Packaging type	measuring index	Level of Taiwan	country leading in technology	level of leading countries
TSOP	Thickness	mass production 0.6 mm	U.S.A. , Japan	Mass production 0.5 mm
QFP	Lead Pitch	mass production 0.3~0.5 mm	Japan	Mass production 0.25~0.4 mm
BGA	Pin Count	mass production 700 Pin	U.S.A. , Japan	Mass production 1156 Pin
Flip Chip	Pin Count	pilot run 1000 Pin	U.S.A. , Japan	mass production 2300
CSP	Ball Pitch	mass production 256 Pin	U.S.A. , Japan	mass production 768 Pin

Remarks: CSP includes BGA of 0.8mm Ball Pitch
Data source: ITIS plan of ERSO, ITRI (May 2000)

Table 6. Comparison of Technology Level in Packaging between Taiwan and Leading Countries

This strategy of overall competitiveness is derived from two important factors in the industrial development process. First, although Taiwan is not a leader in technology, due to its fast-follow capability, it can capture the mainstream technology necessary for mass production almost without delay, which distinguishes it from its Southeast Asia counterparts. Taiwan's quick adaptation of packaging technology is shown in figure 4. This capability to catch up with technology quickly can be attributed to the assistance of government programs in R&D, personnel training, and the creation of a venture capital environment. This environment allows industry players to acquire the technology quickly. In addition, local players can provide customers with the most appropriate product packaging at a suitable total production cost.

	1988	1989	1990	1991	1992	1993	1994	1995	1996	1997
Mini BGA:										48
BGA:							256	500	530	569
VSOP:						48	48	48	48	48
SOP:	28	28	28	40	44	44	44	44		50
QFP:	100	100	160	208	256	304	304	304	304	304
LCC:	84	84	84	84	84	84	84	84	84	84
Year	**1988**	**1989**	**1990**	**1991**	**1992**	**1993**	**1994**	**1995**	**1996**	**1997**
DIP:	40	40	40	40	48	48	48	48	48	48
SDIP:	28	28	28	28	28	28	32	32	32	32
ZIP:				28	28	48	48	48	48	48
PGA:					172	172	172	181	181	

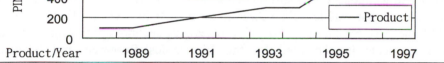

Figure 4. Taiwan's Packaging Technology Capability and the Movement Trends

Secondly, besides the basic capability of providing mass production technology, Taiwan's packaging industries team up with domestic OEM chip fabrication and testing industries to generate a clustering effect of expanded capacity, high quality, transportation cost savings, enhanced efficacy, and increased services. This enables the group to establish the overall performance required by customers and assure itself a competitive position in the market.

The next section will illustrate the developmental elements that have been crucial to Taiwan's packaging industry in attaining its unique competitiveness for strategic partnerships in the specialized global division of labor.

5.   Factors affecting the competitiveness of Taiwan's packaging industry

To position itself as a fast-follower in technology, Taiwan had to respond to technological trends in the shortest possible time as well as create the mass production capability to meet the requirements of IC manufacturers and design houses. This meant it had to first acquire the technology, then obtain capital investments for the production capacity, then allow the technology to realize its capability through sound management and fine-tuning of qualified personnel. These components -- technology, capital investments, and management -- needed governmental support. By means of R&D project assistance, personnel training, and an improved investment and financial environment for technology industries, the effect gradually emerged after 1985.

Technological foundations for strategic competence—government R&D projects support the quick-following technology strategies.

As mentioned, foreign companies established the earliest packaging industries in Taiwan. HuanYu, which was established in 1969, was the first domestic company created in the packaging business. After that, locally invested factories such as OSE and ASE joined the industry. The amount of locally developed technology was still relatively low, however, as shown by a R&D expenditure that was less than three percent of total revenue. Beginning in 1979, the government helped develop packaging technology through special R&D projects implemented by the Electronics Research and Service Organization (ERSO) in the ITRI (Industrial Technology Research Institute). A series of projects on computer product packaging technology was started in 1979, each running for a four-year term. These focused on module packaging engineering, substrate engineering, system packaging engineering, etc. As a result of these projects, the industry developed electronic product packaging technology, electricity engineering analysis, heat dissipation analysis, and other technologies to meet the efficiency and quality requirements for high-speed and high-density IC design.

ITRI's continuous efforts in packaging research helped the industry establish the necessary R&D capability, laying the foundation for rapid technological advances in locally invested packaging factories after 1985. In the 1990s, responding to the demands of VLSI process technology and downsized portable computer and communication products, ITRI combined the resources of its four labs (ECL—Electronic and Communication Lab; ERSO; MRL—Material Research Lab; and EMRO—Energy and Mining

Research and service Organization) to develop technologies to carry out advanced packaging processes. These technologies included systems packaging design and assembly processes, component packaging technology, advanced packaging substrate and materials, and heat transmission effects.

By utilizing products such as card-sized PCs and wireless LANs as carriers, ITRI enabled domestic packaging technologies to expand from the information domain to the communications domain. Related products, processes, and material technologies are transferred to related SMT factories, packaging factories, and substrate factories, enabling local producers to establish core technologies. Although Taiwan is still one to three years behind the leading countries in advanced packaging technology, technology indices of mass production such as lead pitch, pin count, etc., are running almost neck-and-neck with the leading countries.

The capacity advantage—creating an environment for entrepreneurship.

In the second half of the 1980s, the influx of foreign-invested factories came to a halt and was replaced by a new rush of locally invested companies, which brought about the industry's growth. The robust growth of locally invested specialized packaging factories was stimulated by potential business from OEM chip fabrications, with the necessary support of professional personnel and capital investment. During the industrial transformation of the 1980s, Taiwan's standard of living and economic power also were experiencing considerable growth. The economy also was stimulated by a series of government policies such as financial market liberalization and globalization. In addition, venture capital companies were springing up.

The total effect was that personnel from research institutes gravitated toward entrepreneurial enterprises, which had secured funding for new factories and new equipment. Many of these new packaging factories were created by upstream electronics players; for example, Caesar gathered personnel from ERSO, TSMC, and Macronix to form its new company. Some of these resulted from creative combinations from conventional industries; for example, Pan Pacific combined the capital investments of Pacific Construction and HungHe Textile to form a new company, while TI technology and management teams combined with HuaLon Textile to form Chino-Excel. The world's second largest packaging factory, ASE, was established in 1987.

Investment and continuous technological developments have allowed Taiwan's packaging industry to not only survive the impact of rising labor costs without losing steam, but to become more prosperous. In the 1990s, as BGA, Flip Chip, CSP, MCM related technology came out, Taiwan producers entered various specialized markets. Pan Pacific selected ceramic packaging as its niche market, Vate entered into BGA and Flip Chip technology, Kingpaq went into DRAM module packaging, and NanYen specialized in packaging communication-related semiconductors.

On the other hand, to keep up with the competition, senior large factories gathered advanced technology from their international alliances. Siliconware Precision Industries obtained the authorization to use DBGA technology from NEC. These companies also achieved economies through mergers and overseas production. ASE attained an economy of scale by merging Motorola's Chungli factory and the Korean factory. ASE established plants in Malaysia and the Philippines to transfer low-end production lines overseas.

Because of the government's financial and technological support, Taiwan's packaging industry had an abundance of capital resources to keep abreast of advanced technologies and expand its production capacity. As the industry developed, it achieved significant economies of scale and a sound financial basis. Its ability to avoid the Asian financial crisis in 1996 also earned customers' recognition for its risk management capabilities, strengthening Taiwan's position in the global supply chain.

The quality advantage—maintaining good quality and highly trained human resources.

Packaging technology actually involves many diverse disciplines such as electronic engineering, material engineering, mechanical engineering, and chemistry. The industry further demands expertise in high yield rates, capacity planning, and various technologies linking upstream and downstream industries. Because of this, the recruitment of high quality technical personnel and management is essential to maintain competitiveness.

Taiwan's widespread education policy has produced thousands of highly qualified scientists and engineers. In addition, the government has recruited a group of professionals for the research labs in ITRI, technology is disseminated through research results, seminars, technical support services, and professional training. The prosperity of the electronics and information industries has attracted not only domestic talents, but foreign ones as well. As a result, Taiwan's packaging industry has retained the technical expertise to maintain its competitive edge. Although the direct labor cost in Taiwan's packaging industry is higher than in Southeast Asia, it is relatively cheap compared to leading countries in Europe, the U.S.A, and Japan. Taiwan's engineers also are known for their hard work and endurance. The ability to train and attract high-quality employees has enabled the industry to maintain commitments to new technology, production flexibility, and product quality attestations, such as ISO.

The logistical advantage—effects of industrial divisions and clustering.

In evaluating production costs from a global management view, cost has to be measured against service. Taiwan's packaging industry's competitive edge is a result not only of relatively cheap labor cost, but also of the competitive cost of materials, equipment, and transportation. Because the collective industry's demands create an economy of scale, the industry has been able to negotiate better prices for materials and equipment, which reduces the average cost of production. At the same time, the clustering of upstream OEM chip fabrication and specialized design houses and downstream testing factories and IC application system firms saves on transportation costs between the packaging fabricators, testing factories, and end users. The most important contribution to overall competitiveness is the quick delivery time. These factors create a turnkey service that unifies chip fabrication, packaging, and testing services that customers used to have to deal with separately. This one-stop environment enables local packaging firms to deliver good quality service at a relatively cheap cost.

The cost advantage—creating price negotiation capability.

In the normal production cost structure of the packaging industry, direct materials occupy 30 to 40 percent of costs; direct labor takes up 20 percent; manufacturing costs, including equipment, absorb another 20 to 30 percent; and operations cost another 10 percent. This leaves a gross profit margin of 10 to 20 percent. Among these cost factors, manufacturing costs can be reduced by 10 percent if automatic processes are implemented, but since the bulk of product costs lies in materials, the price of materials and equipment becomes a crucial factor in determining the overall production cost.

The total sales value of Taiwan's packaging industry, which comprises close to 30 factories, has reached NTD54.9 billion. These factories range from newly established small niche factories to such world-class large facilities as ASE. Taiwan has gathered so many players that its industry generates a total revenue that ranks second in the world. The size of this aggregated market is obviously very attractive to materials and equipment suppliers, and the sheer volume of the massed industry hands Taiwan's packaging factories a strong price negotiation advantage. As materials and equipment costs take up almost half of the total cost of a final product, savings of 10 to 20 percent in that area is almost equivalent to a 20 to 30 percent savings in labor costs. Even smaller packaging factories can take advantage of the bargaining power of world class factories and the collective bargaining of multiple firms. Through its industry clustering, Taiwan's packaging industry can obtain an upper hand in controlling overall production costs.

The delivery advantage—competitiveness through saving time costs.

Almost 60 percent of the Taiwan packaging industry's main customers are the IC design houses, which includes the top-ranking design industry in North America and Taiwan. The remaining 40 percent are chip manufacturers, almost two-thirds of which are based in Taiwan. IC products after-packaging, including memory chips (around 30%, and mostly with SO packaging) and PC chipsets, are mainly for use by electronics and information customers. The majority of packaging products are delivered to downstream computer system manufacturers in Taiwan. Because of this, when a North American company places an IC design order with an OEM chip fabricator in Taiwan, and the product is to be inserted on Taiwan-made printed circuit boards, it is both convenient and efficient to select Taiwan packaging factories.

Taiwan has upstream- and downstream-related industries such as computer and information industries, chip fabrication, and IC design firms to form a completely integrated system that has developed vigorously (as indicated by black circled portions in figure 1). Packaging firms can take advantage of this industry clustering from order taking to goods delivery. Apart from time and cost savings, another important advantage is the proximity to customers and end users, which allows firms to respond to changes in customer requirements and market demands quickly. This ability to respond quickly is vital at a time when product life cycle is getting shorter and competition among new products is becoming keener. The Taiwan packaging industry can help customers maintain efficiency and save time, thus enhancing its overall competitiveness.

The service advantage—creating specialized customer service performance.

The system of vertical disintegration by specialization in Taiwan's semiconductor industry is unique. The packaging industry not only continually updates its technology and invests in production capacity, it also insists on rigorous quality control in an effort to maintain a high yield rate (almost 99% with mass production technology). Besides keeping competitive in terms of costs (about 10% lower than its main rivals), it also counts on the integration of OEM chip fabrication and testing industries to offer turnkey services. In this integrated environment, customers only need to order once. In turn, customers receive integrated services, from chip fabrication and packaging to testing. This allows customers to save considerable costs by eliminating the need to transfer orders and reduce their inherent risks.

Part of the industry's capacity for customer response results from management information systems that provide on-line, real time customer service through the Internet. Through this system, customers can check the status of their orders, view the actual production schedule, and receive instant responses to their inquiries.

As a result of its performance in efficiency, cost savings, and customer service, Taiwan's packaging industry has established its competitive position of delivering high performance relative to cost.

6. Conclusion

From the early days when Taiwan used low-cost labor to attract foreign capital to set up packaging factories, the industry has been transformed, until domestic firms dominated and expanded the industry. In this way, Taiwan's packaging industry evolved from being a production branch for foreign companies to an important partner in the global semiconductor supply chain system.

It accomplished this transformation by adopting a fast-follow strategy, a production capacity that ranks number 2 in the world, and world-class customer response system. Taiwan's strategic competitive advantage in the packaging industry is the result of government assistance in R&D, an appropriate investment environment, and high-quality manpower. In addition, the clustering of semiconductor and information industries gives Taiwan's industry the ability to control production costs, delivery, and services. Even though Taiwan is not the technological leader, and labor costs are lower in other areas, the unique, integrated production capability has proven advantageous in developing global partnerships.

In the last few years, Taiwan's packaging industry has maintained high growth rates, but it has many challenges ahead. These include competitive pressures from Southeast Asia and the technology leader Annam of Korea. Issues that need to be dealt with include conducting R&D programs that develop advanced packaging technology in the next three to five years and improving the yield rates of MCM, high density 3-dimensional packaging and flip chip technology. Other challenges are developing soldering technology for copper lead wire/low-dielectric layer chips; heat-dissipation of miniaturized chip modules; low contamination packaging processes; and developing materials technology. More effort has to be expended in chip-size packaging technologies.

With respect to human resources, the industry also has to recruit more professionals with interdisciplinary capabilities or practical operational experience. With the trend of further specialization, it is important for packaging players to enhance their technological level and management skills so IDMs will release more packaging orders. As OEM chip factories begin to carry out the initial packaging processing, packaging fabricators should consider how to fine tune the division of labor by specialization among OEM chip fabricators, substrate factories, and testing factories in order to sustain competitiveness in the global supply chain and seek new cooperative models for the survival and growth of the industry.

References

[1] Bowersox, D. J., Closs, D. J. *Logistics Management -- the Integrated Supply Chain Process*, the McGraw-Hill, Singapore, 1996.
[2] Chang, P. L., and Hsu, C. W., "The Development Strategies for Taiwan's Semiconductor Industry," *IEEE Transactions on Engineering Management*, Vol. 45, No. 4, 1998, pp. 349-356.

[3] Chang, P. L., Hsu C. W. and Tsai, C. T., "A Staged Approach for Industrial Technology Development and Implementation – the Case of Taiwan's Computer Industry," *Technovation,* Vol. 19, 1999, pp. 233-241.

[4] Chang, P. L., Shih, C. and Hsu, C. W., "The Formation Process of Taiwan's IC Industry—Method of Technology Transfer," *Technovation,* Vol. 14, No. 3, 1994, pp. 161-171.

[5] Chen, C. F. and Sewell, G., "Strategies for Technological Development in South Korea and Taiwan: the Case of Semiconductors," *Research Policy,* Vol. 25, 1996, pp. 759-783.

[6] Chiang, Jong-Tsong, "Management of National Technology Programs in A Newly Industrialized Country-Taiwan," *Technovation,* Vol. 10, No. 8, 1990, pp. 531-554.

[7] Hou C. M. and Gee S., "National Systems Supporting Technical Advances in Industry: the Case of Taiwan," in Nelson R., ed., *National Innovation Systems: A Comparative Analysis,* Oxford University Press, New York, 1993.

[8] ITRI, *Yearbooks of Semiconductor Industry*, (in Chinese), Taiwan, MOEA, 1992-2000.

[9] Lambert, D. M., Stock J. R. and Ellram, L. M., *Fundamentals of Logistics Management*, Irwin/McGraw-Hill, Boston, 1998.

[10] Lee, Chung-Shing and Pecht, Michael, *The Taiwan Electronics Industry*, CRC Press LLC, Florida, USA, 1997.

[11] Liu, Chung-Yuan, "Government's Role in Developing a High-tech Industry: The Case of Taiwan's Semiconductor Industry," *Technovation*, Vol. 13, No. 5, 1993, pp. 299-309.

[12] Mathews, John A., *High-Technology Industrialisation in East Asia: The Case of The Semiconductor Industry in Taiwan and Korea*, Chung-Hua Institution for Economic Research, Taipei, Taiwan, 1995.

[13] Mathews, John. A., "A Silicon Valley of the East: Creating Taiwan's Semiconductor Industry," *California Management Review,* Vol. 39, No. 4, 1997, pp. 26-53.

[14] Porter, M. E., *Competitive Advantage: Creating and Sustaining Superior Performance*, Free Press, New York, 1985.

Chapter 7

The Notebook Niche

Jen-Hung Huang

Department of Management Science
National Chiao Tung University
HsinChu, Taiwan, R.O.C.

1 Introduction

An industry's overall competitiveness is the result of many factors, two of which are a cohesive fit among facilitating institutions and distinctive resources. This cohesive fit includes those institutions that, combined, create an industry and whose interrelationships determine the industry's success or failure. Institutions that create this interrelationship consist not only of companies but also the national systems in which they function. These national systems' cultures, laws, policies, and procedures encourage or hinder a specific industry. As a result, different actors in an international industry develop different sets of expertise and develop relationships to achieve an overall industry goal. Distinctive resources include such production factors as natural resources, capital, and human resources.

Taiwan has carved out a distinctive niche within this overall industrial system. Its characteristics can be described as flexible, of medium technology, assembly-oriented, cost-driven, and focused on the short-term. Because these traits are suited to the production of information products, information product industries—particularly notebook computers—have flourished in Taiwan. Taiwan is a manufacturing center for information product components and systems and ranks third in information product production in the world, after the U.S. and Japan (Table 7.1)[1].

Notebook computer production has been a successful focus for Taiwan. According to the Market Intelligence Center (MIC) of the Institute for Information Industry (III), the output of notebook computers in Taiwan in 1999 grew

1999 Ranking	Nation	1999 (Thousand unit)	1998 (Thousand unit)	Growth rate in 1999
1	United States	95,162	90,630	5%
2	Japan	44,051	42,558	4%
3	Taiwan	21,023	19,240	9%
4	Singapore	18,473	18,660	-1%
5	China	18,455	14,196	30%
6	England	15,552	15,398	1%
7	Ireland	9,360	8,667	8%
8	Germany	9,197	8,844	4%
9	South Korea	8,862	8,169	8%
10	Brazil	8,227	8,395	-2%

Table 7.1 Ranking of information hardware production in 1999 (Source: III, ITIS)

53.7 percent in a market that grew 23.77 percent overall (Table 7.2)[1][3]. Taiwan surpassed Japan as the world market leader by garnering 46 percent of the market share. The top ten market leaders of notebook computers all currently outsource their manufacturing to Taiwan.

Ranking	Product	Value (Million Dollars)	Value Growth Rate	Unit (Thousand)	Unit Growth Rate
1	Notebook PC	10,198	21.1%	9,355	53.7%
2	Monitor	9,330	24.0%	58,729	17.7%
3	Desktop PC	7,188	11.2%	19,457	35.7%
4	Motherboard	4,854	12.6%	64,378	21.0%
5	Switching Power Supply	1,744	16.4%	80,221	36.6%

Table 7.2 Output of Hardware of Information Products in Taiwan in1999
(Source: MIC, III)

The overall notebook computer industry, or value chain, is comprised of several elements —design, component sourcing, manufacturing, distributing, marketing, and servicing. In this value chain, historically design has been controlled by large U.S. and Japanese firms such as Dell, Compaq, and Toshiba. Intel and Japanese firms such as Sharp have dictated such critical components as CPU and TFT-LCD, and Microsoft has dominated the software used in notebook computers. American and large Japanese firms such as Sharp also dominate the marketing end of notebook computers. According to Acer Chairman Stan Shih's smile curve theory, in the value chain of the notebook computer industry, as in many other industries, components and marketing account for a larger share of added-on value, while manufacturing and logistics account for a far smaller share of added-on value.

It seems obvious now that achieving high profitability in manufacturing computer systems might not be easy; however, it was not evident a few years ago. IBM considered that making PC systems was much more important than making such PC components as operating systems and CPUs, thus clearing the way for Microsoft and Intel, both of which now have higher market values than IBM. In 1987, Microsoft disagreed with IBM on the future direction of the OS/2 operating systems and proposed that IBM invest in Microsoft. That proposal was not accepted.

While the profit margins in manufacturing notebook computers might be less than desired, Taiwanese manufacturers have created a few large manufacturing firms that have succeeded in this niche and hopefully will make strides toward both ends of the smile curve in industries related to or transformed by the notebook industry.

2 Notebook Computers

2.1 A Brief History

In 1981, Osborne, a United States corporation, developed a portable computer called Osborne 1, making it possible to use a computer anywhere. The computer was too heavy for carrying around, however, and disappeared from the marketplace when Osborne collapsed. In 1987, Toshiba Inc. launched the T1000 laptop computer, which weighed less than 6.25

pounds—the first computer to weigh less than 10 pounds. In October 1989, Compaq introduced LTE and LTE/286, which weighed about 7 pounds and had a size of 2" x 11" x 8.5". The computer came with a floppy disk drive and a hard disk, and had a great impact on the industry in terms of the acceptance of this type of computer.

Although notebook computers are the main portable computers in the marketplace today, notebooks are just one type of portable computer. Portable computers can be classified into several categories, including laptop computers, notebook computers, sub-notebook computers, palm-held computers, and personal data assistants (PDAs). According to the product classification of the Ministry of Economy, ROC, a notebook computer is a computer weighing less than 6.6 pounds, includes a modem and battery, and can be carried around easily.

Notebook computers can be classified into three categories: high-end notebooks, value notebooks, and basic notebooks. High-end notebooks emphasize all-in-one capabilities, weigh more than 7.5 pounds, and often are used as a desktop replacement. Value notebooks are the mainstream products and come with various performance levels and price ranges for different market segments. Value computers come in two basic types. The first type is a stripped-down version with options determined by the purchasers. The second type is an all-in-one, with all options included in the case, resulting in a somewhat bulky machine[2].

There is a trend in the marketplace toward ever smaller, thinner, and lighter machines. After Sony introduced mini-notebooks—stripped-down versions of notebook computers—many manufacturers adopted new materials for cases and began to emphasize the color of the cases. Mini-notebooks have been increasing their share in the notebook computer market; however, because of the downward pressure of the price of value notebooks, the line between value notebooks and mini-notebooks is becoming blurred[2].

2.2 Notebook Computers and Desktop Computers

A notebook computer has characteristics that differentiate it from a desktop computer:

The degree of standardization. Notebook computers lack specification standards, which results in lower reliability. Each brand has its own special design and uses its own parts, which makes maintenance difficult. A retail store usually can fix a desktop computer, but not a notebook computer.

Expandability. Due to its small size and lack of standardization, it is more difficult to add a second hard disk drive and other components to a notebook computer. Because of this, a notebook computer is not as expandable as a desktop computer.

Price. The costs of components for notebook computers are higher than that of desktop computers. The costs of designing and producing a notebook computer are also higher than that of a desktop computer. Because of these factors, prices of notebook computers are higher than the prices of desktop computers for the same performance,

Performance. Due to their energy consumption and heat, notebook computers' performance usually falls behind that of desktop computers.

Mobility. Due to the size of a notebook computer, it can be carried around, unlike the bulkier desktop computer. For many people, this is a very important characteristic because it allows people to work without interruption when going between workplace and home, between office and clients, or between library and dormitory. It can also save work space.

3 The World Notebook Computer Industry

According to IDC (International Data Corporation) and MIC, III (Figure 7.1), the production of notebook computers grew by 20 percent in 1997. It grew less than 10 percent in 1998, due to the extreme popularity of low-priced desktop PCs, which squeezed the demand for notebook computers. It was estimated that the growth rate would reach 23.8 percent in 1999, and annual growth rates are expected to be more than 10 percent before 2003.

The market of notebook computers is quite concentrated and is getting more concentrated. In 1999, over 50 percent of the market was shared by the top four notebook manufacturers, and over 65 percent of the market was shared by the top six manufacturers (Table 7.3)[3].

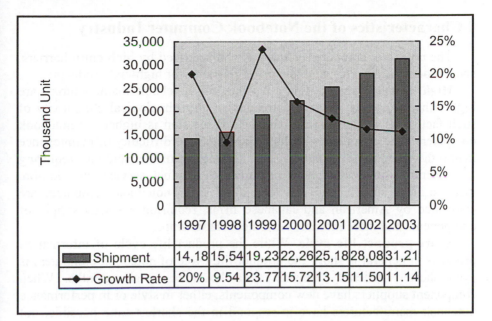

	1997	1998	1999	2000	2001	2002	2003
Shipment	14,18	15,54	19,23	22,26	25,18	28,08	31,21
Growth Rate	20%	9.54	23.77	15.72	13.15	11.50	11.14

Figure 7.1 World Notebook Computer Shipment - History and Forecast

Ranking	Company	Market Share	Cumulative Market Share
1	Toshiba	16.4%	16.4%
2	IBM	12.8%	29.2%
3	Compaq	12.3%	41.5%
4	Dell	10.5%	52.0%
5	Fujitsu Siemens	7.3%	59.3%
6	NEC	7.0%	66.3%
7	Sony	4.5%	70.8%
8	Acer	3.5%	74.3%
9	Apple	3.1%	77.4%
10	Gateway	2.3%	79.7%

Table 7.3 Shares of Top Ten Notebook Computer Corporation in 1999
(Source: IDC and MIC)

4 Characteristics of the Notebook Computer Industry

The notebook computer industry is characterized by high entry barriers, short product life cycles, and low price elasticity for high-end products.

High entry barriers. Entry barriers for notebook manufacturers are higher than those for desktop computers. The technological complexity of such factors as miniaturization and heat dispersion is higher for notebook computers. The complexity of the product and the difficulty of maintenance make the product distribution and service more demanding, requiring manufacturers to devote more resources to product service. In addition, many critical components and technologies for notebook computers are controlled by American and Japanese firms, requiring a steady supply of components and more intimate customer relationships.

Short product life cycle. While the product life cycle of information products in general is short, the product life cycle of notebook computers is even shorter, generally considered to be three to six months. When component suppliers have new components, either in style or in performance, notebook manufacturers have to respond in the shortest time possible, not only to develop a new product but also to mass produce the product and ship it to customers. The product life cycles of such components as CPUs are very brief, making the product life cycle of notebook computers even shorter. If a manufacturer cannot respond very quickly, it will find it cannot meet the needs of the market. This would result in lost profit opportunities, increased inventory levels, and increased costs, all of which would threaten a company's very survival.

Low price elasticity for high-end products. Buyers of high-end notebook computers are businesses, not individual consumers. The purchasing criteria are quality, performance, reliability, and stability of the product, with price playing a less important role.

5 The Notebook Computer Industry in Taiwan

5.1 The Early Efforts

The notebook computer industry emerged early in Taiwan. Many of the original companies had been manufacturers of calculators and electronic dictionaries. Making notebooks turned out to be more complex and technologically challenging than calculators, however, and the many small firms who put their efforts into the notebook computer were not successful. The overall performance of the industry was not impressive, and the made-in-Taiwan image suffered.

In 1990, a joint government-business alliance provided the tools and expertise necessary to develop this industry successfully. The Industrial Services and Technology Institute, a government-sponsored research organization, the Computer and Communications Research Laboratory, the Industrial Technology Research Institute, and the Taiwan Electrical and Electronic Manufacturer's Association initiated "The first generation of notebooks development project," sometimes called "The first generation of notebooks strategic alliance."

The project's objectives were to develop human resources for the notebook industry, standardize notebook specifications, and develop universal machines for participating companies. It was expected that the use of universal machines would minimize the risk to individual companies, and standardization would facilitate the division of manufacturing activities among firms. Many firms enthusiastically joined the project.

The strategic alliance between industries and government organizations accomplished quite a lot. The alliance set the standard of the main machine and developed a prototype for the COMDEX show within three months, setting a performance record and facilitating the further development and growth of Taiwan's notebook computer industry.

5.2 Production and Sales

Taiwan companies have been making notebook computers under contract for such companies as Compaq and Dell and under their own brand name such as Twinhead and Acer since the early 1990s. After the success of the alliance, former producers of calculators and electronic dictionaries successfully adapted their expertise in manufacturing miniature products to producing notebook computers. Engineers in those firms quickly learned how to make complicated notebooks and how to fit components such as floppy disk drives, hard disks, CPUs, and CD-ROMs inside the tiny space and prevent the machine from overheating. Quanta, Acer, Inventec, Compal, Arima, and First International Corporation became top manufacturers for notebooks. The output of those manufacturers is shown in Table 7.4.

1999 Ranking	Firm	Output (thousand unit) 1999	Output (thousand unit) 2000(est.)	Growth rate (%)
1	Quanta	2150	3300	53%
2	Acer	1900	3000	58%
3	Inventec	1200	1500	25%
4	Compal	1100	2200	100%
5	Arima	1100	2200	100%
6	FIC	800	1200	50%
7	Alpha Top	550	1000	82%
8	Twinhead	450	500	11%
9	Mitac	400	800	100%
10	Clevo	390	500	28%
Total		10,040	16,750	67%

Table 7.4 Estimated Output of Taiwanese Notebook Manufacturers in 2000

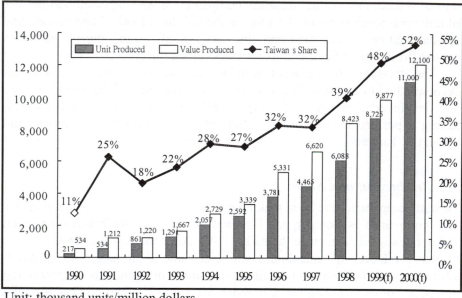

Unit: thousand units/million dollars

Figure 7.2 Output and Share of Taiwanese Notebook Computers (Source: MIC)

According to MIC, Taiwan produced 8.2 million notebook computers in 1999, achieving a growth rate 34.7 percent, which far exceeded the world market growth rate of 15.4 percent. Taiwan's output share of notebook computers increased to 45.8 percent in 1999 and a 34.1 percent growth rate was forecast for 2000, with the share of world output reaching 52 percent (Figure 7.2).

According to IDC and MIC, III, the top brands of notebook computers in the world in 1999 were Toshiba, IBM, Compaq, Dell, NEC, Fujitsu, SONY, Acer, Gateway, and Sharp, every one of which manufactures its notebook computers in Taiwan. Because Taiwan manufacturers' customers are large firms, their increases in market share raise the volume of Taiwanese manufacturers. In addition, new customers continue to come to Taiwan seeking manufacturing bases. Because Taiwanese manufacturers quickly learned and upgraded their skills, customers who used to outsource only their low-end notebook lines to Taiwan now make their higher-end products in Taiwan as well. Toshiba, the top notebook computer manufacturer, which used to produce its own notebook computers, now outsources production to Taiwan[3][6].

5.3 OEM/ODM Models

The notebook computer industry started by selling products to medium and small customers and built its competitive strength along the way. In 1994, when Inventec began manufacturing notebook computers for Compaq, Taiwan became the *de facto* manufacturing center for notebook computers in the world. After that, other top-tier notebook computer brands such as Dell, IBM, and HP came to Taiwan. By 1996, due to the competitive pressure of ever decreasing prices, more orders flowed to Taiwan's notebook manufacturers. By 1999, 87 percent of Taiwan's notebook computers output was for OEM/ODM customers[5].

Company	Brand	Japan Europe and China	United States
Quanta	Q-Lity	Toshiba, Sharp, Siemens	Dell, Gateway, Apple, HP, IBM, Compaq
Compal		Fujitsu, Toshiba, Legend	Dell, HP
ARIMA	ARIMA	NEC	Compaq
Inventec			Compaq
Acer	Acer	Casio, Fujitsu, Hitachi	IBM, Dell
FIC	FIC	NEC, Mitsubishi, Legend	-
Alpha Top		NEC	Apple, Packard-Bell
Clevo		Hitachi	
Twinhead	Twinhead	Sharp	Winbook, Itronic
ASUS	ASUS	SONY	-

Table 7.5 Taiwan Manufacturers and Their Customers

Japanese manufacturers used to be highly vertically integrated, with production covering every step, from producing components such as LCDs, CD-ROMs, and hard disk drives to assembling the finished products. Their competitive advantages had been vertical integration and highly automated production processes. However, a change of environment made these two advantages less important. First, competition among component manufacturers made components readily available to notebook manufacturers, making vertical integration unnecessary and less flexible. Second, the product life cycle became ever shorter and shorter, compressing from nine to 12 months to around three to six months. In addition, speed became a more important competitive factor than mass production. Japanese manufacturers, like their American counterparts, turned to Taiwanese manufacturers for speed, flexibility, and mass production capabilities, and Japanese outsourcing of notebook computers to Taiwan has been steadily on the increase. Table 7.5 lists the manufacturers and their customers from the US, Europe, and Japan.

6 The Role of Taiwan's Notebook Manufacturers

The notebook manufacturers in Taiwan play a key role in the international value chain of notebook computer products and distribution, but this role differs from the roles of large brands from the U.S. and Japan, and these manufacturers face different environmental challenges.

6.1 The Challenges

High Customer Bargaining Power. There are about 10 notebook computer manufacturers in Taiwan, mainly OEM/ODM manufacturers. Many of them do not have their own brand of notebook computers on the market. The market trend is that large manufacturers have become ever larger, which results in a more concentrated market. Manufacturers in Taiwan rely on only a few brands to produce more and more notebook computers, and these large brands rely on fewer and fewer manufacturers to make notebook computers for them. The benefits of relying on a few customers or a few suppliers are reduced transaction costs and enhanced competitiveness, however, the strong relationship between large manufacturers in Taiwan and large brands from the U.S. and Japan raises the entry barrier for small manufacturers. In addition, large manufacturers in Taiwan have to manage the risk of sudden cutbacks of orders from large brands.

Confronting price pressures in the marketplace, large brands not only demand that OEM/ODM manufacturers increase their productivity, they also control the procurement of key components, further decreasing manufacturers' profits. Although manufacturers may dramatically increase their output of notebook computers, their profit margins continue to fall.

Sources of Key Components. The source of key components has been an important issue since the industry started. Because Taiwanese manufacturers do not have control over the technology of key components, these manufacturers periodically have to endure component shortages and reduce their output of notebook computers. Furthermore, the bargaining power of Taiwanese manufacturers is unequal to the key component manufacturers, putting a cap on the profitability of notebook computers.

Key notebook computer components include CPUs, LCD flat panels, DRAMs, and batteries. Of these, LCD flat panels play the most important role because they account for a large percentage of a notebook computer's cost, and Japanese manufacturers dominate LCD production In 1999, a shortage of TFT-LCDs severely reduced the output of Taiwanese notebook computers. Because of Taiwan's dependency on external sources of components and the output size of its notebook computer industry, more than 10 TFT-LCD manufacturers were established in Taiwan. These manufacturers are either already in operation or in the process of building manufacturing facilities. Taiwan is striving to become the world's largest TFT-LCD manufacturing base, a move that should enhance the competitiveness of Taiwan's notebook computer industry.

After the shortages of TFT-LCDs ended, a shortage of CPUs from Intel occurred. Another key component, notebook batteries, all come from Japan, a dependency that increases the costs and uncertainties that notebook manufacturers face.

Ensuring the continuous supply of critical components has been an important issue for manufacturers since the inception of the industry. Due to the strong bargaining power of suppliers of these components, production and profitability are affected by the capability of a manufacturer to deal with these suppliers.

6.2 Critical Success Factors and Core Competencies.

Critical success factors and core competencies can be summarized as follows: gaining critical technology, ensuring the supply of key components, responding quickly to the changing market, and expanding the economies of mass production

Miniaturization is the most critical technology for notebook computer manufacturing. Taiwan's notebook computer manufacturers had a solid foundation in miniature technology from their experience making calculators, such as Compal, or electronic dictionaries, such as Inventec. This expertise was transferred to manufacturing notebook computers. As high-end notebook computers gain popularity, the demand for increased power and ever decreased size places more importance on the technology of miniaturization.

Due to their small size, heat dissipation is an important factor in designing notebook computers. Design also affects the computers' performance and reliability. In addition, notebook computers' portability demands their ability to sustain impacts. Another critical factor is keeping power consumption to a minimum.

Another success factor is the ability to speedily respond to changing markets. There are two aspects of changing market conditions: first, consumer demand for new and higher performing computers; second, as a result, notebook performance improves very rapidly, which results in very short product life cycle. If a manufacturer is unable to respond to these changing conditions swiftly, the loss of customers and accumulated inventory could be fatal.

Compared with Japanese manufacturers, Taiwanese manufacturers can introduce a new product in less time. Japanese manufacturers need nine to 12 months to introduce a new generation of notebook computers, while Taiwanese manufacturers require only six to nine months.

Finally, economies of mass production are important in this industry. A manufacturer needs to have a large enough market and adequate production facilities to operate successfully. Many firms in Taiwan entered the notebook computer arena, only to find themselves losing money and finally exiting the market because of their inability to meet these criteria.

6.3 SWOT Analysis

Examining the notebook computer industry and the firms in it, the following strengths, weaknesses, opportunities, and threats can be identified for the notebook computer industry in Taiwan.

Strengths
- Capability of miniature manufacturing
- R & D capability
- Speedy and flexible manufacturing capability
- Ample components suppliers and their strong supporting capability

Weaknesses
- Lack of key components initiatives
- High bargaining power of customers
- Declining competitive advantage of low costs

Opportunities
- Low-price computers prevail
- High growth potential for Japanese manufacturers to rely more on Taiwanese manufacturers
- Continuous growing demand for notebook computers

Threats
- Fierce competition among domestic manufacturers
- South Korean manufacturers expanding output, challenging the position of Taiwan manufacturers
- Chinese manufacturers trying to dominate the outsourcing market.

7 Directions for the Future

Facing such marketplace challenges as technological advances, ever decreasing prices, and service demands from OEM/ODM customers, notebook computer manufacturers have to continue to improve. Several avenues are considered.

Invest in component manufacturers. After suffering from the shortage of components in the past, many notebook computer manufacturers now invest in component manufacturing. Quanta, Acer, and Compal have all invested in TFT-LCD firms. This investment will help ease the shortage problems.

Global Logistics. Because many customers demand global distribution and service from OEM/ODM manufacturers, firms have to set up plants and service centers around the globe. The objectives are to be close to customers and to provide perfect service by configuration to order (CTO). Qunta first adopted Taiwan Direct Shipping (TDS)[7] – shipping notebook computers directly to customers' customers, and other manufacturers such as Compal, ARIMA, and Twinhead have followed suit.

Diversification to maintain growth. The notebook computer industry is maturing, and most firms in the industry have considered or ventured into other opportunities, such as CDMA cellular phones, PDAs (personal data assistants), or information appliances to maintain their growth. These products have characteristics similar to notebook computers because both require advanced technology and miniature design and production. Table 7.6 lists the new products and investment plans of notebook computer manufacturers.

Company Name	New Products and Investment Plan
Quanta	New Product: motherboards, GSM cellular phone, LCD PCs Investment: TFT-LCD, CD drives
Acer	New Product: network service, communication products, Software Investment: Venture capital, Internet mall, TFT-LCD
Compal	New Product: LCD monitors, CDMA cellular phones Investment: LCD, Communications
ARIMA	New Product: Servers, DSC Investment: Cellular phone sets, LED
Inventec	New Product: Servers, Internet phone, Alliance with Cisco, IA products Investment: Venture capital

Table 7.6 New Products and Investment Plans of Taiwanese Notebook Computer Manufacturers

Profit margins of notebook computers will be squeezed because notebook prices are dropping, while prices for liquid-crystal displays and other components are rising or in short supply. Eventually, notebook computers will follow the path of desktop computers, with ever decreasing margins, resulting in companies' shifting manufacturing sites to Mainland China. Taiwanese no doubt will continue to build on their successes and expand into other products. Many companies are branching into servers or handheld devices such as PDAs.

Vertical disintegration and outsourcing seems to be the trend for many industries, such as PC and semiconductor firms. Vertical disintegration offers flexibility for the firm and allows firms to concentrate their efforts. In this way, firms can grow very rapidly. Dell, for example, does not make any components for its product and concentrates its efforts on making and marketing computers. Dell's high growth rate would be impossible if it tried to make a lot of components at the same time. Firms in Taiwan tend to grow into many related areas. The most obvious example is Acer, whose products encompass the whole spectrum of the information industry, from software, books, Web mall, CD-ROM drives, PCs, and notebooks to servers. Each product is made by a different company within the group. Although firms belong to the same group, no one is obliged to buy products from any other member in the group. In this way, the firm has the benefits of vertical disintegration while at the same time ensuring the supply of important components.

8 Quanta – A Successful Example

Quanta Computer, Inc. is an example of a computer manufacturer that successfully adapted to the notebook computer industry and continues to adapt as the marketplace changes. As the company grew in competence and reputation, it became the largest notebook manufacturers in Taiwan. In 1999 overtook IBM as the world's second largest notebook computer manufacturer. It is estimated the company will produce around 3.5 million notebooks in 2000 and is likely to surpass Toshiba as the world's largest notebook computer manufacturer[9].

8.1 The Origin and the Subsequent Growth

Quanta was established in 1988 with US$1 million and specialized in manufacturing notebook computers. Sales were NT$800 million or about US$26 million in 1989, and Quanta's sales and profits have rocketed upward each year. Sales and profits from 1994 to 1998 are shown in Table 7.7.

Item	1994	1995	1996	1997	1998
Revenue	8,034,366	8,763,765	17,482,203	34,942,654	51,901,508
Gross Profit	869,041	792,672	2,027,673	5,909,251	9,751,687
Operation Profit	584,844	453,715	1,553,862	5,210,371	8,735,673
Income other than operations	69,222	108,826	101,111	1,129,739	1,063,595
Expense	193,962	352,706	572,526	373,707	318,411
Profit before Tax	460,104	209,835	1,082,447	5,966,403	9,480,857
Net Profit	431,677	258,762	915,647	5,444,502	9,213,201

(Unit: NT$ in Thousand)

Table 7.7 Income Statements of Quanta from 1994 to 1998

Notebook computers account for more than 95 percent of Quanta's sales, and more than 98 percent of the notebooks it produces are shipped outside Taiwan. The division of its market is shown on Table 7.8.

Area	1996	1997	1998
America	51.29%	62.80%	65.54%
Europe	27.94%	25.16%	23.98%
Others	20.16%	11.64%	10.28%
Total Export	99.39%	99.60%	99.80%
Total Domestic	0.61%	0.40%	0.20%
Total	100.00%	100.00%	100.00%

Table 7.8 Quanta's Market Division during 1996-1998

Quanta's customers are large firms from the US, Europe, and Japan. In 1996, Its customer base was broad, with no single customer accounting for more than 20 percent (Table 7.9)[8]. By 1997, however, Apple and Gateway accounted for about two-third of the sales. In 1998, big orders from Dell accounted for about 60 percent of sales. In June 2000, Sony gave its order for notebook computers to Quanta. With Sony's notebook computers growing at more than 100 percent and Dell's growth rate around 60 percent, it is expected that Quanta's sales will continue to skyrocket. In addition to those listed in Table 7.9, Quanta's customer base reads like a *Who's Who in Notebook Computers* and includes Toshiba, Sharp, HP, IBM, and Compaq.

Customer	1996		1997		1998	
	Amount	Percentage of Total Sales	Amount	Percentage of Total Sales	Amount	Percentage of Total Sales
DELL	406,171	2.32%	3,332,884	9.54%	30,275,264	58.37%
GATEWAY	3,282,514	18.78%	10,574,878	30.26%	11,437,992	22.05%
APPLE	3,183,495	18.21%	13,030,397	37.29%	6,425,527	12.39%
SIEMENS	2,899,275	16.58%	3,823,632	10.94%	3,297,620	6.36%
AST	2,717,676	15.55%	1,798,526	5.15%	40,897	0.08%

(Unit: NT$ in Thousand)

Table 7.9 Customers and Amounts during 1996-1998

	Quanta	Acer	Inventec	Compal	Twinhead	ARIMA	Clevo
1997 Shipment	734	648	597	391	379	376	334
1997 Share of Taiwan Shipment	16.4	14.1	13.4	8.8	8.5	8.4	7.5
1997 World Share	5.2	4.6	4.2	2.8	2.7	2.7	2.4
1998 Shipment	1,310	850	750	720	450	700	300
1998 Share of Taiwan Shipment	21.5	14	12.3	11.8	7.4	11.5	4.9
1998 World Share	8.4	5.5	4.8	4.6	2.9	4.5	1.9

(Unit: thousand unit; %)

Table 7.10 Market Shares of Taiwan Notebook Manufacturers

Quanta's competition comes mainly from manufacturers in Taiwan who also want the orders from top-tier brands. Those manufacturers include Acer, Inventec, Compal, ARIMA, Twinhead, Clevo, and FIC. Table 7.10 shows that the Quanta's share is increasing, despite the heavy competition

8.2 Turtle Culture

Back in 1988, when notebook computers had limited functionality and few people thought much of the industry, CEO Pi-Lee Lin founded Quanta. Mr. Lin had been chief engineer of an electronics firm, which he left to found Compal, a company that made calculators. Mr. Lin found the technology for making a calculator was highly related to that required for notebook computers in terms of miniaturization and dealing with batteries and LCD displays[9][10].

Quanta pays close attention to new product developments. While OEM/ODM manufacturers of notebook computers abound in Taiwan, Quanta does only ODM. Under this strategy, Quanta designs the products, interests customers in them, and orders the products under the customers' brand names. In 1997, Quanta developed a notebook for Dell, named Latitude CP, which was a runaway best seller for Dell, in sharp contrast to Dell's initial poor showing in notebook computers.

Quanta is very proud of its research and development capacity, and most of its executives have backgrounds in technology. Senior management stress vision in technology and have a "vision team" that is in charge of research and development for the technology needed more than two years in the future.

Mr. Lin stresses a "Turtle culture" for Quanta, meaning the company should be humble, stable, and progress surely each step of the way. Mr. Lin himself does not like to appear in the media or to talk about Quanta, but he likes to talk about vision[9].

In addition to developing excellent products, Quanta has maintenance centers around the globe for speedy after-sales service. The combination of excellent products, speedy delivery, and service has attracted top brands to Quanta for manufacturing.

To prevent component shortages from interfering with on-time delivery of their products, to enhance its bargaining power with customers, and to lower the cost of making notebook computers, Quanta has invested in many companies that make notebook components, including batteries, alloyed cases, and TFT-LCDs. In cooperation with Japan's Sharp, Quanta will invest around US$500 million for a TFT-LCD plant.

Quanta makes a lot of notebook computers that are marketed by its customers under the customers' brands. Mr. Lin considers that customers are Quanta's marketing teams. In this mutually beneficial relationship, customers need Quanta, and Quanta needs its customers. Making a lot of excellent products without recognition seems to have left something to be desired, however, as Quanta recently established a company in the U.S. to market its own brand of PC and notebook computers, Q-Lity. It also collaborates with distributors in Taiwan to market Q-Lity. Time will tell whether Quanta is a good brand marketer or not; however, with the quality of its product and its financial power, Quanta should have the benefit of the doubt[10].

While the notebook computer is Quanta's main product, it knows that a product has a life cycle, and new products are needed to sustain growth. The Quanta group has been selling products such as LCD monitors, LCD PCs, Mini-notebooks, and handheld PCs. Other products in the market include information appliances, GPRS (a wireless service), and GSM, CDMA, and WAP cellular phones. It is estimated that total sales of the company in 2000 will reach NT$100 billion (around US$3 billion), nine percent of which will come from products other than notebook computers[8].

8.3 Pursuit of Global Excellence

Mr. Lin considers the next 10 years crucial for educating Quantaians. He hopes that Quanta will attract talents, and plans to make Quanta a unique company with special Taiwanese characteristics, yet important in the world community. He wants Quanta to be respected by the international community, something no company in Taiwan has yet achieved. Mr. Lin envisions an international company with diverse cultures. For example, IBM is an international company, with special Japanese characteristics in Japan and special European characteristics in Europe. In Mr. Lin's vision, making Quanta a great company is much more meaningful than pursuing money, much like an athlete does not participate in the Olympics for monetary rewards[8][9][10].

References

[1] Wang, T.P., Past、Present and Future of Taiwan's Information Industry: 1999, *Computer Systems and Components*, p.p. 2-22, Jan. 2000.
王子博，1999 年台灣資訊工業回顧與展望，**電腦系統與零組件**，2-22 頁，2000 年 1 月

[2] Chao, C. H., Current(1999) Development & Future Prospects of Taiwan's Notebook Industry, *Computer Systems and Components*, p.p. 2-11, Feb. 2000.
趙建宏，1999 年我國筆記型電腦產業發展現況與未來展望，電腦系統與零組件，2-11 頁，2000 年 2 月

[3] Chao, C. H., Key Success Factors of Taiwan's Notebook Industry, *Evaluation and Analysis of Focus News*, 71, p.p. 13-15, Nov. 1999.
趙建宏，由「全球生產王國」看台灣筆記型電腦產業的成功關鍵，焦點新聞評析，71 期，13-15 頁，1999.11

[4] Chen, W. T., An Analysis of Developmental Trend of Taiwan's Notebook Industry in First Quarter of 2000, *Computer Systems and Components*, p.p. 2-9, Jun. 2000.
陳文棠，2000 年第一季我國筆記型電腦產業發展趨勢分析，**電腦系統與零組件**，2-9 頁，2000 年 6 月

[5] Fang, Y. H., Glory Piled Up by OEM at the End of 20th Century, *Global Views Monthly*, Vol. 164, Feb. 2000.
方雅惠，代工堆砌的世紀末華麗，**遠見雜誌**，164 期，2000 年 2 月

[6] Liu, P. S., From the Positioning of Global Big Companies to Forecast the Future of Taiwan's Notebook Industry, *Computer Systems and Peripheral*, p.p. 20-30, Apr. 1998.
劉培盛，從全球大廠動向看我國筆記型電腦產業之未來，**電腦系統與週邊**，20-30 頁，1998 年 4 月

[7] Tseng, E. W., Global Operational Center Comes True with TDS, *Digital Times*, 21st March, 2000.
曾而汝，TDS 實現全球 NB 營運中心，**電子時報**，2000 年 3 月 21 日

[8] Prospectus of Quanta Computer Inc. , Jul. 1999
廣達電腦公司公開說明書，八十八年七月

[9] Lu, C. F., Quanta Computer Inc., *Common Wealth*, Apr. 1999.
盧智芳，廣達電腦：十年埋名 一鳴驚人，**天下雜誌**，215 期，1999 年 4 月

[10] Lu, C. F., President of Quanta, Lin Pai-Li , *Common Wealth*, Apr. 1999.
盧智芳，林百里（廣達董事長），**天下雜誌**，215 期，1999 年 4 月

Chapter 8

Desktop PCs:
A Project Management Revolution

Chyan Yang

Institute of Business & Management
National Chiao Tung University
HsinChu, Taiwan, R.O.C.

1. Introduction

Although personal computers originally were designed for use at home, they quickly found their way into businesses as a tool to handle office activities. Millions of PCs shipped throughout the world are made in Taiwan[4, 8]. The short life cycles of PC models call for a tight development and manufacturing schedule, and Taiwan has developed a competitive advantage through the years in rapid prototyping, material sourcing, and mass production.

This chapter examines the fundamental reasons Taiwan's desktop PC industry has been able to remain a reliable supplier for the demanding global market. The main focus is flexibility and project management, which are enhanced by their methods of implementing engineering changes quickly[1]. Although most high technology products are quickly replaced by next-generation products, the experiences and methodologies developed in Taiwan's desktop PC industry provide a supporting infrastructure for new products.

2. Facts: Demand and Supply

2.1 Facts: Demand and Supply

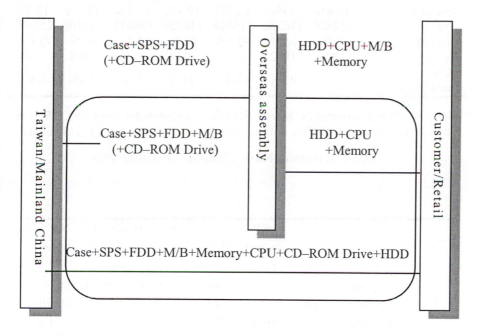

Figure 1 Taiwan's Supply Chain of Desktop PC's

Figure 1 shows Taiwan's main manufacturing processes for providing desktop PC's to meet the worldwide demand. Around 40 percent of the components for Taiwan's companies come from Mainland China, and around 60 percent come from plants in Taiwan. Table 1 shows the IDC statistics for desktop PC demand worldwide, and Table 2 shows the statistics for PC motherboards. A motherboard is the major component for assembling the final desktop PC. Since the most complex process is making motherboards, the discussions in this chapter are applicable to both motherboards and a complete desktop PC system.

	1996	1997	1998	1999	2000	2001	2002
Units	56324	64202	71407	80278	90955	102479	114992
Growth	14.6%	14%	11.2%	12.4%	13.3%	12.7%	12.2%
$value	112429	116356	116058	116250	130632	143106	156077
Growth	32.8%	3.5%	-0.3%	0.2%	12.4%	9.5%	9.1%
$price	1996	1812	1625	1448	1436	1396	1357
%Price reduction		9.3%	10.4%	11%	1%	2.8%	2.8%

Note: Worldwide Desktop PC Market Statistics and Estimates from IDC. Units in thousands, value in US million dollars, growth in %, average price in US dollars.

Table 1 Worldwide Market Statistics of Desktop PC's

	1998	1999	2000(e)	2001(f)	2002(f)
Worldwide	86900	106246	123447	138135	153653
Growth	11.6	22.3	16.2	11.9	11.2
Taiwan	63000	83835	101792	119320	136758
Taiwan exclude system	53220	64378	77860	91080	104000
Growth	19.5	33.1	21.4	17.2	14.6
Taiwan mfg Share %	72.5	78.9	82.5	86.4	89.0

Note: Worldwide motherboard market analysis, MIC ITIS Dec. 1999 Worldwide volume in thousands, growth rate in %

Table 2 Worldwide Market Statistics of motherboards

	97Q4	98Q1	98Q2	98Q3	98Q4	99Q1	99Q2
810	0	0	0	0	0	0.2	2.0
440ZX	0	0	0	0	0	4.3	6.8
440EX	0	0	2.5	8.0	6.0	1.3	1.1
440BX	0	0	17.0	30.0	43.0	60.8	59.2
440LX	9.7	31.9	31.6	26.0	23.0	6.4	4.9
440FX	0.7	0.3	0.1	0.0	0.0	0.0	0.0
430TX	45.6	34.1	25.3	7.0	2.0	0.0	0.0
430VX	14.1	8.7	1.7	0.0	0.0	0.0	0.0
430HX	0.0	0.0	0.0	0.0	0.0	0.0	0.0
Intel	72	75	78	71	74	73	74

Table 3   Percentage(%) of Different Types of Intel Chipsets

Table 3 shows major types of Intel chipsets. Although there are other major vendors of chipsets, such as AMD and VIA, Intel chipsets enjoyed a 71 to 78 percent market share between Q4 1997 and Q2 1999. Table 4 shows a typical evolution of the major types of motherboards between the first quarter of 1998 and the second quarter of 1999. Figure 2 shows the major types of case enclosures for a desktop PC, and Figure 3 shows OEM/branded splits. Because of tariff savings, local market requirements, and flexibility of local prices, many vendors prefer to import motherboards and do the final assembly in local plants.

	1Q98	2Q98	3Q98	4Q98	1Q99	2Q99
Others	0.4%	0.3	1.0	0.1	0.5	0.3
Slot 1	23.9	56.9	64.7	72.2	61.9	56.8
Socket 7	75.4	42.7	34.4	27.0	18.6	20.2
Slot 1 & Socket 370	0.0	0.0	0.0	0.0	14.7	16.3
Socket 370	0.0	0.0	0.0	0.7	4.4	6.4

Table 4.   Percentage(%) of Different Types of Motherboards

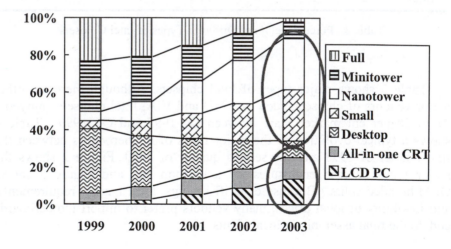

Figure 2 Types of Case Enclosures of Desktop PCs

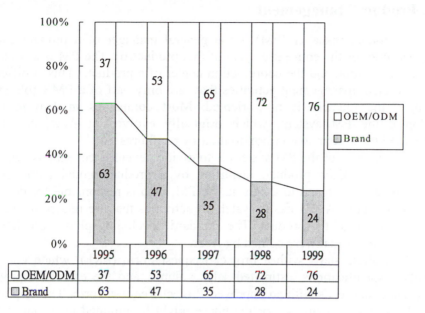

	1995	1996	1997	1998	1999
☐ OEM/ODM	37	53	65	72	76
☐ Brand	63	47	35	28	24

Figure 3 Brand Business is Gradually Depressed

What do we learn from these figures? First, one notices that Taiwan's manufacturing share of desktop PCs is very high. As the price drops, the supply increases, an indication of the cost leadership. Second, the life cycle of a product or a specific model is very short without a stable demand. Third, the many variants of so-called desktop PCs require a good management model with a fast and flexible response mechanism. Taiwan's competitive advantage is partially due to a clustering of related industries, which shortens the cycle time of development and manufacturing. More importantly, there must be a product management system that enables companies to meet the fast changing demands.

3. Product Management

A product manager (PM) is the general manager of a product and is responsible for the entire life cycle of that product[6]. The PM is a product-oriented position and the coordination center of a product. This is different from project management activities that are only part of a PM's job, since project management is task-oriented. Most companies in Taiwan have adopted the PM system, which originally evolved at Acer, and have modified the system to conform to their own cultures

The essence of the PM system is to divide development into assignment phases[3,7]. Each product, identified by a product model name or an equivalent, is assigned to a person, the PM, who is responsible for delivery of the product. A PM has to watch all activities that are related to the on-time delivery of the product. The standard developing phases are labeled C_0—C_6, names that were coined by Acer.

This phase starts with a Project Request Form (PRF), which contains product specifications, estimated sales volume, and the estimated product life cycle, and ends with an approved Project Request Form. The originator might be a sales manager, or the phase might be initiated in response to a request from an OEM customer. The owner of the PRF is a PM. In general, the PM or a sales manager will prepare a market requirement survey (MRS) to support a PRF. A PRF also has to indicate the impact of such a project—for example, what product does this new model replace and how much inventory of the old model is still on hand. These inventory issues are crucial to the company's profitability. For the model to be phased out, a PM has to dig out all the numbers on finished and semi-finished goods, scheduled work, and materials purchased for upcoming production.

A PRF meeting is held at which all related parties discuss their concerns—for example, the R&D department has to consider whether it has sufficient manpower to meet the proposed delivery schedule[5]. In many cases, PRFs are approved with some modifications to reflect the realities expressed in these meetings. In rare cases, PRFs might get turned down due to the shortage of manpower. It also might be rejected if demand is uncertain, as when a customer asks for just few samples.

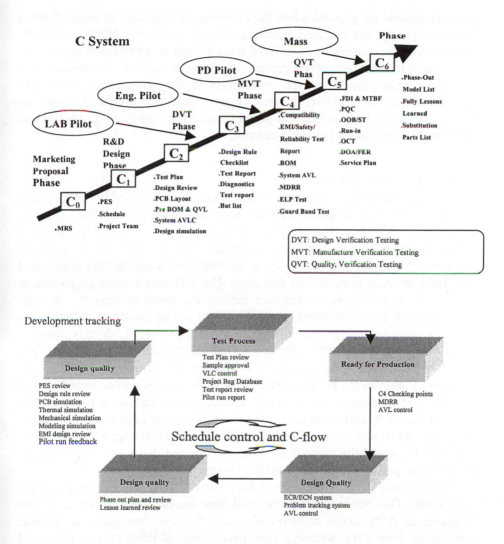

Figure 4 New Product Development Process

Companies in Taiwan are generally very aggressive in responding to OEM requests for new products, because they know that if they don't honor the request, other companies will. This aggressive attitude infuses much of the Taiwan PC industry's competitive advantage. Branded business or product models are granted when the company is less busy or when there is excess capacity, but branded business always yields to OEMs or ODMs because foreign companies often have more effective distribution channels.

Although there are other parties involved in a PRF discussion, key managers are responsible for the final decisions. Key managers in this phase are vice presidents or above. In some companies, a vice president is still too low in the hierarchy to approve a project, since the resources committed are too high for the rank in Taiwan's culture.

3.1 C1: Planning Phase

Only product development proposals approved in C_0 proceed to the C_1 phase. The C_1 starts with an approved PRF and ends with a committed product development schedule. The objective in C_1 is to construct a detailed product development schedule with an emphasis on delivery of a working engineering sample. The PM forms a development team for this phase, and the R&D division is central to this step. The PM coordinates all parties to support R&D engineers so they can deliver the working sample. A fine-tuned timetable is established, and all corresponding tasks are dated. This phase is often very short, but all people are assigned to it. In this phase, a PM often finds that bottlenecks tend to focus around a few people. One reason is that it is difficult to transfer one engineer's skill set to another. The division of labor in the PC industry is very sophisticated and an imbalance of workload often occurs; for example, circuit layout engineers for the PCB (printed circuit board) often have a backlog during the high season, whereas they may have several days with a light workload during early summer. Seasonal workload fluctuations are uncommon now, however, since Taiwan industries experience more demand than it can supply.

A PM needs to know the process time each activity requires to develop a new model. One needs to know the lead time for each key components: for example, an ASIC needs three months; a PCB takes two weeks; a barcode label takes three days; writing a new user's manual takes two months; and thorough product testing needs one month. For a new product using a new ASIC, the uncertainty is much higher. The industry tends to absorb uncertainty in whatever way possible, and a CEO will exercise his power in accelerating the project by motivating or pressuring the vice president in R&D.

The main issue here is the asymmetry among the development team parties. Each party tends to extend the schedule for itself and reduce the time needed for other units. A PM has to mediate any conflicts and settle on a final schedule. For an experienced PM, this is feasible, although it is a tough job for a new PM, and PMs with short tempers tend to quit the job at this phase due to their inability to work out a schedule The timetable has to be optimum: a compressed timetable means lots of overtime, and a stretched timetable means less productivity. With pressure from customers, top management, and even the stockholders, a PM must coordinate multiple objectives simultaneously.

Engineering resources are often in conflict during the C_2 phase. Dozens of models are simultaneously handled by different PMs, and each with its own committed schedule. Some resources, such as hardware engineers, are dedicated. On the other hand, resources such as industry design and PCB layout are shared. To resolve potential conflicts, high-ranking managers must prioritize the projects. Added to this, rush orders are common and definitely impact existing schedules.

3.2 R&D Design Phase

The C_2 phase starts with a committed product development schedule and ends with an approved engineering design. The key design factor in C_2 is to either cost down and/or to feature up. The industry commonly reduces its cost to ensure price competitiveness, and any redesign of a cost-down version on an existing model is always welcome and often required. OEM buyers often request a "price schedule" that guarantees a certain percentage price drop over a specified number of months. These R&D cost-down designs usually result from new-generation components that are better and cheaper—generally from siliconization, size reduction of ASIC, and denser integration of systems components. Since the product life cycle is so short, new products must be released on time. Whenever Intel, for example, announces a new CPU, the corresponding motherboard must be ready within weeks and the desktop PC should be available to customers within months. Regardless of whether a company releases its new product on time or not, the old model is destined to be phased out, so there is a cost of obsolescence inherent to the desktop PC industry. A newly released model will depreciate daily on a retail outlet's shelf if it is not sold.

Like most engineering projects in the world, uncertainty often delays the completion of a design. Engineering design is a task that constantly changes because of changes and uncertainty. The main reasons for uncertainty are new versions of key components or ASICs and new manufacturing processes. For instance, the BGA (ball grid array) ASIC packaging was a great challenge when it first appeared. New design tools for CAD (computer aided design) and new testing instruments also require engineers to take time out for training. Preliminary versions of the BOM (bill of materials), circuit design reviews, test plans, and other engineering-related issues must be settled during this design phase.

In addition, some Japanese companies are concerned about what types of components and power supplies are being used, and any design modifications to an existing product requires approval. To make the situation even more complex, OEM customers often will designate some key components in the design. These customers might even consign key components, mostly key ASICs, so a manufacturer has less room for constructing its BOM costs. Because of the razor-thin profitability that has become the norm, companies either pursue high volume orders to ensure economies of scale in sourcing materials or start shifting their manufacturing capacity to products with higher margins.

3.3 R&D DVT Phase

The C_3 phase starts with a committed product design and ends with a working prototype. With a motherboard, PCBs, and components mounted and inserted, engineers test the product's functionality. C_3 is concerned with the functional correctness of a product, or design verification testing (DVT). C_3 is the main hurdle for R&D engineers, and it is here that hardware, software, and firmware design bugs are fixed.

With a populated motherboard, in the case of a desktop PC, engineers run EMIs (electrical and magnetic interference) conformance tests to comply with the FCC for American products and corresponding regulations for each country to which the products will be exported. Some regulations are more stringent that others, for example, class B EMI compliance is required for a desktop PC instead of the looser class A standard. Different areas around the globe have varying safety requirements, and there are many institutions authorized to issue safety assurance certificates. OEM customers often ask for certified test reports before ordering the PCs. To meet these requirements, test reports of each model must be done by a test lab or its equivalent.

3.4 MVT Phase
The C_4 phase starts with a working prototype and ends with a committed manufacturable design. C_4 concerns a product's manufacturability for mass production. A good working engineering prototype does not necessarily guarantee that the product will easily mass produced, so this phase concerns manufacture verification testing (MVT). A PC's design can be thoroughly verified by R&D engineers, however in mass production, companies must balance testing and productivity. The company faces the dilemma of saving time, yet assuring that quality is not compromised. Every second of savings becomes amplified in mass production, when productivity is measured.

C_4 is the main hurdle that industry manufacturing and testing engineers must pass. Efficient plant layout, work process partitioning, time and motion studies, and major productivity issues are decided at this stage. Fast production lines are required, and automated processes are welcome to assure quality. Because direct laborers are usually less educated than R&D engineers, fault-tolerant designs are needed in the manufacturing process.

Every single step must planned and every variation ensured. European countries will not use a power cord of 110 volts; American customers want the application software installed in English; each box must include a proper user's manual written in the language that user expects. What happens if there are two booklets of user's manuals lying on the packaging bench after you have loaded a full shipment of a container? What happens if the application software loaded in the system is a buggy old version and thousands of these PCs are on the way to customers? These types of nightmares can happen without a good quality assurance system, and that razor-thing profit margin can disappear with a single mistake.

3.5 QVT Phase
The C_5 phase starts with a committed manufacturable design and ends with a work order to the production line. QVT, which stands for quality verification testing, is a pilot run that will detect all possible flaws in manufacturing. In most digital products the system often will keep its power on for a certain amount of time, say 48 hours, as a burn-in process to screen out faulty

products because many faulty electronic parts will not endure the burn-in process. Large production orders would require a large burn-in room. Usually QA (quality assurance) engineers have their own quality tests for finished products and will issue a hold-shipment order if they find the product does not meet the deliverable specifications.

The desktop PC in a very complex system, and if one finds a faulty product one must identify the real cause for the fault. Three major reasons for a faulty product are faulty engineering design, faulty parts, or a faulty manufacturing process. Engineers in the plant or in R&D must locate the fault, though usually there are grey areas for which no one admits responsibility. Regardless of any internal conflicts in providing a good product, customers expect to receive a good quality product and don't care who is responsible when it is not.

3.6 Mass production Phase

The C_6 phase starts with a work order to the production line and ends with a phase out order. This might be expected to be a more predictable phase, but life for a desktop PC is short, and demands change even at this phase. One of the changes occurs when it is necessary to substitute parts, which happen frequently. Parts suppliers also change over time, due to price or performance changes. For large-volume manufacturers, any minor price change or performance enhancement calls for serious consideration before parts from a second source would be considered. Each manufacturer maintains its own database of QVL (qualified vendors list) and QPL (qualified parts list), and the purchasing department makes sure all parts are QPL and QVL. Any single production order will use a corrected BOM for materials and parts preparation. A BOM (bill of materials) is maintained for each model and each version, and any modification to the BOM requires whoever initiated it to issue an engineering change request. The process from issuing an engineering change request to the effective engineering change notice is discussed in the next section.

4. Workflow

Workflow is application software that provides a cooperative working platform. One basic workflow application is the purchase approval. Applicants can log into the purchase workflow system to initiate a purchase order for certain requirements. The most important type of workflow is the processing flow[2]. The processing flow, which requires various databases supporting many functions, is the foundation of electronic business. For instance, enterprise resource planning (ERP) applications require accounting, inventory, and manufacturing information to be supported by the corporate information systems.

In a manufacturing organization, ECR/ECN is the most important workflow application. ECR stands for Engineering Change Request and ECN stands for Engineering Change Notice. Whenever there is a need to initiate an engineering change, one must issue an ECR. All relevant parties are informed of the request when they log in to the engineering change workflow system. Each person can express his or her opinion and suggestion, then a senior manager makes a final decision based on this feedback[9, 10]. Since it is a workflow system, one can get on or off the flow at one's convenience, saving meeting time. Although small organizations with less frequent ECRs hold meetings, for large organization with frequent ECRs an automated workflow system is a necessity to respond quickly to changing requirements. ECR issuers change depending on what phase the product is in: during the design phase a hardware engineer often issues the ECR to have a cost-down redesign to improve a robust circuit or to overcome certain EMI (electrical and magnetic interference) issues.

Any change to the BOM of a product requires issuing an ECR, at least to inform everyone involved. If an ECR is not rejected by anyone in the workflow, it becomes an ECN (engineering change notice) that is effective and enforced by the system. An example is if engineer John Doe found that a capacitor value was incorrectly designed in the previous version, which could damage a PC. John would issue an ECR to reflect a corrective action. Instant response and adaptation is essential. If this ECR were to remain in the workflow for two weeks, any manufacturing work order during that time would still get MO (material orders) from the old BOM, which is incorrect. This illustrates the importance of a workflow system.

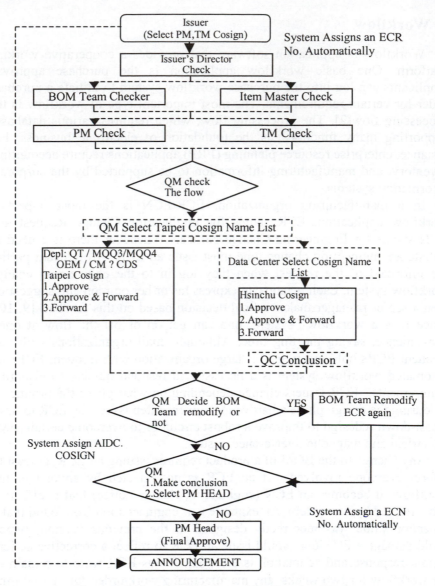

Figure 6 A Typical Workflow of Engineering Change

5. Concluding Remarks

Before Taiwan made desktop PCs, the most complex product supplied by Taiwan was the electronic wristwatch. With the growing demand and rapid changing specifications of PCs, Taiwan's PC manufacturers have developed a good working methodology to manage new product development cycles. Moreover, information systems were developed to manage this fast-moving industry. Experiences and tools developed in the PC industry have been transferred to other products, such as scanners, networking equipment, notebooks, and others.

In addition, the entire supporting industry environment is established and benefits all other systems manufacturers. The PCB industry, the mechanical design industry, the labeling and packaging industries, and LED and electronic parts suppliers have enjoyed the same growth as the desktop PC industry. Today all these supporting industries have developed their own economies of scale and have adapted to the changing environment. Regardless of whether the desktop PC will continue to be the largest information industry in Taiwan, or whether another will displace its position, its historical position is undeniable.

6. References

[1] Betz, Frederick Strategic Technology Management, McGraw-Hill, 1993.
[2] Cortada, James W. and Woods, John A. The Knowledge Management Yearbook 1999-2000, Butterworth-Heinemann, 2000.
[3] Crawford, C. Merle, New Products Management, Irwin, 1994.
[4] Davidow, William H. and Malone, Michael S. The Virtual Corporation, Haper Collins, 1997.
[5] Goldratt, Eliyahu M. Critical Chain, The North River Press, 1997.
[6] Kotler, Philip Mrketing Management, Analysis, Planning, Implementation, and Control, 7th ed., Prentice-Hall, 1991.
[7] Lehmann, Donald R. and Winer, Russel S. Product Management, Irwin, 1994.
[8] Porter, Michael E. Competitive Strategy, Macmillan, 1980.
[9] Robbins, Stephen P. Organizational Behavior, 8th ed. 1998.
[10] Slatter, Stuart Gambling on Growth: How to Manage the Small High-Tech Firm, John Wiley & Sons, 1992.

Part 4: Technical and Capital Innovation

Chapter 9

Competing in the Knowledge Game: Intellectual Property Rights

Liu, Shang-Jyh

Professor & Director, Institute of Technology Law
National Chiao Tung University
HsinChu, Taiwan, R.O.C.

1.Introduction

As Taiwan increases its commitment to the development and manufacture of high-technology products, intellectual property rights have become an issue with international implications. The key to competitiveness in technology depends upon whether a company, or country, can develop products that become the industry standard. In order to set that standard, and gain from other companies' usage of new technology, new methodologies, or new products, a company has to become a leader early in a new product's life.

This chapter looks at the development of Intellectual Property Rights (IPRs) in Taiwan and the importance of IPRs to Taiwan's position in the world market.

2.The Development of IPRs

Taiwan's IPRs are a result of Taiwan's economic development and increasing role in global technological competition. The legal system related to intellectual property rights in Taiwan largely developed as a result of international pressure. The USA was particularly influential, and it employed economic sanctions and retaliation against Taiwan to make concessions during trade negotiations in the1980s.

Taiwan's IPR laws concerning patent and copyright were formulated 50 years and 70 years ago, respectively, and historically Taiwan was not concerned with the concept of IPRs. Since 1950, however, this changed when many Taiwan businesses shifted to high-technology industries and became internationalized. As a player in the global arena, IPR disputes and royalty fees problems followed the adoption and usage of technology and international partnerships. Since that time, Taiwan has developed competitive capability in industrial technologies and has learned from IPR disputes. As a result, Taiwan's own IPRs have been growing and have become the model for developing countries.

IPRs have become a significant consideration in Taiwan's industrial development, but this did not occur immediately. The development of IPRs during the last 20 years can be divided into four stages:
  (1)1978-1985: Government learning — negotiations and trade consultations between the USA and Taiwan;
  (2)1985-1990: Industrial learning — Government introducing the concept of IPRs to industries;
  (3)1990-1995: Industries developing IPRs — Establishment of a legal system;
  (4)After 1995: IPRs' rapid growth within industries.

The impetus for Taiwan's interest in IPRs came from Taiwan-USA trade negotiations in the 1980s. Another factor that appeared about that time was the phenomenon of product imitation and counterfeit products. This became increasingly critical as the global economy developed more freedom. At that time, the issue of product imitations was serious because the concept of IPRs was not a familiar one.

In response to this global threat to patented products, the Chinese National Federation of Industries held an "anti-imitation self-restraint convention" in 1981. The federation invited the prime organizations of importing and exporting trade to sign a treaty and established a group to propagandize anti-imitation. After the government agreed to reinforce intellectual property rights, it was incumbent to get industries to follow suit. On 20 March 1984, the government's Chinese National Federation of Industries and the Chinese National Federation of Businesses founded the National Business Anti-imitation Committee and issued an Alliance Self-restraint Declaration. The committee's purpose was to advance anti-imitation activity in non-governmental organizations. In 1990 the Chinese National Federation of Industries enlarged its organization devoted to IPRs to form the IPR Protection Committee. Although the government supported IPRs during the period of 1980 to 1990, industries did not endorse the concept, did not understand what it meant, and were unaware of the implications.

In 1990, Hsinchu Science Park's industry association established an IPR Committee, which in 1993 was divided into the Guidance Committee and the Working Committee. During this time, the issue of IPRs became an international, hotly debated issue. The incarnation of WTO (World Trade Organization), GATT (General Agreement on Tariffs and Trade), debated, negotiated and consulted for seven years to agree to Trade-related Intellectual Property Rights (TRIPs). Finally, at the end of 1993, it established the key role of IPRs in international trade. Since that time, IPRs, especially patent rights, have become an increasingly important weapon of industrial competition.

The significance of IPRs was underscored in the period of 1985 to 1995, when Taiwan industries faced serious challenges over patent disputes and royalty fees. In 1982, Apple Computer sued Acer, Inc., for copyright infringement when Acer exported Small Professional No.2 to the USA. Apple contended Acer's BIOS (Basic Input/Output System) infringed upon IBM's copyright. In 1985, America National Semiconductor sued UMC (United Microelectronics Corporation) for infringement of patent rights. In 1993-1994, although Philips licensed TSMC (Taiwan Semiconductor Manufacturing Company), Nintendo sued TSMC.

In order to protect themselves, Taiwan's industries began to apply for patents. It was necessary for the Taiwanese government to aid businesses, since the small enterprises that dominated domestic markets and even major enterprises lacked legal professionals and knowledge about IPRs. The Taiwanese government provided financial assistance for corporations and universities to educate businesses about IPRs and to conduct research on intellectual property rights. Organizations to help businesses included ITRI's (Industrial Technology Research Institute) "IPR Development and Management", the Institute for Information Industry's (I.I.I), "Research and Popularization" by Science and Technology Law Center, and NCTU's (National Chiao Tung University) "IPR Management and Patents Engineering Training" by Legal Center for Enterprise & Entrepreneurship.

Education on intellectual property rights has been intense. Since 1986, ITRI has employed IPR as a strategic development. It has established training for personnel, accumulated patents, and interacted with enterprises. At the end of 1999, ITRI had owned 1,259 American patents and organized and generated more than 200 American patents per year. In 1995, III established both the Market Information Center's Law Research Team and the Science and Technology Law Center. These Centers, in addition to cooperating with the Ministry of Economic Affairs to investigate and establish technology development laws, also provide training and services for enterprises. Many universities and colleges offer IPR courses; of these, the one most oriented toward IPR practice is the Credit Class of IPR Management of NCTU. In 1993, NCTU's Department of Management offered IPR courses for graduate students and entrepreneurs. In 1994, NCTU established the IPR management credit class accredited by the Ministry of Education. In addition to professors, NCTU brings in many judges, lawyers and procurators to teach related courses. These courses are very rich and intense—the training courses on patents for engineers have been proceeded for 14 semesters and have trained more than 1,500 professionals.

To recognize the connection between technology and the laws and to enable IPRs to be utilized, NCTU established the Institute of Technology Law in 2000. National Tsing Hua University also established an Institute of Technology Law the same year. During 1997 to 1999, NCTU, the Chinese National Federation of Industries, the Science-based Park Conservancy and the Intellectual Property Office held a joint National IPR Seminar, at which attendance exceeded 1,000. On 7 June 2000, the Institute of Technology Law at NCTU also held a seminar on Internet Business Methods Patents and invited professors and professionals to discuss the issues related to e-commerce.

3.Timely Product Development Essential

Generally, the key to technological competitiveness is not only developing innovative products. The product also must become an industry standard in the product introduction stage rather than later in a product's life cycle. To evaluate a country's industrial competitiveness and innovative characteristics requires an overview of its industry technology, this technology's product's life cycle (PLC), and patent accumulation (Archibugi and Pianta, 1996).

Once a product enters a market and becomes the dominant product, profits increase rapidly. During this growth stage, the continued development of the manufacturing process as well as product improvement will generate the dominant technology. During a product's mature stage, technology becomes diffused. The major competitive factors in the mature stage are price, quality and service, and technology gaps among enterprises are limited. During the decline stage, new technology replaces the product or manufacturing technique, and the original product or industry experiences a decline.

Enterprises wanting to establish a foothold for a new product in the global marketplace require breakthrough technologies. Because of the competition among emergent enterprises during the growth stage, technologies and product developments tend to be diverse, and the quality and quantities of technologies and products increase rapidly. Few organizations compete in this stage because not many are competitive in advanced technologies, and the new product is still non-standardized. Because only a limited number of organizations invest in technology development, most companies adopt a wait-and-see attitude (Chen et al, 2000).

Reflecting the small number of enterprises involved in active technological development, the amount of patent applications in the development stage is relatively small (Figure 1). During the growth stage, however, the number of applicants and the total number of patents grow rapidly. During the maturity stage, the number of enterprises still investing in research and development (R&D) for a product decreases, although technological developments continue. During the decline stage, the total amount of patents filed and enterprise investments decrease rapidly. To gain profit with long term added value, technology leaders must enter into the market early, since competition intensifies in the growth stage, and product life cycles have become shorter. High profits during the growth stage, in particular, are becoming rare (Liu and Shyu, 1997).

Enterprises that enter the market in the introductory stages are called *technology leaders* because they develop new products and new manufacturing processes earlier than others. Enterprises that enter during the growth stage are called *fast followers*, whereas others who enter after the growth stage are technology followers or late-to-markets.

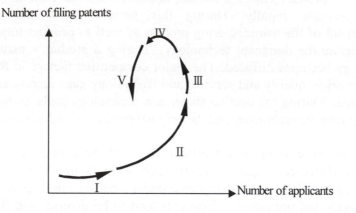

Figure 1 Technology development life cycle.

Enterprises with different technologies and abilities to develop markets obtain different benefits and market risks.   Generally, leaders have the ability to:
(1)Standardize the product, deciding the content of a product.
(2)Gain more experience, decrease learning costs and increase efficiency as they enter the market and use the technology earlier than other competitors.
(3)Increase obstacles for competitors by using the patent's monopoly.
(4)Establish a self-expectant industry environment through technology licenses and cooperative arrangements.
(5)Potentially earn high profits during the introductory and growth stages because of the value-added dimension.

There are also risks and costs associated with being a technology leader and market developer, however. These companies:
(1)Bear the cost of developing new markets and educating users.

(2) Require a high investment in research and development (R & D) to maintain the status of technology leaders, and they bear the costs of R & D failures.

(3) Bear the additional costs of conform to various countries' laws, regulations and environmental impacts. These include environmental protection regulations, inspection and testing on new products, and conforming to product specifications.

(4) Confront lower-cost imitators. Products of technology leaders might be imitated easily in areas where there is less IPR protection.

Followers or late-to-markets can:

(1) Reduce the R & D and learning costs by licensing or learning from others.

(2) Enter into the developed market to reduce the exploration and R & D investment.

In order to be profitable, late-to-markets must reduce their costs and respond promptly to the market. As the marketing channel has been occupied, their profits are not as high as those of the technology leaders.

Taiwan's development and growth in technologies have been major factors in upgrading Taiwan's industry and making it a viable part of global business. In this capacity, its high technology industries have been fast followers.

Taiwan's industrial and economic developments began during the 1950s. They include reconstruction after World War II, import substitutions, an export orientation, two oil crises, an industry upgrade, and the first policy of economic freedom in nearly 10 years. Government played a major role in directing economic development.

Since Taiwan became involved in high technology in the 1980s, the Science-based Industry Park, ITRI, TSMC and UMC have become paragons, and the small- and medium-sized Taiwan enterprises interact actively. During globalization, Taiwan's enterprises have depended upon fabrication, a quick market response, elasticity, and flexible cost controls to respond to overseas competition and international market changes. Despite Taiwan's progress, however, the upstream enterprises in Taiwan have not had sufficient technology and capital to compete with the USA, Japan, and Korea.

4.Indices and Estimates of Technological Capabilities

The technological capabilities of a country can be estimated by statistical indices—the most commonly used being the SCI (Science Citation Index), EI (Engineering Index) and CHI patent index developed by the CHI Research Corporation of USA.

4.1 SCI (Science Citation Index):

SCI surveys global journals in the science and engineering field and calculates the frequencies of citations from different countries. In this way, SCI determines a country's basic science abilities. In 1991, Taiwan ranked number 24 and had reached number 19 by 1998 in the world. As far as social sciences citation index (SSCI), Taiwan ranked number 28 in 19914 and number 25 in 1996. Although Taiwan ranks behind China and Japan, it leads Korea and Southeast Asia combined. Compared with the USA, Japan and Germany, Taiwan has displayed rapid growth since 1985 (Figures 2 to 4). The United States accounts for approximately one-third of all global science papers.

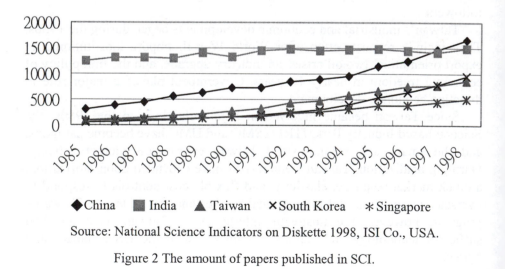

◆China   ■India   ▲Taiwan   ✕South Korea   ✳Singapore

Source: National Science Indicators on Diskette 1998, ISI Co., USA.

Figure 2 The amount of papers published in SCI.

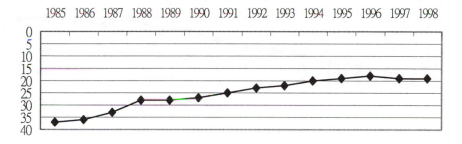

1985 1986 1987 1988 1989 1990 1991 1992 1993 1994 1995 1996 1997 1998

◆Taiwan: Germany ■Taiwan: Japan ▲Taiwan: U.S.

Source: National Science Indicators on Diskette 1998, ISI Co., USA.

Figure 3 International comparisons on the amount of papers published in SCI.

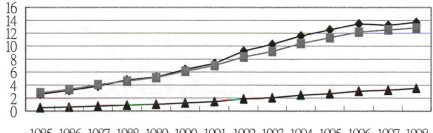

Source: National Science Indicators on Diskette 1998, ISI Co., USA

Figure 4 Rank by country for the amount of papers of Taiwan published in SCI.

4.2 The EI (Engineering Index):

The engineering index (EI) reflects the vigor of Taiwan's engineering technology, and its engineering academic ability is stronger than in any other science. In 1992, Taiwan ranked number 13 globally and in 1999 progressed to number 11. The next highest-ranked country, India (number10) is less than five percent higher than Taiwan, which expects to be number 10 within five years. The development of engineering papers began in 1985, and, compared with the USA, Japan and Germany, shows progress in both quantity and quality (Figures 5 to 7).

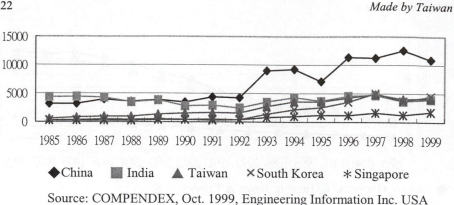

◆China   ■ India   ▲ Taiwan   ✕ South Korea   ＊ Singapore

Source: COMPENDEX, Oct. 1999, Engineering Information Inc. USA

Figure 5 Amount of papers published in EI.

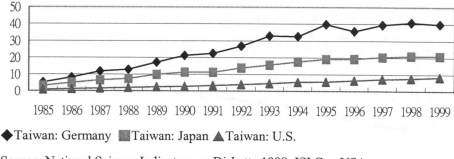

◆Taiwan: Germany   ■Taiwan: Japan   ▲Taiwan: U.S.

Source: National Science Indicators on Diskette 1998, ISI Co., USA

Figure 6 International comparisons on the amount of papers published in SCI.

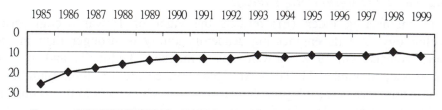

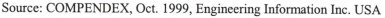

Source: COMPENDEX, Oct. 1999, Engineering Information Inc. USA

Figure 7 Rank by country for the amount of papers of Taiwan published in EI.

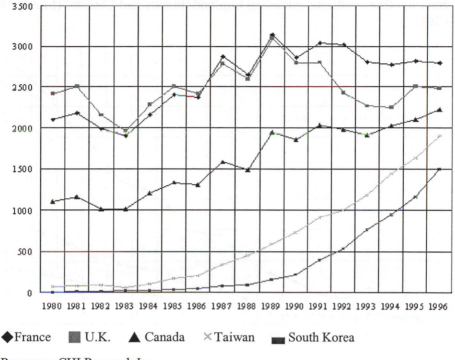

France ◆   U.K. ■   Canada ▲   Taiwan ×   South Korea ▬

Resource: CHI Research Inc.

Figure 8 CHI index

4.3 The CHI patent index:

CHI Research Corporation has developed indices to evaluate technological competitiveness of each country and each company. The patent evaluation indices designed by CHI include quality and quantity dimensions. The basic method of estimating a patent's quality depends upon the frequency with which others cite the patent. If a patent is cited or compared with a later innovation, this implies that it is a significant patent and therefore earns a higher weighting.

Since the USA is one of the largest global markets, the number of patents filed in the USA reflects that country's technology industry. As the number of Taiwanese patents increases, Taiwan's CHI index is getting nearer to other countries, including England, France and Canada (Figures 8 to 10).

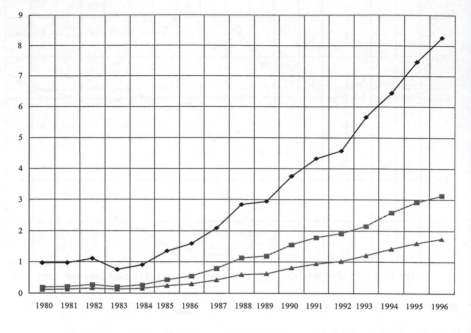

◆Taiwan: Japan ■Taiwan: U.S. ▲Taiwan: Global

Resource: CHI Research Inc.

Figure 9 International comparisons on the CHI index

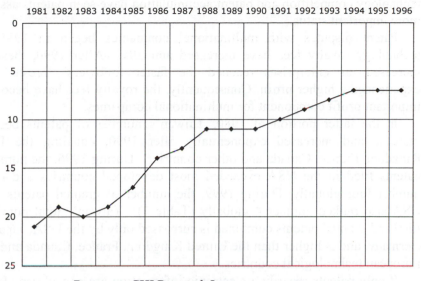

Resource: CHI Research Inc.

Figure 10 Rank by country for Taiwan on the CHI index.

5.Taiwan Patent Numbers Increase

Taiwan's industrial development, especially in the electronics and information industries, is reflected in patent accumulations. Taiwan at first depended upon low-price laborers and effective management and competed with other countries by offering a low-cost advantage. When compared with the USA and Japan, Taiwan's product lines were more diverse and had shorter production cycles. Although this created a competitive advantage, it was not an advantage that resulted in patents. Taiwan's industries at this time were followers.

At the beginning of the 1980s, Taiwan entered into the high-technology fabrication era, and after 1990, its enterprises became fast followers rather than simply followers. Several semiconductor manufacturing technologies are global leaders. Due to the accumulation of capital and the number of products entering into the market, industries in Taiwan that encompass technology competition and patent accumulation have seen patents assume a more important status.

Patent disputes with multinational companies began in 1985, and technology royalty fees have increased annually. After 1990, these fees increased, as enterprises reached the faster followers' threshold and experienced a higher profit. Consequently, the royalty fees have become an important profit component for multinational companies.

In the latter portion of 1980, Taiwan's number of patents began to increase and increased exponentially after 1990, equaling the United Kingdom, France, Canada and other countries. During 1996, the number of patents filed in the USA exceeded most developed countries and ranked number four globally. During 1999, the number of granted patents in the USA also ranked number 4 globally (Table 1). Taiwan's total number of filed and granted patents combined is surpassed only by the USA, Japan and Germany, and is higher than the United Kingdom, France, Canada and other European technological countries.

If only patents regarding electronic information are considered, Taiwan ranks ahead of Germany but after the USA and Japan. In the last decade, granted patents have been concentrated in the electronics area (Figure 11 and Table 2). Taiwan's industries and research organizations have had an impact on related patents as well. UMC and Hon Hai Precision and TSMC ranked in the top 50 in U.S.-granted patents. Most of the patents in Taiwan are for improvements (Figure 12).

The proportion of filed and granted invention patents increases annually (Figure 13). In the 1980s, the patents focused on toys and electronic toys; however, in the 1990s the focus shifted to electronics and semiconductor manufacturing techniques. In 1996, 54 percent (5942 pieces) of utility patents filed were in the field of electrical engineering, such as computer information, semiconductors and telecommunications. Foreign patents for the same period amounted to 58 percent (2514 pieces) compared to 42 percent domestic patents (2514 pieces). When compared with the fact that 80 percents of invention patents are held by countries other than Taiwan, Taiwan's domestic high technology, semi-conductor and telecommunication technology industries have shown the most progress.

1992			1993			1994		
rank	Countries	number	rank	countries	number	rank	countries	number
1	Japan	23164	1	Japan	23411	1	Japan	23517
2	Germany	7605	2	Germany	7186	2	Germany	6989
3	France	3282	3	France	3155	3	France	2985
4	U. K.	2632	4	U. K.	2521	4	U. K.	2469
5	Canada	2218	5	Canada	2231	5	Canada	2380
6	Italy	1446	6	Taiwan	1510	6	Taiwan	1814
7	Switzerland	1294	7	Italy	1453	7	Italy	1361
8	Taiwan	1253	8	Switzerland	1198	8	Switzerland	1244
9	Netherlands	974	9	Netherlands	944	9	South Korea	1008
10	Sweden	727	10	South Korea	830	10	Netherlands	998
1995			1996			1997		
rank	countries	number	rank	countries	number	rank	countries	number
1	Japan	22871	1	Japan	24059	1	Japan	24191
2	Germany	6874	2	Germany	7125	2	Germany	7292
3	France	3010	3	France	3016	3	France	3202
4	U. K.	2681	4	U. K.	2674	4	U. K.	2904
5	Canada	2447	5	Canada	2639	5	Canada	2817
6	Taiwan	2087	6	Taiwan	2419	6	Taiwan	2597
7	Italy	1242	7	South Korea	1567	7	South Korea	1965
8	South Korea	1240	8	Italy	1385	8	Italy	1417
9	Switzerland	1187	9	Switzerland	1192	9	Switzerland	1179
10	Sweden	914	10	Sweden	971	10	Sweden	970
1998			1999			2000		
rank	Countries	number	rank	countries	number	rank	countries	number
1	Japan	32119	1	Japan	32515	1	Japan	32,924
2	Germany	9582	2	Germany	9896	2	Germany	10,822
3	France	3991	3	Taiwan	4526	3	Taiwan	5,806
4	Taiwan	3805	4	France	4097	4	France	4,173
5	U. K.	3726	5	U. K.	3900	5	U. K.	4,090
6	Canada	3537	6	South Korea	3679	6	Canada	3,925
7	South Korea	3362	7	Canada	3678	7	South Korea	3,472
8	Italy	1820	8	Italy	1686	8	Italy	1,967
9	Netherlands	1382	9	Sweden	1542	9	Sweden	1,738
10	Switzerland	1373	10	Netherlands	1396	10	Switzerland	1,458

Resource: U.S. Patent and Trademark Office, Office of Information System, TAF Program.

Table 1 Total counts of granted patent for top ten countries during 1992 to 2000

1990	1991	1992	1993	1994
B60	H01	H01	H01	H01
H01	A63	A63	A63	A63
A63	A47	F16	A47	A47
F16	F16	A47	F16	F16
A47	B60	B60	E05	B62
1995	1996	1997	1998	1999
H01	H01	H01	H01	H01
A63	A63	A63	A63	A47
A47=F16	A47	A47	A47	H04
B60	F16	F16	F16	B65
B62	B62	B65	G06	G06

Note:

A47: furniture; domestic articles or appliances; coffee mills; spice mills; suction cleaners in general

A63: sports; games; amusements

B60: vehicles in general

B62: land vehicles for travelling otherwise than on rails

B65: conveying; packing; storing; handling thin or filamentary material

E05: locks; keys; window or door fittings; safes

F16: engineering elements or units; general measures for producing and maintaining effective functioning of machines or installations; thermal insulation in general

G06: computing; calculating; counting

H01: basic electric elements

H04: electric communication technique

Table 2 Top Five classes of USA granted patents obtained by Taiwan during 1990 to 1999

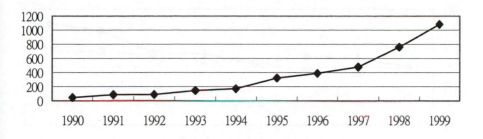

Resource: United States Patent and Trademark Office

Figure 11 The progress of granted U.S. patents of Taiwan in the IPC H01.

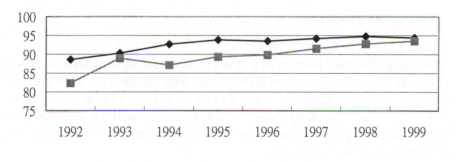

◆filed improvement patents   ▪granted improvement patents

Resource: Chinese Taipei Intellectual Property Office

Figure 12 The proportion of filed and granted improvement patents held by Taiwan's companies and people (%)

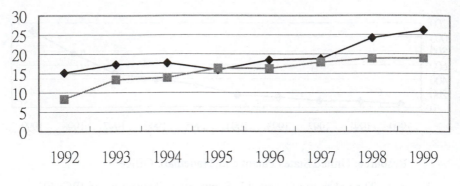

filed invention patents   granted invention patents

Resource: Chinese Taipei Intellectual Property Office

Figure 13 The proportion of filed and granted invention patents held by Taiwan's companies and people (%)

Although the total number of patents in information and electronics held by Taiwan is impressive, most patents can only be used as tools for self-protection or cross-licensing. The amount of patents of companies in the USA, Japan and Korea exceeds Taiwan's, and it will be necessary for Taiwan to enter patent alliances to produce greater R&D and marketing power for domestic enterprises.

Taiwan's patents primarily involve the use of manufacturing process techniques or other similar innovations. Since Taiwan has yet to establish product regulations, its technologies vacillate between the roles of fast followers and followers. These two types of innovations are dissimilar. The risk of failure is high for fast followers, since breakthroughs in product technologies are difficult, and capital investment is high. Continuous development in manufacturing process techniques and product improvements also requires innovation.

Extra efforts are necessary to improve the quality of Taiwan's industry patents. As mentioned, the quality of patents is judged by the frequency with which they are cited. US patents obtained by Taiwan's enterprises and research organizations are primarily not pioneer or basic patents, and have been only recently obtained, but Taiwan has the potential to develop its patent quality.

6.Taiwan and Asia: A Possible Growth Path

In recent years, some scholars consistently predicted high growth in Asian economies when predicting the future economic perspective for a single Asian country. Their argument was that they were on a lower-level economic scale and could develop economic bodies to obtain a higher economic development since they had such a broad range for improvement. Initially, this appeared to be a good theory; however, since the 1990's Japan has sunk into a period of constitutional adjustments after the economy was ruined. Furthermore, since World War II, Japan has experienced a long-term economic recession, and it appears there will be no recovery in the near future. At the same time, through the advantage of low cost laborers, Mainland China and the countries of Southeast Asia have achieved considerable progress.

6.1 Cooperative Alliances Could Advance Taiwan's Interests

Since the 1990s, Japan has been at a standstill in the amount of published SCI papers and on the CHI index, which represent basic research abilities and technology inventions, respectively. This implies that Japan's domestic research system has been saturated; however, if Japan's population and economic scale is considered, there is a gap between Japan and Western Europe and North America in research outcomes. In order to develop its economy and increase its quality of life, Japan needs to establish a research system comparable to Western Europe's and North America's to supply the requisite innovative technology. Globally, Japan owns the largest domestic manufacturing industries, and these require long-term, large-scale research efforts to maintain their production efficiency.

Japan must respond flexibly to global market changes to maintain its competitive ability. When Japan's domestic research system can not provide sufficient innovative knowledge for industry, Japan needs to seek these resources elsewhere. Japan requires Asia's resources to develop its economy and will not prosper economically if it becomes isolated from other Asian countries. The research strength and capabilities in Northeastern Asia, including Mainland China, South Korea and Taiwan, have increased to become a source of innovative knowledge in Asia. Of all Asian countries, Taiwan's research abilities rose dramatically in the mid-1980s and 1990s, and Korea has experienced rapid research growth as well. The levels of industry developments in South Korea and Taiwan now differ only slightly from Japan's.

At the same time, beginning in the 1990s, Japan's economy began to decline. Caught in an economic depression, Japanese companies sold many of their mid-lower-level technologies, capital assets, and even advanced technologies to other Asian regions. Many provinces in Mainland China, including those in outlying rural areas, bought Japan's technologies and capital equipments at a high cost. These purchases were not utilized, however. A lack of professional techniques, a lack of accessory systems, a fondness for grandiosity, and the exceedingly high purchase prices resulted in no chance to utilize their assets.

Japan would achieve more benefits by becoming partners with South Korea and Taiwan, which have complete industries, strong and flexible manufacturing capabilities, and rich business experiences. Japan could consider South Korea and Taiwan as partners in developing technology, strengthening technology transfers and cooperating to develop new products, manufacturing techniques, capital assets and software services. By forming partnerships with South Korea and Taiwan as transformation centers of technology trade, Japan could experience several advantages. It could: (1) share the risks of economic development, (2) use local research resources, and (3) extend Japan's research systems. South Korea and Taiwan would benefit by changing their product-oriented economies to market-oriented economies with a higher added value.

A further benefit for a Japanese-Taiwanese association is it would allow Taiwan to evolve from a purely manufacturing center to a technology service center, which markets quality of life. Japan's achievement in the global market is due to its philosophy of "produce for life, not produce for production." Its viewpoint on markets is very delicate and complete—to promote quality of life by developing products, services or technologies that enhance this quality. It creates the required technology for this end and improves that technology gradually. Conversely, Taiwanese technological developments are based on sales volumes of existing markets; quality of life is not a factor. Taiwan's seeks to reduce production costs through efficiency, not through the adding the value of quality. Because of this, there is an unsatisfied demand in Taiwan for an increased quality of life. Vast production capabilities and profits are meaningless if technology fails to contribute positively to one's quality of life.

In addition to providing a quality dimension to Taiwan's processes, Japan and Taiwan have compatible technologies. This includes the accessory functions of product planning, industry design, and human factor engineering and marketing.

6.2 An Asian Manufacturing Center

Taiwan has an opportunity to develop as a manufacturing center in the global market by using the Asian-Pacific region as a base. Due to its skills in facility and process planning, establishment of operation standards and quality control, Taiwan has the ability to become the engineering management center of Asia. In the USA, the contribution of manufacturing to the GDP decreased from 41 percent in the 1950s to 20 percent, the lowest point since American Civil War. The USA has gradually given up expanding its manufacturing facilities, choosing instead to rely on importing various products and is now the largest importer of industrial products in the world. Taiwan has the opportunity, given its ability in engineering management, to become the global center for manufacturing, providing numerous, high-quality products at reasonable prices.

Although countries such as Japan, Australia and Singapore have strong technological capabilities and geographical regions in which to house similar jobs, Taiwan is best suited for this endeavor. Japan is too conservative to accept orders. Australia's fastidiousness in everything causes high costs and lack of competition. Singapore's technology and R&D are not competitive. Although Taiwan is famous for winning orders by offering lower prices, the products continue to have a certain quality, delivery is satisfied, and the price remains attractive. These capabilities have established Taiwan as the largest production system of personal computers and accessories in the world. Taiwan's techniques in mechanical manufacturing and material-forming fields lead the world.

Taiwan has developed the human resources to be able to become the most important source of innovative technology knowledge in Asia, excluding Japan. It can integrate Asia's production capabilities to provide services for one-time purchases, gaining profit from engineering management. Taiwan can become the operations center of a Big Chinese Economic Circle, acting as an intermediate commercial dealer for Mainland China and Japan and gaining technology skills to strengthen its technological capability.

To emulate Japan, Taiwan needs to adjust its attitude to accurately predict market trends and search for the most suitable technology to satisfy the demands of the market. Taiwan's nimbleness in commerce and its professional accomplishments in technology management will help it enter as an advanced country and become a great technological nation.

References

[1] Archibugi, A. and Pianta, M., "Measuring technological change through patents and innovation surveys," Technovation, Vol. 16, No. 9, pp 451-468, 1996.

[2] Chen, J. L., Liu, S. J., and Tseng, C. H., "Technological Innovation and Strategy Adaptation in the Product Life Cycle," *Technology Management: Strategies & Application*, Volume 5, No. 3, pp. 183-202, 2000.

[3] Liu, S. J. and Shyu, J., "Strategic planning for technology development with patent analysis," *International Journal of Technology Management*, Vol. 13, No. 5/6, pp. 661-680, 1997.

Chapter 10

Investment: The Life Blood of Growth

(Taiwan)

Chih-Young Hung

Institute of Information Management
National Chiao Tung University
HsinChu, Taiwan, R.O.C.

514 016
G31 521
L63
L11

1. Introduction

This chapter looks at the source of funding for Taiwan's conversion to a high-tech economy. An abundant supply of capital resources is a critical factor in the successful development of an industry because this growth requires a constant influx of funds. To support increases in sales, a manufacturing firm inevitably will need to increase its holdings in cash, inventories, equipment and facilities, which results in a depletion of usable funds. To balance this drain on usable funds, a firm needs to raise funds from external sources.

In Taiwan, 30 years of industrial growth has enabled companies to obtain these funds from investors. This chapter looks at the institutions and mechanisms that have provided the funds for Taiwan's growth. Sources of these funds have changed over the decades, along with the changes in the industrial sector itself.

2. The Growth of PC /IC Industries in Taiwan

Taiwan's IC and PC industries have evolved from a humble beginning into a world-class manufacturing muscle. The number of PC or IC related firms that are listed in the Taiwan Stock Exchange (TSE) and the Over-the-Counter (OTC) Exchange increased from 22 in 1985 to 196 in 1999. Figure 1 depicts the pattern of this increase. The largest number of 213 occurred in 1996; however, 17 firms were removed from these two exchanges for various reasons in 1999. The reduction in number might reflect partly the lagged adverse effect on Taiwan of the Asian financial turmoil since 1997.

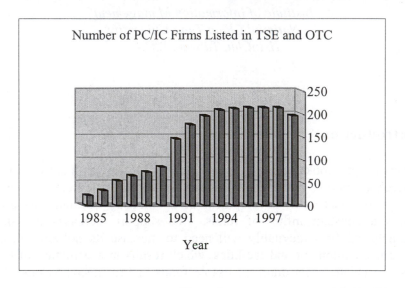

Figure 1

As shown in Figure 2, the total assets of the listed firms in the PC and IC industries had reached 2.06 trillion NT dollars in 1999. In other words, these two sectors of PC and IC related firms have absorbed two trillion NT dollars from the public, equivalent roughly to 70 billion US dollars,. Apparently, investors in Taiwan are very friendly and generous to the PC and IC industries.

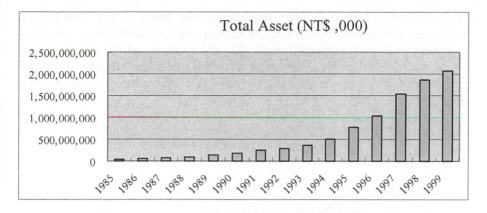

Figure 2

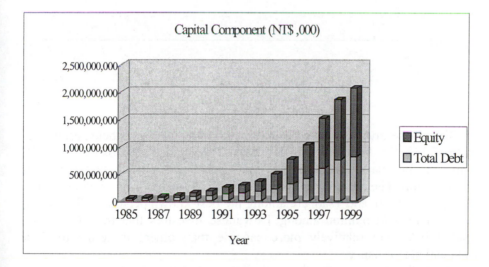

Figure 3

These massive needs of capital were raised in the form of debt and equity. Based on our analysis, the distribution between debt and equity is roughly half and half, as shown in Figure 3.

Noticeably, the debt ratio of these listed firms had declined consistently from around 70 percent in 1985 to 40 percent in 1999. The pattern of this change of financing behavior is demonstrated by the declining trend of the

TD/TA ratio in Figure 4. The tendency of the firms to use less debt in financing reflects two facts. First, the management of technology firms was becoming more and more concerned with the riskiness of their business and thus reduced their financial leverage. Second, the equity market in Taiwan had become very popular among investors. Listed companies were able to raise capital relatively easy in the stock market.

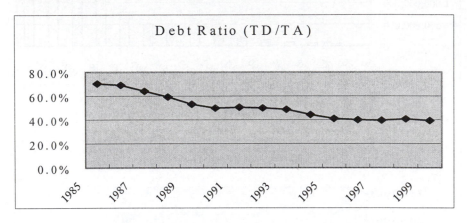

Figure 4

Taiwanese investors have been attracted to technology stocks, especially in the IC sector, for more than 10 years. The intensive exposure of the IC firms in the mass media might have been one crucial factor in this phenomenon. The personages associated with PC or IC firms, such as Morris Chang, Stan Shih, and Tsao, are among the best-known persons in Taiwan. It is a widely held opinion among Taiwanese investors that the PC- or IC-related firms are relatively more capable than others in terms of their financial performance.

According to one study, the performance of electronics firms over a five-year period is moderately superior to that of other firms in various measures, as depicted in Table 1.

	Measures/Year	1995	1996	1997	1998	1999
IC/PC Firms	EPS (NT$/share)	2.5	1.69	2.08	1.43	1.21
	EBIT/Sales (%)	24	20	19	19	16
	ROS (%)	13	9	7.7	7.5	5
	ROA (%)	11.4	8.7	8.5	7.4	5.8
Others	EPS (NT$/share)	1.01	0.8.	1.21	0.76	0.55
	EBIT/Sales (%)	25	22.6	22.9	22.5	21.7
	ROS (%)	10.1	7.4	7.4	6.8	5.9
	ROA (%)	6	4.7	5.2	4	3.6

Table 1 Financial Performance of TSE-Listed IC/PC Firms vs. Other TSE-Listed Firms

Investors are rational in general and are attracted to certain stock sectors because of the higher expected returns these stocks provide. Average investors, however, could have difficulty analyzing the performances of the firms in which they are interested and might simply assume that past performance will be repeated in the future. Thus, past performances of these firms can be valuable information to investors. For reference, the financial performances of Taiwan's PC and IC industries are summarized in Figure 5. Over the 15 years from 1985 to 1999, the average annual rates of ROS (return on sale), ROA (return on total assets), and ROE (return on equity) are 6.2 percent, 6.4 percent, and 11.5 percent, respectively.

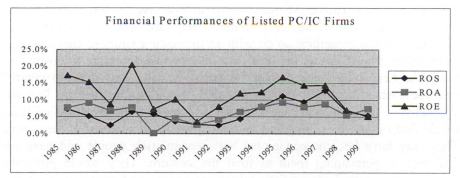

Figure 5 Financial Performances of Listed PC/IC Firms
Source: AREMOS database of financial statements of listed companies

The results reveal several interesting things. First, the relatively low and declining values of the ratio of the ROS (return on sale) indicates that these two sectors are not performing impressively in terms of adding value. One possible explanation could be that most PC- and many IC-related firms devoted most of their capacity to OEM activity. Because the competition for OEM orders is fierce, the profit margin for those businesses is not likely to be high.

Second, the value of the ROS is roughly the same as that of the ROA (return on total asset). Since the value of ROA is derived by multiplying the value of ROS times the value of total asset turnover, the ROA will be greater than ROS if the turnover ratio is greater than unity. In the current case, it appears that the asset turnover ratio is roughly only one. The results suggest that there is ample room for Taiwan's PC/IC firms to improve their performance in term of asset management.

Third, the level of ROE (return on equity) ratio has gradually declined relative to the ROA ratio. As commonly known, ROE is the product of ROA and the equity multiplier (TA/E). The results thus indicate that PC/IC firms are using more equity capital for funding. This result is consistent with the findings documented in Table 4.

3. Profiles of Typical PC/ IC Firms

The PC and IC firms in Taiwan vary dramatically in terms of size and performance, but Taiwanese tech firms, irrespective of their differences, seem to share one thing in common—they are quick to react. This phenomenon has something to do with an interesting Chinese characteristic exemplified by a Chinese proverb that says people are more interested in being the head of a chicken than the tail of a cow. This proverb vividly describes what happened in the PC and the IC industries in Taiwan. Typically, a few engineers working for a company for a period of time would find t is more exciting and rewarding to start a business of their own. They may have become acquainted with several rich people and have no difficulty in persuading them to fund the venture. They would probably make the same products as their former company, and competition in the same market soon becomes fierce. To survive, they are forced to respond very quickly and become very flexible.

To further understand these firms, we report the balance sheets of six typical firms. These typical firms are actually portfolios of firms derived from our database of all listed PC/IC related firms. First, we ranked the firms by size based on total assets. Second, three equally weighted portfolios were formed—the large, the medium and the small. The large portfolio consists of those firms in the upper 10 percentile, the medium portfolio consists of firms in the middle 20 percentile, and the small portfolio consists of firms in the bottom 10 percentile. We performed this process twice, one time for firms listed in the TSE (Taiwan Stock Exchange) and the other for the firms listed in the OTC-Exchange. Balance sheets of these typical firms are given below:

(1) Balance Sheet of a typical small firm listed in the OTC exchange

Assets (NT$ M)		Liabilities and Equities (NT$ M)	
CA	263	CL	36
Investment	91	LT Debt	9
FA	358	Equity	810
Discrepancy.	143		
TA	855	Liability & Equity	855

(2) Balance Sheet for a typical medium size firm listed in the OTC Exchange

Assets (NT$ M)		Liabilities and Equities (NT$ M)	
CA	844	C.L.	376
Investment	254	LT Debt	82
FA	444	Equity	1,022
		Discrepancy.	62
TA	1,542	Liability & Equity	1,542

(3) Balance Sheet for a typical firm listed in the OTC Exchange

Assets (NT$ M)		Liabilities and Equities (NT$ M)	
CA	4,023	C.L.	1,875
Investment	942	LT Debt	3,582
FA	8,338	Equity	7,827
		Discrepancy.	19
TA	13,303	Liability & Equity	13,303

(4) Balance Sheet for a typical small firm listed in the TSE

Assets (NT$ M)		Liabilities and Equities (NT$ M)	
CA	1,113	C.L.	581
Investment	250	LT Debt	87
FA	454	Equity	1,136
		Discrepancy.	13
TA	1,817	Liability & Equity	1,817

(5) Balance Sheet for a typical medium firm listed in the TSE

Assets (NT$ M)		Liabilities and Equities (NT$ M)	
CA	3,760	C.L.	1,639
Investment	2,056	LT Debt	596
FA	1,573	Equity	5,042
		Discrepancy	112
TA	7,389	Liability & Equity	7,389

(6) Balance Sheet for a typical large firm listed in the TSE

Assets (NT$ M)		Liabilities and Equities (NT$ M)	
CA	21,048	C.L.	7,307
Investment	18,499	LT Debt	13,501
FA	24,242	Equity	42,278
		Discrepancy	703
TA	63,789	Liability & Equity	63,789

As shown in these six balance sheets and also illustrated in Figures 6, 7 and 8, the scale of these typical firms varies widely. For example, total assets of a typical large TSE-listed firm are on the level of 63.79 billion NT dollars, while total assets of a typical small OTC-listed firm are on the level of 855 million NT dollars.

We also calculated six financial ratios for these firms, three for the asset side and three for the liability side. These three ratios—current asset to total asset (CA/TA), long-term investment to total assets (Invest/TA), and fixed assets to total assets (FA/TA)—are summarized in Table 2. Several observations regarding the results in Table 2 are in order. First, there appears to be a pattern for the ratio of CA/TA in that the ratio declines as a firm grows larger. Smaller firms are less inclined to use operating leverage and probably resort to outsourcing for their manufacturing needs. There is one exception, however; the ratio for the OTC-small firms (39%) is less than that of the OTC-medium firms (55%). One possible reason for this phenomenon is revealed in the ratio of FA/TA. Notice that the fixed assets-to-total-assets ratio for the OTC-small firm is relatively large at 48 percent. This indicates that for a manufacturing firm to run its business, there is a minimum requirement for its investment in fixed assets. Since smaller firms have smaller total assets, the fixed assets to total assets ratio be upward-biased. In turn, this would thus cause the current ratio for smaller firms to be less than that of larger firms. This result also seems to suggest that a basic requirement of 400 million NT dollars in fixed assets for a manufacturing firm to run a business.

Second, cross-investments among PC/IC related firms are very common. The ratios of investments to total assets increase as the firms get bigger; for example, the ratio is 13 percent for the OTC-small firm and 29 percent for the TSE-large firm. A typical large PC/IC firm listed in the TSE would invest 18 billion NT dollars in stocks of other companies. An examination of these firms' reports reveals that most of these companies are closely related, either in business or in ownership.

Third, larger firms are definitely more capital intensive. The fixed assets to total assets ratio for the OTC-large firm, at 63 percent, is the highest. Even though the ratio for the TSE-large firms is not impressive, at 38 percent, it is worth noting that these firms devoted 29 percent of their total assets in other companies' stocks. Apparently, as firm grows larger, they opt not only to grow internally but also to expand externally.

	OTC-Small	OTC-Med.	OTC-Large	TSE-Small	TSE-Med.	TSE-Large
CA/TA	39%	55%	30%	61%	51%	33%
Invest/TA	13%	16%	7%	14%	28%	29%
FA/TA	48%	29%	63%	25%	21%	38%

Table 2 Ratios Reflecting Investment Activities of Taiwan's PC/IC Firms

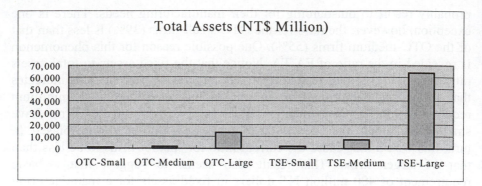

Figure 6 Comparisons of Sizes of Six Typical PC/IC Firms

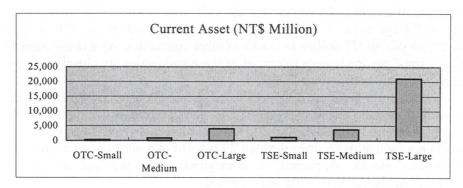

Figure 7-a

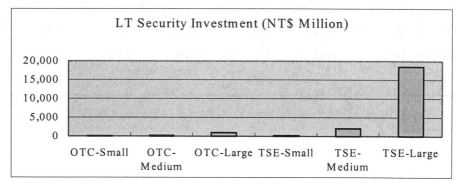

Figure 7-b

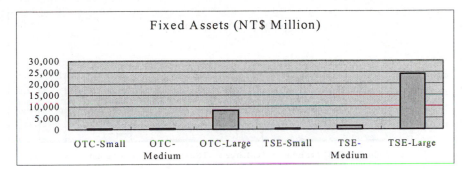

Figure 7-c

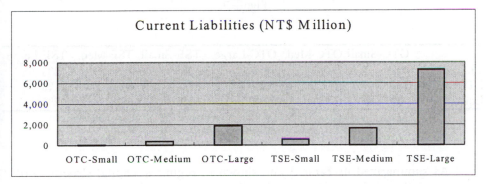

Figure 7-d

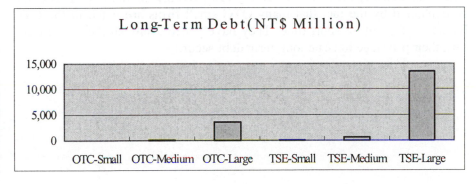

Figure 7-e

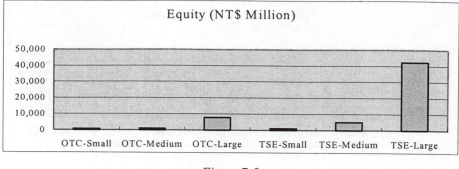

Figure 7-f
Figure 7

	OTC-Small	OTC-Med.	OTC-Large	TSE-Small	TSE-Med.	TSE-Large
CL/TA	5%	25%	14%	32%	23%	12%
LTDebt/TA	1%	6%	27%	5%	8%	21%
Equity/TA	94%	69%	59%	63%	69%	67%

Table 3

As summarized in Table 3 and shown in Figure 8, capital structures of the listed firms are closely related to their sizes. The OTC-small firms rely almost exclusively on their own equity (94 percent) for funding. This could be explained by the fact that many OTC small firms are listed in the OTC Exchange for only a short time. They have yet to establish their credit and earn their privilege to issue long-term debt security.

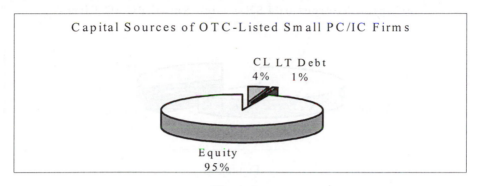

Figure 8-a

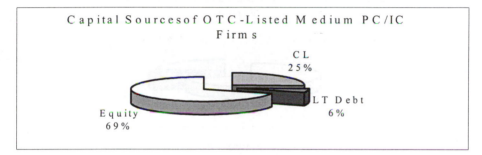

Figure 8-b

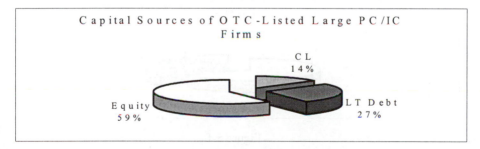

Figure 8-c

Figure 8 Capital Structures of Typical PC/IC Firms of Different Sizes

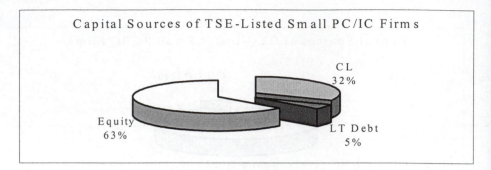

Figure 8-d

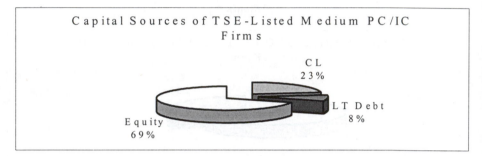

Figure 8-e

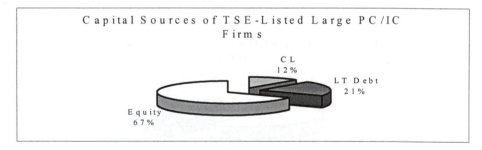

Figure 8-f

Figure 8 Capital Structures of Typical PC/IC Firms of Different Sizes

The equity ratios (equity to total assets) for other firms are also on a relatively high level, roughly in the neighborhood of 65 percent. Obviously, IC/PC related firms in Taiwan are very conservative about using financial leverage. As pointed out earlier, the debt ratio (total debt to total assets) for all firms as a whole has declined steadily from 70 percent in 1985 to 40 percent in 1999. This result is best explained by the argument that Taiwanese investors are very interested in owning stocks of PC/IC-related firms. These firms have found that the primary stock market is very receptive to new issuance of their stocks.

The results also indicate that larger firms are able to raise debt funds through either issuing long-term debt securities or borrowing long-tem debt. Ratios of long-term debt to total assets are five percent, eight percent, and 21 percent for TSE-listed small, medium, and large firms, respectively. For smaller firms that have not been able to raise sufficient long-term debt, short-term credits become an important source of funds.

4. Fundamental Economic Strengths of Taiwan

The PC/IC industries in Taiwan were fortunate in several respects. First, there is a plentiful supply of well-trained and hard-working engineers. Second, the economy has been growing very strongly for a long period of time. The massive amount of savings by the public is funneled to the manufacturing sectors through several major mechanisms. In this section, we present data on the fundamental economic strength of Taiwan.

GDP. The IC manufacturing industry is a capital-intensive industry. Its nickname of "money furnace" illustrates how fast money can be consumed. The PC and IC industries in Taiwan, especially the IC, have been fortunate because Taiwan's GDP has experienced dramatic growth for an extensive period of time. Taiwan also has enjoyed huge trade surpluses for many years. The people in this island are diligent, and the rate of savings among the general public is relatively high. These savings are continuously funneled to these sectors through various channels and mechanism. From the analysis, we found evidence that might explain why Taiwan is able to sustain the growth of its IC industry and stay basically unharmed by the fire of Asian financial crisis. The key is Taiwan's financial strength.

The GDP (gross domestic product) of Taiwan in 1951 was a humble 12.33 billion NT dollars. It had grown 755 times, to 9.3 trillion NT dollars in 1999. The annual compounded growth rate of the GDP over this period of 49 years is a respectable 14.5 percent. Figure 9 shows the history of Taiwan's GDP. To further understand how Taiwan's GDP has been performing, we also show the GDP growth rate over the same period of time. This is given in Figure 10.

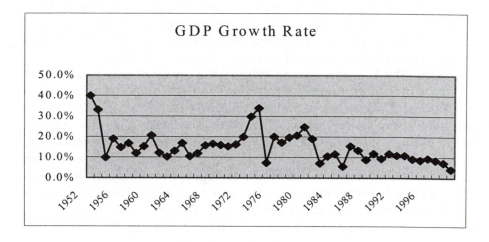

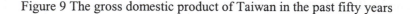

Figure 9 The gross domestic product of Taiwan in the past fifty years

Figure 10 The growth rates of Taiwan's GDP in the past fifty years

As shown in Figure 10, Taiwan's economy has enjoyed double-digit growth rates for an extensive period. One setback occurred in1975 when the growth rate dropped from its previous high of 34 percents to 7.3 percents, but the growth rate bounced back to 20 percent the next year and remained at that level another five years. This pattern of the GDP growth rate demonstrates how resilient Taiwan's economy has been. In the six years between 1994 and 1999, the GDP growth rate declined to the single-digit neighborhood. There could be two major reasons for this decline.

First, the increasing costs of land and labor have stimulated many firms to move their manufacturing facilities from Taiwan to either Mainland China or Southeast Asian countries. Second, Taiwan's economy has gradually reached its mature stage. Its previous policy of building an expansionary and export-oriented economy has been modified to a more moderate one. The government now spends more money in environmental protection, pollution control, public health care programs, and various social welfare programs. Most of these programs are not "producing" in that they do not create products. In the past, the expansion of Taiwan's economy was achieved at the expense of water pollution, air pollution, working conditions long working hours, etc. Now, society is making corrections and learning to enjoy life more.

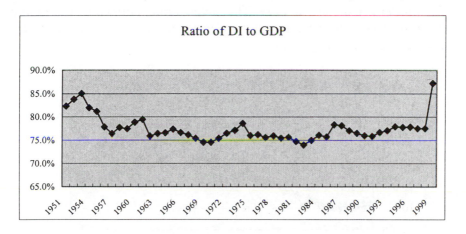

Figure 11 The ratio of disposable income to GDP in Taiwan

Disposable Income. Disposable income, normally defined as the sum of consumer expenditures and savings, has been a major part of Taiwan's GDP. Figure 11 shows that this ratio fluctuated between 75 and 85 percent over the past 48 years and jumped to 87 percent in 1999. Figure 12 shows the disposable income and its components of savings and consumption.

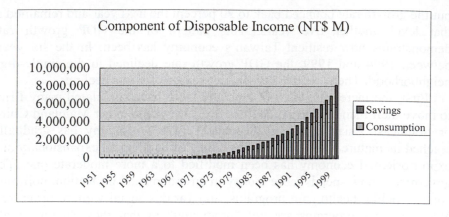

Figure 12 The distribution of disposable income in Taiwan

Savings. The massive amount of consumer savings has become an important source for businesses that need capital resources. Figure 13 shows that savings have grown steadily from a mere 1.2 billion NT dollars in 1951 to 2.5 trillion NT dollars in 1999. The savings rate, defined as the ratio of savings to disposable income, has a mean value of 24 percent. Its pattern over time is shown in Figure 14.

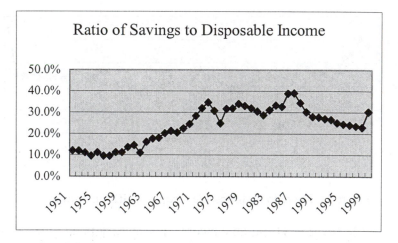

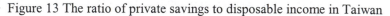

Figure 13 The ratio of private savings to disposable income in Taiwan

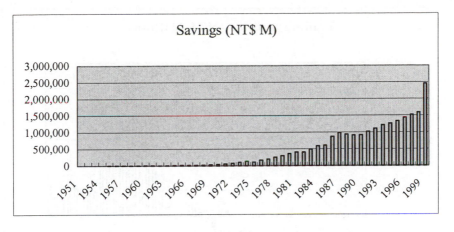

Figure 14

Trade Surpluses. As pointed out in Baumol and Blinder (1997), the trade surplus is a major contributor to a nation's savings (S). The reason is that income (Y) must be either spent on consumer goods (C) or saved (S). Since Y= C+S always, and since Y=C+I+(X-M) when Y is at its equilibrium value. (Note: I is the gross domestic private investment and X-M is the trade surplus). We can describe equilibrium by the condition that C+S = C+I+(X-M), thus S=I + (X-M). It becomes apparent that the main reason Taiwan is be able to maintain a high level of saving (S) is because of its trade surplus.

Figure 15 depicts the trade deficit/surplus of Taiwan for the period between 1951 and 1999. Taiwan's economy was pretty small in the period after World Was II, and the economy was basically in the farming sector. For 20 years Taiwan ran a trading deficit. A turning point occurred in 1971, and from 1971 to 1987 the trade surplus grew at an impressive speed, with only three years of trade deficits. The surplus reached its climax in 1987 at 561 billion NT dollars (equivalent to 20 billion US dollars). After that, the surplus began to fall, but despite its dramatic decline between 1987 and 1992, Taiwan has maintained a trade surplus of between 100 and 200 billion NT dollars (three to eight billion US dollars).

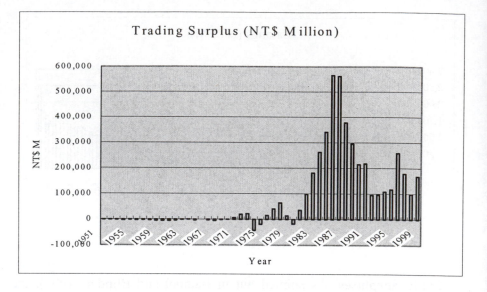

Figure 15 Net exports of Taiwan in the past fifty years

The large balance of trade surplus has played a very important role in the development of Taiwan's economy. For one thing, the trade surplus translated into wealth for the general public. With plenty of money at their disposal, people started investing. First, the focus was in real estate. Then, the stock market caught the eye of investors.

4. Profile of Funds Providers

Taiwan's financial system roughly consists of two subsets, namely, the organized and the unorganized. The unorganized subset is the so-called underground financing mechanism. This is the direct transfer of funds between borrowers and lenders. The underground financing mechanism historically has played an important role in Taiwan's traditional economy. The direct transfer of funds consists of collateralized- or non-collateralized short-term borrowings between business firms and private individuals. This kind of financing used to be an indispensable source of funds for many small-sized firms; however, along with the progress of Taiwan's financial system, the importance of this underground financing mechanism has faded.

The organized subset of the financial system consists of two major branches. The first is related to financial intermediaries. The second is related to the issuance of financial securities. These two branches of Taiwan's financial system are subject to relatively tight control by two government agencies, the Central Bank and the Ministry of Finance.

Roughly speaking, the Central Bank is the major government agency involved in regulating the banking system, and the Ministry of Finance is the major regulatory agency for securities firms and capital markets. Funds needed by PC/IC firms are formed and allocated to them through either the banking system or the primary security markets. In the remainder of this section, we will describe the profile of four major providers of funds for PC/IC firms. They are the financial intermediaries, the primary bond market, the primary stock market, and venture capital funds.

Financial Intermediaries. There are many types of financial institutions in Taiwan, and not all of them are involved with the functions of intermediaries, i.e., capital formation and fund allocation. For completeness, all types of financial institutions are listed below:

1. The Central Bank
2. The Central Deposit Insurance Company (CDIC)
3. The Central Reinsurance Company
4. Domestic banks
5. Local branches of foreign banks
6. Medium business banks
7. Credit Cooperative Associations
8. Credit departments of Farmers' and Fishermen's Associations
9. Postal savings system
10. Investment & Trust companies
11. Life insurance companies
12. Bills finance companies
13. Securities finance companies
14. Others.

Among these 14 types of institutions, there are eight —from item 4 to item 11 on the list—that that play the role of financial intermediaries. To visualize the growth or decline of these intermediaries and their role in intermediating public funds, we present their total assets, loans to private enterprises, and loans to the government over the past 10 years. As shown in Figures 16-a and e, domestic banks and life insurance companies are expanding their territory, both in terms of total assets and outstanding loans. On the other hand, as shown in Figures 16-c, f, and h, the role of the credit cooperatives, the medium business banks and the credit departments of the FFA all are declining, a descent that started roughly in 1995.

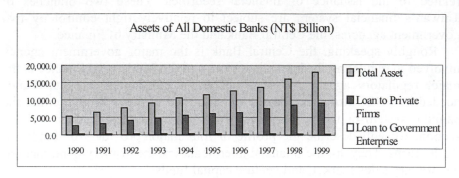

Figure 16-a

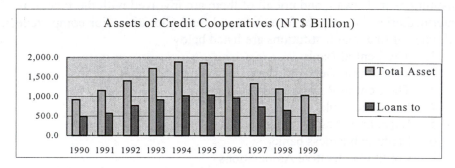

Figure 16-b

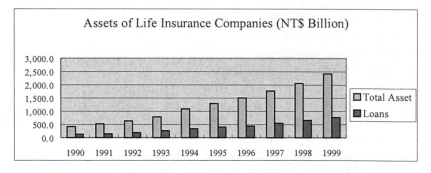

Figure 16-c

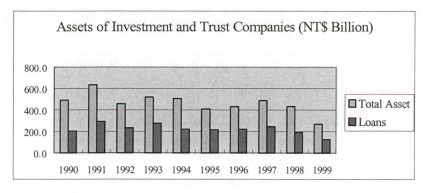

Figure 16-d

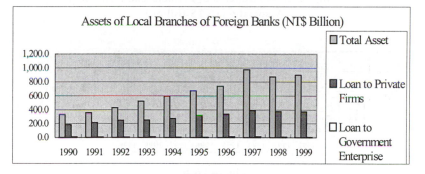

Figure 16-e

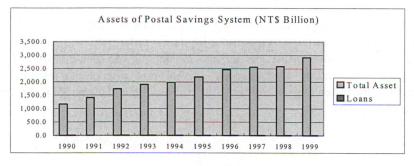

Figure 16-f

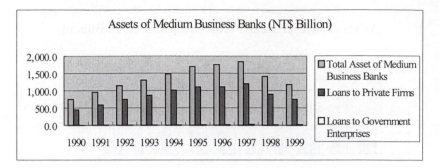

Figure 16-g

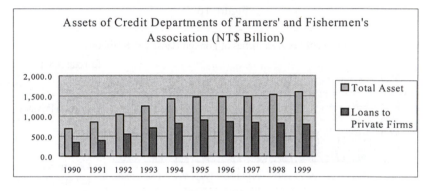

Figure 16-h

To gain a further understanding of the relative importance of these financial intermediaries in transferring funds from the public to the industrial sectors, the pie charts in Figures 17 and 18 depicts the distributions of total assets and outstanding loans among these eight intermediaries in 1998. Figure 17 illustrates the distribution of total assets, and Figure 18 illustrates outstanding loans.

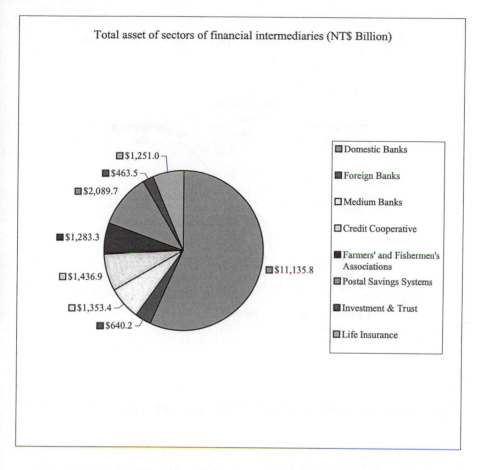

Figure 17 Distribution of Total Assets among Eight Types of Intermediaries

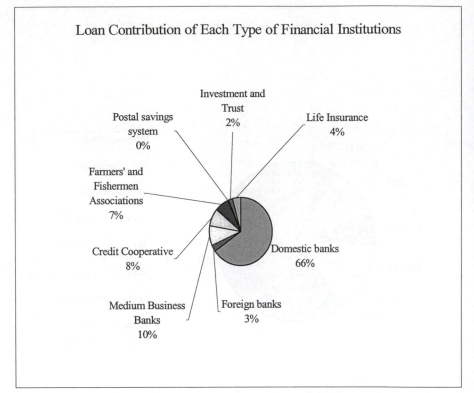

Figure 18 Distribution of Loans Outstanding among Eight Types of Intermediaries

To illustrate the relative importance of these institutions to the development of Taiwan's industries, we also chose to describe the relative importance of these institutions in terms of four measures: number of headquarters, number of branches, total assets, and total outstanding loans. The number of headquarters can be an indication of competition; the greater the number, the greater the competition. The number of branches, on the other hand, can serve as an indication of quality of service—the more, the better. Total assets reveal the public acceptance of a particular type of financial institution. Finally, outstanding loans represent the commitment of the financial institution to allocating funds in the interest of the public. The profile of these financial institutions is summarized in Table 3.

Type	Number of Headquarter	Number of Branches	Total assets (NT$ Billion)	Loans outstanding (NT$ Billion)
Central Bank	1	1	4,140	2 (to government)
Central Depository Insurance Company	1	1	18.6	0
Central Reinsurance Company	1	1		
Domestic banks	47	2,288	18,080	9,588
Foreign banks	41	70	900	383
Medium Business Banks	5	288	1,179	765
Credit Cooperative Associations	50	416	1,035	547
Credit departments of Farmers' and Fishermen's Associations	314	1,020	1,603	793
Postal savings system	1	1,296	2,912	4
Investment and Trust companies	3	36	269	127
Life insurance companies	31	108	2,420	764
Bills finance companies				0
Securities finance companies				0
Total	495	5,525	32,556.6	**12,973**

Table 3 Summary of financial institutions of Taiwan as of December 1999

As shown in Table 3, the primary loan fund providers are domestic banks, with total loans of 9,588 billion NT dollars, or about 74 percents of all outstanding loans. The next most important providers are the credit departments of the Farmers' and Fishermen's Association, the medium business banks, and the life insurance companies, respectively.

Even though the credit departments of the Farmers' and Fishermen's Association, as a whole, have lent 793 billion NT dollars, they are not an important source of funds for most PC/IC firms. These credit departments primarily are interested in real estate mortgage loans. Since most PC/IC firms do not invest much in land, they are not favored by the FFA.

Note that the postal savings system has total assets of 2.9 trillion NT dollars; however, has outstanding loans of only 4 billion. This is because the postal savings system is prohibited from extending loan to individuals or businesses. The postal savings system is required by regulation to deposit all of its funds in the Central Bank.

Medium business banks have been an important source of mid-term funds for most PC/IC firms. For firms that apply for loans at medium business banks, the government may provide bank loan guarantees. Credit cooperatives are active in real estate loans and are relatively conservative about lending to high-tech industries.

For high-tech industries, the investment and trust companies have become an important source of funds. As an example, the China Development Corporation has been very aggressive in both lending to and investing in PC/IC firms. These have done very well in their investments. Even though there are only three investment and trust companies in Taiwan at present, they have earned the confidence of investors and have accumulated 269 billion NT dollars in assets.

Foreign banks also play an important role in providing loans to local companies. Loans by these branches of foreign banks amount to 383 billion NT dollars; however, it is worth noting that foreign banks have played down their role in local lending somewhat. This is evidenced by the fact that the lending ratio, defined as the ratio between total loans to total assets, declined from 59 percent in 1990 to 43 percent in 1999. The lending ratio was at its lowest level of 41 percent in 1997 when the Asian financial turmoil began.

Foreign banks in Taiwan have adjusted to the society very well. We show in Table 4 two interesting ratios; namely, the public-source ratio (PSR) and the intermediary ratio (IR). The PSR measures the degree to which a bank is able to absorb public savings in funding its total assets and is the ratio between public savings and total assets of that bank. The IR of a bank is defined as the ratio of total outstanding loans to public savings in that bank and measures how active a bank is in playing its role of financial intermediary. An IR ratio of one indicates that public savings in that bank have been totally funneled to borrowers. Thus, an IR ratio of one would imply that the institution is a genuine financial intermediary.

Year	PSR (%).	IR (%)
1990	23	253
1991	21	295
1992	24	249
1993	23	215
1994	25	189
1995	28	172
1996	32	146
1997	37	113
1998	41	107
1999	45	93

Table 4 Public Savings Ratio and Intermediary Ratio of Foreign Banks

Over the 10-year period, the average IR percentage for all financial institutions in Taiwan was 77 percent. the IR for an average foreign bank was 253 percent in 1990, and this ratio declined almost steadily, with the exception of 1991, to 91 percent in 1999. As to how foreign banks sustained those high IRs, we learned through interviews with some of the foreign banks that they had encountered two obstacles. First, they had difficulty in attracting local deposits. Second, they were limited by regulations regarding their capital movement. To expand their presence in the local loan market, foreign banks had resorted to local money markets for funds. By continuously rolling over short-term debt securities, they raised sufficient funds to support their expanding loan business and were very successful. Some of these loans had gone bad, however. In addition, the risk of rolling over short-term debt securities is high, even for foreign banks known for their expertise in risk management. Foreign banks now are becoming more popular among depositors, especially among those who had been frightened by local bank runs. Foreign banks are noted for better internal control and are less subject to interference from various sources.

Table 4 indicates that local depository money now funds more of foreign banks' assets—from 23 percent in 1990 to 45 percent in 1999. They also reduced their loan portfolio from 59 percent in 1990 to 43 percent in 1999. The ratio of IR had declined from an unusual number of 259 percent to a relatively normal level of 93 percent.

The Primary Bond Market. Businesses in Taiwan are not active in issuing bonds to raise funds. Various reasons have been offered for this phenomenon. One of the reasons cited is the Ministry of Finance's relatively stringent regulations concerning issuance of bonds. Currently, business firms need to maintain a period of good performance to be eligible for issuing bonds. Another reason is the low liquidity of bonds in the secondary market. Trading in bonds is very inactive, and bonds simply are not popular among most investors in Taiwan. The following table shows the number of bond issues and the total value of bonds outstanding in Taiwan in each year from 1989 to 1999. There are three types of issuers in Taiwan: the government, the corporate sector, and foreign institutes.

Year	Government Bonds		Financial Debenture		Corporate Bonds						Foreign Bonds			
					Common		Convertible		Total Amount	Growth Rate(%)				
	I	OSN	I	OSN	I	OSN	I	OSN			I	OSU	OSY	OSN
1989	64	212.02	3	0.25	42	43.35	-	-	43.35	-	-	-	-	-
1990	25	169.06	2	5.38	39	48.78	2	2.50	51.28	18.3	-	-	-	-
1991	26	327.64	3	11.60	36	52.20	10	6.79	58.99	15.0	1	300	-	-
1992	31	533.60	5	18.51	35	50.11	20	12.56	62.67	6.2	2	600	-	-
1993	35	707.74	-	-	29	37.14	20	10.65	47.79	-23.7	3	600	30	-
1994	34	787.11	-	-	23	22.71	18	9.32	32.03	-33.0	3	600	30	-
1995	38	860.95	-	-	28	41.79	16	6.95	48.74	52.2	4	600	30	26
1996	42	995.05	-	-	95	108.34	17	15.99	124.33	155.1	5	600	30	96
1997	44	1,034.40	-	-	188	177.21	44	41.90	219.11	76.2	7	300	30	294
1998	45	1,042.00	-	-	487	298.61	70	85.18	383.79	75.2	11	-	-	631
1999	50	1,243.82	-	-	907	386.17	79	65.5	451.67	17.7	18	-	-	911

Table 5 The Number of Issues and the Total Value of Bonds Outstanding in Taiwan

Source: The SEC, Ministry of Finance, Taiwan, ROC, 2000
OSN : Outstanding(NT $Billion) OSY : Outstanding(YEN $Billion) OSU : Outstanding(US $Million) I : Number of Issues

Note: 1. Financial debentures are traded in the OTC market only. 907 common corporate bonds with a total amount of NT$386.17 billion are traded on the OTC market. Of 79 convertible corporate bonds, 68 with a total amount of NT$59.39 billion are listed in the Taiwan stock exchange. The other 11 convertible corporate bonds with a total amount of NT$6.11 billion are listed in the OTC market. **2.** Except the paperless government bonds with an amount of NT$20 billion issued in June 1992, all government bonds and foreign bonds are allowed to trade concurrently in the TSE and OTC. **3.**The bond securities above are listed either on TSE or OTC market.

In addition to domestic bond issues, there is an increasing interest in the issuance of bonds in European bond markets. Most firms that have taken advantage of the European bond markets are PC/IC firms, which have a profound interest in the use of convertible bonds (the ECB). European capital markets have offered several favorable terms that Taiwan firms found to be irresistible. First, interest rates generally are very low because of the call option embedded in the ECB. Second, special deals can be arranged between the issuers and the buyers of ECBs so holders of these ECBs can vote along with management when ECBs are converted to stocks. The latter benefit could be very attractive to Taiwan's management teams.

Table 6 reports ECB issues in the past seven years. The number in each cell indicates the total value of ECB issues that year. The number inside the parenthesis indicates the number of issues in a particular year. It is clear that most ECBs are denominated in US dollars. ECB values fluctuated significantly during the period. Japanese-Yen-denominated and the Swiss-Franc-denominated bonds have lost favor among Taiwanese firms because of the relatively strong value of these two currencies in recent years.

Year	1994	1995	1996	1997	1998	1999	2000
US$ denominated	1,484 M (12)	250 M (1)	775 M (8)	2,244 M (16)	852 M (9)	475 M (5)	1,110 M (6)
Swiss Franc *denominated*	504 M (9)	40 M (1)	0 (0)	50 M (1)	0 (0)	0 (0)	0 (0)
JP Yen *denominated*	4 B (1)	0 (0)	3 (1)	12.5 (1)	0 (0)	0 (0)	0 (0)

Table 6 The Issues and the Values of Taiwanese' ECB Outstanding
Source: Grand Cathay, Taipei, 2000

The Primary Stock Market. The stock market has played an indispensable role in the growth of Taiwan's PC/IC firms. Investment and trading in stocks have been termed "the national sport" in Taiwan in the last 15 years. This vividly describes the popularity of stocks among average people. Heated activity in the secondary stock market has, in turn, built up momentum in the primary stock market. Most PC/IC firms took advantage of the popularity of the stock market and successfully raised large amounts of capital during this period, as depicted in Figure 2 earlier. Table 7 gives some statistics of interest regarding the issues of new equities in the TSE and the OTC.

Year	(TSE Listed Companies)					OTC Companies					Unlisted Companies	
	No.	CI	CGR	PV	MC	No.	CI	CGR	PV	MC	No.	CI
1989	181	439.23	24.60	421.30	6,174.16	1	0.17	-	0.17	1.35	318	449.55
1990	199	533.33	21.42	506.43	2,681.91	4	1.45	752.94	1.45	8.39	567	645.42
1991	221	643.08	20.58	616.71	3,184.03	9	3.78	160.69	3.78	10.52	717	766.81
1992	256	761.09	18.35	735.63	2,545.50	11	4.47	18.25	4.47	9.79	803	1,019.28
1993	285	908.37	19.35	891.02	5,145.41	11	3.96	-11.41	3.96	9.61	852	1,133.67
1994	313	1,099.81	21.08	1,071.10	6,504.37	14	9.79	147.22	9.79	26.92	917	1,204.80
1995	347	1,346.68	22.45	1,324.62	5,108.44	41	173.01	1,667.21	173.01	245.73	999	1,218.17
1996	382	1,661.27	23.36	1,626.80	7,528.85	79	264.13	52.67	264.13	833.46	1,110	1,345.51
1997	404	2,106.29	26.79	2,066.32	9,696.11	114	314.89	19.22	314.89	1,026.86	1,501	1,462.06
1998	437	2,734.07	29.81	2,696.66	8,392.61	176	382.39	21.44	381.39	887.63	1,810	1,518.79
1999	462	3,083.02	12.76	3,056.54	11,803.52	264	514.76	34.62	504.96	1,468.44	2,018	1,609.6

Table 7 The New Issues of Stocks in the TSE and the OTC

CI : Capital Issued   CGR : Capital   Growth Rate (%)   PV : Par Value   MC : Market Capitalization

Units: $NT Billion

Source: The SEC, Ministry of Finance, Taiwan, ROC, 2000

Note:

1. 13 Companies are listed as full delivery stocks and traded under separate bracket with a total par value of NT$ 42.93 billion. **3** List Companies are suspended stock trading by TSEC with a total par value of NT$ 17.34 billion. **2.** 1 TDR is listed in TSEC with a capital amount of USD $19.3 million and a market value of NT$ 12.85 billion.

Venture Capital Firms. Venture capital (VC) firms are another source for some PC/IC firms in Taiwan. Though the total amount of funds provided by VCs is not large compared to that provided by the banking system or the stock market, it nevertheless helped many new ventures survive their first few years. The VC industry experienced its fastest growth during the past three years, and we expect the trend to continue for the coming five years.

The concept of venture capital firms was introduced into Taiwan from America roughly in 1982. In 1983, the Executive Yuan put into effect Projects for Promoting Venture Capital Investment Enterprises and Regulations of Governing Venture Capital Investment Enterprises and formally allowed domestic enterprises to establish VC firms in Taiwan. The first venture capital firm in Taiwan was established in November 1984.

To stimulate the establishment of VC firms, the government designated NT$800 million from the Development Funds of the Executive Yuan as seed funds for prospective ventures. The response was great, and the fund was depleted in a very short time. The government then provided a second seed fund of NT$1.6 billion. The government's move roused the awareness and willingness of the public to invest in domestic VC firms. Since then, venture capital investment has played an increasingly important role in the development of high technology industries in Taiwan.

As depicted in Table 5, the number of venture capital firms in Taiwan grew from one in 1984 to 153 in 1999. Their accumulated capital increased from 200 million NT dollars in 1984 to 103 billion NT dollars in 1999.

Tax Incentives and its Consequences on the Portfolios of VC Firms. As part of the effort to promote venture capital firms, Taiwan's government offered generous tax incentive programs. Individual or corporate investors were entitled to a 20 percent tax concession upon investment in strategic industries. Although this program has been replaced by the Statute for Encouragement of Investment and the Statute for the Upgrading of local Industry, this benefit has been preserved.

To qualify as a venture capital firm and be entitled to tax benefits, a venture capital firm has to invest at least 70 percent of its funds in so-called high-tech companies, as defined by the government in item 4 of Regulations Governing Venture Capital Investment Enterprises. According to a survey done in 1999 by the Taiwan Venture Capital Association, IC and PC companies alone have received 53 percent of venture capital fund.

Year	Number of VC Firms	Capital Accumulated (NT$ Billion)
1984	1	.2
1985	2	.4
1986	3	1.2
1987	6	1.8
1988	9	3.3
1989	13	5.3
1990	20	8.9
1991	22	10.6
1992	24	11.8
1993	27	13.6
1994	28	14.7
1995	34	18.7
1996	47	25.5
1997	72	42.6
1998	107	72.9
1999	153	103.1

Table 5 The Growth of Taiwan's VC Industry

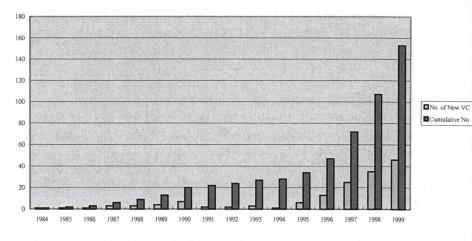

Figure 18 Number of Venture Capital Firms

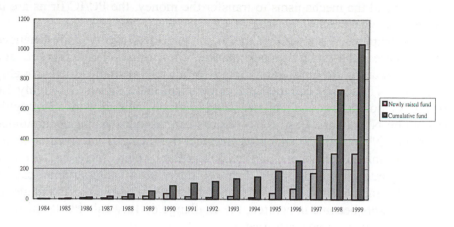

Figure 19 Newly Raised and Cumulative Fund of Venture Capital Firms

Sources of Funds for VC Firms. Generally, pension funds and insurance companies are major providers of funds for VC firms in developed countries, but this is not the case in Taiwan. Insurance companies and various banks had been prohibited from investing in VC firms, but in 1994, the government permitted them to invest in VC firms. Currently an insurance company is allowed to invest up to 25 percent of its capital in a VC firm; for banks, there is a ceiling of five percent of the capital to be invested.

5. Concluding Remarks

In this chapter, we reported the financial strength that has sustained the growth of Taiwan's PC/IC industries. It is commonly known that the development and growth of an industry requires a constant influx of funds. Taiwan's PC/IC firms are very fortunate in two aspects. First, the economy of Taiwan has been very strong for the past 30 years and in this time a positive trade surplus has enabled Taiwanese investors to invest heavily in the stock market. Second, the financial system in Taiwan is relatively healthy. Even though academia has debated the issue of the efficiency of Taiwan's financial markets, there is no doubt that public funds have been effectively transferred to the manufacturing sectors. With a plentiful supply of money and the mechanisms to transfer the money, the PC/IC firms are in very good environment to blossom.

This chapter has shown that the major providers of funds are financial intermediaries, the primary stock market, the primary bond market, and venture capital funds. Outstanding loans for all intermediaries totals roughly 13 trillion NT dollars. The total par value of all listed stocks is roughly 3.6 trillion NT dollars, and the total par value of all outstanding bonds is roughly 450 billion NT dollars. Lastly, the venture capital industry has accumulated 110 billion NT dollars. Thus, on the surface, the financial intermediaries are still the dominant providers of funds. In recent years, there has been an increasing interest among IC/PC firms to make use of international capital markets for raising funds, and we expect the trend to continue. As the global capital markets become integrated, the challenge of Taiwan's PC/IC firms to raise funds may become even greater.

References

[1] Baumol, William J. and Alan S. Blinder, *Economics: Principles and Policy*, Fifth Ed., Harcourt Brace Jovanovich, 1991,
[2] AREMOS, *The National Income Database*, Taiwan, 2000
[3] AREMOS, *The Production of Industries in Taiwan Database*, 2000
[4] AREMOS, *The Financial Sectors in Taiwan Database*, 2000
[5] AREMOS, *The Financial Statements of Listed Companies Database*, 2000
[6] AREMOS, *The Stock Market Database*, 2000
[7] Published materials, the SEC, Ministry of Finance, 2000

Part 5: Education and Government Policy

Chapter 11

The Industrial Park: Government's Gift to Industrial Development

514 516

532

538

L63

(Taiwan)

Pao-Long Chang

Institute of Business and Management
National Chiao Tung University
Taipei, Taiwan, R.O.C.

Chiung-Wen Hsu

Industrial Economics and Knowledge Center
Industrial Technology Research Institute
HsinChu, Taiwan, R.O.C.

1. Introduction

Taiwan's government has been instrumental in the country's growing success in technology. The first step in transforming Taiwan's economy was for the government to establish a science-based industrial park, the Hsinchu Science-Based Industrial Park (HSIP). Taiwan built this park for the sole purpose of making high-technology industries a reality in a country whose traditional economic bases no longer seemed adequate.

Taiwan realized the major factors for developing high-tech industries were workers highly trained in science and technology, an advanced technology, and the swift acquisition and absorption of information. Because of this, Taiwan selected Hsinchu as the site for its science-based park. Academic and research organizations in Hsinchu, such as the National Chiao Tung University, National Tsing Hua University, and the Industrial Technology Research Institute (ITRI), provided human resources to help factories break through the bottlenecks of technology and provided convenient and rapid transportation.

After 20 years, the Hsinchu Science-based Industrial Park is recognized by domestic and foreign businesses as a crucial factor in Taiwan's growth. As it enters the 21st century, Taiwan needs to maintain its economic growth through concentrating on and accelerating the growth of high-tech industries [1]. This chapter describes the policies that created the Hsinchu Science-based Industrial Park as it promoted high-tech industries to both businesses and investors. It concentrates on five major factors—technology resources, human resources, capital demand, profit margin, and the operational environment.

2.   Industrial Development: The Logical Option

Industrial development for economic growth can result from the judicious use of a country's resources as it determines how it can prosper in a global economy. In the mid-1970s, Taiwan realized the limitations imposed by its scarce natural resources and the small scale of its domestic market. Taiwan's industry in the 1950s had focused on commodities; in the 1960s industries were dominated by exporting for light industries. At the time, research and development activities were rare in both industries and academic communities [1].

Because of its limited natural resources and small domestic market, Taiwan decided a logical course was to develop technology-intensive industries. Following this course required that the Taiwanese government help its industries evolve its economic base. To accomplish this, the government enacted such measures as subsidizing and developing research institutes, granting preferential taxes for industrial research and development, and enacting financial incentives for investment and development.

In addition to technology, developing high-tech industries required investors and a place to breed. In the 1960s, the science-based industrial park was considered an effective instrument for development, as it supplied a locus around which technological development could cluster. Taiwan adopted this idea after the success of America's Silicon Valley, located near Stanford University. Silicon Valley's reputation was established by the research abilities of its professors, the quality of its graduates, and the high-tech industries that flourished in this environment. After Taiwan had developed light industry, created foreign exchanges with import substitutes, and encouraged exports by establishing the Export Processing Zone, the government decided to establish a science-based industrial park (SIP) to build on these bases and develop high-tech industries. In this way, Hsinchu Science-based Industrial Park (HSIP) was established adjacent to the National Chiao Tung University, National Tsing Hua University, and the Industrial Technology Research Institute.

It has been 20 years since the Taiwan government decided to develop high-tech industries. In that time the semiconductor, computer, communications and opto-electronic industries have prospered from their link with HSIP. The policy of utilizing science-based industrial parks for development is expected to benefit Taiwan's future growth in high-technology industries.

Hsinchu Science-based Industrial Park. Enterprises were not in a position to develop high-tech industries themselves; therefore, the government adopted models from advanced countries to establish an environment that would develop and motivate high-tech industries. HSIP was created to provide an environment suitable for science and technology research, with comfortable living facilities, and that was conducive to investment in high-tech industries. The goal was to attract investors and technical personnel from home and abroad to upgrade the nation's industrial technological capability and help high-tech industries take root in the R.O.C. On July 27, 1980, the Science-based Industrial Park Installation and Management Regulation was announced, and in September 1980, HSIP was established. In April 1983 and June 1990, the second and third stages were launched as HSIP expanded. At the end of 1999, 605 hectares of land had been developed, but because of the speedy growth of high-tech industries in the area, more land was needed. In the fourth stage the Chunan and Tungluo sites were added, adding 117 hectares and 353 hectares, respectively [3].

Firms that wished to enter HSIP had to be approved to set up, manufacture, research, and develop high-tech products that could develop Taiwan's industrial base. The park's administration stipulated other requirements as well, which included employing or cultivating domestic science and technology personnel, reaching a certain level of research and laboratory equipment, and not producing pollution. In addition, the enterprises were to meet one of the following conditions:

(1) Have the ability to design and develop products;
(2) Manufacture products that already had been researched and developed.
(3) Produce with the potential for development and innovation.
(4) Have a well-established research institute to engage in innovative research and development.
(5) Be able to import and cultivate high-tech personnel in the production line and need large amount of investment and development.
(6) Benefit the economic construction or national defense in Taiwan.

The science-based industries set up and operated in HSIP fall into the following categories [4]:

1. Integrated Circuits: The integrated circuit (IC) industry has been the fastest growing industry in HSIP. It includes design, manufacturing, material, packaging testing, and processing equipment for integrated circuits.

2. Computers and Peripherals: The computer and peripherals industry includes computer systems, storage equipment, input equipment, output equipment, network equipment, special software, and related mechanical and electrical components.

3. Telecommunications: The telecommunication industry in HSIP imported four categories of products—telecommunication systems (including telephone sets, modems, and switchboards), microwave systems and components, fiber optics systems and components, and satellite communication systems.

4. Opto-electronics: The opto-electronic industry in HSIP imported opto-electronic system components (e.g. TFT flat displays, color display tubes, CD-ROM drives, digital still picture cameras, contact

image sensors, photoelectric semiconductors, photodiodes) and optical system components such as instruments and lenses.

5. Precision Machinery: The precision machinery industry imports automation systems (e.g. CNC tool machines, industrial controllers, robots, aquatic knives, vacuum instruments, factory information automation systems) and automation components such as castings and surface treatment components.

6. Biotechnology: The biotechnology industry in HSIP imports vaccine reagents, medical appliances, inoculating vaccines, etc.

Since HSIP was founded in 1980 to the end of 1999, it had attracted 292 high-tech firms, with a total of 82,778 employees and a total capital of NT$618.3 billion. After 20 years' development, HSIP has become the most important area for high-tech industries with a ratio of R&D expenditures to revenue far beyond that of the entire manufacturing industry. The flourishing growth in HSIP has been reflected in revenue, number of firms, invested capital, employee productivity and educational level, and R&D expenditures, as expanded upon below [5].

Revenue and number of firms. The revenue of firms in HSIP was initially NT$3 billion in 1983 and grew to NT$650.9 billion in 1999. It grew 217 times, with an average annual growth rate of 46 percent (Figure 1). HSIP's rate of output value to that of the whole manufacturing industry grew from 0.15 percent in 1983 to 8.63 percent in 1999. The biggest output value is the IC industry, which constituted 55 percent of HSIP's total output value in 1999. The second largest was the computer and peripherals industry, followed by the opto-electronics and telecommunications industries. The precision machinery and biotech industries were just beginning, so their output values were small (Figure 2).

There were 17 firms operating in HSIP in 1981; this number had grown to 292 by 1999 (Figure 1). Most of these—118—are IC firms, which comprise 40.4 percent of the firms in the HSIP. The next most numerous are the computer and peripheral industries, which had 51 firms in 1999.

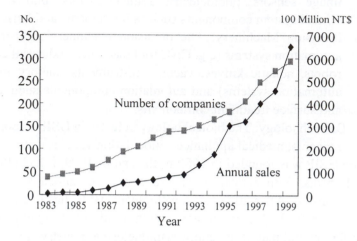

Figure 1: Number of firms and combined sales in HSIP

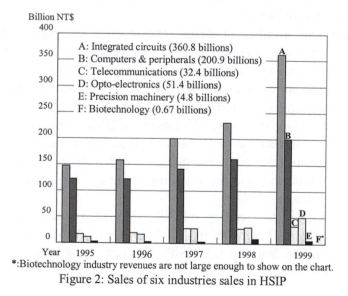

*:Biotechnology industry revenues are not large enough to show on the chart.

Figure 2: Sales of six industries sales in HSIP

Amount and source of invested capital. The total amount of invested capital for HSIP firms was NT\$2 billion in 1983. This grew rapidly to

NT$566 billion in 1999, a growth rate of 44.4 percent per year. The biggest source of investment was domestic, followed by foreign capital (Figure 3). Foreign capital constituted more than 20 percent of total capital investment between 1986 and 1991. After 1998, domestic capital exceeded 90 percent of total capital.

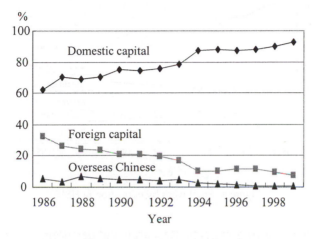

Figure 3: Capital sources in HSIP

Employees and productivity. The number of employees in HSIP firms rose from 1,216—or 0.06 percent of manufacturing employees—in 1983 to 82,822—or 3.43 percent—of manufacturing employees in 1999.

The educational level of employees increased as well in this time. In the early stages half of the employees had a high school education; the number with high school educations has decreased to 30 percent as more employees have obtained at least a junior-college level of education. As shown in Figure 4, more than 60 percent of employee have junior college degrees or above. The number of employees with masters degrees has increased significantly, reflecting the increase in educational levels needed for these types of business. The higher educational level correlates with higher productivity. Comparing the number of employees with the output value, the number of employees in HSIP was 3.43 percent of the total number of manufacturing employees, but these employees accounted for 8.63 percent of the total manufacturing output value. The average productivity of employees in HSIP was NT$2.06 million in 1986, and this grew to NT$7.86 million in 1999. The average annual growth rate was 11.86 percent.

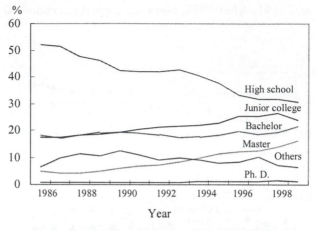

Figure 4: Employees by education in HSIP

R&D and recruiting experts. Research and development are the lifeline for the survival and expansion of high-tech industries, and firms in HSIP emphasized research and development. The average ratio of R&D expenditures to sales had been more then four percent in the past years and reached 7.03 percent in 1998. This rate exceeded that of the electronics industry as well as the whole manufacturing industry. In the decade from 1989 to 1998, the ratio of R&D expenditure to sales was between 1 and 1.4 percent. In the electrical and electronic machinery industry in the five years from 1994 to 1998, the ratio was between 2.1 percent and 2.9 percent [6]. R&D expenditures in HSIP in 1998 reached 31.8 billion, which constituted 28.5 percent of the R&D expenditures for the entire manufacturing industry (see Figure 5). HSIP's emphasis on R&D attracted scholars and experts from abroad. Accumulated to the end of 1998, there were 3,056 scholars and experts who took positions in HSIP firms. These returning experts established 109 enterprises.

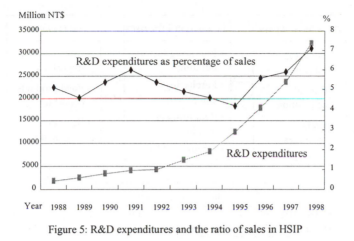

Figure 5: R&D expenditures and the ratio of sales in HSIP

3. The role of science and technology

Taiwan's government and general population realize that science and technology will play a key role in the 21st century to meet the challenge of developing the country. At first it was impossible for individual enterprises to carry out the necessary innovation and high-tech development with their limited resources. Government not only provided the assistance to develop high-tech industries that could compete internationally, it also constructed a suitable environment for investing in research and development. It did this through many strategies, including favorable taxes, loan assistance, and training of personnel. The flourishing development of HSIP became the motivator and engine for the development of high-tech industries in Taiwan

The main purpose of establishing the science-based industrial park was to promote the development of high-tech industries. Taiwan's government carried out the essentials to develop high-tech industries and encourage the firms or founders in this path. HSIP's policies can comprise four aspects of decision-making by the firms: investments, production, sales outcomes, and basic environments (see Figure 6).

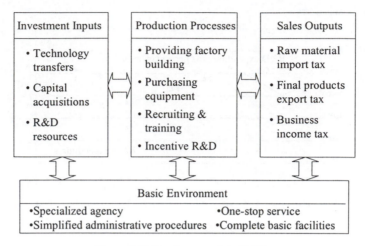

Figure 6: Policy framework in HSIP

Encouraging investments. HSIP encouraged investments through technology imports, fund obtainment, and utilization of academic and research resources [7]. Technology imports were encouraged from foreign and overseas Chinese investors by granting certain protections. Foreign and overseas Chinese investors enjoyed the same rights and privileges as investors who were ROC nationals and could hold a 100 percent ownership in HSIP enterprises. They also could enter into a joint venture with the ROC government or local enterprises. Investors could invite the ROC government to participate in equity investments of up to 49 percent of the total capital for an approved investment project. Agencies that could participate in equity investments on behalf of the ROC government were the Scientific & Industrial Development Fund or other development funds such as the Development Fund of the Executive Yuban. These investors could apply to have their profits, capital gains, and interest from their investments remitted overseas.

The ROC government guaranteed that an HSIP enterprise would not be expropriated within 20 years after the commencement of its business if 45 percent or more of the enterprise's stock was owned by foreign and overseas Chinese. In addition, after one year of investing had passed, foreign investors could remit out their entire invested capital at one time. Investors could contribute a patent right or technical know-how as an equity investment, but that value was limited to 25 percent of the total capital investment. Lastly, ownership rights and intellectual property rights were protected by law.

A science-based industry could apply to the Bank of Communication for a low-interest loan to purchase equipment for constructing factories. The interest rate on these loans is approximately two percent lower than bank prime rates. The amount of such a loan could not exceed 80 percent of the capital required to purchase the equipment, or 65 percent of the total cost of the investment project. The maximum period for repayment of such a loan is 10 years including a grace period of one to three years. When enterprises in HSIP imported machinery equipment for their use, the import tax and commodity taxes were exempted. In addition, businesses in HSIP enjoy an accelerated depreciation rate on equipment.

When a science-based industry uses its earnings to purchase or replace machinery, equipment or transportation facilities to produce goods, or upgrades to conform to industrial safety or sanitary standards, stockholders are exempt from paying income tax on newly issued stock certificates for the year the recapitalization took place. Shareholders must pay income tax on those stocks if they are subsequently transferred. Industries designated by the ROC government may retain earnings of up to 200 percent of their paid-in capital. Profits in excess of this are subject to a 10 percent tax, and the remainder may be retained and is not required to be distributed.

After deciding to enter the science-based industrial park, firms faced the issues of factory buildings, facilities, manpower, and research and development activities. The government was prepared to assist in these start-up issues. [7]. To shorten set-up time, the government offered standard factory buildings to be rented. If the standard building was not satisfactory, a firm could rent the land and construct its own building. Once an enterprise in HSIP built a new factory or requisitioned a building through the Science-based Industrial Park Administration (SIPA), property taxes were exempted. SIPA was established in 1980 to oversee the operations and management of HSIP.

Sales and outcomes incentives include import duties, export taxes, and profit-seeking enterprise income taxes [7]. No import duties can be levied on machinery, raw materials, fuels, supplies or semi-finished products imported by an HSIP enterprise for its own use, and the importer is not required to file for exemption for import duties. Business taxes are computed at a rate of zero percent for goods and services exported by an HSIP enterprise, and no commodity taxes can be levied. Newly established science-based industries enjoy a five-year exemption from the profit-seeking enterprise income tax. A science-based industry may, within two year of the date on which it begins to market its products or renders services, select a fiscal year in the four-year period beginning on said date for a fiscal year in the four-year period beginning on said date for a continuous five-year period of exemption from the profit-seeking enterprise income tax fiscal year.

Encouragement of research and development is also important for developing high-tech industries, and the government offered several incentives to promote R&D. The SIPA provides grants for innovative technological research and development activities undertaken by a science-based industry that has been duly registered and is operating in the HSIP. To apply, an industry must submit a comprehensive plan for R&D activities over the next five years. If approved, the industry may receive up to NT$5 million for each project. The amount for the grant, however, may not exceed 50 percent of the total cost required for the project. In addition R&D expenses may be credited against income tax to a certain limit. Import duties on machinery and equipment used on R&D can be exempted, and the donation of R&D equipment is tax-deductible.

When a science-based industry carries out a capital expansion project, it also enjoys some tax advantages. Income generated from the new facilities may be exempt from the profit-seeking enterprise income tax for four years. Alternatively, a business can apply 15 percent of the cost of new production or servicing equipment as a credit against the profit-seeking enterprise income from the newly added facilities for five years. After the tax exemption period expires, the profit-seeking enterprise income tax and its surcharges can not exceed 20 percent.

Human resources. Recruitment and training of high-tech personnel is another critical aspect of high-tech industries. The number of domestic high-tech personnel in a HSIP industry should grow annually and comprise 50 percent of the work force or above within three years from the day a product is marketed or a service provided. Employees are encouraged to attend domestic academic institutes to take related courses and training, or to obtain a higher education. The government subsidizes academic research institutes to train high-tech personnel.

Interchange about instruments, facilities, and personnel are encouraged between firms and academic research institutes. Nearby academic institutes such as NTHU and NCTU assist in academic research and supply and train manpower. The nearby applied research institute ITRI provides help in research and development; in fact, ITRI was charged with promoting domestic industrial technologies. ITRI receives R&D projects from the government, then transfers them to industry for commercialization.

Incentive policies for basic environments. A specialized supervising committee in HSIP supervises, guides, and decides policies and provides one-stop services and public facilities. This committee is composed of the vice-president of relevant ministers in the government and experts. The chief of the committee is chairman of the National Science Council. The committee submits policy decisions on planning and important issues to Executive Yuan to be authorized [3]:

The SIPA was established to manage HSIP, to handle operations in the park, and to provide a one-stop service for HSIP enterprises. SIPA's duties include encouraging management policies, guiding and servicing businesses, attracting investments, testing products, certifying the place of production, examining telecommunication trades, certifying evidence of passports, verifying and transferring immigrant affairs, issuing certificates of tax exemption, issuing business registration and industrial electricity certificates, managing storage and transportation, and bonding warehouses.

SIPA simplifies administrative procedures such as the cargo automation system. Firms can transact import and export business on an integrated on-line computer system. To improve service quality, a cargo automation system integrates visas, storage, and declarations. It offers one-step freight declarations, 24 hours a day and on holidays to facilitate the timeliness of imports and exports. Waste sorting and recycling are reinforced. In addition, the e-commerce environment and a wide-range frequency ATM were available to enhance competition.

The park provides complete basic facilities, including a stable quality and quantity of water and power. Regarding workers' safety and environmental protections, the park supplies sewage disposal, with safety and sanitation conventions managed by the firms.

Education is a priority in such an environment. A national experimental high school was established to educate children of HSIP employees, to attract investment, and to encourage scholars and specialists to return to Taiwan.

4.   Factors impacting policies and investments

There are five important factors that directly impact high-tech firms' policies and investments—technology resources, human resources, demand for funds, business profits, and the business environments. Taiwan's government policy impacts all five factors:

Technology resources. In the 1970s, when high-tech industries were being developed in Taiwan, few institutions, including academic institutions, had experience in research and development. The demand for technology was great, and in 1973, the government created a subsidy for ITRI to provide basic research for domestic industries to develop technology. ITRI was established to accelerate the development of industrial technologies in Taiwan and was an important technology source for HSIP, which was established in 1980. Firms could count on ITRI to develop technologies for the products or to solve technical problems. ITRI, which was near HSIP, conducted research and transferred it to industry for commercialization. An example is the IC industry [8]: ITRI transferred technology from abroad then assimilated and processed it through in-house R&D activities. After it came into full possession of the relevant technology, ITRI spun off new companies and transferred relevant technology and technical staff to HSIP. In this way, the first domestic IC maker was established—United Microelectronics Corporation (UMC). To accommodate the demands for a foundry for IC designs, ITRI transferred technologies for a plant, and Taiwan Semiconductor Manufacturing Company (TSMC) was formed to provide foundry services to HSIP's IC design companies. This was the first IC specialized foundry company. After ITRI successfully developed sub-micron technology, a DRAM manufacturing company named Vanguard International Semiconductor Corporation was spun off in HSIP [9]. The government put a large emphasis on technology transfer from ITRI to the nascent industries. In the high-tech arena, the best technology transfer is talent transfer, and ITRI was a key source of HSIP electronic and information talents.

As a neighbor of HSIP, ITRI functions similar to a university close to a science-based industrial park in advanced countries, where cooperation between industry and university is extremely close. The establishment of Science Park helped utilize the results of university research. After the growth of HSIP, firms could get their technologies either by transferring them from abroad, through cooperation, or from neighboring NCTU or NTHU.

Initially, then, technology for HSIP firms came from domestic research institutes, enterprises abroad, and the technologies of the founders. Government policies impacted this research and development by subsidizing research institutes to engage in R&D, recruiting talented persons to start businesses, and encouraging firms to be involved in R&D.

The government policy was for ITRI to be rooted in industrial technologies [10], but this had an unexpected consequence for ITRI and HSIP. Some firms recruited ITRI talent to gain the technology and accelerate their commercialization. The effect was that ITRI was unable to effectively accumulate technology for industry as a whole; instead, the technology and staff that developed it were lost to a specific factory. Although this helped some high-tech industries in HSIP start quickly, the industry as a whole lost the benefit of ITRI's innovations. Nowadays, the technical supply from ITRI can't satisfy industries' demands, so companies increasingly depend on the their own R&D. The government has adjusted the research institute's direction to advanced innovations and generic research and development activities, giving industries the responsibility for technological development. Firms in HSIP still access information from IRTI to explore new technology fields; however, ITRI's role has evolved from leading and guiding firms to inspiring innovation and providing information to help technological problem-solving.

As companies recruited ITRI researchers to join them, other ITRI researchers were lured by the success and prestige Taiwan's newcomers had achieved. As a result, many high-level, technically talented persons in the research institute founded businesses in HSIP. In 1982, ITRI personnel founded the first private domestic IC design company, Syntek Semiconductor Co., Ltd. The general manager had been manager of the Digital Circuit Design Department of the Electronics Research and Service Organization

(ERSO)/ITRI, and the R&D manger and layout engineers all came from ITRI. Research personnel also founded Wel Trend Semiconductor Inc. and the Silicon Integrated Systems Corporation (SIS).

In addition to providing the assistance of ITRI, the government provided financial assistance for firms to research and develop innovative technologies. This assistance, which began in 1986, was an important resource for technological competitiveness for industries in HSIP. There were 24 R&D projects subsidized in 1999 at a cost of NT$67 million, which was 28.1 percent of the total NT$241 million R&D expenditure in HSIP. Up to 1999, there were 478 R&D projects subsidized, at a cost of NT$896 million. At the same time, the government provided grants to encourage firms to research and develop key components and products. There were 88 projects approved from July 1992 to June 1999. The total amount of R&D was NT$6.333 billion. The approved subsidized amount was NT$2.472 billion [5].

HSIP firms gradually enhanced their R&D capabilities, and the number of approved patents increased commensurately. Among the top ten approved domestic patents in 1997 were ITRI (296 items), UMC (515 items), and TSMC (178 items). Half of top ten are firms in HSIP [3].

Human resources. Human resources were an important factor in the growth of high-tech industry, and ITRI and overseas recruits provided HSIP's ability to develop and build its expertise. In the early days, HSIP had an urgent need for high-tech entrepreneurial talents and research and development capabilities. As a result, it went abroad to recruit professionals, especially from the Silicon Valley in the USA. This brought in technical abilities, marketing expertise, and information on establishing facilities. In addition, these professionals brought experience in technology transfers, alliances, branch offices, and technical seminars. These recruits imported technology and created high-tech enterprises.

Recruiting talented persons from abroad had multiple positive effects. For the 1980s and 1990s they were crucial in creating and developing industries. Recruited staff developed new products and improved existing products. During the industries' growth stage, especially in the 1990s, there was a continuous influx of new technology, and progress was rapid. Although these talented people were responsible for jump-starting the Taiwanese economy and growing it quickly, domestic Taiwanese felt excluded from these research and development activities, and morale was affected, especially when native

Taiwanese witnessed the high positions and prestige these returning people held. Another issue accompanied these talents' homecoming—intellectual property rights—a subject addressed in another chapter of this book.

The strategy of recruiting overseas personnel turned out to be very advantageous to Taiwan, as scholars and experts from abroad returned to Taiwan to make a significant contribution to the economy. Some 3,056 scholars and experts returned to Taiwan and established 109 companies in HSIP. The technology and concepts they brought with them were developed in HSIP.

ITRI's pool of talented people was another key element in nurturing high-tech industries. ITRI at first provided the human resources to help companies meet their recruiting targets, access on-the-job training facilities, and attract talented employees. Taiwan's government selected Hsinchu—a suburban area that housed NCTU, NTHU, and ITRI—as the SIP site to serve the high demand for talented skills. As mentioned above, many HSIP companies are spin-offs of ITRI, and significant numbers of NCTU and NTHU graduates joined HSIP companies. In this way, the government's decision to place a science-based industrial park in an area of universities and research institutes achieved its goals.

HSIP's need for both middle- and entry-level talents has grown progressively. In the early days, HSIP only recruited experienced talents. ITRI had been a key resource for HSIP's middle-level talents, and NCTU and NTHU graduates were the key entry-level talents. New graduates usually joined ITRI to get experience, then switched to HSIP after three to five years of experience. As HSIP companies matured, they began hiring new graduates and providing in-house training. New graduates were eager to join HSIP companies because of their bright futures, good salaries, and good benefits.

ITRI's mission has been to upgrade Taiwan's overall technological capabilities. ITRI had a significant influence on HSIP in its infancy, as described above. As the HSIP companies mature and develop their own R&D capabilities, the government wants to retain ITRI talents and focus on research and development. HSIP companies, on the other hand, prefer to hire the key members from ITRI ongoing projects. Although this expedites commercialization of a specific technology, it is not in line with the idea of open technology. In the future, the government may require companies to pay a licensing fee in receiving ITRI key talents.

To satisfy the demand for training, SIPA, NTCU, NTHU, and ITRI jointly conduct professional technical training programs in such fields as sub-microns, communications and computers, computer automation, management, second majors, and evening on-the-job training. These training programs are designed to meet the needs of technological development and industrial human resources, upgrade human resources, and shorten pre-job training time for new hires. From 1993 to 1998, 24,390 person participated have been trained. Of these, 18,271 have been in management programs and topical seminars [5]. This attendance reflects HSIP's demand for training in the face of rapid technology changes. Recently, the Ministry of Education authorized a Masters-Degree-on-the-Job program to make higher education more accessible.

Employee Stock Option Plans. To attract more talented employees, HSIP companies have adopted employee stock option plan. Employee stock option plans allow profit sharing among employers and employees, simplifying employer-employee relationships, and reducing company internal transaction costs. On the positive side, these plans help attracted and retain talented employees.

Before 1990, when HSIP companies adopted stock options, employees were not particularly eager to participate because of the risk involved in domestic high-tech industries. As companies started making profits and went public, stock options became attractive to employees—so much so that many employees make job-changing decisions based on the stock options or use them to negotiate a better financial package. This has been advantageous for employees with professions with a shorter technology life. Employees are productive capital for current companies and assets for future companies. The ability for employees to change easily to other companies puts more emphasis on building professional management. It is not unusual in HSIP to switch jobs frequently, to share companies' information, transfer corporations' technology, and to form strategic alliances. This mobility allows companies with bright futures to acquire capital investments through informal connections.

The impact of government on capital acquisition. Initially HSIP provided land for companies to build factories because capital acquisition is relatively difficult, especially in risky high-tech industries. Gradually the capital market has built up in Taiwan sufficiently to provide needed capital.

The following looks at the impact from the government providing seed and operation capital.

In the beginning, the government, working with the Chiao Tung Bank, provided loans to and/or invested in high-tech industries, and an Executive Yuan Development Fund was set up to invest in high-tech industry. At the same time, the government established regulations for venture capital investments to encourage investment in high-tech industries. This law significantly influenced HSIP high-tech investments; in 1996, nine domestic venture capital investment enterprises invested in 10 out of 32 HSIP companies [11].

Of the government's monetary measures to stimulate high-tech investments, the most significant in reducing capital costs has been low interest loans. The Chiao Tung Bank, with its start-up investment promotions, helped a lot companies to build factories in early stages. Today, most companies have their own factories, so there is not the urgency for start-up investment funds. These low-interest loans, along with sharing risks, have been a controversial issue, especially when they are perceived as favoring a business or industry.

HSIP companies, promoting their business operations and professional management teams, now go public in the domestic market to acquire needed capital. In addition to founders' capital, venture capital, bank capital, and corporate investments, employee stock options have helped supply capital.

One of the major sources of capital is other companies. HSIP electronic companies set up or invest in companies that manufacture their key components, establishing a closed network among companies. Once the market is prosperous, this network can quickly give birth to a new company. In this situation, it is relatively easy for the company to capture capital, increase market share, assure product deliveries, recruit high-level managers, and set up management systems to reduce the cost and time involved in starting a new company.

The government helps company acquire operating capital by shortened depreciation periods. In this way, HSIP companies with heavy equipment investments enjoy tax deferrals and interest-free operating capital. These measures have been particularly advantageous for electronic and optic companies. As acquiring capital resources in the domestic market becomes easier, relaxing of the regulation regarding retained earnings distribution has fewer benefits for HSIP. Also the government provides mid- and long-term low-interest loans for investing in high-tech key products. This practice can encourage companies to invest in risky, advanced high-tech products and can still satisfy the companies' capital needs.

Taiwan has adopted free import and free commodity taxes to reduce equipment and material costs for high-tech companies and to increase their profits. These measures encourage HSIP companies to import materials, components, apparatus, and equipment from developed countries. Purchasing foreign goods can bring related technologies; on the other hand, it can decrease the demand for domestic products. The effect on high-tech industries is generally positive because these companies rely heavily on specialized equipment, and the domestic equipment market for this equipment has not yet been developed. On the other hand, these measures block opportunities for domestic materials, components, and apparatus industries and put control of material supplies in the hands of foreign suppliers. These drawbacks impacted DRAM/SRAM industries in early 1990 and semiconductor equipment industries in recent years.

The government also offers several significant tax deduction incentives—five (or four) years' exemption from taxes, accelerated depreciation, tax ceilings, investment tax deductions, and others. Also the government gives duty and commodity tax refunds to companies that produce exports. In return, companies enjoy higher after-tax profits because of these tax incentives.

The biggest benefit for newly established firms is the five- or four-year exemption from enterprise income taxes for income generated by the new facilities. This allows companies to avoid an income tax that averages 25 percent in Taiwan. Taiwan government considers this 25 percent income tax loss as an investment because it encourages HSIP companies to invest in high-tech industries. These tax incentives have achieved their goal of encouraging investments in high-tech industries and allowing HSIP companies to quickly accumulate needed capital. Critics on the fairness of these tax incentives to HSIP companies are not uncommon. HSIP companies are allowed to invest only in risky high-tech industries and are expected to contribute significantly to upgrading the level of domestic industry technology. Since these companies could act as a locomotive pulling a train of high-tech followers and could face high R&D costs, the government has assumed the responsibility of sharing risks and costs with them.

The government gives five years of tax exemptions for companies to create emerging technology in key industries. The government exempts new facilities investments in HSIP for four years. Almost all HSIP companies have qualified for both incentives. Because the government only provides tax incentives to selected industries, critics say these tax incentives interfere with market functions and impact resource utilization efficiencies. In recent years HSIP companies have grown rapidly and produced large profits, and the fairness of these incentives have been questioned. The tax incentives need to be considered in a larger, international perspective. Compared to Singapore and Mainland China, Taiwan's government gives less attractive tax incentives to high-tech industries. With globalization, liberalization, and profit-oriented business cultures, if Taiwan's government did not offer competitive tax incentives to high-tech industries, domestic tech companies would move to foreign lands. In addition, foreign high-tech companies would have no interest in investing in Taiwan. Debate on the fairness of tax incentives for high-tech industries needs to consider the influence of high-tech industries, their impact on non-tax policies, and competing foreign tax and non-tax incentives.

5. Government policies and the environment

The government has adopted such measures as one-stop services, simplified administrative processes, and improved basic facilities in order to provide a favorable foundation for high-tech industries to grow. This section analyzes the impact of the government's export service and environmental protections on HSIP companies operations.

For export services, Taiwan's government provides a time-saving, automated cargo system for HSIP companies. This automated cargo system uses a HSIP network that connects SIPA, warehousing, companies, custom services, post offices, and software inspection stations. The network provides cargo imports/exports approval processing, warehouse operations, and converting approval paperwork and cargo shipping lists into an electronic data format. This network also connects to the Trade-Van transport network for fast and convenient transportation. These services increase companies' competitiveness and simplify government administration.

With SIPA providing a one-stop service that saves time and reduces red tapes, companies can focus on their core businesses and increase their market shares. Both domestic and foreign high-tech companies are eager to move into HSIP so they can access these services, reduce business operation costs, provide good living environment for their employees, and enjoy information exchanges. The government provides these services from a NT$ 400 million annual budget.

Taiwan's government environmental protection measures cover sewage disposal, waste recycling and classification, safety, and sanitation. However, HSIP's rapid growth, high-tech product cycle reductions, and fabrication processes put increasing demands on environmental protection measures. The IC fabrication process consumes large amounts of lethal chemicals. In the future, TSMC and UMC will be the world leaders in the IC fabrication process and will pioneer the handling of IC fabrication process lethal chemicals. Semiconductor industries create serious concerns in industrial safety and sanitation, sewage disposal, air contamination by lethal chemicals, and health hazards in the clean room. Since half of HSIP revenues comes from the semiconductor industry, environmental protection has become an important issue. A bundle of relevant environment protection measures was recently enacted. On July 1, 2000, the Semiconductor Industry Air Contamination Control and Emissions Standards became effective. HSIP has more stringent environmental protection standards than other businesses in Taiwan, but environmental protection will become an increasing challenge for the HSIP.

6. Conclusions

In the 1980s, Taiwan adopted various measures as catalysts to encourage the development of high-tech. After 20 years, the high-tech industry has grown from seeds into trees in HSIP and from trees into woods in Taiwan. As high-tech woods have rooted in Taiwan, these original catalysts have had little effect in growing high-tech woods into forests.

In the last 18 years Taiwan's government has invested NT$18 billion in software and hardware in HSIP to attract high-tech companies. In general, Taiwan has achieved its goal, establishing a high-tech industrial zone. Now, however, it has come to a point to question the wisdom of the government's continuing to invest in HSIP. It is logical to consider investing in a new science-based industrial park (SIP) for a better return. HSIP could serve as a model for other SIPs in Taiwan. The government has adopted measures to nurture opto-electronics, telecommunications, biotechnologies, and precision machinery industries. These government measures serve as catalysts to these high-tech industries as they did to the semiconductor industry. Whether these new high-tech industries will sprout in Taiwan depends on market demand; however, if Taiwan did not adopt these measures, it would miss the chance for these industries to sprout when the market demand arrives.

Taiwan government did not hand pick the electronic and information industries as target industries. These two industries enjoyed the fastest growth because of strong market demand. Global demand for electronic and information products—especially in the semiconductor industry—has driven high-tech industrial growths. In the foreseeable future, telecommunications and the Internet will become the next high-tech industries to be developed in Taiwan. Because of its exclusive involvement in HSIP, however, the government has been unable to capitalize on these opportunities because of land shortages, water shortages, a declining environment, insufficient public facilities, clogged transportation, and long waiting lists for companies to move into HSIP.

After 20 years of devotion to developing HSIP, Taiwan's government receives good comments for its efforts to develop high-tech industry and is working on policies to create or enhance high-tech industry development. There are limited resources, however, and policies will affect the way these resources are allocated. Since various policies compete for the same resources, the government needs to establish a pre-request list and a time limit for each policy, monitor each policy's status and effects, and make any necessary adjustments. Indeed, frequent policy adjustments are hard to make and can discourage high-tech companies. With the benefits from its experience with HSIP, future government policies on SIPs can better benefit high-tech industries entering their growth stages.

Current planning focuses on meeting demands for technology innovation and providing a better environment for R&D employees in high-tech companies. The goals are to promote an industrial zone that offers an attractive domestic entrepreneurial R&D environment, invites investments from multinational corporations to develop high-tech industries, and provides integral software and hardware facilities.

A second SIP, the Tainan Science-based Industrial Park (TSIP), was approved in February 1995, and in 1997 high-tech companies began moving in. In October 1998, the first TSIP high-tech enterprise started production. By March 2001, 57 high-tech companies had been approved, 25 of these invested by HSIP companies. In 2000 TSIP reached NT$24.7 billion. Comparing TSIP's early growth rate with that of HSIP, it is obvious that the lessons learned from HSIP have been utilized in TSIP.

References

[1] *The Annual Report of Science and Technology R.O.C. 1996.* National Science Council, Executive Yuan, Taiwan, R.O.C., (NSC), 1998.

[2] *Development of Industries in Taiwan, Republic of China.* Industrial Development Bureau, MOEA, 1995.

[3] *National Science Council Review 1997.* National Science Council Executive Yuan, Taiwan, R.O.C., (NSC), 1998.

[4] *The Annual Report of Hsinchu Science-based Industrial Park.* Science-based Industrial Park Administration, NSC, 1998.

[5] *The Statistics Quarterly Report of Science-based Industrial Park.* Science-based Industrial Park Administration, NSC, 1999.

[6] *Science and Technology Indicators.* National Science Council, Executive Yuan, Taiwan, R.O.C., (NSC), 1998.

[7] *Enforcement Rules of Science-based Industrial Park Installation and Management Regulation.* National Science Council, Executive Yuan, Taiwan 1987.

[8] Chang, P.-L., Shih, C., Hsu, C.-W., 1993. "The Formation Process of Taiwan's IC Industry-method of Technology," *Technovation* 14 (3), 161-171.

[9] Chang, P.-L., Hsu, C.-W., 1998. "The Development Strategies for Taiwan's Semiconductor Industry, *IEEE Trans. Eng. Management* 45 (4), 349-356.

[10] *MOEA Technology Development Program 1998.* Ministry of Economic Affairs, Taiwan, R.O.C., (MOEA), 1999.

[11] *White Book of Industrial Technology 1998* (in Chinese). Ministry of Economic Affairs, Taiwan, R.O.C., (MOEA), 1999.

Chapter 12

Intellectual Capital in the Information Industry

Gwo-Hshiung Tzeng and Meng-Yu Lee

Institute of Management of Technology
National Chiao Tung University
HsinChu, Taiwan, R.O.C.

1. Introduction

In traditional economic theories, land, labor and capital are the essential industrial activity investments, and their costs are computed as rent, wages and interests. These models may have been applicable when agriculture and industry were the main economic forces, but with the advent of high-tech industry, classic investment essential theories and their applications are inadequate. Traditional theories fail to evaluate human brainpower, or "intellectual capital," which is the knowledge and skill that provide a competitive advantage[1]. Richness of intellectual capital and human resources is the reason that Taiwan, a small island with few natural resources and only 23 million people, was able to become the third largest world producer of information hardware[2] and achieve the 19th highest GDP among the 192 countries of the world.

---

[1] Stewart, 1997, p1.

[2] Lin, Nov. 30, 1999, "Taiwan's Information Hardware Production Value Posts Dramatic Growth of 18% in 1999 (Chinese Edition)".

This chapter explains the role of human resources in the development of Taiwan's technology industry from two viewpoints. First, it analyzes the sources of Taiwan's competitive advantage—the high ratio of R&D employees, the investment in education and advanced R&D, the cultivation of high-tech professionals, the establishment of special training for technical professionals, and the recruitment of foreign-educated talents. Specific data compare conditions in Taiwan with those in the US, Germany, Japan, Thailand, Malaysia, Indonesia, Philippines, Singapore, Hong Kong and Israel.

The chapter also examines the HsinChu area's contribution to the development of information industry, especially the impact of the National Chiao Tung University (NCTU), National Tsing Hua University (NTHU), the Industrial Technology Research Institute (ITRI), and the HsinChu Science-Based Industrial Park (Science Park). These institutions created a human resource network that led to the flow and distribution of techniques, information, capital and creativity. This network propelled the development of the Taiwan high-tech industry. This chapter also focuses on the ACER Group and its positive effect on the general industrial development of Taiwan.

In the end, the chapter shows that to achieve continued progress in the high-tech industry Taiwan needs the proper distribution and development of human resources and larger research and development staffs and budgets.

2. Human Resource Factors For Leading to Industry Development

Human resources clearly contributed to the rapid development of Taiwan's information industry. Human resource factors that led to the development of Taiwan's high-tech industries include the following:

2.1 The market economy system

After Martial Law was lifted in 1987, Taiwan began to move away from a planned economy to a market economy system, using the "invisible hand" of the market to resolve poor market efficiencies. Despite several problems with its execution, the advantages of this change outweighed the disadvantages, and the change was the primary factor behind Taiwan's US$ 13,000 per capita GNP achievement[3].

Incentive is the nature of economy. With the right incentives, a market economy can stimulate human self-interest and urge individuals to pursue their personal interests, while at the same time promote general socioeconomic growth.[4] In a market economy system, assets and labor utilization are relatively efficient. A match of asset ownership and usage rights will maximize asset surplus values. A user with asset ownership rights will attempt to maximize the surplus value; on the contrary, a user owning no assets rights will not exert efforts to preserve the maximal surplus value. For instance, a taxi driver who owns the taxicab will drive more carefully and avoid damaging the cab than a driver who only rents the cab.

In the labor market, performances are the basis of wages or compensation for skills. Hence, one may urge individuals to work hard to optimize their own interests, reduce supervisory costs and uplift society.[5] High-tech companies in Taiwan have implemented a profit-sharing system that not only allows employees to own shares, thus integrating stockholder ownership and usage-rights, but also issues stocks based on employee performance, thereby upgrading the operating performance and overall social values. This indicates that "matching asset ownership and usage rights" and "performance-driven salary remuneration" are effective tools in a market economy.

History has now shown that the market economy is more effective than Marx's communism. During the competition between the US and the USSR in the 60s, it was not clear which system was more effective; but now we know. USSR Premier Nikita Khrushchev postulated the slogan "bury the US with communism," but in 1999, his son Saichi Khrushchev made a choice that undermined the premier's stance when Saichi pledged loyalty to the US as its citizen.[6]

Powered by the market economy, Taiwanese have chosen maximal utility for themselves and used industry to gain prosperity and enrich their lives.

---

[3] General of Budget, Accounting and Statistics Directorate website (www.dgbasey.gov.tw), May 19 2000.

[4] Milgrom and Roberts, 1992, p 166.

[5] Milgrom and Roberts, 1992, p. 256.

According to a Lausanne Institute for Management Development survey, Taiwan has the fourth highest home ownership rate worldwide.[7] This pursuit of individual excellence also created maximum utility for the society, creating social prosperity and industrial development.

2.2 Cultural diligence

A special cultural characteristic has fostered the Taiwan economic miracle. Taiwanese work extended hours and possess an enterprising spirit that would "rather become the king of a small domain than a follower in a huge dominion." Other hallmarks of the Taiwanese character are a flexible work mode and a high degree of environmental adaptation. On one hand, these characteristics laid the cornerstone for the traffic congestion and environmental pollution of Taiwan; on the other hand, they fostered the strong work involvement and flexible workmanship with which the Taiwanese coped with industrial changes to achieve "the Taiwan miracle."

These personality traits are also reflected in multinational surveys. Taiwan holds the world's record for longest work hours and lowest unemployment rate and has a sense of entrepreneurship that is second only to Hong Kong and Finland. Taiwanese also show the highest flexibility and adaptation skills for environmental changes and possess such values as industry and willingness to innovate(See Table 12.1.). Professor Yu makes a clear presentation and analysis of the Taiwanese human nature in Chapter 13.

2.3 Contributions of education, research and overseas Taiwanese

The primary factors propelling the high-growth information industries of Taiwan are the high percentage of R&D personnel, cultivation of professionals needed for national competition, and recruitment of foreign-educated professional talents. This chapter evaluates this aspect of development.

---

[6] China Times General Editor, May 27, 1999.
[7] Institute for Management Development (IMD), 1999. p. 506.

2.4 The special HsinChu setup

The communication, exchanges and interaction of the people working in the companies, educational establishments and research institutes of the HsinChu area form a human resource that has fostered the growth of Taiwan information industries. Later, a special feature of this topic is going to presented later in this chapter.

3. Contributions of Education, Research and Overseas Taiwanese

The high number of trained professionals has been a primary factor for Taiwan's high-growth of information industries. Aside from the higher percentage of R&D personnel in research institutes, other important cornerstones of Taiwan's industrial development are the number of R&D professionals with a higher education, skilled workers with high school educations, special technology training courses and institutes, and returning overseas Taiwanese. In the following, we evaluate their contributions to the industrial development, as well as compare Taiwan with other nations to highlight the special aspects of Taiwan's case.

3.1 Higher percentage of R&D personnel

In 1996, the annual R&D budget of Taiwan was NTD 138.6 billion (US$ 4.62 billion), that was 1.85 percent of the GDP. Of this, 42.5 percent was invested in government agencies, and more than 75 percent was invested in the field of engineering. A total of 72,000 researchers was employed in government authorities, universities, research institutes and companies[8]. The educational attainment, age structure and fields of research of these researchers are shown in Fig. 12.1, 12.2 and 12.3.

---

[8] National Science Council, 1997, p. 14 , p. 28.

According to the Lausanne Institute for Management Development (IMD) analysis of the 1999 World Competitiveness Report, Taiwan had a competitive advantage in the "R&D personnel" and "R&D budget" categories. In the "corporate R&D personnel," "corporate R&D personnel ratio," "technical human resource availability," and "share of R&D budget in GDP" categories, it was found that Taiwan performed quite well in the R&D field. A comparative study of the above-mentioned categories is provided in Table 12.1.

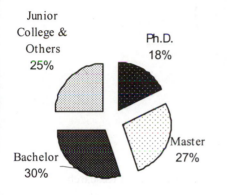

Data source: National Science Council,1997

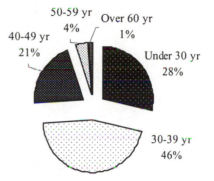

Data source:National Science Council, 1997

Fig. 12.1 1996 R&D Manpower by Degree   Fig. 12.2 1996 R&D Manpower by Age

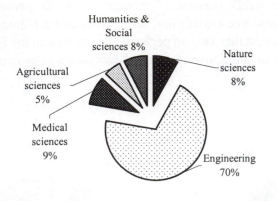

Fig. 12.3 1996 R&D Manpower by Field of Research

The input from R&D personnel, together with suitable R&D budgets, helped spur innovations in products and manufacturing processes. These factors not only support the rapid growth of companies and industries, but also improve Taiwan's competitiveness. Emphasis on R&D personnel and expenditure stimulates business growth and the ability to create new technology and products.

3.2 Advanced Education

Advanced educational institutions in Taiwan include junior colleges, colleges, universities and graduate schools. Junior colleges teach applied sciences and develop skilled technicians. Colleges, universities and graduate schools provide further research and develop professionals. Taiwan had a total of 191 higher education establishments in 1999, and 44 of which were universities. The student population for the same year exceeded 200,000 students, including 1,300 doctoral students and 15,000 masters students.[9] In 1997, around one-fourth of educational resources, or NT$126.5 billion (US$ 4.22 billion), including government budgets and private investments, were directed into higher education.[10] Since 1995, some national universities have funded 15 percent of their budgets, to reduce universities' reliance on government and to upgrade their operating flexibility and efficiency.

The success of advanced education in Taiwan has been striking. Compared with other nations, Taiwan has a higher registration ratio, with education and training in accord with national competitiveness requirements, as indicated in Table 12.1. This advanced education achievement has been one of the primary factors in the vigorous development of the information industry.

3.3 Senior high school education and compulsory education

Senior high school educational establishments include senior high schools, senior vocational schools and comprehensive senior high schools. The senior high school course curriculum consists mainly of academic subjects aimed at preparing students for a higher education. The senior vocational school course curriculum teaches skills, cultivates professional ethics and develops trained technicians. The comprehensive senior high school course curriculum is a combination curriculum offering both academic and vocational courses. As of 1999, there were 452 of these establishments in Taiwan, producing around 250,000 graduates.[11]

---

[9] Ministry of Education website (www.edu.tw), 2000b.

[10] Ministry of Education 1998, p. 39.

[11] Ministry of Education website (www.edu.tw), 2000c.

Country	Science and education		Science & technology and youth		Public expenditure on education		University education		The education system		Advanced education enrollment		Secondary school enrollment	
	Score	Rank	Score	Rank	US$	Rank	Score	Rank	Score	Rank	%	Rank	%	Rank
Taiwan	7.533	5	7.6	2	653.4	25	7.07	6	6.978	4	12[13]	12	94[14]	5
Hong Kong	6.036	20	6.071	21	655.7	24	5.54	23	5.228	22	—	—	71	23
Singapore	8.727	1	7.727	1	857.5	22	7.58	3	7.636	3	—	—	—	—
Japan	6.909	11	5.603	30	1360.9	11	3.09	45	3.868	35	—	—	96	2
South Korea	4.259	39	5.963	24	370.8	28	2.81	47	2.963	44	13.7	6	96	2
Philippine	4.909	31	5.709	29	23.4	44	6	18	5.891	15	9.6	19	60	24
Indonesia	4.571	36	5.111	39	13.9	45	3.11	44	2.952	45	—	—	42	30
Thailand	4.721	33	5.302	36	114.6	40	3.98	43	3.907	33	—	—	—	—
Malaysia	7.020	9	6.531	14	237	32	5.55	22	5.776	17	5.2	26	—	—
Israel	7.107	6	7.286	4	1029.4	17	7.32	4	6.071	13	—	—	—	—
United States	5.073	28	5.982	22	1385.6	10	6.62	11	4.909	25	16.2	2	89	12
United Kingdom	4.850	32	4.617	44	1009.7	18	5.23	27	4.25	32	9.4	20	92	9
Germany	5.846	22	5.949	25	1404.2	9	5.51	24	5.615	19	9.4	20	88	14

Table 12.1 Comparison of the National Society, Research and Education[12]

---

[12] For details regarding the index definition and year references, see Appendix 12.1.

	Demographic Characteristics										
Country	Access to property		Working hours		Entrepreneurship		Unemployment		Flexibility and adaptability		Values of the society	
	%	Rank	Hours	Rank	Score	Rank	%	Rank	Score	Rank	Score	Rank
Taiwan	82.5	4	2330	1	7.11	3	2.69	1	7.978	5	7.438	9
Hong Kong	52	31	2312	2	7.61	1	5.3	16	8.246	1	8.702	2
Singapore	80	6	2028	17	6.09	23	3.2	5	8.06	3	8.866	1
Japan	61.7	23	1799	34	3.49	47	4.2	11	5.058	41	7.23	11
South Korea			2253	7	3.96	46	7.4	25	5.352	38	7.926	4
Philippine	79.5	7	2238	9	5.71	31	11.1	36	7.579	8	6.596	23
Indonesia	16.8	39	2121	13	4.32	45	4.68	13	4.921	43	4.54	44
Thailand			2245	8	5.23	39	3.41	8	6.8	21	6.094	30
Malaysia	85	3	2157	11	5.8	29	4.9	15	7.163	15	7.49	8
Israel			2128	12	6.84	6	8.7	31	7.088	16	7.088	14
United States	64	22	1916	21	6.2	18	4.5	12	7.37	10	7.626	6
United Kingdom	67	18	1839	28	5.17	40	6.6	21	5.833	33	6.383	25
Germany	37	37	1699	46	5.69	32	9.6	34	4.872	44	6.359	26

Table 12.1 (Cont.)

[13] Data based on IMD reports. 1999 Advanced Education Registration Ratio is 15.03%.

[14] Ministry of Education website (www.edu.tw), 2000c. 1999 high school education registration ratio in Taiwan is 96.52%.

| | Research and Develpoment | | | | | | | | | | | | | |
| Country | Availability of it skills | | Total R&D personnel nationwide | | Total R&D personnel nationwide per capita | | Total expenditure on R&D | | Total R&D personnel in business enterprise | | Total R&D personnel in business per capita | | Business expenditure on R&D per capita | |
	Score	Rank	1K persons	Rank	Per1K population	Rank	%	Rank	1K persons	Rank	Per1K population	Rank	US$M	Rank
Taiwan	7.3.3	8	98.6	13	4.565	15	1.922	12	65	10	3.01	8	154.84	20
Hong Kong	6.509	20	—	—	—	—	0.288	40	—	—	—	—	5.16	35
Singapore	7.091	11	12.1	37	3.226	20	1.489	22	7.9	28	2.121	17	236.59	13
Japan	6.267	24	891.8	3	7.091	3	2.829	2	598.5	3	4.689	3	735.25	2
South Korea	4.833	43	135.7	10	2.98	22	2.791	3	89	8	1.954	19	317.38	14
Philippine	8.182	2	15.6	32	0.239	38	0.218	41	1.7	41	0.026	43	0.04	44
Indonesia	4.127	47	239.7	8	1.322	31	0.092	45	33.7	16	0.186	34	0.5	42
Thailand	4.814	44	12.8	35	0.216	39	0.18	44	0.8	42	0.013	43	0.71	41
Malaysia	5.755	34	4.4	41	0.2.5	40	0.199	42	2.4	39	0.108	36	6.56	33
Israel	7.636	4	—	—	—	—	2.29	8	6.4	31	1.224	23	181.52	16
United States	7.138	10	962.7	1	3.729	18	2.546	6	764.5	1	2.962	9	573.69	4
United Kingdom	5.717	35	279	7	4.795	14	1.9	13	139	7	2.364	14	247.16	12
Germany	6.205	26	459.1	5	5.624	8	2.401	7	291.8	5	3.556	6	418.1	6

Data source: Institute for Management Develop (IMD), 1999.

Table 12.1 (Cont.)

The principal contribution to the Taiwan information industry of a senior high school education is the foundation it establishes for advanced education and the development of technicians. These technicians are mainly senior vocational school graduates, whereas senior high school graduates are mainly trained for higher education. Senior high schools provide English language classes, teaching the basic English language skills needed in high-tech work environments such as reading English labels, instructions for machinery, materials, work procedures, or to some extent, conversing in English.

An overview of the Taiwan educational system reveals that, in 1997, the government alloted 18.97 percent[15] of its budget to education; moreover, the 1995 educational fund allocation per person amounted to US$ 653.40, ranking Taiwan number 24 worldwide. Public education enrolment rates reached 98.24 percent[16] in 1999, an achievement that compares favorably with other nations. The incorporation of science into the compulsory curriculum and the development of students interest in technology also fosters the rapid development of science. In terms of satisfying the economic system's requirements, the general education system ranks number four in the world, as shown in Table 12.1.

Educational levels of Taiwanese people over the age of 25 for the year 1995 are shown in Fig. 12.4. The table indicates that 18 percent received higher education; a ratio that is lower than that of Japan, South Korea, the US and Canada, but higher than Mainland China and Singapore.[17]

---

[15] Ministry of Education 1998, p. 41.

[16] Ministry of Education website (www.edu.tw), 2000c, "Population of the Schooling Population".

[17] General of Budget, Accounting and Statistics Directorate website (www.dgbasey.gov.tw), 1999,Others' ratios: Japan 20.7% (1990), South Korea 21.1% (1995), US 47.8% (1995), Canada 21.4% (1991), Mainland China 2.0% (1990) and Singapore 4.7% (1990).

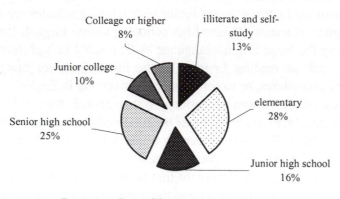

Data source: Dept. of Census Administration, Taiwan

Fig. 12.4 Educational Attainment of Taiwan People over Age 25 (1995)

3.4 Special technology training courses and institutes

Human resource development takes a long time in the formal educational system, and the Ministry of Education must approve any quota changes. Because of these restrictions, formal education was not sufficient to supply the demands of the fast-developing information industries. Many training courses and institutes are available to fulfill the gap between the supply of schools and the requirements of information industries.

The majority of training courses and institutes in Taiwan cater to the requirements of high-tech industries. Among these are training courses of the Institute for Information Industry (III), the National Nano Device Laboratories (NDL), the NCTU Submicro Professional Training Center, and the Second Skill Training Program for College Graduates of the National Youth Commission.

Institute for Information Industry (III) is the biggest information resource training provider in Taiwan and provides in-service training courses for information professionals. In addition to training information industry personnel, it also provides training for communications and network professionals in response to industry changes. Aside from the courses opened to the public, III also conducts in-service training courses in a number of large corporations such as Citibank and Taiwan Fuji Xerox Corp. From 1980 to 1996, III trained more than 175,000 professionals[18], most of whom received full-time six-month training courses.

Parallel to the III's information, communication and network courses, the National Nano Device Laboratories (NDL) located inside the NCTU campus and the NCTU Submicro Professional Training Center offer courses specializing in semiconductor training. NDL annually trains around 730 professionals in engineering, IC technology and semiconductor equipment[19]. The Submicro Professional Training Center admitted over 4,000 trainees in 1999 and trained more than 11,000 persons from 1991 to 1998.[20] The National Youth Commission's Second Skill Training Program for College Graduates and the training courses of other universities or training establishments catering to high-tech industry professionals had fewer trainees in information industry.

During the rapid development of Taiwan's technology industries, these technical training courses and institutes compensated for the inadequacies of the higher education system. Taiwan ranks eighth worldwide for availability of high quality information technology human resources, and a good part of this accomplishment may be attributed to the special technical training institutes.

3.5 Returning overseas Taiwanese professionals

Oversea Taiwanese who returned to resume their careers in Taiwan not only arrived at the right time to provide professional, technical and business management skills for Taiwan's industrial development, they also imported

---

[18] III website (140.92.88.45), 2000.
[19] Chiang, December 23, 1999.
[20] NCTU Submicro Professional Training Center (www.ee.nctu.edu.tw/~submic), 2000.

technological and business concepts. The principal source of this influx was the United States, and their contributions to Taiwan's technology industry is greater than the contributions of other US-educated nationals who later returned to serve their countries. They proved to be extremely useful in terms of both technological expertise and knowledge about managing human resources.

ITRI Director Chintay Shih is an overseas-educated professional who obtained a doctoral degree in electrical engineering at Princeton University and an MBA degree at Stanford University and who observed the industrial development conditions of Taiwan and South Korea. He stated excitedly "Compared with South Korea, Taiwan has many success stories of US-educated Taiwanese returning to work in local industries. Chen Ta-chi of Samsung Electronics Co., Ltd. is one foreign-educated Korean who made significant achievements in the Dynamic Random Access Memory (DRAM) industry in South Korea. But in Taiwan, notable figures in the semiconductor industry such as Nicky Lu in Etron Technology, Ting-hua Ho and Min-chiu Wu of Macronix International Co., Ltd., or Morris Chang of Taiwan Semiconductor Manufacturing Co., Ltd. (TSMC), Ting-yuan Yang and Chin-Cu Chang of Winbond Electronics Corp., Hsiao-ming Liu and Chun-yuan Tu of Silicon Integrated System Corp. are examples of overseas Taiwanese who achieved outstanding accomplishments in the US then returned to Taiwan to serve the local industries. Their contributions for Taiwan were immeasurable."

One of these returning Chinese is Morris Chang, chairman of the board of TSMC. A native of Shanghai, this US-educated senior vice president of Texas Instruments came to Taiwan in 1985 to become director of the Industrial Technology Research Institute (ITRI). In 1987 Chang started his own business, a spin-off company of the ITRI, the Taiwan Semiconductor Manufacturing Company (TSMC). Popularly known as the "godfather of the Taiwan semiconductor industry," Morris Chang introduced his business management experience and professional background to Taiwan and fostered the growth of the semiconductor industry. He created the semiconductor -dedicated foundry industry and made TSMC the fourth largest semiconductor company in the world (1999) and the most valuable company in Taiwan.[21]

The massive influx, partially spurred by a depressed US economy in the early 90s, created a positive effect on Taiwan industries. Table 12.2 shows that the US economic growth rate reached rock bottom in 1991. The same table also shows how the depressed US economy influenced the number of returning Taiwanese; the number rose from 2,800 persons in 1991 to 5,700 persons in 1995 but gradually subsided by 1996. The ratio of graduates returning from the US to all returning graduates rose as high as 91 percent in 1992, an extraordinarily high ratio compared to 74 percent in 1997. When the US economy was flourishing, only a small number of US-educated students returned, hence it may be said that the economic depression played an influential role. Fig. 12.5 shows the inverse relationship between number of returning students and the US economic growth rate.

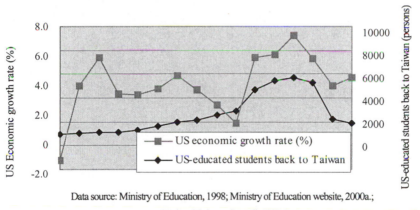

Data source: Ministry of Education, 1998; Ministry of Education website, 2000a.;
National Science Council, 1997.

Fig 12.5 Returned US-Educated Graduates & US Economic Growth

According to the 1998-1999 study by the US Institute of International Education (IIE)[22], 31,000 Taiwanese are studying in the US, the fourth largest

---

[21] Lin. April 21, 2000.
[22] Ministry of Education website (www.edu.tw) , 2000a.

student group in the US. Table 12.2 shows that from 1983 to 1987, the Taiwanese student population even ranked first. This figure is far higher than the number of students coming to the US from Thailand, Indonesia, Malaysia or the Philippines. Table 12.3 indicates that the ratio of Taiwanese students in the US is far higher than that of Japanese or Korean students. Over the years, many of these students would bring back advanced technology and management. They returned either immediately after graduating or after decades working in the US and became a major force in the development of Taiwan's industries.

Year	82	83	84	85	86	87	88	89	90	91	92	93	94	95	96	97
Taiwan economic growth rate (%)	3.55	8.45	10.6	4.95	11.64	12.74	7.84	8.23	5.39	7.55	6.76	6.23	6.54	6.03	5.67	6.68
US economic growth rate (%)	-2.2	3.9	6.2	3.2	2.9	3.1	3.9	2.5	0.8	-1	2.7	2.2	3.5	2	2.8	3.8
Overseas students back in Taiwan (persons)	1106	1257	1329	1350	1583	1920	2296	2462	2963	3264	5157	6172	6510	6272	2760	2526
New US-educated students from Taiwan (persons)	20770	21960	22590	23770	25660	26666	28760	30960	33530	35552	37432	37581	36407	32702	30487	30855
World rank in overseas students in the US	2	1	1	1	1	1	2	2	3	3	3	3	3	4	5	5
Science & eng'g overseas students back in Taiwan (persons)	441	455	440	443	523	634	770	935	1023	1036	1657	1839	1806	1701	776	670
US-educated students back to Taiwan (persons)	932	1079	1158	1142	1334	1637	1984	2150	2580	2888	4681	5472	5716	5262	2200	1875
Ratio of US-educated students back in Taiwan (%)	84	86	87	85	85	85	86	87	87	88	91	89	88	89	80	74

Data source: Ministry of Education, 1998; Ministry of Education website, 2000a; National Science Council, 1997.

Table 12.2 Economic Growth Rate vs. Overseas Students Statistics

Rank of population of students studying in US	Country	Total students studying in the US (persons)	Total population (million)	Ratio of students in US against total population (%)	Rank of ratio of students in US against total population
1	PRC	51,001	1,255.5	0.004062	9
2	Japan	46,406	125.5	0.036977	6
3	S. Korea	39,199	46.4	0.084481	4
4	Taiwan	31,043	21.8	0.142399	1
5	Thailand	12,489	61.2	0.020407	7
6	Indonesia	12,142	203.0	0.005981	8
7	Malaysia	11,557	22.2	0.052059	5
8	Hong Kong	8,735	6.7	0.130373	2
9	Singapore	4,030	3.9	0.103333	3
10	Philippines	2,846	75.2	0.003785	10

Data Source: Institute for Management Development, 1999; Ministry of Education website, 2000a.

Table 12.3 1998 Statistics of Asian Students Studying in US Universities

According to AnnaLee[23] (1990), more than one-third of the engineers in the Silicon Valley were born outside the US, and two-thirds these were Asians (51 percent Chinese), the majority of whom came from Taiwan. Considering the number of Taiwanese students in the US, it became easy to form their own group affiliations, such as the Mt. Jade Science and Technology Association[24] and alumni associations. In the 60s these associations provided learning and employment assistance, but in the 90s their main concerns became technology, capital, business ideas and business management experience. US-educated Taiwanese engineers created an invisible social and economic link between Silicon Valley and HsinChu. The trust and knowledge existing in these associations transcended national boundaries and caused the Silicon Valley

---

[23] AnnaLee, 1999.

[24] Mount. Jade is the highest mountain in Taiwan and in Southeast Asia.

experience to flow into Taiwan, providing Taiwanese industries with human resources as well as capital, technology, creativity and marketing information. This was another major force behind the development of Taiwan's technology industry.

Managers and engineers that returned to Taiwan played a dominant role in developing Taiwan's HsinChu Science-Based Industrial Park. March 2000 statistics indicate that 115 of the park's 297 companies were established by overseas-educated graduates, who comprised around five percent, or 4,000, of the 72,000 employees working in the park.[25]

Another notable individual in the overseas Taiwanese group is Yuan-Tseh Lee -- the 1986 Nobel Prize winner and Academia Sinica President. Lee completed his college and masters education in Taiwan, then went to the US to obtain his doctorate. After 32 years of research and teaching experience and receiving a Nobel Prize, he returned to Taiwan to fulfill the mission of upgrading Taiwan's academic research. He became director of the highest academic research establishment in Taiwan, the Academia Sinica. Lee personally raised funds from corporations to establish the Yuan-Tseh Lee Outstanding Scholar Development Foundation. This foundation subsidizes the salary differences between Taiwan and other countries, attracting successful overseas Taiwanese scholars and experts in the fields of anthropology, biology, botany, etc. to continue their careers in Taiwan. Attracted by equivalent pay of contemporary and Director Lee's encouragement, more than 30 outstanding scholars have returned to Taiwan since 1995 and assumed positions in the Academia Sinica and universities.

Although the scholars and experts that returned to Taiwan under the persuasion of Dr. Yuan-Tseh Lee may not have contributed as much to applied research in the technology industry, their contributions were outstanding in terms of upgrading Taiwan's fundamental research standards. The return of experts in fundamental and applied science research not only created hope for the realization of rapid industrial development, it also laid the cornerstone for longer lasting national and industrial development.

---

[25] HsinChu Science-Based Industrial Park Administration website(www.sipa.gov.tw), 2000.

3.6 Factors of Taiwan's Prominence

The unconditional surrender of Japan at the end of World War II resulted in Taiwan's return to the Republic of China (ROC). The February 28 Incident, White Terror and the Formosa Incident after surrender had a negative impact on knowledge transmission and human resource cultivation in Taiwan. These events were not as devastating, however, as the 10-year Cultural Revolution of Mainland China (Peoples Republic of China, PRC) and the Pol Pot government of Cambodia that killed over millions individuals, mostly were educated elites, and eradicated the intellectual class activities totally [26]. Despite the lingering shadow of the February 28 Incident on the victims' families and the ongoing rehabilitation work from the White Terror, Taiwan was able to preserve its educational system and human resources. The educational system and human resources developed during the Japanese Occupation formed the foundations for higher levels of human resources. This is indicated by the fact that more than 20 public elementary schools celebrated their centennial anniversaries in the past two or three years, and National Taiwan University (NTU) and the National Cheng Kung University (NCKU) are now more than 70 years old. A cross-nation comparative study is provided in Table 12.1 to analyze the factors behind Taiwan's prominence in the international arena.

Compared with Hong Kong and Singapore, the people of Taiwan and Hong Kong are both strongly entrepreneurial; the education systems of Taiwan and Singapore are equally capable of meeting international competition requirements. However, since Taiwan has a much larger population than either Hong Kong or Singapore, Taiwan is capable of producing more researchers and engineers.

Compared to Japan and Korea, there are several factors that enabled the vertical disaggregation and cooperative business relationships in Taiwan's information industries. The university education and compulsory education systems of Taiwan are more capable of meeting the requirements of competitive economic systems. The compulsory education curriculum

---

[26] Lao Human Rights Council, Inc. (home.earthlink.net/~laohumrights/laohdl21.html) July 1,1997, "Genocide in Cambodia and Laos". The Pol Pot regime killed more than 2 million Cambodians during the 1975-1979 period.

includes science courses that direct students' interest toward technology. In addition, higher skilled technicians availability and higher oversea-educated personel help information industries in Taiwan. Besides, Taiwan people are more flexible and adaptable, with a stronger entrepreneurial spirit than their Japanese and Korean counterparts.

A comparison with Southeast Asian nations, namely the Philippines, Indonesia, Thailand and Malaysia, shows Taiwan's higher enrollment ration in advanced education and secondary school, higher emphasis in investing in education, as shown by the relatively higher public education budget. Taiwan's emphasis on education and proper resource investment has been a prime factor in Taiwan's prominence in high technology compared to these four Southeast Asian nations. Taiwan's university and compulsory education also are more capable of meeting international competition requirements. Taiwan's ratio of human resources engaged in R&D, national or corporate, vis-à-vis the total population is higher. John Hsuan, who assumed the position of United Microelectronics Corp. (UMC) Chairman in May 2000, evaluated Thailand's factory investment environment. He stated that "the number of skilled-technical persons in Thailand educates and trains annually is not sufficient to meet the requirements of a wafer factory."

A comparison with Israel, another nation of adept businesspersons facing a high degree of military threat from a neighboring country, reveals that both nations have a high regard for investment in education and human resource cultivation. In terms of entrepreneurship, the people of both nations shows similar personality traits, although Taiwan has a higher ratio of human resources in R&D, as well as more foreign-educated engineers in technology and business management. Hence, compared to Israel, Taiwan has achieved more significant accomplishments in high-technology fields.

It is evident from a bird's eye view of Taiwan that the abundance of high-quality human resources is an important factor in the success of Taiwan's information industries. Taiwan compensates for its scarcity of natural resources through infusing more human resources into R&D work, paying attention to education and training investments, cultivating the human resources capable of meeting international competition, offering special skills training courses, and introducing advanced technology and concepts through returning foreign-educated professionals. These have formed the basis of the fast-developing information industries in Taiwan.

4. The Special HsinChu Community

Relative to the preceding broad view, this section focuses on how the human resources gathered in the HsinChu area have contributed to the development of Taiwan's industries. This is the foremost factor behind the successful development of the Taiwan technology industry. The community formed by the National Chiao Tung University (NCTU), National Tsing Hua University (NTHU), the Industry Technology Research Institute (ITRI), and the HsinChu Science-Based Industrial Park (HSIP) served as the cradle of Taiwan's information industry. This area is popularly referred to as the Taiwan Silicon Valley.

Access to this special community is provided by two expressways, a railway running north-south on one side, and a county road cutting across it. It is 40 minutes away from the Chiang Kai-Shek International Airport (CKS), and around 75 km to its north and south are Taipei and Taichung, respectively. The Keelung and Taichung harbors are around two hours drive from the area, so the area is near international class cities, harbors and airports. The principal reasons behind its Taiwan Silicon Valley tag are not just its accessibility or geographical location, but the close community relationship between neighboring schools, research institutes and the science park.

As shown in Fig. 12.6, there are two universities (three campuses), a research institute (seven offices, five centers, and two institute grounds), four national-class labs and a Science-Based Industrial Park containing almost 300 companies located within a five kilometer radius. The total area is around 840 hectares. Moreover, there are more than 100,000 professionals with higher education working in the community.

The following provides a brief introduction to this special community and explains the interaction among the elements that fostered the rapid development of the technology industry.

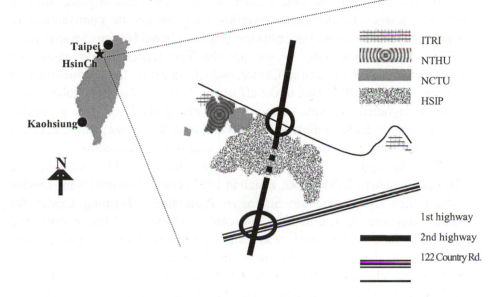

Fig. 12.6 The HsinChu Community Location Map

4.1 NCTU and NTHU

Neighboring NCTU and NTHU have a lot in common. Originally established in Taiwan under the name of noted Mainland China universities, these two universities specialize in science and technology and are transformed toward comprehensive researches. When the central government moved to Taiwan in 1949, it saw military grade nuclear science and peacetime electronics science as the most important directions in contemporary science field. Consequently, NTHU was established in 1956, setting up a graduate school in atomic science; and NCTU was established in 1958 with a graduate school in electronics. The two universities hoped that they would complement each other with breakthroughs in electronics and nuclear research, providing a good foundation for Taiwan's development.

In 2000, NCTU had a faculty of 550 and a student population of more than 9,000. The university is well known for its electronics engineering and computer science. In addition to government support and the contributions of overseas and domestic alumni, plus the original United Nations Special Fund (1961), NTCU was able to set up the Far Eastern Electronics and Telecommunication Training Center, which became the Semiconductor Research Center (SRC). Due to the efforts of local and foreign scholars, SRC not only upgraded corporate technology, but also trained high-tech personnel for the semiconductor industry. The top and middle management executives in Taiwan's semiconductor industry come mainly from this center.

With the support and subsidies of the government, NCTU established the National Submicro Lab in 1992, which in 1993 became National Nano Device Laboratories (NDL) and the Submicro Professional Training Center for further submicro studies. In 1994, Taiwan's first Electrical Engineering and Computer Science College[27] was established, and faculty, students and alumni made significant achievements in electronics engineering, computer science, and telecommunications. NTCU has a solidarity and is an important part of students' lives from the time they enter as students through their careers as alumni, when they help and support each other in the field of high-tech industry.

Parallel to NCTU's achievements in the field of applied engineering, NTHU has excelled in natural science research and studies[28]. In 2000, NTHU had a faculty of 500 instructors and a student population of more than 7,200. The university started as an Atomic Science Research Institution in 1958, with a 1,000 power fountain-type nuclear reactor that was decommissioned in 1993. NTHU has specialized in natural science research and electrical engineering studies. In addition to government subsidies, funding also is provided by the Tsing Hua Fund set up from Boxer Indemnity rebates received during the early years of the university[29].

---

[27] NCTU website (www.nctu.edu.tw), 1997.

[28] Chiang and Chang, May 16, 1999.

[29] NTHU website (www.nthu.edu.tw), 1999

The two universities have established camaraderie through several channels. NTHU and NCTU started a joint "Plum-Bamboo Championship Meet" in 1969. Meet competitions include ball games, relay races, tug of wars, bridge, chess, debates, etc. The effect is similar to the boat rowing contest between Oxford and Cambridge Universities of the United Kingdom. The meet has become a tradition for the two universities, and students and alumni join in with pride. The Plum-Bamboo meets build esprit de corps, interaction, teamwork and rapport between students of the two universities, and these relationships prove to be beneficial in students' careers.

There is both a competitive and cooperative relationship between the two neighboring universities similar to the relationship between Harvard University and the Massachusetts Institute of Technology (M.I.T.). They share teaching and research resources and support and upgrade each other's research and teaching levels. On the other hand, they compete for students and government aid. For instance, the two universities recently aggressively vied for an affiliate College of Medical Science permit from the Ministry of Education. With their mutual competition, support and encouragement, NCTU and NTHU bolstered the development of the HsinChu Science-Based Industrial Park into the Silicon Valley of the West Pacific.

4.2 The Industry Technology Research Institute

At its establishment in 1973, the ITRI was only an electronics research and development center; however it became a quasi-government corporation as a result of the accelerated upgrading of industrial technology and the promotion of industrial performance. Now after 27 years, ITRI is composed of seven research institutes and five technology development centers handling research in electronic engineering, computer science, telecommunications, machinery, chemistry, aerospace, biotechnology, and material science. The research infrastructure employs more than 6,000 people, whose educational attainment and tenure for 1999 are shown in Fig. 12.7 and 12.8, respectively.

For years, the ITRI served as a bridge between academic studies and industrial applications and provided strong backing to develop industries. Successful technology transfer operations were numerous, benefiting companies such as UMC, TSMC, Winbond Electronic Corp., Sampo Corp.,

Mustek Systems Inc., and Chunghwa Picture Tubes. Achievements in electronics, computer science, telecommunications, machinery, chemistry and medicine were outstanding.

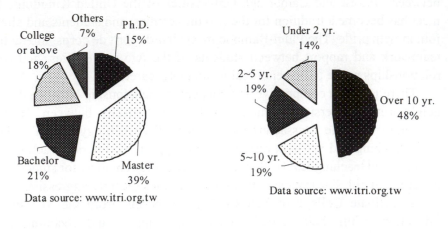

Data source: www.itri.org.tw

Data source: www.itri.org.tw

Fig.12.7 1999 ITRI Employee   Fig. 12.8 1999 ITRI Employee Tenure

Education Attainment

The institute's One-on-One Policy asked each research project to gain equivalent funding from both the government and companies, thereby creating a close association between institute technology and industrial requirements. Under this arrangement, the technologies ITRI developed were able to meet the needs of industries, providing them the means to operate successfully and profit. The total research budget for 1999 reached NTD 16.54 billion (US$ 551 million), 52.8 percent of which came from the government technology project income and 47.2 percent of which came from joint development contracts with businesses.[30]

As the private sector experienced human resource shortages, numerous high-tech companies recruited ITRI personnel through attractive salary and stock dividend packages; however, ITRI was still able to retain a team of personnel dedicated to research by offering them more space for individual

---

[30] Data source: Technology Service Department of ITRI, 2000.

development, a free and open work environment, and a humane management system.

4.3 HsinChu Science-Based Industrial Park

HsinChu Science-Based Industrial Park was developed in 1980 under the government's high-tech industry development policy. The government provided complete infrastructure facilities and investment incentives to attract companies into the park. As of March 2000, there were 297 companies in the park conducting research and production operations, including TSMC, UMC and ACER Group. The park generated an income of NTD 650.9 billion (US$ 21.7 billion) in 1999, posting a growth of 43.1 percent over the previous year. It is regarded as the most successful science-based industrial park outside of Silicon Valley, California. The park contains three national-grade labs, including a national high-speed computer center, a synchronized laser research center and a national aerospace planning center. The status of the industries in the park is shown in Table 12.4. The average age of the 82,000-plus employees in the park is 31 years, and around 4,000 engage in R&D. Details of employees' educational background are shown in Fig. 12.9.

Industry	I.C.	P.C.	Telecom.	Opto.	Precision equipment	Biotechnology	Total
1999 revenue (US$ Million)	12026.7	6,696.5	1,079.9	1,712.9	159.8	22.1	21697.9
1999 revenue proportion (%)	55.43	30.86	4.98	7.89	0.74	0.1	100
Ratio of 1998 R&D expense against. total revenue (%)	9.49	3.85	5.52	6.6	3.23	2.15	7.03

Data source: HsinChu Science-Based Industrial Park Administration, 2000.

Table 12.4 HsinChu Science-Based Industrial Park Industrial Statistics

4.4 The Interaction among Universities, ITRI and the Industrial Park

It is only natural that the universities near the HsinChu Science-Based Industrial Park (NCTU and NTHU) would interact constructively with the park. The universities obtain timely information regarding industry requirements and adjust their academic curriculum designs. Case studies provide students with the opportunity to conduct field interviews and do observation work, becoming familiar with the industrial environment. As a result, students often seek employment at the Science-Based Industrial Park after their graduation.

Successful entrepreneurs in the park also both add to the universities'

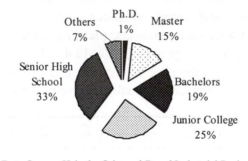

Data Source: Hsinchu Scienced-Based Industrial Park
Administration, 2000

Fig. 12.9 The HsinChu Science-Based Industrial Park Employee

Education Attainment on March, 2000

knowledge base and seek specialized information there. Many of NCTU and NTHU graduate courses, including EMBA, were designed in response to the huge enrollee population coming from the science park. In addition, many seminar speakers come from the HSIP and exchange experiences with members of the audience. Outstanding entrepreneurs also serve as professors, teaching for years without regard for payment. Two good examples are the chairman of TSMC -Morris Chang and the chairman of ACER Group -Stan

Shih. Those two hold chair professor positions at NCTU and taught business management courses at the NCTU Management School in 1999 and 2000. Their classes were full, and students who wanted to take their classes had to enroll through special procedures. The dedication of these successful entrepreneurs went beyond the pursuit of business profitability; these qualities are also manifested in their teaching attitude. Morris Chang would prepare his own teaching materials, then conduct a preliminary rehearsal class with executive managers in TSMC.[31]

Outstanding entrepreneurial experiences are not only conveyed in classrooms but also applied in teaching techniques, course curriculum design, and faculty selection. NTHU awarded Morris Chang an honorary doctorate degree in 1999. He took a seat on the Consultant Committee of the NTHU Technology Management School and introduced his management concepts into the university's curriculum and teaching techniques.

In addition to knowledge and experience, creative ideas and capital flow between campuses and the industrial park, and alumni contribute significantly to the universities. For example, NCTU and NTHU alumni hold most of the executive positions at Stark Technology, Inc., a successful computer service company, and the company provides staff development and venture capital funds. Stark encourages innovative and enterprising students to join with them and help them realize their ideas. Furthermore, with the support of alumnus Robert Tsao, chairman of UMC Group, NCTU was able to conduct special projects, support technology seminars, and subsidize participation of professors in top international conventions and exchange programs with Mainland China. Robert Tsao also donated NTD 15 million to NTHU after playing Chinese chess with former NTHU president Chun-shan Shen. In 2000, the chairman of Microelectronics Technology Inc., Hua-yen Wang, another NCTU alumni, solicited a donation to NCTU of US$ 5 million from Dr. Lee Li, a Taiwanese entrepreneur in the US, then personally contributed US$ 500,000 to NCTU. Their donations were to fund NCTU's network and telecommunications technology studies. TSMC donated about US$6.5 billion for the teaching hall of the Technology Management School in NTHU and also created an intellectual property rights scholarship fund that sponsors outstanding students who wish to pursue a law degree in the US.

---

[31] Chin, Mar. 20, 2000.

In addition to the flow of graduates to the science park, NCTU and NTHU also aggressively introduce research findings to companies in the Science-Based Industrial Park. According to HSIP administration statistics, the research outcome of these two universities led to the establishment of 15 HSIP companies in 1999. Aside from the outcome of their research projects, the two universities also established incubators to assist innovative and technology groups, enabling these groups to successfully start business enterprises under HsinChu's special environment. Besides, NCTU solicited corporate donations for a fund in order to help student groups find entrepreneurial success in technology at HsinChu in 2000.

The HSIP developed another type of interaction with ITRI different to the exchange setup with academic establishments. Under this interaction model, industries provide the capital for ITRI technology research projects, enabling the transfer of ITRI research accomplishments to the electronics, computer and telecommunications industries, creating very significant results. In 1998, ITRI was able to gain 537 patents, develop joint technology ventures with 344 companies, provide 27,825 technology services, transfer technology 538 times, complete commissioned research projects from 1,080 companies and provide seminar training to 82,225 persons[32]. These statistics make ITRI's contribution to the companies of the HsinChu area clear.

Another ITRI model is the establishment of spin-off companies. The two most valuable companies of the Taiwan Stock Market, TSMC and UMC, are ITRI spin-off companies, attestating to the 27 years of ITRI research efforts. In 1999, 31, or more than 10 percent, of the companies in the Science-Based Industrial Park were ITRI spin-off companies.

Aside from providing techniques and skills to HSIP companies, the ITRI also "passively supplied" them with technology-based human resources, despite the effects on ITRI's research work. According to ITRI internal records, around 76 percent (more than 8,300 persons) of the employees who resigned from ITRI were absorbed by companies in the park, with most of them assuming high executive and management positions, especially in the IC companies. These employees also carried significant knowledge from ITRI to

---

[32] Data source: Technology Service Department of ITRI.

their new companies, contributing significantly the development of Taiwan industries.[33]

ITRI's success in fostering industry and promoting development has become an example for other nations. In 1998, the Chief Executive's Innovation Technology Committee of the Hong Kong Special Administrative Region Government concluded that "the establishment of a state-funded institute in the applied technology research field should be proposed to make up for the applied technology gap between universities and industries. The institute shall serve as part of the technology infrastructure." This suggestion came from Chintay Shih, who was present in his capacity as ITRI director, and the comment was inspired by ITRI's successes.

A system for exchange of experience and knowledge was established between the ITRI and NCTU & NTHU. Similar to the classes taught by ACER Chairman Stan Shih, ITRI director Chintay Shih taught to fully-packed classrooms at the NCTU Management School as he shared his experiences with the future industrial human resources. On the other hand, the schools provide new knowledge and concepts to ITRI personnel. ITRI personnel, from basic-level researchers and administration personnel to top management executives are familiar faces in the classrooms, absorbing new ideas and knowledge and discussing their experiences with teachers and students.

4.5 Silicon Valley of the West Pacific: HsinChu

The first unit that NCTU established was the electronics institute. NTHU, on the other hand, started as an atomic science graduate institute, while ITRI began as the Electronics Research and Service Organization (ERSO). Prior to the official establishment of the Science-Based Industrial Park 20 years ago, UMC already had planned to construct its factory in the reserved "science park" land. Far-sighted entrepreneurs and leaders had directed industrial development toward electronics and information, and subsequent development showed that direction was the road to success.

NTHU and NCTU graduates have become dominant figures in the high-tech industries here and abroad. According to the current NCTU

---

[33] ITRI website (www.itri.org.tw), 1997.

president Dr. Chun-Yen Chang, "the income of NCTU alumni holding important positions in high-tech companies has now exceeded NT 1 trillion (US$ 32.3 billion)." "25 percent of the entrepreneurs in the US Silicon Valley are Asians, and 60 percent of these Asians are Chinese, around 50 percent of which came from NCTU. For instance, five of the nine Chinese-owned companies listed in the US stock market in 1999 were opened by NCTU alumni."[34]

In this special community, human resources were able to achieve substantial success in terms of information and capital flow. During its second year, after UMC encountered a capital shortfall, its president, Robert Tsao, returned to ITRI to make a fund-raising speech. His efforts raised NT$ 60 million, resolving the company's financial problems[35]. This kind of flotation, corporate cooperation or fund solicitation is made possible by the concentration of human resources, which enables an accurate and speedy information flow within Taiwan's Silicon Valley.

The principal factor behind the "vertical disaggregation" in the Taiwan information industry is its high degree of human resource concentration. The rapid dissemination of information allows people to have an early idea of market opportunities, making it possible to draw capital from individuals familiar with the market or invite investment from upstream or downstream companies. This creates an efficient, flexible network.

In HsinChu, NCTU and NTHU act as the cradle of fundamental academic research and human resource development. The ITRI serves as a bridge between academic research and practical applications. The ITRI researched and developed technology applications, as well as cultivated an advanced level of researchers. Companies in the Science-Based Industrial Park applied the technology and produced merchandise. The complete chain of human resource and technology resources from academic research to applied research to practical applications was an essential factor in the creation of "West Pacific Silicon Valley: HsinChu".

---

[34] Ko, Feb. 2000.
[35] Chen and Wang, 1999, p. 41.

5. The Contributions of ACER Group in Taiwan's Human Resource Development

This section focuses on ACER Group, since this conglomerate not only contributed substantially to Taiwan's human resource development, it also launched internal ventures that are rare in other corporations.

Mr. Stan Shih established the Multitech In. Co. in 1976 and moved it to the HsinChu Science-Based Industrial Park in 1981. In 1987, English versions of the company and product brand names were changed to ACER. ACER started as a producer of microprocessors and endeavored to promote information technology. The company has developed into a global high-tech conglomerate that develops and manufactures PCs, motherboards, peripheral equipment, telecommunication products, consumer electronics, and Internet and software programs. At present, ACER Group is the maker of one of the 10 top PC brands in the world. It was in the top five Taiwan Group[36], generating a net income of almost NT$ 180 billion (US$ 5.81 billion). In 1999, ACER Inc. rose from its rank of number four the previous year to become the largest manufacturing company in Taiwan. Annual income amounted to NT$ 127.8 billion (US$ 4.12 billion), the only private corporation to break the NT$100 billion (US$ 3.23 billion) income mark[37], and its income was projected to grow to NT$150 billion (US$ 4.84 billion) in 2000. The entire group is organized in six parts—ACER SoftCapital Group, ACER Information Products Group, ACER Peripheral Group, ACER Sertek Service Group, ACER Digital Services Group and independent business enterprises. The group now is comprised of more than 100 companies.

In 1978, two-year-old ACER set up the Hung Ya Microprocessor Learning Center to train information technology engineers. In 1985 it started the first computer chain store in Taiwan, ACER Information Square. The chain stores not only sold computers, peripherals and components, they also offered software and hardware training courses, providing a learning venue for engineers, families and individuals. From 1990 to 1995, Acer promoted its Dragons Project, which was aimed at training future leaders. It planned to

---

[36] China Credit Information Service, LTD website (www.credit.com.tw), 1999.
[37] Huang, Jan. 14, 2000.

train 100 future corporate presidents in five years. In 1997, it started promoting the second stage of its Dragons Project, which planned to train 200 possible future corporate presidents in the next five years, thus providing the massive human resource requirements of companies in this Internet Era.

In order to develop managers for Taiwan and Asia, as well as upgrade the area's international competitive power, in October 1999 ACER Group established the Aspire Academy, a non-profit corporate educational organization inside the Aspire Park in Taoyuan. Aspire Academy was established to pursue the mission of "upgrading the competitive power of Taiwan and Asian corporations." Principal offerings included mid- and high-level management training, corporate management consultation, Asian management case studies and course development, and the dissemination and sharing of management knowledge. It conducted joint research ventures with Michigan University, Harvard Business School, M.I.T., the University of Southern California, and the Lausanne Institute for Management Development (IMD). These pursuits show ACER's programmed development of better human resources.

From its establishment to its present global high-tech status, ACER has concentrated on cultivating human resources. Under the 1-2-3 ACER principle (customer first, employee second and stockholder third), employees take precedence over stockholders. In ACER's contributions to human resource development, the contributions of its founder and chairman, Mr. Stan Shih, are especially significant. One of the first NCTU graduates, Mr. Shih possessed a high degree of charisma and humility, which led to the implementation of human resource training regardless of ability to pay. Regardless whether the person is a home PC user, a computer engineer, or a top management executive or researcher, he/she may enjoy meticulous ACER training.

Aside from Mr. Stan Shih's insistence on cultivating human resources, ACER also resolutely upholds the principle of "risk sharing and profit sharing," in which every ACER employee is a stockholder. Allowing employees to own stock places them in the same "interest consortium" as the company, hence ACER not only reduces the drain of human resources, it also promotes internal enterprise. This satisfies employees' yen to overcome challenges and difficulties and provides them with the means to increase their wealth while remaining within the corporation.

ACER Group[38] with 35,300 employees on May 2000 cultivated many elites while it contributed to society in many ways. The group's emphasis on research and development earned the acclaim of users and international magazines worldwide. Companies opened by former ACER employees applied the company's spirit to their enterprise as well; for example, the technology and innovation expert Asustek Computer Inc. became the leading brand in the motherboard industry. Mr. Shih Chung-tang, chairman of motherboard and notebook PC maker Asustek Computer Inc., once proudly stated that the chairman of the board, the vice-chairman of the board, Tung Tze-hsien, and three other company vice-presidents all came from the R&D department of ACER Group. He even stressed that the technological concepts they used came out of the same mold as ACER's.

ACER also developed its massive professional core of technology experts and top management for internal new ventures through internal promotions. Besides, the 190 ACER Information Square stores located throughout Taiwan trained numerous computer engineers and hobbyists in the past 15 years, satisfying the needs of office and home computer users as well as preparing Taiwan for the digital revolution of the 90s.

As it grew, ACER continually gave back to society, donating computers to NCTU and other teaching establishments and fostering the integration of information technology applications and technology into daily living. Since February 2000, Stan Shih has shared his business experiences as a lecturer of International Business Management and Strategies at NCTU. Under the urging of founder Stan Shih, the ACER campaign of providing versatile technology and management resource development through schools and corporations has been justly referred to as the cradle of technology and management.

Another ACER trait is promoting internal ventures in developing fields instead of mergers and acquisitions. ACER's internal ventures allow the company to cope with industrial changes and increase employees' promotional opportunities. Internal ventures give opportunities to core technology and management personnel, not only allowing the company to cope with industrial and environmental changes, but also increasing employees' promotional and developmental opportunities. Although ACER

---

[38] Data source: ACER Group, May 2000.

does employ more experienced outside professionals, it does so to a significantly lesser degree than many companies, reflecting ACER's special competence in personnel training, organizational commitment, corporate culture and organizational flexibility. ACER's top level-executives rose from within its ranks, including the CEO of ACER Information Products Group, Simon Lin; the CEO of ACER Peripheral Group, K. Y. Lee; the CEO of ACER Sertek Service Group, J. T. Wang; and the CEO of ACER Digital Services Group, George Huang.

ACER's encouragement of internal ventures not only provided employees with developmental opportunities, it also allowed a huge organization to remain innovative, pursuing high profits and growth under changing technical and social environments. ACER became a "mega-incubator" that provided capital, technology, human resources, management skills and experience to its start-ups. ACER's new companies have contributed significantly to the Group's income and net profit, allowing the Group to encourage more internal ventures. This policy has provided ACER third-generation subsidiaries such as Aopen Inc., the motherboard, storage, multimedia product designer and manufacturer.

To counteract the high employee mobility in the information industry, ACER shares stocks with employees and urges internal enterprising to provide proper incentives, adequate career development and promotional opportunities, thereby attracting high quality personnel and developing a higher level of satisfaction and cooperation among employees. Its employee development opportunities and high degree of affinity have given ACER Group its business edge.

6. A Prosperous Future

In this section, we introduce the infulence of HsinChu community in Taiwan, the risk it faces and the proposed solution.

6.1 Expansion and cloning of the HsinChu Community

The success of the HsinChu community allowed it to spread its roots outside. Not only it has the original unit expanded in size, but also has attracted other units to join the community. Ten kilometers away from the science park, the Hukou Industrial Park has become a part of the Taiwan Silicon Valley and the base of numerous electronics and information manufacturers. The National Science Council, which governs the HsinChu Science-Based Industrial Park, selected nearby Chunan and Tunglo as the sites for the HsinChu Science-Based Industrial Park spin-off. The council plans to double the site area within four years, resolving the land shortage problems and industrial development bottlenecks in the original park.

The university-business relationship also intensifies with industrial growth, as institutions of higher education increase their ability to serve the evolving economic base. Taiwan's leading university, National Taiwan University(NTU), also has established a new campus in HsinChu County. The campus will serve mainly as the NTU management school and electronics engineering training facility. It is hoped that bringing education to the doorstep of high-tech industries and maintaining a closer interaction with industries will upgrade the university's research and educational levels. Faced with limited space, NCTU has set up a branch campus in Chupei, near the future site of NTU's new campus. NTHU also has sought the assistance of the HsinChu City Government to acquire an additional 16-hectares for its campus.

Aside from the NTU, other educational establishments either have established or altered their orientation towards technology in HsinChu areaduring the past decade—e.g., Chunghwa University, Hsuan Chuang University, Ming Hsin Technology College, Yuan Pei Science and Technology College, Ta Hua Technology College and Chin Ming Industrial & Commercial College.

The success of the HsinChu "university-research institute-industrial park" model not only bolstered the national competitive power of Taiwan, it also became a model for other parks. The Tainan Science-Based Industrial Park was set up in 1998 and surrounded by the National Cheng Kung University, the south branch institute of ITRI, the Metal Industry Development Center and the Asian Vegetable Research Center. Moreover, National Chung Cheng,

National Chiayi Universities and National Sun Yat-Sen University were only 40 kilometers. Other likely future communities include the Chungli Industrial Park of Taoyuan and the Aspire Park, which is near the Chung Shan Institute of Science & Technology and Central, Chung Yuan, and Yuan Chih Universities. The parks in Tainan and Taoyuan replicate the successful HsinChu model. With emphases on wireless telecommunications and biotechnology, they aspire to find success in these fields, thereby creating more production value and competitive power for Taiwan.

6.2 The human resource vortexes and industrial black hole

The information industry has upgraded the national competitiveness of Taiwan, contributing to its industrial transformation and maintaining its economic growth; however, the number of human resources attracted to high-profit industries resulted in an overconcentration of human resource in these fields and shortages in such new industries as telecommunications and networks. This problem may affect new industries' development.

TSMC and UMC continue to compete and expand their domain in the foundry industry. By holding a dominant position in the world market, the semiconductor industry has become Taiwan's new favorite industry. Young graduates with different degrees or people already with positions in other industries are eager to accept jobs to join this high-profit, high-growth industry. They are even willing to work as engineers of "One-touch" equipment.

Another industry, the computer peripheral liquid crystal display (LCD) industry, is considered to hold the most promise for growth and profitability for the next three to five years. At present, there are at least six companies expanding their business in Taiwan and massively recruiting new graduates and other high-tech company or research institute personnel.

The two mainstream industries, semiconductor and computer peripherals, are like *human resource vortexes* in that they attracted so many human resources through the lure of stock ownership that an over-concentration of human resources occurred in these fields. Since this development could be detrimental to future industrial growth, it is necessary to invest capital and human resources in future stellar industries and encourage existing businesses to grow.

In face of these human resource shortages and imbalances, the Taiwan Government should increase its higher education capacity, attract internationally renowned engineers to work in Taiwan, and offer incentives and legislation to keep human resources inside research institutes and future stellar industries and prevent the overconcentration of human resource in certain industries.

Taiwan also faces a serious threat from Mainland China. Mainland China is developing high-tech industry and possesses an oversupply of excellent researchers, low labor wages and an oversized market. It has become an important computer hardware producer and after its admission into the World Trade Organization (WTO) will deregulate its high-tech industry restrictions, easing the development of the semiconductor and other high-tech industries. This is bound to become an *industrial black hole* for the Taiwan high-tech industry, absorbing investments and having a serious impact on Taiwan.

Although silicon chip makers and other high-tech industries are prohibited by Taiwan's law from setting up factories in Mainland China, the Hung Jen Group has invested in the construction of a foundry factory in Mainland China. The restricted industries such as the semiconductor manufacturing are in the high-growth stages in Taiwan and generate major economic benefits. Hence, in the absence of early planning and governmental assistance in an industry transition from production to R&D, future manufacturers will rapidly move to the Mainland.

The negative side of the human resource vortexes caused by the semiconductor and computer peripheral industries is in a human resource imbalance, which affects other industries' pace of development. But Mainland China's siphoning off industries from Taiwan will cause greater impact. This possible challenge could be another turning point in that the government could capitalize on Taiwan's management strength and help companies change into investment holding or consulting companies. Then, through job specialization, Taiwan should transfer the production of low value-added products to Mainland China or other Southeast Asian countries. Taiwan should focus on market and marketing studies, R&D and other high value-added work that could not be easily copied. These companies cannot be easily replicated by a transition to more profitable upstream and downstream industries, such as semiconductor equipment manufacturing, semiconductor material or marketing agenccies. This would ensure that Taiwan will not be overwhelmed when Mainland China's market is deregulated and incorporate Mainland China with Taiwan to a "win-win" future.

6.3 Juncture to Success

Taiwan recently enacted reforms to upgrade educational quality and the level of human resources. The traditional rigid entrance examination is being replaced by a diversified admission method to encourage various interests and support more creative thinking. In addition, the Ministry of Education has allowed universities and colleges to open in-service training courses and consolidate channels and organizations to promote "life-long learning." This is intended to provide more channels, so individuals can absorb new information and satisfy their thirst for learning as well as help upgrade Taiwan's industries. Besides, the government appropriated NT$ 12 billion (US$ 387 million) in its 1999 budget for university "pursuing excellence" projects to urge universities to study advanced fields. These reforms are aimed to upgrade Taiwan's human resources and increase Taiwan's "intellectual capital."

However, there is room for improvement in Taiwan. As shown in Table 12.5, the proportion of R&D personnel and expenditures is relatively low compared to the US and European developed countries. R&D personnel constitute 0.4565 percent of personnel, while the proportion of R&D expenditures against GDP is 1.922 percent. This figure may have been suitable for the subcontract production mode, but it is inadequate for high-tech industries focusing on R&D. Compared to Switzerland, Sweden, Finland and Denmark, Taiwan has a larger population and therefore more R&D personnel, but proportionately they are a smaller percentage. Likewise 7.03 percent of average annual revenues in the high-tech companies of HsinChu Science-Based Industrial Park went to R&D expenditure, whereas in other countries the R&D expenditure proportion is as high as 20 percent. If Taiwan manufacturers wish to become first-rate global companies, they should direct more effort, budget and personnel into R&D.

Country	Total expenditure on R&D (%)	Business expenditure on R&D per capita (USD1M)	Total R&D personnel nationwide (per 1K persons)	Total R&D personnel (per 1K persons)	Total R&D personnel in business enterprises (1K persons)	Ratio of Total R&D personnel in business (per 1K persons)
Taiwan	1.922	154.84	98.6	4.565	65	3.01
Japan	2.829	735.25	891.8	7.091	589.5	4.687
US	2.546	573.69	962.7	3.729	764.5	2.962
Germany	2.401	418.1	459.1	5.624	291.8	3.556
UK	1.9	247.16	279	4.795	139	2.364
Switzerland	2.739	807.92	50.3	7.11	34.5	4.873
Sweden	3.594	699.05	62.6	7.093	41.6	4.715
Finland	2.711	434.64	33.6	6.582	20.8	4.054
Denmark	1.937	388.22	31.5	5.96	17.8	3.371

Data source: Institute for Management Development, 1999.

Table 12.5 Comparative Table of R&D Personnel and Expense[39]

In addition, the HsinChu Science-Based Industrial Park was initially developed as a "research & development park". Under the contemporary environment of the times, however, some companies in Industrial Park were unable to focus their most effort on R&D, as a result, these companies were converted into manufacture factories. Twenty seven years of effort has allowed HsinChu Science-Based Industrial Park to drive the Taiwan high-tech industry development, as well as foster the establishment of other science parks in Tainan. Possessing highly skilled human resources from the nearby universities and research institute, the HsinChu Science-Based Industrial Park

---

[39] Definition and year of the indices used in this table are shown in Appendix 12.1.

should be able to fulfill its founding objectives and become a research and development park now.

As of 1996, and only 10 percent of the more than 12,000 researchers with doctorate degrees were in corporations. Sixty-six percent are in universities and colleges, and twenty-four percent are in technology research institutes[40]. Corporate R&D personnel mainly have bachelors or masters degrees. The government should provide more incentives and work environments to attract researchers with doctoral degrees from universities to companies. This move will help upgrade industrial technology research capacities and levels

Finally, the enlargement and enhancement of human resource are critical issues for Taiwan. The shortage of qualified engineers for the boosting industries is a serious problem and will limit the growth of industries. The leverage of human resources through recruiting capable people from Mainland China or other countries is a feasible soultion. Besides, the increasing rate of students studying abroad is less than prior periods. To keep the progressive human flow from Taiwan to abroad and the reverse is also a good way to maintain Taiwan's strength. The development and improvement of intellectual capital will supporting continuously the competitiveness of Taiwan and its industries.

---

[40] National Science Council, 1997, p.34.

Appendix 12.1

Item	Unit	IMD Index No.	Page	Year	Definition
Access to property	%	8.37	506	1994	Homeownership rates proportion of households that are owners
Working hours	Hours	8.19	497	1998	Average number of working hours per year
Entrepreneurship	Survey scores	6.35	470	—	Managers generally have a sense of entrepreneurship.
Unemployment	%	8.20	497	1998	Percentage of labor force
Flexibility and adaptability	Survey scores	8.42	508	—	People in this country are flexible enough in adapting to new challenges.
Values of the society	Survey scores	8.44	509	—	Values of the society (hard work, innovation) support competitiveness.
Availability of it skills	Survey scores	7.11	479	—	Qualified information technology employees are available in this country's labor market.
Total R&D personnel nationwide	FTE (1000s)	7.06	476	1997	Full time work equivalent (FTE)
Total R&D personnel nationwide per capita	FTE (1000s)	7.07	476	1997	Full time work equivalent (FTE) per capita
Total expenditure on R&D	%	7.03	475	1997	Percentage of GDP
Total R&D personnel in business enterprise	FTE (1000s)	7.08	477	1997	Full time work equivalent (FTE)

Table 12.6 Explanation of Comparison of Nations

Item	Unit	IMD Index No.	Page	Year	Definition
Total R&D personnel in business per capita	FTE (1000s)	7.09	478	1997	Full time work equivalent (FTE) per capita
Business expenditure on R&D per capita	US$ millions	7.05	476	1997	US$ millions per capita at current prices and exchange rates
Science and education	Survey Scores	7.20	483	–	Science is adequately taught in compulsory schools.
Science & technology and youth	Survey scores	7.21	484	–	Science & technology arouses the interest of youth.
Public expenditure on education	US$	8.29	502	1995	US$ per capita
University education	Survey scores	8.25	500	–	University education meets the need of a competitive economy.
The education system	Survey scores	8.22	498	–	The education system meets the needs of a competitive economy.
Advanced education enrollment	%	8.24	498	1996	Net enrollment in public and private tertiary education for persons 17-34
Secondary school enrollment	%	8.23	498	1995	Percentage of relevant group receiving full-time education

Data source: Institute for Management Development (IMD), 1999.

Table 12.6 (Cont.)

References

[1] AnnaLee, Saxenian (1999), "The Silicon Valley-HsinChu Connection: Technical Communities and Industrial Upgrading", Stanford Institute for Economic Policy Research (SIEPR), Stanford University, SIEPR Discussion Paper No. 99-10.

[2] Chen, Hung-chi and Wang, Chun-Cheng (1999), "The Information Industry News of Taiwan"(Chinese Edition), China Credit Information Service, LTD..

[3] Chin, Li-ping (March 20, 2000), "Has Morris Chang Changed?" (Chinese Edition)" *Commerce Weekly*, Vol. 643, pp. 44-48.

[4] Chiang, Chao-ching and Chang, Chih-ching (May 16, 1999), "Tsing Hua Leads in University Prestige Survey" (Chinese Edition), *China Times.*

[5] Chiang, Hsin-yi (December 23, 1999) "The Ten Year Education Plan of the National Science Council: Cultivate Semiconductor Human Resource" (Chinese Edition), *The Commercial Times.*

[6] China Credit Information Service, LTD website (www.credit.com.tw)(1999), "Taiwan Corporate Business Research " (Chinese Edition).

[7] China Times General Editor (May 27, 1999), "Son of Former USSR Premier Nikita Khrushchev Turns American" (Chinese Edition), *China Times.*

[8] General of Budget, Accounting and Statistics Directorate website (www.dgbasey.gov.tw) (1999), "Summary of Popular Education Standards" (Chinese Edition).

[9] General of Budget, Accounting and Statistics Directorate website, (www.dgbasey.gov.tw) (May 19, 2000), "Important Socioeconomic Indices" (Chinese Edition).

[10] Huang, Chuan-chen (January 14, 2000), "Taiwan Semiconductor Manufacturing Co., Ltd. can Look Forward to Becoming the Largest Private Manufacturer" (Chinese Edition), *Business Weekly.*

[11] HsinChu Science-Based Industrial Park Administration website (www.sipa.gov.tw)(2000), "The HsinChu Science Park Guide" (Chinese Edition).

[12]Lao Human RightsCouncil,Inc.(home.earthlink.net/~laohumrights/laohdl21.html (July 1, 1997), "Genocide in Cambodia and Laos".

[13] Lin, Chiu-ling (April 21, 2000), "The Profitability Race of Semiconductor Manufacturers" (Chinese Edition), *Electronic Times.*

[14] Lin, Ling-fei (November 30, 1999), "Taiwan's Information Hardware Production Value Posts Dramatic Growth of 18% in 1999" (Chinese Edition), *China Times.*

[15] Institute for Information Industry (III) website (140.92.88.45) (2000), "What is an Education & Training Center"(Chinese Edition).

[16] Institute for Management Development (IMD)(1999), *The World Competitiveness Yearbook,* IMD.

[17] ITRI website (www.itri.org.tw) (1997), "The Contributions of ITRI to the Development of Taiwan's Industries" (Chinese Edition).

[18] Ko, Hsin-ying (February 2000), "NCTU Alumni in Silicon Valley Talk of Their Business Successes" (Chinese Edition) , *Voice of NCTU Alumni*, Vol. 378, pp. 48-52.

[19] Milgrom, Paul and Roberts, John (1992), "Economics, Organization & Management", Prentice-Hall, Inc.

[20] Ministry of Education (1998), "Education Statistics, 1998 " (Chinese Edition), Ministry of Education.

[21] Ministry of Education website (www.edu.tw) (2000a)," East Asia Pacific students in US universities 1998-99" (Chinese Edition)

[22] Ministry of Education website (www.edu.tw) (2000b), "Population Students and Graduates of Colleges" (Chinese Edition).

[23] Ministry of Education website (www.edu.tw) (2000c), "The Schooling Population "(Chinese Edition).

[24] NCTU Submicro Professional Training Center (www.ee.nctu.edu.tw/~submic) (2000), "Trainee Population from 1991 to 1998 "(Chinese Edition).

[25] NCTU website (www.nctu.edu.tw) (1997), "History of the National Chiao Tung University"(Chinese Edition).

[26] National Science Council (1997), "Indicators of Science & Technology in Taiwan, 1997 Edition" (Chinese Edition), National Science Council.

[27] National Tsing Hua University website (www.nthu.edu.tw)(1999), "History of the National Tsing Hua University"(Chinese Edition) .

[28] Stewart, Thomas (1997), Intellectual Capital: the new wealth of organizations", Bantam Doubleday Dell Publishing Group, Inc.

Part 6: Culture and People

Chapter 13

Five Life Experiences That Shape Taiwan's Character

Po-Lung Yu

C. A. Scupin Distinguished Professor
School of Business, University of Kansas and
Chair Professor, Institute of Information Management
National Chiao Tung University
HsinChu, Taiwan,R.O.C.

Chieh-Yow ChiangLin

Associate Professor, Department of Industrial Engineering and Management
Tahwa Institute of Technology
HsinChu, Taiwan,R.O.C.

1. Introduction

Using the concept of habitual domains, we can identify five life experiences in Taiwan that form the special characteristics of Taiwan competitiveness. In order to facilitate our discussion, let us first introduce some important habitual domain concepts. It is well known that our thoughts and attitudes determine our actions and behaviors, which in turn determine our success or failure. Indeed, without good habits it is difficult to succeed, and without bad habits it is difficult to fail.

The collection of all ideas, memories, thoughts and thinking paradigms that can be activated in our mind and brains, together with their organization and dynamics is known as our Habitual Domain (HD). [14-15] Thoughts or paradigms that are used repeatedly became stronger and stronger and are more easily activated to occupy our attention. Thoughts or paradigms that are seldom used are weak and not easily activated to occupy our attention, but this does not mean they are not useful.

Our thoughts and thinking paradigms are represented by circuit patterns of our billions of neuron cells. These circuit pattern are our mental programs or human software, which drive our brains (a very super computer) to work. Our habitual domain or software development is a function of our experience and learning. It goes with us wherever we go and has a great impact on our behavior and on our competitiveness.

Mathematically, it can be proven that unless there is an extraordinary event, or we set our mind to break through it, our HD will become stabilized in a certain domain. [3] As a consequence, we develop predictable reactions to or judgments about external events or information. In this way, people gradually development their attitudes, personality and characteristics, which in turn affect their lives.

One of the important questions of competitiveness is how a company can maximize its value of existence by producing products and services that are really needed by potential customers. Since customers, producers and intermediate sellers are human beings, to answer this question we should study the behavior of the consumers, the producers and the sellers. In other words, we must study human behaviors.

Like individuals, organizations also have habitual domains, and the concepts of habitual domains can be applied to organizations to maximize their value. The tools of expanding an individual's habitual domain [14-15] can be applied to organizations, industries and nations. Historic tradition, geographical environment and daily life experiences shape our HD. We can say that in ever-intensifying competitive situations, the key factor for organizations, industries, societies or nations to succeed and prosper is to continuously upgrade, expand and enrich their competence or habitual domains.

We shall focus on some almost unique daily life experiences of Taiwanese and how they shape the characteristics of competitive behavior in doing business. In this article, we shall first observe five almost unique life experiences in Taiwan. These are: a belief in higher education, motorcycling, a sense of crisis, compulsory military service, and going abroad to study and coming back. We will describe these life experiences and how they may build and rebuild strong circuit patterns or thinking paradigms in Taiwanese minds, patterns that affect their competitiveness.

To verify our observations, we surveyed college students to obtain a more detailed relationship of these life experiences to Taiwanese competitive characteristics. Finally, we make some suggestions on how to upgrade Taiwanese industrial competitiveness from a habitual domain point of view.

2. Belief in higher education—Life Experience 1

There is a strong belief in Taiwan that nothing is more important than continuing to study and pursuing higher scholarship, and that no job is nobler than a job related to scholarship. Even though they are not highly paid, scholars are highly respected and enjoy a high social status and reputation. As a consequence, almost all the parents directly or indirectly motivate their children to pursue a higher education. Every youngster by law must have at least nine year of education, and, except for a small number of senior citizens, most people in Taiwan are well educated. Even illiterate senior citizens have the opportunity to go to night schools or community schools to make up the education they lack.

Beginning in kindergarten, parents give incentives, including awards and threats, for their children to study hard to pass examinations to enter one of the best grade schools, and then one of the best high schools. In their high school years, many parents pay expensive fees for makeup education, paying instructors to help children to get higher grades in the entrance examinations. Once they get into college, pressures continue from parents, peers and instructors to get into good graduate schools to earn a masters or doctorate degree.

These pressures from parents, peers and teachers may be invisible but exist almost everywhere and almost all the time. Through competition with peers in school examinations, children are encouraged to work hard to get into good schools. Many parents even tell their children, "You don't have to do anything else, just focus your energy on studying in order to enter a good high school or good college." They want their children to become outstanding scholars. In the examinations, they want their children to be one of the best. In so doing, their children gradually neglect other aspects of life and pay little attention to social problems. As a consequence, they neglect pursuing truth, perfection and beauty in their lives. Some commentators say that Taiwan's college students are good at examinations but not so successful in daily living. As their studies advance, they focus on deeper and narrower subjects in a specialized area. As a consequence, many may lose the vision of life and the creativity they need in the future, even though they have acquired a deep technological knowledge. They may not explore many aspects of their lives or develop the capability to integrate a variety of technologies, something needed to become a well-rounded manager.

Because of Taiwan's belief in higher education and its competitive education system, there is an abundance of well-trained and well-educated engineers and professionals. Taiwan's high-tech industries offer better jobs and better pay, but they demand higher education. In this way, higher education helps the high-tech industry, which in turn forces the educational system to have more specialized training. These engineers and specialists have helped Taiwan develop light industries, consumer-oriented industries, and IC and PC industries in designing, production and marketing. Because of their effort and productivity, the products made in Taiwan are competitive, of good quality and low-cost.

Some of the special characteristics that shaped up by this belief in higher education are as follows:

(i) Having clear, specific and measurable goals for life.

All students from kindergarten, grade school, junior high, high school, college, and even graduate school have a clear goal and time schedule for entering a good school. The goal is clear, specific and measurable. The measurement of whether they can get into a good college or graduate school is almost completely determined by their performance on examinations. In order to enter a good college or good graduate school, each student must do well in almost every exam, especially those subjects that are closely related to entrance exams. They know how to prepare for the exams and study those subjects that will be tested. Unwittingly, they develop a habit of continuing to learn and working hard to reach clear, specific and measurable goals.

(ii) Enjoying the sweetness of success only after the pains of hard work.

Working hard and being willing to "pay the price" are fundamental for success. Parents and teachers continuously encourage their children and students by saying, "Work hard and tolerate the pains of learning. Once you get in the best school, you can enjoy the sweetness and happiness of success and have a bright future." Many students develop a habit of getting up early and studying. Once their school is over in the afternoon, they go to makeup schools to keep on studying, even at night. The joys of eating, drinking, and playing are deferred until they finish their exams. As a consequence, they develop a strong habit of working hard, paying the price and tolerating the pain in order to succeed.

(iii) Be mentally focused and move toward a goal without distraction.

In order to get high grades in examinations to enter a good school, students must focus mentally and concentrate on their studies. Under the supervision and encouragement of their teachers and parents, many students focus on their studies day and night and are not easily distracted by other daily activities. Gradually they develop a habit of self-motivation and hard work to move toward their goals.

(iv) Lifelong learning to get new knowledge.

To get good grades on the examinations, students must be able to keep up with new knowledge. After studying day and night for so long, they develop a habit of continuing to learn new things. Many feel uncomfortable if they aren't studying and learning new knowledge, even after graduation. Some study subjects outside their field purely for entertainment or relaxation. Thus the habit of continuous studying and acquiring new knowledge is shaped.

(v) Keen awareness of competition.

Examination grades determine whether a student can enter a good school or not, and instructors make up some difficult problems to distinguish good students from ordinary students. Examinations are competitive, so students achieve success relative to other students' performance. Since there is such a strong emphasis on doing well on examinations, students are always aware of their competition. Because there may be hundreds or thousands of competitors in entrance exams, students study day and night until the examinations are over. As a consequence, they develop a very keen sense of competition.

The cultural belief in higher education has generated a large number of highly educated professionals who have made a great contribution to

Taiwan's industrial competitiveness. But this value also produces some attitudes that may become handicaps in the arena of industrial competitiveness. Some of these are discussed as follows:

(i) Lack of team spirit.

Individual performances determine the grades of most examinations, and students outperform if other students do not do as well. Because of this, studying for examinations has a tendency to develop a personality trait of doing everything just for oneself. Students seldom consider that they also must work for other people. As this circuit pattern of individualism strengthens, the circuit pattern of working for the group or the larger self becomes relatively weak, and a team spirit is difficult to develop. In the extreme, it is not easy for students accept different concepts from other people.

(ii) Narrowed vision and short-term gratification.

Everything students do is for examinations and entering a good school, so students only pay attention to subjects relevant to examinations. They pay little or no attention to subjects not covered by the examinations; consequently, they tend to have a restricted vision and work for short-term gratification. They might neglect many important aspects of their lives, including pursuing living wisdom, moral values, truth, and beauty, and pay little attention to social problems or contributing to society.

3. Motorcycling—Life Experience 2

In August 1999 [1], there were more than 10 million motorcycles in Taiwan, and this number of motorcycles increases drastically every year (see Table 3.1). There is almost one motorcycle for every two persons. According to statistics, most cyclists are young people in the age group of 20 to 25, who are full of energy and quick to react. In addition, Taiwan is the largest producer of motorcycles in the world.

Year	Quantity
1991	7,409,175
1993	7,867,394
1994	8,034,509
1995	8,517,024
1996	9,283,914
1997	10,027,471
1998	10,503,877

(Source: Ministry of Transportation and Communications, Statistics Department)

Table 3.1 Motorcycles registered in Taiwan

In the crowded streets of Taipei and other cities, we can see motorcycles congested on the streets, waiting for their owners to drive them around the city. These motorcycles, on one hand, give their owners the convenience and flexibility to move around; on the other hand, they make traffic difficult for automobiles, other motorcyclists, and pedestrians. The result is chaotic, congested traffic.

Motorcycles are small, relative to automobiles, and agile. They accelerate quickly and move fast. As all they need is a path of two to three feet wide to move, motorcycles move in and out quickly in a small space. Some cyclists drive their motorcycles like a snake, swinging swiftly from left to right, and right to left frequently. Some motorcyclists even zigzag on the fast automobile designated lane. This, of course, takes special courage and risk.

Since they are young, most children ride motorcycles with their parents and watch the motorcycles moving around swiftly on busy streets, sometimes illegally. The corresponding circuit patterns of these experiences become ingrained strongly and unwittingly in their minds. As they grow up, they learn to drive motorcycles as their parents did, subconsciously developing their circuit patterns, which help shape their personalities. The fallowing are some personality characteristics shaped up by this life experience of motorcycling.

(i) Moving accurately and swiftly with clear, specific goals.

Every motorcyclist knows that it is difficult to find space to drive on the road or to park. Their actions must be swift and accurate; otherwise, they could not get on the road or get a desired parking space at their destination. As a consequence, they develop the attitude that action must be quick and accurate with a clear and specific goal.

(ii) Looking for opportunities almost anywhere and anytime.

Motorcyclists at any moment try to move their motorcycles wherever it is advantageous. Their eyes continuously scan, and their ears listen in every direction. Their eyesight is very clear, and their sense of smell is also very keen in the search for an opportunity to move ahead.

(iii) Be adaptive and flexible.

In order to move quickly to their destinations, the motorcyclist must drive adaptively and flexibly. If it is more convenient and advantageous, they will move adaptively and speedily wherever possible, and in so doing may not observe traffic regulations one hundred percent. When they need to deliver goods to customers, they know how to find the shortcut to deliver the products in five to 10 minutes.

(iv) Be tough and take risks.

Many motorcyclists keep a very short safety distance from others and drive as if they were not afraid of a collision with other motorcyclists or even with moving automobiles. Because they drive with a full awareness of approaching vehicles, they expect others will do the same to avoid a collision. In order to move fast, it is important to identify and occupy a vacant space quickly, so they move swiftly, not afraid of a potential collision with other vehicles. In the case of a standoff, whoever persists longer will occupy the position or space.

Motorcycling shapes some other personality traits that might not be advantageous for industrial competitiveness:

(i) One-person operation with small scale of vision.

Usually one motorcycle is for one person, who drives it. The driver alone decides where to go and where to park. Motorcyclists do not have to stop and move like automobiles or buses, considering riders' opinions and preferences. As a consequence, motorcyclists tend to be independent and want to be the boss. They tend to act individually without much spirit of teamwork. They also tend to consider problems on a small scale and in the short-term and limit their vision, perhaps unwittingly, to a small scale.

(ii) They tend to walk in the gray areas of the law.

As long as it is safe, doesn't hurt other people, and they perceive the police cannot catch them, they can act illegally, even though they know it violates traffic laws. This unwittingly develops the attitude that they don't have to strictly obey the law or regulations.

4. Crisis consciousness—Life Experience 3

Ever since 1622, various foreign forces had occupied Taiwan. The Dutch invaded and occupied part of Taiwan from 1622 to 1661. Spain invaded and occupied part of Taiwan from 1624 to 1642. China's Ming Dynasty forced out the Dutch in 1661 and governed Taiwan until 1683. The Ching Dynasty of China then occupied Taiwan from 1683 to 1895. From 1895 to 1945, Japan occupied and ruled Taiwan. The Republic of China accepted the surrender of Taiwan from the Japanese in 1945 and has governed Taiwan until now.

Because of frequent changes of external ruling powers, people don't feel very secure and possess a high degree of crisis consciousness. Even since Chiang K. S. retreated to Taiwan from Mainland China in 1948, the ROC of Taiwan and People's Republic of China have been engaged in direct or indirect fighting for reuniting China. Even though Taiwan has been transformed into a democratic nation, it is continuously threatened by China, creating a keen sense of imminent crisis in Taiwan.

As a consequence, large budgets for national defense are a necessity for survival, and people search for opportunities to migrate to countries that might be safer than Taiwan. For those who have no opportunity to migrate, this keen sense of crisis has prepared Taiwanese psychologically and physically for war.

They must work hard and save money in case war breaks out between Taiwan and China.

In Table 4.1, we see that the Taiwan's savings rate is the second highest among developed countries, second only to Japan. These savings provide the needed capital for Taiwan's economic development.

Period	Taiwan	U.S.A	Japan	Germany	France	U.K.	Italy
1989	31.10	12.46	32.71	25.44	21.17	18.15	19.11
1990	29.33	11.18	33.01	26.43	21.06	17.62	19.15
1991	29.40	11.95	33.83	21.97	20.47	16.11	18.14
1992	28.99	14.30	33.01	21.61	19.40	15.50	17.03
1993	28.83	14.82	31.95	20.15	18.17	14.80	17.20
1994	27.68	15.50	30.75	21.15	18.68	15.71	17.76
1995	27.11	15.52	30.06	21.54	18.65	16.61	19.56
1996	26.83	15.79	30.44	22.62	18.33	16.32	19.50
1997	26.50	16.31	29.91	23.45	19.71	17.27	19.49
1998	26.08	16.03	28.76	31.02	--	17.14	--

(Source: International Financial Statistics (IMF), Oct. 1999 Economic Statistic Monthly (Japan))

Table 4.1 the Saving Rate of representative developed Countries (Ref. 11)

This crisis consciousness directly and indirectly makes Taiwanese prepare, physically and psychologically, for changes. Changes are not new to them, and they can adapt to changes. This awareness of crisis makes them willing to work hard and face challenges in order to survive. As a consequence, they know how to adapt and protect themselves in the rapid changes of the information technology era. The following are some personality characteristics shaped by this high degree of crisis consciousness.

(i) Prepare and be ready for changes.

Because they live in a high degree of uncertainty and insecurity, Taiwanese must be highly sensitive to future events and prepare for the worst that could happen. This instills a capability to adapt quickly to changes. It also makes industrial organizations pay attention to potential changes and economic trends and prepare for them. In highly competitive environments, they know that the only thing that doesn't change is change itself.

(ii) Act and react quickly and swiftly.

In order to survive in crisis, people must build the capability to adapt. Because of Taiwan's lack of natural resources, knowledge and skills have become Taiwan's main resources for competition. Taiwanese must continuously and actively learn new ideas and professional knowledge. As the success factors in competition changed from efficient low-cost production to high quality, then to customer satisfaction, management focus must adapt accordingly. This acting and reacting quickly offers Taiwanese some competitive advantages in the global supply chains of vertical integration and diversification. This competitive advantage could be vital for Taiwan's industries in the information technology era.

(iii) Work hard now for future success; save now and enjoy later.

Over the last 50 years, Taiwan's economy transformed itself from agricultural to industrial, then to the current post-industrial one. As there are no rich natural resources, in order to survive and prosper, Taiwan has to work hard and work smart. Brainpower must be continuously updated. Taiwanese are willing to spend much time, pain and effort to work and learn new knowledge and skills because they understand their future depends on their skills and knowledge and because of their crisis consciousness. As a consequence, they can habitually delay the joys of consumption to accumulate saving for future investments, as evidenced by the high rate of savings of Taiwan.

(iv) Influence on government policy: Economic growth with security and stability.

Taiwan faces potential verbal or military attacks from China, so it needs to develop new ways to defend itself. Taiwan has found that a democratic system and economic development are powerful weapons to defend itself. Because of past painful experiences of losing control of the mainland, the government has emphasized security and stability in order to develop the economy. Over the last 50 years, Taiwan has accumulated a high level of foreign exchange and very little debt. Although such a foreign exchange policy may be overly conservative, it helped Taiwan to overcome the oil crisis in the 1970s and the financial crisis in 1998.

(v) International networking.

Because of the need to know about and adapt to changes, Taiwanese are highly interested in external events and world developments, especially changes in information technology. By using the Internet and telecommunications, they gain insight into future market, management and technology changes. Such interest and motivation make Taiwanese industry more ready to adapt to changes. In addition, in order to survive changes, many people are willing to sacrifice their individual interests to organizational success; for instance, many employees habitually accept overtime work without complaint in order to finish products on time.

Crisis consciousness may have developed attributes that help Taiwan's competitiveness in production, technology development, marketing, distribution and management innovation. This crisis consciousness, however, has also contributed to the following, less desirable personality traits.

(i)A focus on short-term interests and a lack of interest in long-term development and planning.

Because Taiwan's limited resources and capability must be used to adapt to endless changes, it is more interested in short-term than long-term consequences. Many people are not very interested in taking the high risk involved in long-term development and research. Without long-term direction, people may make money in activities that involve short-term interests but are unable to set the tone for future development. From a competitive point of view, this focus might not be good for the nation.

(ii)The government might over-emphasize economic development and sacrifice the environment and social welfare.

When Chiang K. S. was forced to retreat to Taiwan in 1949, the government did not plan to stay in Taiwan for the long term, and the government's goal was retaking the mainland. For political stability and economic development, the government sacrificed environmental protection and social welfare and paid little attention to industrial pollution. They focused on short-term economic development and earning foreign exchange in order to stabilize political power. Under the slogan of retake the mainland, the environment was sacrificed. Taiwan would produce what other nations did not want to produce because of pollution. This policy continued until the last two or three decades, when most people realized that retaking the mainland is hopeless. The policy gradually has shifted to focus more on local construction, environmental protection, and quality of life, but the damage that had been done may not be easily recovered.

(iii) Loss of talents to other country because of migration.

Under the threat of attack by China, many Taiwanese believed war might break out any time. In order to have security, many talents, including college graduates, emigrated thousands of miles to foreign countries. Each year, hundreds or thousands of college students went to the USA to study, and many decided to stay there. This loss of talent to foreign countries certainly would have a negative impact on economic development. When many emigrant scholars came back to Taiwan in the late 1980s and 1990s, however, they brought back new technologies, a new democratic mentality and a knowledge of management systems, which directly and indirectly helped Taiwan transform itself from an authoritarian government to a democratic society. The new technology and management systems also transformed Taiwan's IC industries.

5. Compulsory military service system—Life Experience 4

Taiwan adopted a compulsory military service system in the face of the continued threat of a possible military invasion from China. All healthy young men must serve in the military for about two to three years shortly after they graduate from high school, college or graduate institutions. These services are usually performed before the young men enter formal employment.

This compulsory military service is a result of the following considerations: Because Taiwan needs to defend itself against a potential military invasion from China, it needs military power. Since Taiwan has only

23 million people, it needs all capable young men to serve. In Table 5.1, we can see that Taiwan has a relatively high ratio of military personnel to the population. Because the country cannot pay all military men at market wages, the government pays most non-career military men minimal wages.

Military training and service emphasize that everyone should be able to undertake and overcome challenging assignments by hard work, persistence and perseverance. In order to win, teamwork and strict discipline are emphasized. Organizational abilities, law and order, and decisive action are paramount virtues. In addition to increasing physical vitality, this military training also helps many young men prepare themselves psychologically for the highly competitive industrial work environment. The following are some of important influences on personality that result from this military service:

(i)Absolute obedience to the supervisor.

In war and in military training, absolute obedience is required to win battles. Soldiers who do not obey orders may be executed. This creates a very strong disposition for obedience to the supervisor or boss, a mentality that can be important in teamwork.

(ii)Finish an assigned mission with 100% effort, even if it involves sacrificing lives.

In a complex military war, everyone must finish the assigned task in a coordinated way in order to have a winning conclusion. They are repeatedly trained and indoctrinated to devote 100% of their effort spiritually and physically to finishing a task or mission on time, even if this requires sacrificing their lives. As a consequence, they develop a clear-cut goal orientation, perseverance and a high degree of discipline in focusing on their jobs and not being distracted by the other desires.

(iii)Authority and obligation are clearly specified.

In the military, the authority and obligation of each position is clearly specified. Military men recognize the role and position of their jobs, which helps them act properly and promptly in complex military organizations and in industrial organizations.

	China	South Korea	Taiwan	Japan	Vietnam	Indonesia	Thailand	Malaysia	Philippines	Singapore
GNP (Billion)	560	422	262	4700	21	170	157	78	74	67
Population (Million)	1210	45	21	126	76	195	61	24	71	3
Defense Budget (Billion)	8.4	15.6	13.6 (1995)	45.1	1.0	3.0	4.0	2.4	1.1	4.0
Troops (Thousand)	2940	660	376	239.5	572	299	254	114.5	107.5	53.9
GNP/Capita (Thousand)	0.46	9.38	12.48	37.30	0.28	0.87	2.57	3.25	1.04	22.33
DB/GNP	1.50%	3.70%	5.19%	0.96%	4.76%	1.76%	2.55%	3.08%	1.49%	5.97%
DB/Capita (Thousand)	6.94	346.67	647.62	357.94	13.16	15.38	65.57	100.00	15.49	1333.33
Troops /Capita	0.24%	1.47%	1.79%	0.19%	0.75%	0.15%	0.42%	0.48%	0.15%	1.80%

Table 5.1 Military Expenses and Troops of Asia Countries (1996) adapted from (Ref. 2)

(iv) Working together, suffering together and sharing together assures the success of the team.

No matter what their background, whether they are from a poor or wealthy family, all military men must obey strict military discipline. They work and suffer together and share their team's success. As a consequence, they can identify with each other and be able to accept people of different backgrounds.

(v) An awareness of enemies and protecting intelligence against spies.

In order to win, the military must be able to know itself and its opponents and keep opponents from learning military information. The military is aware of the enemy and continuously gathers intelligence about opponents, which develops the skills to know themselves and know their enemy. "Keep secrets from the spies" is a typical slogan, which certainly impacts the psychology of military persons.

(vi) A plan is needed to accomplish a mission.

In order to accomplish an assigned mission, planning is emphasized. Timing and feasibility of each plan are carefully studied. This kind of training in goal orientation and planning could impact their lives in business management.

Although military training has the above positive impacts, it also has some potential negative impacts:

(i) There is a fundamental difference between military goals and business goals.

In the military, protecting the security of the country is the ultimate goal, for which there is no substitution. To defend national security, cost considerations become secondary. Even precious human lives could be sacrificed for national security. Defeat is not acceptable, even in the short term. On the other hand, in industrial organizations, the primary goal is to make money or profits, which is more flexible. Organizations can tolerate a short-term loss for future profits.

(ii)Lack of opportunity for developing creativity.

In order to win in a military war, all units must obey their commanders. They are trained to act in an orderly and uniform manner, and diversity in thinking and action is not encouraged. As a consequence, their thinking becomes relatively rigid. Gradually they could become less creative, flexible and adaptable to life's changes.

(iii)Interruption of continuous studying and learning for nonmilitary career.

In order to mold servicemen into a uniform group, daily activities are rigidly scheduled, and servicemen have little energy or time for nonmilitary study. Since new knowledge emerges rapidly in the information technology era, after two to three years of military service many people find their technical knowledge is behind or even obsolete. They have to relearn in order to adapt into the new society.

The above three potentially negative attributes are well known in Taiwan. The government is planning to improve the system, including an option that allows people with technical training in colleges and graduate schools to perform their military service by working at selected high tech companies.

6. Studying abroad and returning of well educated talents—Life Experience 5

Education is a quick way to gain knowledge about developed nations. Because of Taiwan's history of occupation by the Dutch, Spanish, Japanese, and Ming and Ching Dynasties, Taiwanese have a high degree of acceptance of various cultures. Through sending students to study abroad, returning students can help Taiwan quickly and effectively absorb the experiences, skills and knowledge of advanced nations.

Taiwan and the USA have had a very close relationship in many dimensions since 1950. Early on, American Aid helped Taiwan's economy. Later, a large number of students were sent to study in the USA. These students have helped Taiwan accept different cultures and advanced knowledge.

Taiwan and Japan also have had close historical relations. Because Taiwan was occupied and ruled by Japan for 50 years, many Taiwanese have no difficulty understanding the Japanese language and culture, and many students study in Japan.

In addition, since many students study in European countries, including Britain, France, and Germany, European languages and cultures are not strange to Taiwan.

As a result of these study-abroad experiences with western countries and Japan, Taiwan has become an important locale for multinational businesses. These experiences have greatly expanded and enriched Taiwanese Habitual Domains, and help the advancement of technology and management and help build markets around the world.

Having a large quantity of students studying abroad correlates with Taiwan's emphasis on education. Overseas Taiwanese, although they live abroad, still have a strong emotional tie with Taiwan. They continuously bring in new manufacturing technologies, scientific discoveries, technical skills and capital. They help upgrade industries to catch up with the developed nations. More importantly, they help Taiwanese to have a vision that goes beyond Taiwan to encompass the entire world.

Yang and Chen [13] assert that Taiwan's booming electronics and information technology is to a large degree the result of well-educated talents returning from the USA, bringing with them professional skills and knowledge. Table 6.1 shows statistics on the number of people that returned from abroad to settle in Taiwan. From the table, we notice the number of these returning talents greatly increased in the early 1990s. On one hand, they were attracted by Taiwan's incentive policy. On the other hand, because of the economic downturn in the USA in the late 1980s and early 1990s, these talents could not find good job opportunities. In order to start and upgrade the electronic industry, the government offered generous incentives to well-educated talents to come back and start businesses. Nowadays many well-established companies regularly send their important employees to study abroad to learn advanced professional knowledge or management skills. These returning employees help Taiwan strengthen its high tech economy.

Year	Total	Direct employment assisted by government					Self employment	Assisting returning by government		
		College or University	Government Institution	Research Institution	Public Enterprise	Non-public Enterprise		Doctor Degree	Master Degree	Research
1972	564	303	56	35	67	26	77	103	380	81
1976	722	303	81	34	77	46	181	215	405	102
1981	937	229	132	82	92	254	148	131	732	74
1986	1583	466	191	173	122	327	304	235	1286	62
1990	2863	691	325	374	202	728	543	395	2441	27
1991	3264	768	373	428	229	840	626	456	2780	28
1992	5157	892	472	618	331	1387	1457	835	4277	45
1993	6172	846	219	100	116	877	4014	1099	5036	37
1994	6510	754	130	98	49	1200	4279	1085	5379	46
1995	6272	611	69	102	99	1040	4351	1010	5247	15
1996	2760	78	38	24	1	322	2297	338	2422	-
1997	2677	42	44	10	1	294	2286	403	2274	-
1998	2341	78	25	8	1	292	1967	247	2094	-

(Annual Statistics of Taiwan, ROC, 1999) (Ref. 1)

Table 6.1 People returned and employed in Taiwan by the government assistance

The following are some contributions by returning well-educated talents:

(i)New and effective systems of management.

Traditional companies in Taiwan are run by family members, but this practice cannot compete with multinational systems. People who worked abroad brought back multinational management systems, which changed the scale and management styles of newly formed companies. Many incentive systems, such as bonuses and stock options, have been adopted from western management.

(ii)Various professional skills.

Most students who study abroad are pursuing a masters or doctorate degree, and they learn the most advanced scientific, engineering, professional and management skills. When they return to Taiwan, these students bring this knowledge with them. Whether they work in the academic world and continue studying there or work in industry, they directly or indirectly help upgrade Taiwan's industries.

(iii)Customer orientation.

Taiwan's economy depends on exports. To be successful, customers must accept exporters' products and services. Because of their experience in other countries, returning talents know people's needs in the countries where they stayed. This gives them the ability to develop products and services that are more satisfactory to customers.

(iv)Expanded connections, operations and thinking paradigms.

Because of emigration, we find immigrants from Taiwan around the world, and these overseas Taiwanese have strong ties with their native country. Through the exchange of information and capital, Taiwanese have developed a strong global network, which gives a worldwide perspective to business operations. In this way, their operational domains as well as their mental domains greatly increase and expand their paradigms.

(v)Democracy, law and order.

After the Second World War, the USA and Soviet Union were engaged in a cold war for more than four decades, and Taiwan becomes a front point for the democratic bloc against the communist countries. Through returning talents from the USA, democracy, freedom, law and order became an important part of Taiwan's defense against the threat from China. Now, Taiwan's president is elected directly by citizens. Political power has transferred democratically and peacefully, and democracy is well established in Taiwan. As democracy and a free market system are the best way for a people's creativity to grow, one may expect that becoming democratic will help Taiwan's competitive edge.

(vi)The multicultural impact.

Returning talents not only brought back the advanced technology and professional knowledge that upgraded Taiwan's industries, they also brought with them the cultural influence of various nations, which expanded and enriched Taiwan's habitual domains. This has increased Taiwan's ability to absorb professional skills, understand customers' needs, and manage markets. It also has increased the capacity to understand, manage and direct change and has enlarged Taiwan's vision of business operations.

7. Relation between the five life experiences and characteristics of competitiveness

From the discussion of Taiwan's life experiences above, we could form a picture of the special characteristics of the Taiwanese habitual domain. These special characteristics also are reflected in the dynamics of Taiwan's industries.

About 97 percent of companies are medium- or small-sized. These companies are vertically as well as horizontally diversified. Through competing and complementing each other, they work quickly to adjust to changing market needs. Employees and owners work hard, often 10 to 14 hours a day and six to seven days a week. Owners share profits with employees. These companies have a habit of continuous learning to keep up with changes. These special characteristics seem to be self-reinforced: the people who live in Taiwan need to develop such characteristics to succeed.

In order to have a competitive edge, a company must be able to have insight into potential customers' needs both currently and in the future. A business must understand customers' real pains and desires and produce and deliver products or services that satisfy their needs and relieve their pains and frustrations. In order to reach such a state of competitiveness, a company must become insightful about potential customers' needs and changes in those needs. In addition, it must have maximum flexibility and liquidity to reorganize resources—including human resources, skills, and information—to produce excellent, low-cost goods and services that satisfy the customers' needs ahead of its competitors.

Nowadays, especially in high tech industries, the competition is increasingly intensified. A company can compete and survive only by continuously renovating and improving. The company needs to be effective and efficient to produce products or services with a lower cost but higher quality. The company needs to continuously innovate in all areas, including production skills, production procedures, channels of distribution, services and management reengineering, so it can be ahead of its competitors.

In order for an industry to be competitive, its employees must be competitive. In Table 7.1, some important characteristics of personal competitiveness (or competitive characteristics) are listed in column 0.

In Columns 1 through 5, we list those five life experiences discussed in previous sections and show their relationship with the characteristics listed in Column 0. We use 0 to mean that they have no relation or little relation and use positive (or negative) 2 to mean there are significantly positive (or negative) influences or relations, while positive (or negative) 1 to mean that they have a moderately significant positive (or negative) relation. A sample list is given by Table 7.1. The table indicates, for instance, belief in higher education and motorcycling significantly influence Knowing market needs and individual interest focus, as shown by the score of 2 each. The compulsory military system significantly influences team interest focus with a score of 2. Crisis consciousness makes people significantly more sensitive and able to manage changes, as reflected in a score of 2, and makes people have less self-confident and optimistic (score -1). Studying abroad and returning of the well-educated talents has a significant positive impact on knowing market needs and knowing technology trend etc.

(0) Competitive Characteristics	(1) Belief in higher education	(2) Motorcycling	(3) Crisis consciousness	(4) Compulsory military service system	(5) Studying abroad and returning of the talents
Vitality	-1	2	1	2	1
Clear and specific goals	2	0	0	2	2
Knowing market needs	2	2	1	0	2
Knowing technology trends	1	-1	1	0	2
Sensitivity and managing changes	-1	2	2	1	2
Professional Knowledge	2	0	1	0	2
Working hard for Success	2	0	2	2	0
Perseverance	2	-1	2	2	0
Flexibility and Liquidity	-1	2	2	2	1
Elevated Ambition	2	0	1	0	2
Caring for society	0	0	1	2	1
Devotion to work	2	0	2	1	2
Team work spirit	-2	-2	0	2	0
Organizing ability	1	0	0	2	2
Team interest focus	-1	-1	0	2	0

Individual interest focus	2	2	2	-1	2
Creating cost advantage	0	2	2	0	2
Creating technical advantage	2	0	2	0	2
Creating market advantage	1	1	2	0	2
Creating efficiency advantage	2	2	2	2	2
Creating distribution advantage	0	2	2	0	2
Creating management innovation advantage	1	1	2	0	2
Creating capital advantage	0	1	2	0	2
Bravery and resoluteness	2	2	1	2	0
Enjoying helping others	0	0	0	2	0
Being creative	1	0	1	0	2
Self-confidence and optimism	1	2	-1	1	2

Table 7.1 Influence on competitive characteristics by the 5 life experiences

In order to further understand the relationship, we surveyed about 100 college students about their views on the relation indices of Table 7.1. The figures in Table 7.2 are the average values of these relation indices from the survey. The average values show the influence of life experiences to personal competitiveness, as perceived by 100 sampled college students in Taiwan. For instance, the average value of motorcycling's impact on vitality is 1.43. The last column gives the average value of the influence of the five life experiences on competitive characteristics. For instance, the total average value of the five life experiences on vitality is 0.87. This number is the average of 0.72, 1.43, 0.37, 0.55 and 1.26.

From Table 7.2, we observe the following:
- Belief in higher education has a significant positive impact on those items with average values larger than or equal to 1: Professional knowledge, Clear and specific goals, Individual interest focus, Hardworking for success, Perseverance, Elevated ambition, Sensitivity and managing changes, Knowing technology trend, and Devotion to work. It has a small negative impact on those items with average values smaller than 0.29 such as Enjoying helping others.
- Motorcycling significantly and positively impacts Vitality, Flexibility and Liquidity, Creating efficiency advantage, Bravery and resoluteness, and Clear and specific goals; and negatively impacts Caring for society, and Teamwork spirit.
- Crisis consciousness has a significant positive impact on Sensitivity and managing changes, Hardworking for success, and Knowing technology trend and has a slightly negative impact on Self-confidence and optimism, Bravery and resoluteness, and Vitality.

(0) Competitive Characteristics	(1) Belief in higher education	(2) Motorcycling	(3) Crisis consciousness	(4) Compulsory military service	(5) Studying abroad and returning of educated talents	(6) Row Average
Vitality	0.72	1.43	0.37	0.55	1.26	0.87
Clear and specific goals	1.43	1.09	0.80	0.59	1.09	1.00
Knowing market needs	0.98	0.76	0.91	-0.32	1.11	0.69
Knowing technology trend	1.04	0.30	1.00	-0.27	1.48	0.71
Sensitivity and managing changes	1.09	0.98	1.50	0.02	1.30	0.98
Professional Knowledge	1.52	0.54	0.83	0.64	1.65	1.04
Hard working for Success	1.33	0.61	1.09	1.82	0.54	1.08
Perseverance	1.33	0.48	0.74	1.66	0.57	0.96
Flexibility and Liquidity	0.35	1.33	0.59	0.73	0.85	0.77
Elevated Ambition	1.22	0.43	0.70	0.11	1.22	0.74
Caring for society	0.48	-0.20	0.83	0.66	0.67	0.49
Devotion to work	1.00	0.57	0.85	1.25	1.17	0.97
Team work spirit	0.26	0.20	0.83	1.73	0.72	0.75
Organizing ability	0.83	0.35	0.83	1.50	0.89	0.88
Team interest focus	0.09	0.22	0.59	1.57	0.80	0.65
Individual interest focus	1.39	0.80	0.78	0.32	1.17	0.89

Creating cost advantage	0.74	0.78	0.59	0.05	1.13	0.66
Creating technical advantage	0.85	0.57	0.59	-0.02	1.35	0.67
Creating market advantage	0.63	0.76	0.78	-0.09	1.46	0.71
Creating efficiency advantage	0.78	1.26	0.76	0.32	1.30	0.88
Creating distribution advantage	0.63	0.98	0.89	-0.02	1.26	0.75
Creating management innovation advantage	0.76	0.67	0.72	-0.25	1.22	0.62
Creating capital advantage	0.54	0.54	0.72	-0.14	1.35	0.60
Bravery and resoluteness	0.67	1.11	0.28	1.02	1.04	0.82
Enjoying helping others	0.28	0.59	0.50	1.16	0.72	0.65
Being creative	0.74	0.89	0.54	0.18	1.39	0.75
Self-confidence and optimism	0.70	0.91	0.20	0.59	1.24	0.73
Column Avg	0.83	0.70	0.73	0.57	1.11	0.79

Table 7.2 Average Influence on competitive characteristics by the 5 life experiences

- Compulsory military service system has a significantly positive impact on Hardworking for success, Team work spirit, Perseverance, Team interest focus, Organization ability, Devotion to work, Enjoying helping others, and Bravery and resoluteness. It has a negative impact on Knowing market needs, Knowing technology trends, Creating management innovation advantage, Creating capital advantage, Creating technical advantage, Creating distribution advantage, Sensitivity and Managing changes, Creating cost advantage, and Elevated ambition and a slightly negative relationship to Being creative.

- Studying abroad and returning of the well-educated talents have a significantly positive impact on Professional knowledge, Knowing technology trends Creating market advantage, Being creative, Creating technical advantage, Creating capital advantage, Sensitivity and managing changes, Creating efficiency advantage, Vitality, Creating distribution advantage, Self-confidence and optimism, Elevated ambition, Creating management innovation advantage, Devotion to work, Individual interest focus, Creating cost advantage, Knowing market needs, Clear and specific goals, and Bravery resoluteness. It does not have a negative impact on competitive characteristics.

From the table, we notice that although some individual life experiences may have a negative impact on competitive characteristics, the overall impact of the five life experiences on competitiveness is positive.

From the last column (row average), we notice that the six highest average values are Hard working for success (1.08), Professional knowledge (1.04), Clear and specific goals (1.00), Sensitivity and managing changes (0.98), Devotion to work (0.97), and Perseverance (0.96).

The five lowest scores on the last column are Caring for society (0.49), Creating capital advantage (0.60), Creating management innovation advantage (0.62), Team interest focus (0.65), and Enjoying helping others (0.65).

The above observations are pretty consistent with our discussion. They also can be observed from the dynamics of Taiwan's industries.

In addition, from the last rows of column average, the survey shows that "studying abroad and returning of educated talents" has most important impact on competitiveness, while "compulsory military service" has the least influence on compositeness.

8. Suggestions and Conclusion

Today, many companies are under ever-increasing competition, especially in high tech industries including the IC, PC and information technology industries [4-10, 12]. They are under pressure to respond rapidly to changes in customer demands and technological advancements.

In order to succeed and prosper, a company must have the insight and capability to know its customers' needs and be able to produce high-quality goods and services to satisfy those needs or release customers' pains or frustrations at the right time and right place. To do so, it must continuously expand its learning and innovate its competence and operations. In other words, it must continuously expand and enrich its habitual domain (HD) and competence.

From the previous sections, we have gained a general understanding of Taiwan's competitive characteristics. In order to upgrade or expand the habitual domains and competence of Taiwan's industries, individual HDs of Taiwanese must be upgraded and expanded.

Taiwan's human resources reveal strengths in Hard working for success, Professional knowledge, Clear and specific goal, Sensitivity and managing changes, Devotion to work, and Perseverance. They reflect weaknesses in (A) Caring the society, (B) Creating capital advantage, (C) Creating management innovation advantage, (D) Team interest focus and (E) Enjoying helping others. Note that (A), (D) and (E) imply that the teamwork spirit could be weak and too individualistic, while (B) and (C) shows creativity could be improved.

Teamwork, law and order and creativity are necessary to increase industrial capability and competence to produce goods and service efficiently and effectively. To enhance teamwork, law and order and creativity in Taiwan's HD, we can take the following actions.

(i) Improve the educational system. Some changes would be restructuring the admissions criteria for high schools, colleges and graduate schools. Entrance exams are important, but they should not be the only means to decide which students are admitted. Incentives should be offered to encourage students to be creative and care for other people and help solve social problems. Pursuing truth, beauty and serving other people should be important goals, in addition to professional knowledge.

(ii) Improve the traffic infrastructure. Except for Taipei, the public rapid transportation system is far from adequate. Too many private cars and motorcycles congest in busy streets, and people tend to drive illegally in order to move. This slows traffic and develops the bad habit of not observing laws as long as you are not caught. In addition to having invisible public costs, the traffic situation can be a major barrier to upgrading the competence and HD of Taiwan's industries.

(iii) Improve law enforcement. In Taiwan, laws and regulation are not strictly and effectively implemented and enforced. This indirectly encourages people to act and work in gray areas. The lack of strictly enforced law and order may create chaos and make upgrading and expanding the HD of Taiwan's industries more difficult.

(iv) Finally, as Taiwan becomes a developed nation and people get richer; the value of working hard for success, clear and specific goals, perseverance, etc., may quickly deteriorate. Certain mechanisms, such as crisis training, may be needed to prevent such deterioration.

References

[1] *Annual Statistics*, Taiwan, ROC, 1999

[2] Calder, K. E., *Asia's Deadly Triangle*, Classic Communications Co., 1998

[3] Chan, S. J. and Yu, P. L., "Stable Habitual Domains: Existence and Implications," *Journal of Mathematical Analysis and Application*, Vol. 110, No. 2, pp. 469-482, September, 1985

[4] Davidow, W. H., and Malone, M. S., *The Virtual Corporation*, Harper Collins, 1992

[5] Drucker, P. F., *Post-Capitalist Society*, Harper Business, 1993

[6] Du, C. H., *Theory and Practice of the Asia Operating Center*, Hwa-Tai, 1995

[7] Garelli, S., "From Competitive Enterprises to Competitive Societies: How Much Competitive Can A Country Take?," *IMD Perspectives for Managers*, 1995

[8] Kotler, P., Jatusripitak, S., and Maesincee, S., *The Marketing of Nations – A Strategic Approach to Building National Wealth*, Yuan-Liou, 2000

[9] Leinberger, Paul and Tucker, Bruce, *The New Individualists*, Harper Collins, 1991

[10] Porter, M., *The Competitive Advantage of Nations*, Free Press, 1990

[11] *Quarterly Statistics of National Economic Trends*, 1999

[12] D'Aveni, R. A. *Hyper-Competition: Managing the Dynamics of Strategic Maneuvering,* 1998

[13] Yang, D. Y. and Chen, F. L., "Competition and Evolution of Hi-Tech Industry," *Industry and Business Times*, 1996

[14] Yu, P. L., *Forming Winning Strategies, An Integrated Theory of Habitual Domains*, Springer-Verlag, 1990

[15] Yu, P. L., *Habitual Domains: Freeing Yourself from the Limits of Your Life*, High Water Edition, Kansas City, 1995

[16]Yu, P. L., and Wang, M. C., *Relationship between Taiwan Industrial Competitiveness and Belief in Higher Education and Motorcycling*, the 7th Conference on Habitual Domain, Shinchu, Taiwan, 1999

List of Contributors

Chun-Yen Chang
President and National Endowed Chair Professor
National Chiao Tung University
HsinChu, Taiwan,ROC
cyc@cc.nctu.edu.tw

Pao-Long Chang
Professor, Institute of Business and Management
National ChiaoTung University
Taipei, Taiwan, R.O.C.
paolong@cc.nctu.edu.tw

An-Pin Chen
Associate Professor, Institute of Information Management
National Chiao Tung University
Hsinchu, Taiwan, ROC
apc@iim.nctu.edu.tw

Hubert Chen
Electronic Research and Service Organization
Industrial Technology Research Institute
HsinChu, Taiwan, ROC

Chieh-Yow ChiangLin
Associate Professor, Department of Industrial Engineering and
Management
Tahwa Institute of Technology, HsinChu, Taiwan,R.O.C.
clcy@iim.nctu.edu.tw

Chiung-Wen Hsu
Industrial Economics and Knowledge Center
Industrial Technology Research Institute
HsinChu, Taiwan, R.O.C.

Jen-Hung Huang
Professor, Department of Management Science
National Chiao Tung University
HsinChu, Taiwan, R.O.C.
jhh@ms1.hinet.net

Chih-Young Hung
Institute of Information Management
National Chiao Tung University
HsinChu, Taiwan, R.O.C.
cyhung@cc.nctu.edu.tw

Meng-Yu Lee
PH. D Student, Institute of Information Management
National Chiao Tung University
HsinChu, Taiwan, R.O.C.
mongyu@ms22.url.com.tw

Han-Lin Li
Professor, Institute of Information Management
National Chiao Tung University
Ta Hsieh Rd., HsinChu 30050, Taiwan, R.O.C
hlli@cc.nctu.edu.tw

Shang-Jyh Liu
Professor & Director, Institute of Technology Law
National Chiao Tung University
HsinChu, Taiwan, R.O.C.
sjliu@cc.nctu.edu.tw

Jia-Jane Shuai
PH.D. Student, Institute of Information Management
National Chiao Tung University
Ta Hsieh Rd., HsinChu 30050, Taiwan, R.O.C
jjs@mis.mhit.edu.tw

Charles V. Trappey
Professor, Department of Management Science
National Chiao Tung University
HsinChu, Taiwan, ROC
trappey@cc.nctu.edu.tw

Chien-Tzu Tsai
Dept. of Industrial Engineering & Management
MingHsin Institute of Technology
HsinChu, Taiwan, R.O.C.

Gwo-Hshiung Tzeng
Professor, Institute of Management of Technology
National Chiao Tung University
HsinChu, Taiwan, R.O.C.
ghtzeng@cc.nctu.edu.tw

Shinn-Wen Wang
PH. D. Student, Institute of Information Management
National Chiao Tung University
Hsinchu, Taiwan, ROC
daviwen@sinamail.com

Muh-Cherng Wu
Professor, Department of Industrial Engineering and Management
National Chiao Tung University
Hsin-Chu, Taiwan, ROC
mcwu@cc.nctu.edu.tw

Chyan Yang
Professor, Institute of Business & Management
National Chiao Tung University
HsinChu, Taiwan, R.O.C.
chyan_yang@yahoo.com

Po-Lung Yu
C. A. Scupin Distinguished Professor
School of Business
University of Kansas and
Chair Professor, Institute of Information Management
National Chiao Tung University
HsinChu, Taiwan, R.O.C.
yupl@cc.nctu.edu.tw